To the students

and young physicians

for whom it was prepared

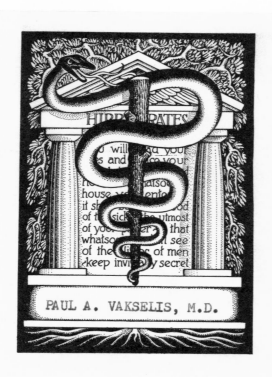

HIPPOCRATES

...u will ...d you...
...s and ...ce your...
... ...atso...
house ... ...ente...
it sh... ...od
of t... sick... ...utmost
of you... ...er... that
whatso... ...l see
of the ...s of men
...keep invi... secret

PAUL A. VAKSELIS, M.D.

FUNDAMENTALS
OF ROENTGENOLOGY

FUNDAMENTALS OF ROENTGENOLOGY

Lucy Frank Squire, M.D.

Lecturer on Radiology, Harvard Medical School

With Drawings and Diagrams by Francis deL. Cunningham Jr.

Published for **The Commonwealth Fund** by
Harvard University Press, Cambridge, Massachusetts

Preface

In undertaking the writing of a textbook in roentgenology, I have been concerned with providing not a compendious reference work in which one might hope to find the roentgen "signs" by which diseases are diagnosed, but rather an instruction manual which would help young physicians learn how to look at x-ray films. The student will find that radiology affords him a memorably graphic means of correlating and retaining material of all kinds learned in other disciplines. It is important for every graduating physician to know how to examine a radiograph and to be able to derive certain kinds of fundamental information from it. He should be able to study a chest film, a plain film of the abdomen, and films of bones without being overwhelmed by a sense of confusion, and he should recognize the shadows produced by some of the commoner types of pathologic change, relating those shadows to the pathology in a logical way and with modest confidence. The young practitioner finds that he can discuss his own patients' films with the radiologic consultant best if he has learned in medical school to expect the pathology to relate to the shadows, and that if they do not seem to tally, it is the nature of the pathology which must be questioned and reconsidered. He should recognize in the radiologist another consultant in the whole-patient study, and not an oracle issuing incomprehensible diagnostic statements. He will be a better physician if he understands enough about roentgen shadows to want to discuss and rediscuss the details of the films on his patients with the experts who have made and interpreted them, until both are satisfied that the roentgen method has been applied ideally to the problem at hand.

In designing this book for use as a manual of instruction rather than as a reference book, I have purposely omitted an index because it was my feeling that it would be unsuitable and improper to index a book in which some fairly esoteric items are used. When they would serve just as well as commoner conditions to illustrate roentgen principles, it has often seemed to me they might offer an element of surprise and color which would function as a mnemonic, for it is in that fashion that I have used them in the past in teaching radiology. To index such a collection of illustrative examples would place a wrong emphasis upon some of them.

Accordingly, the book is intended to be read from front to back, and basic concepts which are covered in early chapters are referred to later more succinctly. The reader will find it most expedient to study the chapters in the order in which they appear for reasons related to the structure of the book as a plan for learning.

Finally, I would like to invite the comments and suggestions of students, many of whom have in the past been immensely helpful to me in evolving better and clearer ways of presenting the material.

L. F. S.

One West 72nd St.
New York, N. Y. 10023

Acknowledgments

The manuscript for this book was produced with the help of a grant from the Commonwealth Fund, and the gentle hand of Mr. Roger Crane, Director of the Division of Publications, is responsible for much that is professional in the final product. Mr. Burton Stratton of the Harvard University Press and Mr. Daniel Briggs of The Case-Hoyt Corporation recognized the value of making each double-page spread a teaching unit so that illustrations being discussed would be immediately before the reader. Their patience and skill in helping me to translate this design was more than any author can expect. To Mr. William Cornwell of the Eastman Kodak Company, Editor of *Medical Radiography and Photography,* and his staff, go my profound thanks. They arranged for the re-use of several hundred copper engravings and made available to me extensive files of unpublished prints of radiographs. Mrs. Alice Russell in particular spent many hours helping to organize the material. From the files of the Strong Memorial Hospital, Dr. Stanley M. Rogoff kindly allowed me to select material which I had used during my years of teaching at the University of Rochester School of Medicine. Medical colleagues who contributed illustrations so generously are individually noted at the end of each chapter, where the source of each previously published illustration is also acknowledged. The largest number of such illustrations came from *Medical Radiography and Photography.* Others came from *Radiology* and *The American Journal of Roentgenology, Radium Therapy and Nuclear Medicine.* I am especially grateful to Dr. John Hope for the large number of excellent illustrations he contributed, to Dr. Bernard Epstein for his very helpful laminagrams, and to Dr. Henry Jaffe for permission to reproduce the beautiful color plates in the bone chapter. To all my friends in the profession who were ready to share their material, again my warmest thanks.

Dr. Lewis Etter suggested, in the fall of 1960, that I write a basic textbook for students. Dr. Laurence Robbins gave me not only his valued opinion on the manuscript but also constant encouragement without which the work might never have been completed. Dr. William Colaiace served as a test subject while interning and represented to me the reactions of the recent graduate. Many times he rescued me from the blind assumptions a teacher must guard against. Dr. Theodore Tristan, a gifted and dedicated teacher, read every word of the manuscript with great intelligence and helped to correct or improve the phrasing of innumerable details, a labor for which no words could thank him. Where I have failed to live up to his very high standards, it was probably because I was too stubborn.

In preparing the work for a second printing, Dr. Alice Ettinger has been of great assistance, bringing up to date a number of items throughout the book. Finally, I would offer to Dr. Richard Schatzki the most important thank you: I owe him the satisfaction and excitement of teaching the logic of roentgen shadows.

May 1966   L. F. S.

Contents

Free air in the peritoneal space; detection of large and small amounts; use of the decubitus and other special projections in the very ill patient; differentiation of 'contained' and 'uncontained' air

Clinical judgment applied to the selection of procedures

Naturally occurring contrast substances

Studies using barium sulfate

Principles of barium work; filling defects; niche detection; rigidity of the gut wall; intraluminal masses and the shelf margin; distensibility

The validity of barium work observations, a function of their being consistently present and redemonstrable

The gastric ulcer, benign and malignant

Duodenal ulcer; scarring patterns

Lesions in small and large bowel, similarly demonstrated; special techniques

Herniation of abdominal structures

Fluoroscopy, its limitations and hazards

The discovery of cholecystography

Present-day technique and physiologic implications of findings

The intravenous urogram and its retrograde pyelographic counterpart not interchangeable examinations

Interpretation of urographic findings in the light of renal physiology

Concept of fluid-flow through the kidney

The obstructed kidney, one kind of decreased fluid flow

Compromised arterial supply, another cause of decreased flow through the kidney

Depressed kidney function, the result of neither obstruction nor ischemia

Integration of excretory contrast studies with split function tests, radio-isotope scans, and complex special procedures, a new key to understanding renal physiology

Roentgen study of bones involves much more than gross structure of the supporting skeleton

A multitude of detailed roentgen findings contribute to understanding the role of the bony skeleton as an organ involved in most generalized disease processes. Role of microradiography, autoradiography, etc.

General principles of roentgen shadows applied specifically to the bones. Three-dimensional thinking still of importance

Orientation of this chapter: learning to think from the gross level appreciated from routine clinical radiographs of bones down to the microscopic level; to understand at the microscopic level both normal structure and changes in that structure in response to disease; then to return to the conventional radiograph and relate the two levels of visualization

Clinical radiography of patients with special address to study of the bones. Projection

Fractures. Roentgen findings. Differentiation from epiphyseal growth plate, from sutures in the skull

Joint structure, normal and abnormal. Chronic and irreversible changes in old age

Pathological fractures and their relation to changes in the bone resulting from disease. The cortex thinned and thickened. Aberrations in the radiograph which reflect either cortical or trabecular bone changes or both

Osteoporosis defined and exemplified as a transition to the microscopic level

Microscopic structure of compact and trabecular bone. Change in structure at different ages throughout life. Bone-building and bone-destroying influences. The constantly changing structure of bones, a difficult concept but very important

Return to the clinical radiograph via magnification studies. Demonstration of the degree to which changes seen so dramatically at the microscopic level actually can be appreciated from routine bone films

The skull, a special province of radiography. Contrast studies: the encephalogram, the ventriculogram, the arteriogram

A final unknown and a final word

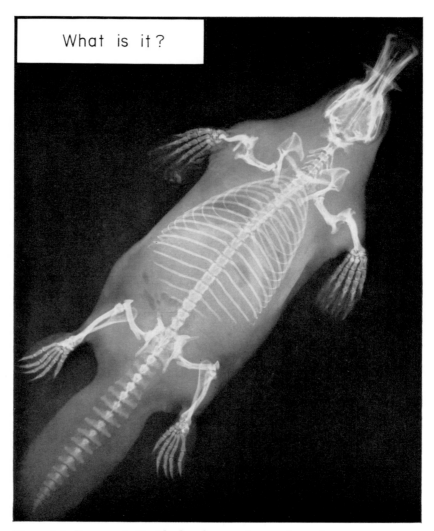

Figure 1-1. Its name is *Ornithorhynchus anatinus,* and you have never seen an x-ray portrait of it before. Nevertheless, there is one creature and one only in the animal kingdom which could give this x-ray appearance, and you can reason out its identity.

CHAPTER 1 Introduction and Basic Concepts

As you probably already know, x-rays are produced by bombarding a tungsten target with an electron beam. They are a form of radiant energy similar to visible light in several respects. For example, they radiate from the source in all directions unless stopped by an absorber. Like light rays, a very small part of the beam of x-rays will be absorbed by air, whereas all of the beam will be absorbed by a sheet of thick metal. The fundamental difference between x-rays and light rays is in their range of wave lengths, all x-rays being shorter than the wave length of ultraviolet light. The useful science of radiology is based on this difference, since many substances which are opaque to light are penetrated by x-rays. It was this attractive property which caught the attention of Professor Roentgen of the University of Würzburg on a cold November night in 1895 when he first observed certain physical phenomena he could not explain.*

Roentgen had been experimenting with an apparatus which, unknown to him, caused the emission of x-rays as a by-product. Accustomed to the darkened laboratory, he observed that whenever the apparatus was working a chemical-coated piece of cardboard lying on the table glowed with a pale green light. We know now that fluorescence, or the emission of visible light, can be produced in a variety of ways by complex nuclear energy exchanges. But in 1895 Roentgen recognized at first only the fact that he had unintentionally produced *a hitherto unknown form of radiant energy which was invisible, could cause fluorescence, and passed through objects opaque to light.* When he placed his hand between the source of the beam and the lighted cardboard, he could see the

Figure 1-2. Staged version of the discovery of the roentgen ray.

bones inside his fingers within the shadow of his hand. He found that the new rays, which he named x-rays, penetrated wood. Using photographic paper instead of a fluorescing material, he made an "x-ray picture" of a hand through the door of his laboratory.

*A more complete account of the discovery of x-rays is to be found in Appendix B.

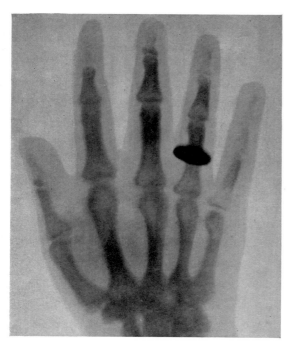

Figure 1-3. Radiograph of hand with ring made in Roentgen's laboratory on January 17, 1896.

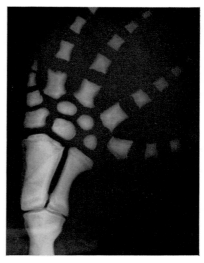

Figure 1-4. Actually, not a hand. Guess what it might be. (Note: Throughout this book you will find rhetorical questions and unanswered propositions. Sometimes they will be found answered in the text immediately following; sometimes, if you read straight along, you will find the answer several pages later buried in the text or incorporated into the legend of a related illustration. It is my intention to help you to learn by reasoning.)

Six years later the first Nobel prize in physics was awarded to Roentgen for his discovery, and by then this remarkably systematic investigator had explored most of the basic physical and medical applications of the new ray.

The idea of being able to see through opaque objects caught the public fancy all over the world, and a great deal of nonsense was written on the subject in many languages within the first decade after its discovery. There is a fascinating file of cartoons and articles in the Library of Congress documenting this fever. It was even predicted that the mind would be explored by the radiologist, but, in time, others seem to have pre-empted that field.

Are you quite sure you can imagine exactly what Roentgen saw when he first observed that he could "see through his hand" with the help of the new ray? In order to grasp this clearly, you must first understand the important difference between what the discoverer saw in the fluorescent shadow (Figure 1-3) and what you see today in an x-ray film of the hand, such as the one in Figure 1-4.

When light hits photographic film, a myste-

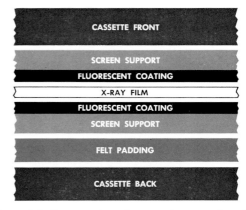

Figure 1-5. Cross section of a cassette, or modern film holder. The x-ray film in use today consists of an acetate sheet coated on both sides with photographic emulsion, and the cassette is constructed so that cardboard fluorescent screens are applied in contact with each side of the film. In this way light rays reinforce the photochemical effect on the film of the x-rays themselves.

rious photochemical process takes place in which metallic silver is precipitated in fine particles within the gelatin emulsion, rendering the film black when it is developed chemically.

Figure 1-6. Modern radiograph of a hand. *(a)* Blackened area where only air is interposed between beam and film. *(b)* Soft tissues absorb part of the beam before it reaches the film. *(c)* Calcium salts in bone absorb even more x-rays, leaving film only lightly exposed and relatively little silver precipitated in the emulsion. *(d)* Dense metal of ring absorbs all rays; no silver is precipitated. (Note: This, like all x-ray illustrations in textbooks and periodicals published in this country, is a doubly reversed print, so that what you see here is what you will see whenever you hold a film of the hand against the light.)

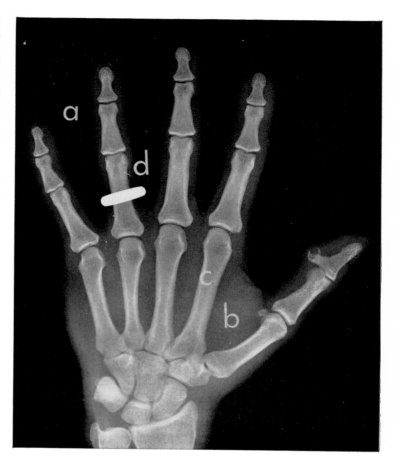

Places on the film which are not exposed to light remain clear. When a "positive" paper print is made of this "negative" film, the values are reversed: the black, silver-bearing areas prevent light from reaching the photosensitive paper, while clear areas in the film permit the paper to be blackened.

The x-ray film you will see in medical school is equivalent to the negative film you may have worked with in your own photographic darkroom. X-rays, like light rays, precipitate silver in a photographic film, but they do so much less rapidly than light. A patient cannot be expected to hold still long enough for films to be made using x-rays alone, and too much exposure to radiation is both dangerous and technically undesirable. Therefore, an ingenious reinforcing technique has been worked out using a special film container, or *cassette.*

The cassette contains a fluorescent screen which is activated by the x-rays and in turn emits light rays which reinforce the photochemical effects of the x-rays themselves upon the film. In this way the silver-precipitating effect of the x-rays combined with that of the light rays they generate work together to blacken the film. Where an object interposed between the x-ray beam source and the cassette has absorbed the rays, no light activation of the fluorescent screen will take place; neither x-rays nor light rays will reach the film, and no silver will be precipitated.

In Figure 1-6 a woman's left hand has been placed over the cassette and exposed to a beam of x-rays. Notice that the film not covered by any part of the hand has been intensely blackened because very little of the beam was absorbed by the *air,* which was the only absorber interposed there between x-ray tube and film. The fleshy parts of the hand, or *soft tissues,*

as they are called by the radiologist, absorbed a good deal of the beam so that the film appears gray. Very few rays reached that part of the film directly under the *bones* because bones contain large amounts of calcium. All *metals* absorb x-rays to an extent depending on atomic number and thickness. No x-rays at all were able to pass through the gold ring, and the film underneath it was not altered photographically.

What Roentgen saw, on the contrary, was the reverse of all the light-dark values you have been looking at in the film of the hand. X-rays reached the coated cardboard in abundance all around his hand so that the background fluoresced vigorously while the shadow of his hand emitted less light and appeared gray-green. The cardboard underneath the bones of his fingers appeared darkest of all, since it received almost no activating x-rays.

Figure 1-4 is not a human hand but a whale's flipper.

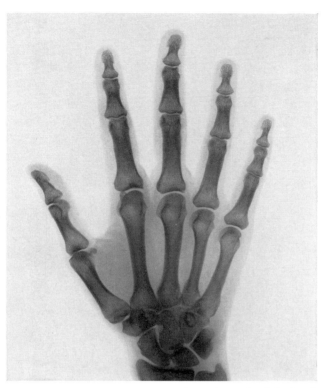

Figure 1-7. Positive print of a radiograph of the hand, made by singly reversing the values. This is also approximately as the hand would look on the fluoroscopic screen, except that the whole would be in various shades of pale green.

What Roentgen saw was, except for modern technical improvements, precisely what the radiologist sees today in the fluoroscopy room. Instead of the coated cardboard, the *fluoroscopic screen,* composed of chemical-coated plate glass, is interposed between the examiner and the patient. The radiologist, working in a darkened room, watches the light and dark areas of the screen, the patient's bones appearing darker and his soft tissues lighter. You will be disappointed the first time you visit a conventional fluoroscopy room because you will see little or nothing unless you have adapted your eyes to dark for some time beforehand. Fluoroscopic light is very faint, unless it is amplified electronically. Equipment of this type is rapidly replacing the usual fluoroscope.

You may not see much fluoroscopy in your lifetime, but you will see many thousands of x-ray films. For this reason, I suggest that you make a practice of thinking in terms of the white and black values that relate to the usual x-ray film as you saw them in the hand in Figure 1-6. Think of dense objects as white and of those more easily penetrated as gray or black. All the illustrations in this book are printed like Figure 1-6, and you will find that most American journals and books print x-ray illustrations in this way. When you have occasion to study from British and certain Continental journals, you will find that positive prints are often employed (see Figure 1-7).

While it is essential to understand which are the more dense (or *radio-opaque*) substances and which the more transparent (or *radiolucent*) ones, your concern, even as you first begin looking at x-rays, should not be only with density. One often makes quite reasonable and useful deductions from the *form and shape* of roentgen shadows. If you figured out that Figure 1-1 was, and could only be, an x-ray of a duck-billed platypus, you have experienced the sort of educated guessing one uses all the time in radiology. One guesses imaginatively and then subjects one's own guess to a rigorous logical analysis based on roentgen and medical data. Putting together expected density and expected form, you will soon find that you can predict the appearance of the x-ray picture of an object or structure.

Begin, then, by applying imagination and judgment to a variety of nonmedical objects. Try to predict the type of shadow that would appear on the film if you x-rayed (1) a coin, flat and then on edge; (2) a paper cup, empty and then containing a teaspoonful of buckshot; (3) a wooden box containing a watch; (4) an electric heating pad.

Figure 1-8 is an x-ray of a woman's purse. Although the cloth from which the purse was made offered almost no obstruction to the x-rays, anything made of metal inside it, including the frame of the purse, absorbed the rays and left a white profile on the film. You will be able to identify from their outlines alone a paper clip, a bobby pin, a safety pin, a pair of rimless spectacles (the glass casts almost no shadow), coins, a lipstick case, two locker keys (overlapped), a nail file, and a metal pencil.

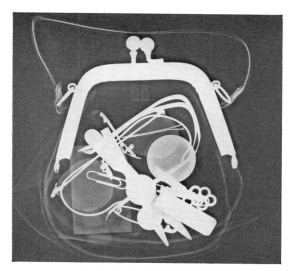

Figure 1-8. Radiograph of a woman's purse.

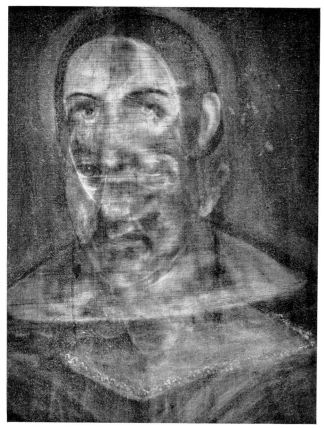

Figure 1-9. Radiograph of a portrait in oils painted over an earlier portrait. The woman with the pale eyes was visible on viewing the painting.

You can almost construe the girl: a poverty-stricken, myopic individual who is taking two lab courses but wears make-up. One might, of course, be mistaken as to the state of her finances: folding money, even in pounds sterling, would be quite radiolucent.

Pure metals are relatively radio-opaque and so are their salts. Consequently, so also are the mixtures of oil and brilliantly colored metallic salts responsible for the whole field of oil painting. The radiography of paintings and other works of art is a fascinating and technically useful branch of the science. Frauds, inept reconstructions, masterpieces painted over by amateurs may sometimes be detected by x-ray studies.

In Figure 1-9 two painters have used the same canvas, or, dissatisfied with his portrait of the man whose eyes appear as the lower pair, the same painter may have done the portrait of the woman with light eyes and severely dressed hair, covering over the earlier portrait. Only the lady was visible as one looked at the painting.

Variations in the precise metallic composition of artists' colors used at different times in history may help in the identification and dating of such works of art. The pigments in use since about 1800 have been made of the salts of metals with much lower atomic numbers than the older pigments and for that reason will x-ray quite differently. Thus a modern forgery of an old master, no matter how adroit a copy, will have an entirely different radiograph from the original. On the other hand a copy made by a pupil of the master or another artist of the same school, painting at about the same time in history with the same hand-ground, earth-mineral colors, could be expected to x-ray in about the same way.

The characteristic use of brush strokes, which, even better than his signature, often stamps the work of a great artist, may also help to identify a concealed painting covered over by a lesser artist. You will be able to imagine the radiograph of a contemporary canvas with the vigorous, heavy brush strokes of Van Gogh showing through, for example.

5

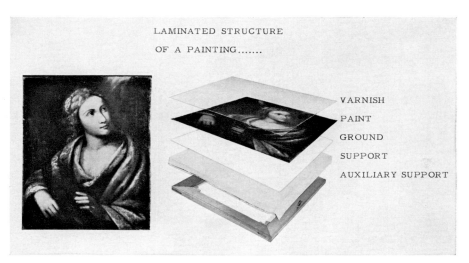

LAMINATED STRUCTURE
OF A PAINTING.......

VARNISH
PAINT
GROUND
SUPPORT
AUXILIARY SUPPORT

Figure 1-10

Remember, too, that any radiograph of a painting represents the addition of not only the various paint densities but the x-ray shadows of the canvas itself and the supporting structures. The wooden frame on which the canvas is stretched will cast some shadow, and if there are any nails in the wood, they will appear in the x-ray, too. Figure 1-11 shows an x-ray of a painting supported on wooden strips. The curious white areas are worm holes which have been filled with white lead. The x-rays have

been completely absorbed, you notice, by the white-lead *casts* of the worm holes, and under them no rays have reached the film to blacken it. The white areas on the film are actually, therefore, *shadow-profiles* of these white lead casts. Remember this; it has an important parallel in barium work in medical x-ray studies.

The industrial uses of x-ray are many and important. Flaws, cracks, and fissures in heavy steel can be shown by x-raying big equipment or building materials. Especially powerful machines are needed for this sort of work, ones which will produce a more penetrating beam of x-rays of very short wave length, often called "hard x-rays." X-rays of long wave length, or "soft x-rays," are used to study thin or delicate objects. Longer- and shorter-length x-ray waves each have their appropriate uses in the field of medicine. Very soft x-rays are used to study tissue sections of bone 1 or 2 micra in thickness (microradiography), while very hard x-rays are used to penetrate deep into the body and destroy malignant tumor cells (radiation therapy). In between these two extremes fall the wave lengths which are used in medical x-ray diagnosis.

The *electromagnetic spectrum* in Figure 1-12 is a scaled arrangement of all types of radiant energy according to wave length. Within the range used in diagnostic radiology, the x-ray technician is trained to select and use the particular wave length suited to the penetrability

Figure 1-11

and thickness of the part he is filming. He does this by varying the kilovoltage of his machine: the higher the kilovoltage, the harder or more penetrating the beam of rays produced. He can also vary the amount of radiation in the beam by altering the milliamperage used, and, finally, he can control the time of exposure. Thus, for instance, for a thin object like the hand he uses a soft beam for a short time, and for a dense object like the head, a hard beam and a long exposure.

An interesting parallel can be drawn by comparing this form of radiography with neutron radiography, a relatively new branch of nuclear science in which a beam of low-energy neutrons is used to penetrate objects which are opaque to x-rays. The images produced in this way are interesting for a special reason: the absorption characteristics for neutrons are quite different from those for x-rays, not simply an extension of the spectrum of penetration you see in Figure 1-12. Heavy elements like lead and barium, which are opaque to x-rays, are penetrated readily by such a neutron beam, while hydrogen-rich substances absorb neutrons but allow x-rays to pass through them with ease. Thus, if you will imagine a pair of lead pipes, one filled with water and the other with air, you will be able to predict both their x-ray image and their neutron-beam image: the lead pipe would in both cases absorb all of the x-ray beam, and no rays would be left to penetrate the water and air differently. The neutrons, on the other hand, would pass easily through the lead casing, would be heavily absorbed in one pipe by the water and much less so by the air in the other. You would, accordingly, have two pairs of images, the x-ray images being identical and the neutron images quite different.

This is not to say that living tissues can feasibly be studied with neutrons in humans; there are dangers implicit in the production of secondary radiation, as you will learn when you study radiation therapy. However, certain biologic studies using neutron beams may indeed prove useful in medicine, since the location of hydrogen-rich areas or the displacement of such areas can be appreciated in this way, even in a delicate structure like a leaf.

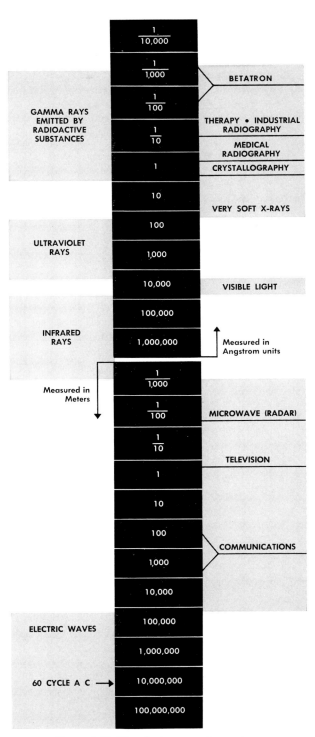

Figure 1-12. The electromagnetic spectrum.

Consider now the contribution of *form* in more detail. Figure 1-13 is a radiograph of three roses which we can use as an example of the basic logic of the roentgen shadows of complex objects. Flowers require only a very soft beam, of course, because they are both thin and delicate. A glance will tell you that one rose is full-blown and the other two more recently opened. You can deduce a great deal of information from form, outline, shape, and structure of x-ray shadows. This is so true that in time you will learn to recognize with confidence the identity of certain shadows in medical x-rays because of their shape or form. Just so, you can say from their outlines that one of these roses is just about done, while the other two will last a bit longer.

Now study the density of various parts of a single petal and compare the radiodensity, or whiteness, of the petals with that of the leaves. The leaves look less dense than the flowers and stems. Notice, too, that the veins within each leaf are denser than the rest of it. Veins of leaves have, of course, a structure independent of the cells composing the flatter part of the leaf. Stems are thicker and they also convey fluid. In both medical and nonmedical x-rays you can anticipate added density, in general, wherever there is fluid.

The main reason for the denser appearance of the petals compared with the leaves is that they do not lie flat against the film but are curved and folded and overlap one another. This gives you a clue to a very important facet of radiologic interpretation. A sheet of any uniform composition, if it lies flat and parallel to the film will have a uniform x-ray density and cast a homogeneous shadow. If it is curved, however, those parts which lie perpendicular to the plane of the film will radiograph as though they were much more dense.

This is perfectly simple. X-rays pass through a complex object and render upon the film not a picture at all but a "composite shadowgram," representing the sum of the densities interposed between beam source and film. Thus a sheet of rose petal which lies perpendicular to the film, or in the plane of the ray, is equivalent to many thicknesses of petal laid one upon another and, quite logically, is much more dense than a single sheet lying flat. Find the leaf which is turned on edge.

Curved sheets, considered geometrically, compose themselves into groups of planes, if you will, and should be so considered in imagination when you are interpreting an x-ray film. Of course, in nature, and consequently in medicine, the curved plane is common and the symmetrical plane rare. In the x-ray of any curved-plane structure, therefore, learn to think in terms of those parts of it which are *relatively parallel to the film* and those which are *roughly perpendicular to it.*

Try to imagine the x-ray of an egg about to hatch. The calcium in the eggshell will absorb the rays, and where those rays are absorbed by a tangential segment of shell, even fewer rays will reach the film to blacken it. You are imagining correctly, then, an oval white shadow outlined by a more intensely white rim, and, inside it, a cluster of white embryo bones, adding together their densities where they overlap. From such a systematic pattern of thought it is not far to the reverse: the deduction of identities from roentgen shadows.

Observe, finally, that the shadow of the stem of the rose in Figure 1-13 has a form you will find characteristic of any *tubular structure* of uniform composition. The margins are relatively dense because they represent long, curved planes radiographed tangentially, and the center area between them appears as a darker, more radiolucent streak. Rose stems are not truly hollow as one looks at them with the naked eye, but the central core, like that of tubular bones, is filled with a structure having less radiodensity. Hence the stem looks hollow and tubular on the film, just as a hollow tube containing air would look. As an exercise try to imagine, now, a tube filled with a denser core and one filled with a substance of the same radiodensity. The last would, of course, be identical with the shadow cast by any cylinder of homogeneous composition.

By this time you have several important principles clearly in mind, although you have learned them largely from examples. *First,* you know that x-rays are radiant energy of very short wave length, beyond light in the electromagnetic spectrum, and that they penetrate,

8

Figure 1-13

differently according to their wave lengths, substances opaque to light.

Second, you know that a beam of x-rays penetrates a complex object like the hand in accordance with the relative radiodensities of the materials which compose the object. You know that it produces on the film a composite shadowgram representing the sum of those radiodensities, layer for layer and part for part. You know that radiodensity is a function of atomic number and of thickness.

Third, you have realized that the parts of an object may become recognizable as to form, and their structure deduced, according to whether they are constructed most like solid or hollow spheres, cubes, or cylinders, or like plane sheets lying flat or curved upward away from the film.

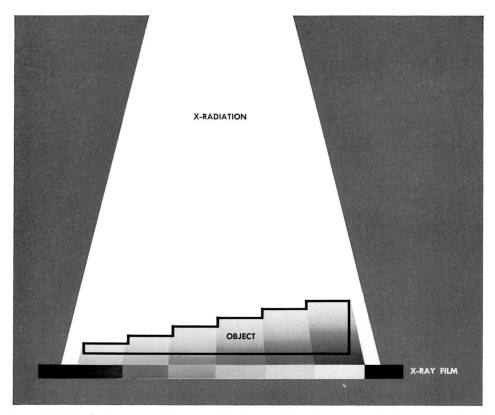

Figure 1-14. Radiodensity as a function of thickness of the object. Here the object to be filmed is of homogeneous composition and has a step-wise range of thicknesses. Gray shading indicates degree of absorption.

Having reasoned through all this, you must now return to the matter of density and consider in greater detail the *relative radiodensities* of various substances and tissues. In order to do so most easily, let us eliminate form for the moment completely. Consider an imaginary row of 1-centimeter cubes of lead, air, butter, bone, liver, blood, muscle, subcutaneous fat, and barium sulfate. Can you arrange them in the order of their radiodensity, decreasing from left to right?

If they were all pure elemental chemicals, you certainly could do so by looking up their atomic numbers. Only one of them is quite so simple as that, and a judicious guess will surely place first to the left the cube of lead as most

dense, with an atomic number of 82.

Are you hesitating between bone and barium sulfate? Barium has an atomic number of 56, and calcium in the bone cube has an atomic number of 20. However, bone is not pure calcium salt. It has a functioning physiologic structure with holes and spaces to accommodate body fluids and marrow. It is composed of an organic matrix into which the complex bone mineral is precipitated. All such organic substances will reduce the radiodensity of the cube of bone, and it would consequently have even less radiodensity than a similar cube of packed bone dust. The cube of barium sulfate must be placed next after the lead cube, and after it, the cube of bone.

10

As to the most radiolucent of all, you can have no trouble with that: surely you will have put the cube of air far to the right, at the opposite end of the scale from the lead. The square of film under the lead, unaltered because no rays penetrated the cube to reach it, will be clear white, while that under the bone will show a tinge of gray. The film under the air cube will be black, since the sparse scattering of air molecules offers almost no obstacle to the rays.

Butter and subcutaneous fat have very similar x-ray densities. They are extremely radiolucent and must be placed next to air in the scale we are considering. Neither butter nor fatty tissue is homogeneous, since one is never quite free of water and the other contains both circulating fluids and a supporting network of fibrous connective tissue. Their squares on the radiograph would be almost the same very dark gray.

In between the three very dense cubes and the three very lucent ones there remain to arrange the three cubes of blood, muscle, and liver. These will all x-ray an almost identical medium gray, and you can remember that all moist solid or fluid-filled organs and tissue masses will have about the same radiodensity, greater than fat or air but considerably less than bone or metal. Thus the muscular heart with

its blood-filled chambers could be expected to x-ray as you see it on the chest film, a homogeneous mass much denser than the air-containing lung on both sides of it, but showing no differentiation between muscular ventricular wall and blood within the ventricle.

Remember that in the above discussion of relative radiodensities, we have kept thickness and form constant, as well as such technical factors as kilovoltage and time of exposure. I have planned this deliberately so that you might more easily build a working concept of the relative densities of different tissues. In practice, the radiologist adjusts the technical factors to accentuate these differences. Upon this useful spectrum of differing radiodensities of human tissues is based the whole field of medical radiography.

Once these considerations are learned, radiology becomes an exercise in logical deduction and an absorbing habit of mind. More importantly for you, it is also a delightful extra dimension in learning, a sort of custom-tailored illustrative tool related to nearly everything you will study in medical school. If you wish, you can use it to help you learn from the first day you begin to study anatomy, through your courses in physical diagnosis, pathology, medicine, and surgery, as a means of comprehending and remembering medical facts.

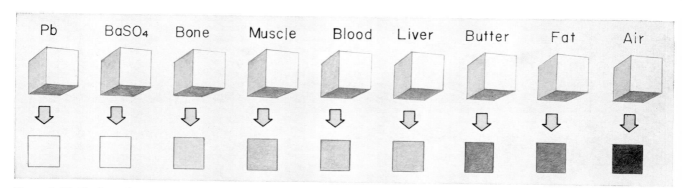

Figure 1-15. Thickness kept constant while composition varies.

Because I believe that the working of problems and puzzles will greatly increase your enjoyment of this book, I have included some in every chapter. They are geared to the chapter in question both in subject matter and in difficulty. In general, they are presented with a few details about the patient, and you should imagine yourself the intern or practicing physician in charge of that patient. Often, especially in the early chapters, you are asked not for a diagnosis but, rather, for an impression of variation from the normal of a particular structure. You will see that this will help you to gauge as you go along just how roentgen shadows can be reasoned out and used as a mnemonic device in learning medicine. I think it will also persuade you that you know more and can reason better than you had realized (a comforting thought). The answers are provided in Appendix A at the back of the book, and the Unknowns are numbered, 1-1, 1-2, 1-3, etc., 2-1, 2-2, 2-3, etc., in relation to the chapter in which they appear.

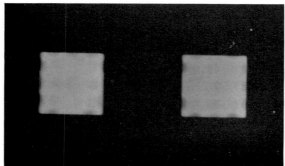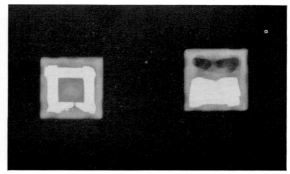

Figure 1-16 (*Unknown 1-1*). Sometimes the radiologist figures in criminology as an adjunctive source of information. The lucky throw you see in the innocent looking pair of dice in the photograph was actually not luck at all but planned economy. Below are two radiographs, one of a pair of loaded dice and one of a pair of unloaded dice for which they could be switched. It is simple enough to decide which are the loaded dice, but can you figure out precisely what has been done?

Figure 1-17 *(Unknown 1-2)*. This is not a familiar object, and though you can figure out what its structure is from this, its radiograph, you will be very gifted indeed if you can say where it was when found.

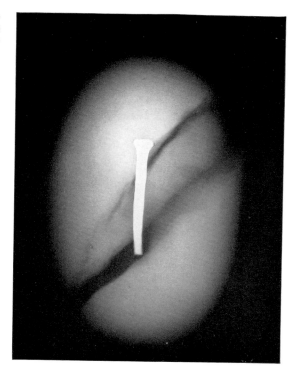

Credits: Illustrations this chapter.

Frontispiece. The late Dr. Merrill Sosman brought this from Australia.

Figure 1-3. From *Medical Record* 149, Feb. 15, 1896.

Figure 1-4. Courtesy Dr. W. Felts, Minneapolis, Minn.

Figure 1-5. From *Fundamentals of Radiography*, p. 25, published by Eastman Kodak Co., Rochester, N. Y.

Figure 1-8. Courtesy Dr. D. Eaglesham, Guelph, Ontario, Canada.

Figure 1-9. Courtesy Dr. E. Comstock, Wellesville, N. Y., and Mr. C. Bridgman, Rochester, N. Y.

Figure 1-10. Courtesy Messrs. C. Bridgman and S. Keck, and the publisher, *MR&P* 37:64.

Figure 1-11. Courtesy Messrs. C. Bridgman, Rochester, N. Y., and S. Keck, New York, N. Y.

Figure 1-12. From *Fundamentals of Radiography*, p. 8, published by Eastman Kodak Co., Rochester, N. Y.

Figure 1-14. From *Fundamentals of Radiography*, p. 6, published by Eastman Kodak Co., Rochester, N. Y.

Figure 1-16. Courtesy Mr. C. Bridgman, Rochester, N. Y.

CHAPTER **2**   An Invitation To Think
Three-Dimensionally

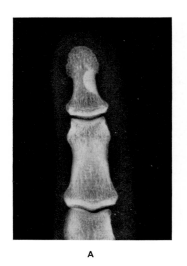
A

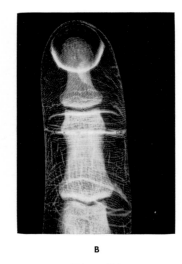
B

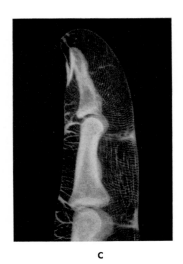
C

Figure 2-1

These three radiographs of a finger in Figure 2-1 will illustrate at once how important it is for you to learn to think in depth about x-ray shadows. Note that the soft tissues in *A* compose a uniform gray outline encompassing the bones. In *C* and *B*, however, the skin with its wrinkles and folds as well as the crevice between cuticle and nail all seem to become visible. This is because they have been coated with a creamy substance containing a metallic salt. Actually, the skin itself is no more visible than it was before, but the radio-opaque cream collecting on its patterned, irregular surface forms a visible coating which marks the position of the skin. Fingerprints can be studied in this way by x-ray, although it is less practical than the usual method of making ink impressions. *A* and *B* were made in the *antero-posterior projection; C,* made from the side, is called a *lateral view.*

Although *A* now probably looks very flat to you and *B* and *C* give an illusion of depth, you will have realized that you can look at a medical x-ray film and *think about it three-dimensionally* even though you do not see it that way. Since the radiograph is a composite shadowgram and represents the added densities of many layers of tissue, just so one must think in layers when looking at it.

The most striking contrasts in radiodensity exist in the region of the chest, where air-filled lungs (radiolucent) on both sides of muscular, fluid-filled heart (relatively opaque) occupy the inside of a bony cage (a fretwork of crossed radio-opaque strips). It is practical, therefore, to discuss the chest first, in this book, and to outline for you a system by which you can learn to study the chest from its radiographs. Later in the book, discussions of the abdomen, bones in

14

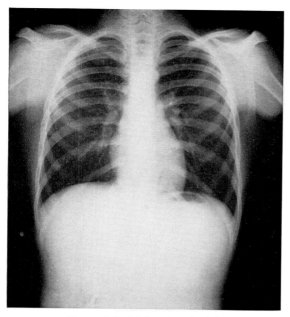

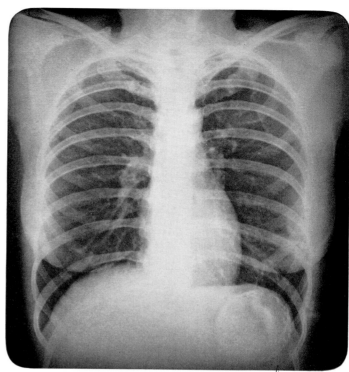

Figure 2-2. *A* (above); *B* (right).

ref: Fig 12-52

general, and the skull will come much more easily because you have thought through the basic problems of adding roentgen densities to account for shadows on the chest film.

In studying Figure 2-2A and *B* you will find that you can best think three-dimensionally about chest films by imagining the structures through which the x-ray beam passed from back to front. You can say to yourself, "Ah, yes: skin of the back; subcutaneous fat; lots of muscle encasing the flat blades of the scapulae, the vertebral column, and posterior shell of the rib cage; then the lungs with the heart and other mediastinal structures between them; the sternum and anterior shell of ribs; pectoral muscles and subcutaneous fat; significant amounts of breast tissue in certain members of the species; and finally, skin again."

In the two chest films on this page note the additional crescents of density that are added in Figure 2-2B, where the x-rays have had to traverse breast in addition to all the other tissue layers. Note that below the shadow of the breast and above that of the diaphragm the film is blacker where more rays have reached it.

One of the problems which will worry you as you begin looking at chest films and handling them will be how to put them up on the light boxes against which they are viewed: since they are transparent, you can look through them from either side. This will be much easier if you *remember always to place them so that you seem to be facing the patient.* This is the conventional manner of viewing films, and you will find that throughout this book, as throughout your professional lifetime, films will be viewed in this fashion if they have been made with a sagittal or near-sagittal beam.

You will find that x-ray films are usually marked by the technician to indicate which was the patient's right side, or, in the case of films of the extremities, whether it was his right or left leg, for example. In chest films one can usually be somewhat independent of the marker because the left ventricle and the arch of the aorta cast more prominent shadows on the left side of the patient's spine. Always view a chest film, then, so that the patient is facing you with his left on your right, and remember that when one says "left" in speaking of a finding on the film one means the patient's left, invariably. When you read "the right breast is missing" you are going to check the breast shadow to your left, automatically.

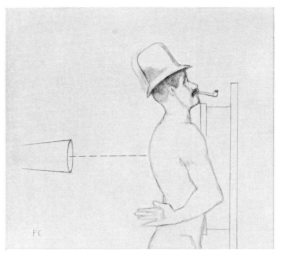 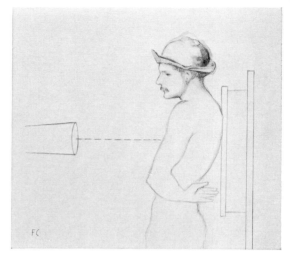

Figure 2-3. *A* (above, left). Postero-anterior beam produces a PA chest film, the conventional view you see most often. *B* (above, right). Antero-posterior beam produces an AP film. Note that the film is named for the direction the beam takes through the patient. (Drawings after Cézanne.)

Most of the chest films you see will have been made with the beam passing in a sagittal direction "postero-anteriorly," the x-ray tube behind and the film in front of the patient. This is the standard PA chest film, and films of all kinds are called *PA views if the beam passes through the patient from back to front*. It has become customary to make a PA chest film of any patient who is able to stand and be positioned.

Figure 2-4. (below, left). PA chest film.

Figure 2-5 (below, right). AP chest film. Note enlargement of the heart, the result of projection; also note difference in the appearance of the posterior ribs and clavicles. This particular film is centered off the midline in order to permit study of the posterior ribs.

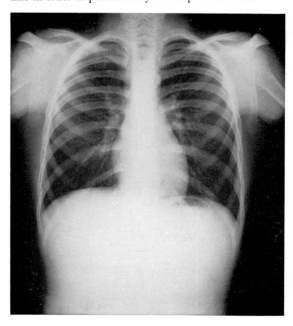 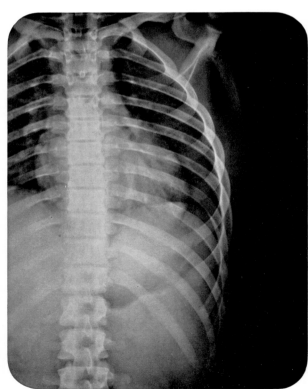

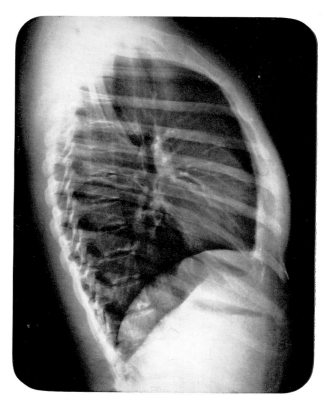

Figure 2-6 (right, above). Right lateral chest film.

Figure 2-7 (right, below). Labeled tracing of Figure 2-6: (1) clavicle, (2) medial end of the first rib, (3) pair of third ribs superimposed, (4) manubrio-sternal junction, (5) anterior and posterior surfaces of the heart, (6) the scapulae, (7) air in the trachea, (8) pair of sixth ribs not superimposed, (9) and (10) right and left diaphragms.

Less satisfactory but often valuable AP films are made of the chest when the patient is too sick to leave his bed. The patient is propped up against his pillows, and the film is placed behind him, the exposure being made with a portable x-ray machine at the foot of the bed. Thus the ray passes through the patient "antero-posteriorly." You will be seeing such AP films of your very sick patients, and although they do not compare in quality to the PA films made with better technical facilities in the x-ray department, they do offer important information about the progress of the patient's disease. Sometimes a patient who cannot stand is not too sick to be taken in his bed to the x-ray department and filmed AP with the equipment available there, a better film being obtained in this way than is possible with the portable unit.

You will want to learn how to recognize an AP film because it is not precisely comparable with the standards for normal which your eye will have set up for you based on the larger number of PA films you see. This is true partly because the divergence of the rays enlarges the shadow of the heart, far anterior in the chest and therefore well away from the film (Figures 2-3, 2-4, and 2-5).

After the standard PA film, the next most common view of the chest is the "lateral." It is marked with an "R" or an "L" according to whether *the right or the left side of the patient was against the film.* You should view either one as though the beam were coming toward you. Always put up a right lateral film, for example, as though the right side of the patient were toward you and he faced to your right. As you look at Figure 2-6, review the structures the beam passed through in order to reach you (the film). Note how the ribs all seem roughly parallel, some pairs superimposed by the beam, forming a single denser white shadow. Mark

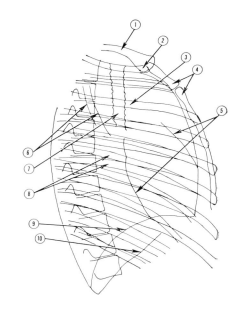

how far the vertebral column projects into the chest, so that the mediastinal structures actually occupy only the anterior two-thirds of the mid-line chest. Large segments of lung extending further back on either side of the spine are superimposed on it in the lateral view.

17

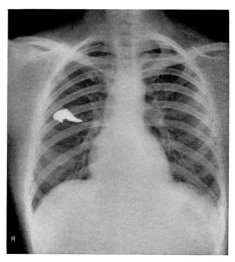

Figures 2-8 (above) and 2-9 (below). Before you read the text on this page try to figure out what is going on in these two films.

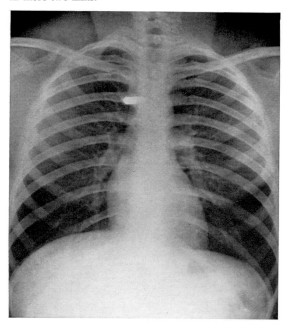

The two chest films in Figures 2-8 and 2-9 offer you an opportunity to test your progress in three-dimensional thinking. Study them both. Each has an obvious artifact of metallic radiodensity. In the upper film the shape of the metal object tells you nothing about its nature. (Perhaps the object in the lower film might be a bullet, and, if it is, might not that in the upper film be shrapnel?)

Figure 2-9 was made, in fact, during World War II of a soldier wounded in the Sicilian campaign. He was invalided out to a hospital, where the surgeons observed what you observe. They requested, as you are about to do, a lateral view to determine the location of the bullet. It might, of course, be in any of the structures whose roentgen shadows superimpose in this view on the origin of the fifth rib.

The importance of localizing a bullet is illustrated by the cross-section drawing, Figure 2-10. If the bullet is lodged in the spinal cord or the trachea, or in one of the major vascular structures at this level, there may be less hope of saving the patient. In point of fact, the bullet was located harmlessly in the anterior mediastinum, had not injured any vital structure, and was removed without incident. (For lateral view see Figure 2-11.)

Figure 2-8 was quite a different matter. Before you read any further, try to estimate what structures could have been injured. Actually there was no injury to any of the structures in the chest, because this film was made of a perfectly well person lying *on* a piece of metal foil. You can never know precisely where a foreign body is located from a single radiograph. A film made at right angles to the first is essential, and minute metallic foreign bodies in the eye are localized very accurately by a refinement of this procedure. Fractured bones, you will find, can appear to be in good position, end to end, in one film, although a second film made at right angles shows that the fragments are separated and do not align. Often the taking of such supplementary lateral films is a routine matter. At other times you will have to ask that they be taken on your patients. Always ask for a right lateral if you think the lesion is on the right, and vice versa, so that the structure to be studied is as close as possible to the film.

Figure 2-10 (right, above). Diagram showing several possible locations of the bullet in Figure 2-9: (1) spinal cord, (2) trachea, (3) superior vena cava, (4) ascending arch of the aorta.

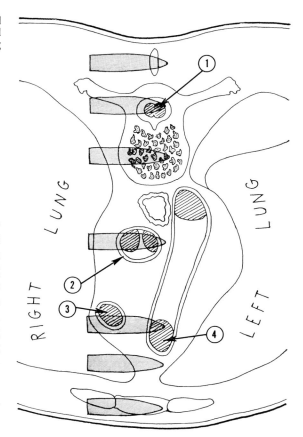

At about this point you will begin to say to yourself, "How am I going to know which views are important for me to understand and learn to use?" If, in the course of your 4-year training in medicine, you can familiarize yourself with the chest structures and their shadows *as seen in the standard PA and lateral views,* you will have built yourself a very useful and satisfying tool, and you should have no trouble in doing so. But do not feel confused or defeated if occasionally you see a chest film, for example, which looks like nothing you have ever seen before. Some of these will be, in fact, films of grossly abnormal chests. Others, however, will turn out to be films made by special or rarely used x-ray projections and procedures with which you are not familiar. You should rely comfortably on your acquaintance with the standard views but not be incurious or resistant to the possibilities of other modes of examination.

There are all sorts of ingenious obliquities of projection and many fascinating special procedures in the armamentarium of the radiologist which you will want to know about. Two of them, the anterior obliques of the chest, are very commonly used in studying the heart and will be discussed later. Others, designed for visualizing a particular structure in a particular way, also offer anatomic information not otherwise available. Sometimes these views or procedures are carried out at the discretion of the radiologist and on his initiation. At other times you will ask for them specifically or, better yet, discuss with a radiologist the chances of their being useful in the study of your patient's particular problem.

Figure 2-11

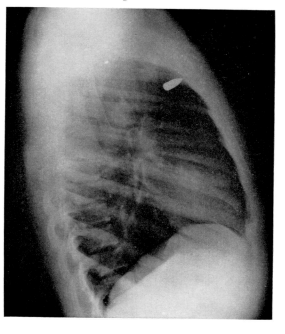

Let me give you an example of the excitement that is basic to such special views. Here is a patient who was admitted to the hospital with a persistent cough, one episode of blood-streaked sputum, weight loss, and a daily fever. The routine PA chest film in Figure 2-12 is not strikingly abnormal at first glance, but the intern had heard some abnormal sounds over the apex of the left lung (on your right, remember) which tended to reinforce the strong clinical suspicion of pulmonary tuberculosis. Unfortunately, the apex of the left lung in this film is obscured by the superimposed shadow of the left clavicle. Accordingly, a special projection, called a "lordotic view," was made, the patient positioned as in Figure 2-14. Here, because the patient stands leaning backward in exaggerated lordosis, the horizontal beam of AP x-rays foreshortens the chest by penetrating it at such an oblique angle that the anterior and posterior segments of the same ribs are superimposed. (If you tilt an articulated skeleton into this position and look at it from the side, you will see why.) The result of this maneuver is, of course, to project the clavicles upward so that by looking between the ribs, one can much more effectively visualize the lung tissue of the apex.

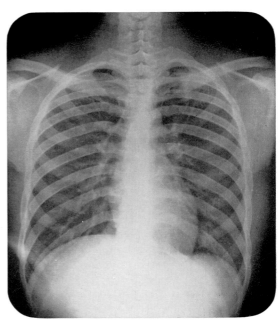

Figure 2-12 (above). Standard PA view of the chest of a patient with cough, fever, weight loss, and hemoptysis.

Figure 2-13 (below). Special lordotic view of the chest of the same patient.

Figure 2-14 (below, left). Position in which Figure 2-13 was made.

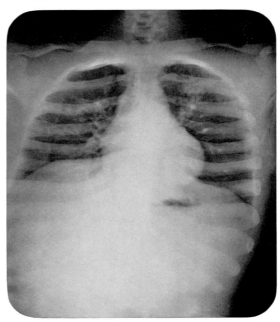

20

With this view (Figure 2-13), one is able to see that there *is* a fluffy white shadow in the upper part of the left lung, best seen in the second interspace. Note that there is nothing like it in the same interspace on the other side. This fluffy, increased density, as you will learn later, is characteristic of early tuberculosis in this location. Analysis of the patient's sputum subsequently confirmed the diagnosis.

You have just learned another important basic principle in looking at radiographs: the use of bilateral symmetry (or the lack of it) in recognizing abnormalities. The shadow of the heart is *not* symmetrical and no comparison of the two sides of its profile will be helpful. The two sides of the bony thorax *are* symmetrical, though, as are the two halves of the skull when viewed sagittally. The two hands ought to be able to be used for comparison with each other, and, for practical purposes, the right and left lungs cast symmetrical shadows on a chest film. You will learn to look back and forth from one interspace to the same part of the same interspace on the opposite side.

As you learn to look at x-rays in general, you will find that you build your idea of the expected normal appearance of various structures in various ways. You are informed by instructors that a given x-ray film is normal. You compare what you see with what you know about normal anatomy. You compare a problem film with one you know to be normal. And, as you have just learned, you can often use the opposite side of the same patient as a norm standard. I grant you, this *could* on occasion be misleading, since abnormality can exist on both sides and often does. However, bilateral abnormality is not very often perfectly symmetrical, and you will find that it is useful and convenient to make a habit of comparing any structure you are studying with the same one on the opposite side whenever possible.

Stop here and try your hand at these two unknowns.

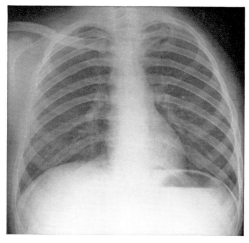

Figures 2-15 and 2-16 *(Unknowns 2-1 and 2-2)*. Using expected bilateral symmetry, make a diagnosis with regard to structure in these two patients.

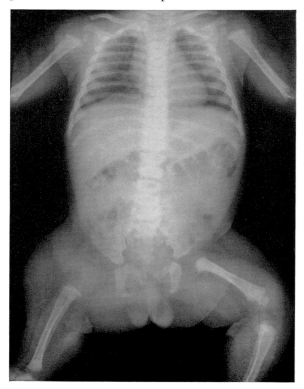

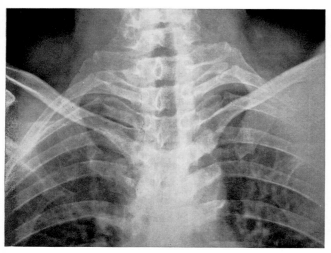
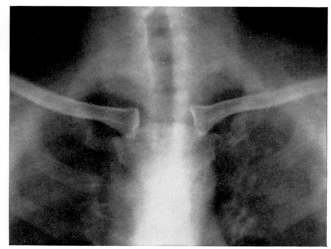

Figure 2-17   A   B

The two films in Figure 2-17*A* and *B* were made of the same patient. *A,* on the left, is an ordinary PA radiograph; *B* is a special procedure film called a "body-section radiograph." This type of study is going to be very useful to you throughout this book and will help you to visualize better the shadows which must be added together to make up the usual x-ray film. It is important, therefore, to understand how body-section radiographs are made.

Imagine that a frozen cadaver is sawed into coronal slices about 1 inch thick and that you then make a radiograph of each slice. Each film will have on it only the shadows cast by the densities of the structures in that slice. There will be no confusing superimposition of the shadows of structures from other slices to trouble you. How much simpler it would be, for example, to study manubrium and medial halves of clavicles if they were not superimposed upon the shadow of the thoracic spine as they are in the standard PA chest film. On the next few pages you will find some radiographed slices of such a cadaver to study. They are arranged in order from front to back, the very first slice having been omitted. It included the anterior chest wall, sternum, and rib cartilages. You will find it helpful to refer back to these slices many times as you learn the x-ray appearance of various organs and structures. Notice how well you can see, in the first slice (Figure 2-20), the shadows cast by the clavicles where they join the manubrium. Now look back

at the body-section radiograph of this area in Figure 2-17. Had you realized earlier that the patient's clavicles were dislocated upward? You cannot even now be certain of it from the standard x-ray in Figure 2-17*A.*

Body-section studies effectively slice the living patient so that you can study the shadows cast by certain structures free of superimposed shadows. Technically, this is done by moving both the x-ray tube and the film, but in *opposite directions, during the exposure.* They are moved about a pivot point calculated to fall in the plane of the object to be studied. In this

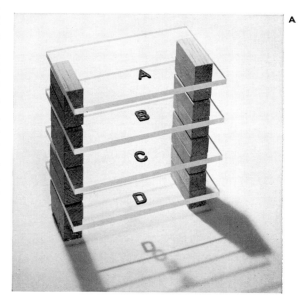

22

way the shadows of all the structures *not* in the plane selected for study are *intentionally blurred* because they move relative to the film. Thus, in the diagram (Figure 2-19), the object to be studied, *b,* will be "in focus" on the film, while the shadow of an object at *a* will be magnified, blurred, and distorted to lie between *a'* and *a"* on the film. This process is repeated for each plane to be studied.

Only the structures in the plane of the pivot point will be recognizable (as in Figure 2-17*B*); the shadows representing organs in front of or behind it are distorted in such a way that shape and form are no longer recognizable and the blurred images are easy for your eye to ignore. Thus you "see" the manubrium and its junction with the clavicles much better in this figure

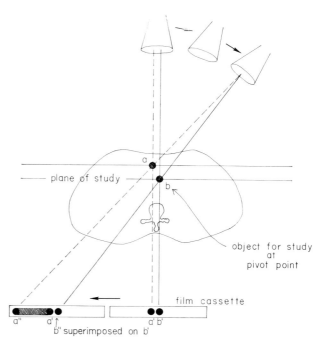

Figure 2-19. One method of body-section study.

Figure 2-18. Demonstration of the effect obtained with body-section studies. *A.* Series of plastic shelves each holding a lead letter superimposed vertically. *B.* Conventional radiograph superimposes the shadows of the letters. *C.* Body-section study at level of "C" shows that letter clearly but distorts and blurs the others.

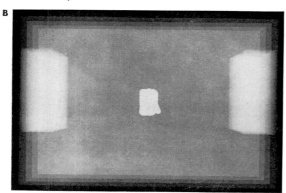

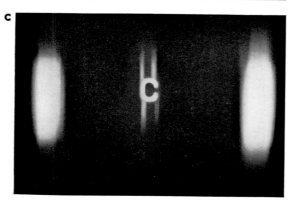

because the shadow of the spine and posterior ribs has been "rubbed out" for you.

The term body-section radiograph is a general one, and there are different types of sectioning studies, the techniques of which depend upon the result desired, that is, the shadows intended for study and those one wishes to distort. You will hear the terms laminogram, tomogram, and planigram. All are body-section studies. On first acquaintance they will all look confusing to you, but in this book you will be shown only paired studies so that you always have the usual x-ray for comparison. Whenever you are puzzled by one of them, try coming back to the cadaver slices to get your bearings, remembering that only the structures in one plane will be in focus in the section study. Remember, too, that the thickness of these particular cadaver slices may not have matched perfectly the chosen plane of the section study you happen to be looking at, since the pivot point determining the plane of a body-section study is calculated arbitrarily for a certain distance in centimeters from the surface of the chest. You will find that these cadaver slices match well enough to help you recognize anatomic structures and their relationships.

23

Figures 2-20, 2-21, and 2-22. Radiographs of a series of coronal slices of cadaver, arranged from front to back. Identify the following:

Junction of manubrium and clavicles
Superior vena cava (empty and filled with air)
Fundus of the stomach
   (Each of the above locates the level of the slice just as a body-section study would identify the level of the slice by including certain structures and excluding others.)
The symphysis pubis
Empty cavity of the left ventricle
Trachea, carina, and major bronchi with the air-filled left atrium immediately below them

Note the change in shape of the liver from section to section.

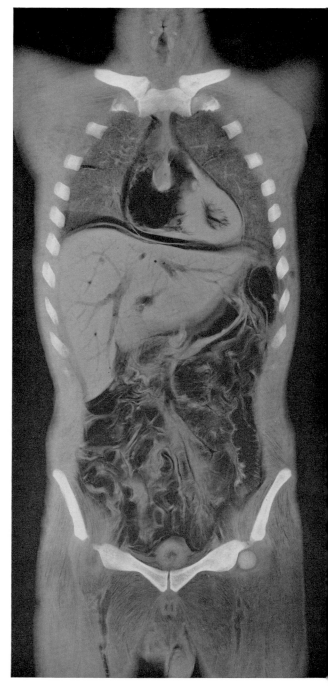

Figure 2-20

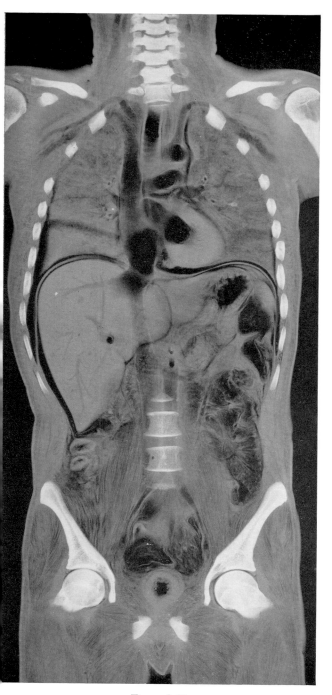

Figure 2-21

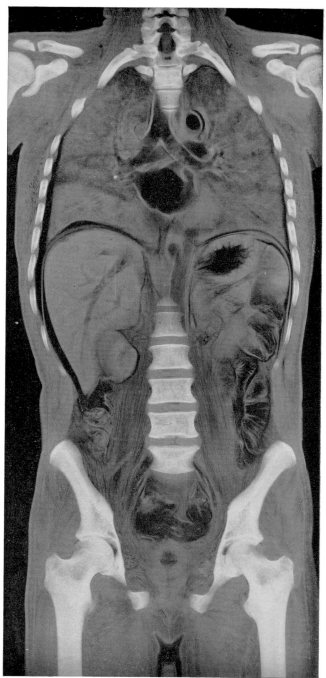

Figure 2-22

25

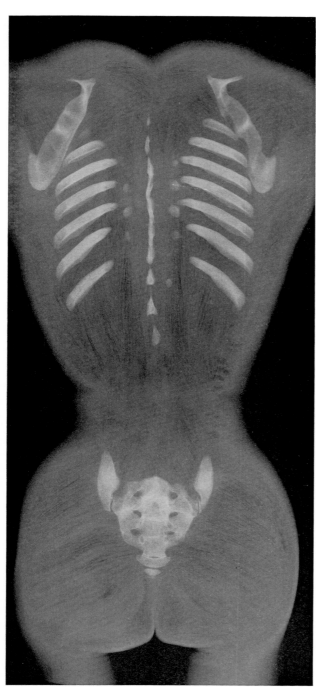

Figure 2-23

The end in view in showing you body-section radiographs and x-rays of cadaver slices is not novelty, though novelty, to be sure, makes study easier. It is, rather, a deliberate attempt to help you to learn to "focus down intellectually" through various layers as you look at any radiograph, thinking in terms of superimposed shadow masses and the anatomic structures responsible for them.

When you first turned the page, for example, did you "see" Figure 2-23 as a posterior view of a human being? If you did, old habit tricked you, because we *were* talking about x-rays of cadaver slices, and there was one left which you needed in the series to account for the scapulae, posterior ribs, and sacrum.

Although you are urged to think in three-dimensional perspective about radiographs which your eyes see as flatly as one eye alone sees any picture, I must not let you leave this chapter without knowing that stereoscopic techniques are also used successfully in radiology, one of those special procedures for special purposes. There was a great resurgence of interest in binocular viewing during the nineteenth century. The binocular telescope had been invented during Shakespeare's lifetime and the binocular microscope soon after, but both were forgotten for two centuries. In the first half of the Victorian era stereoscopes for viewing pairs of drawings in perspective were popular, and a little later with the advent of photography the stereopticon and pairs of photographs mounted on cards became a part of parlor entertainment.

Just so, within 5 years after the discovery of the x-ray, an article appeared in a German journal describing "Die Perspektive in den Röntgenbildern und die Technik der Stereoskopie," indicating that two films made by shifting the position of the tube by a distance equal to the interpupillary distance could be viewed in a stereoscopic projector to give true three-dimensional x-ray vision. The stereoscope is still in common use today in most x-ray departments, particularly for studies of the skull. If you are interested in appreciating for yourself the sensation of roentgen perspective, I suggest you hunt up a member of the department of radiology in your hospital and ask him to show you a stereoscopic pair of films in the viewer. If you do so, you will be better able to appreciate the intellectual procedure by which you can learn to look at regular monocular roentgenograms while thinking of them in depth and reconstructing the shadows that are added together to produce them.

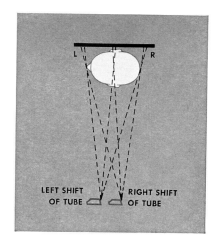

Figure 2-24 (immediately below). A pair of stereoscopic films is viewed with the help of angled mirrors so that they fuse for binocular vision.

Figure 2-25 (right). Diagram to show how stereoscopic films are made.

Figure 2-26 (bottom). Diagram to show how stereoscopic films are viewed.

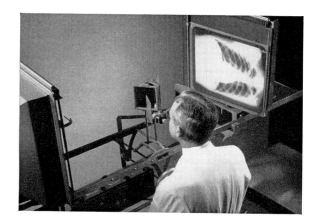

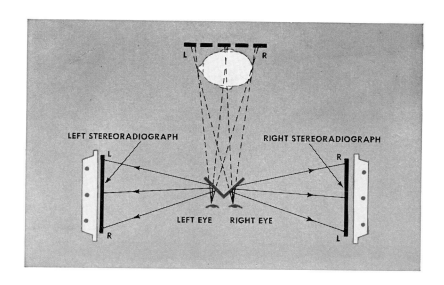

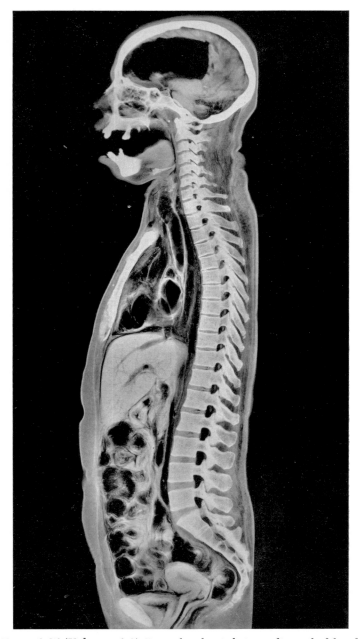

Figure 2-27 *(Unknown 2-3)*. Precisely what is being radiographed here?

Credits: Illustrations this chapter.

Figure 2-1. Courtesy Dr. A. Richards and the publisher, *MR&P* 32:28.

Figure 2-2*B*. Courtesy Drs. W. Macklin, Jr., H. Bosland, and A. McCarthy, and the publisher, *MR&P* 31:91.

Figures 2-5, 2-6. Courtesy Mr. C. Bridgman, Mr. E. Holly, Dr. M. Zariquiey, and the publisher, *MR&P* 32:53, 49.

Figures 2-9, 2-11. Courtesy Dr. C. Behrens, Bethesda, Md.

Figures 2-12, 2-13. Courtesy Dr. H. Forsyth, Jr., and the publisher, *MR&P* 25:38.

Figure 2-15. Courtesy Dr. J. Tollman, Omaha, Neb.

Figure 2-17. Courtesy Dr. B. Epstein and the publisher, *MR&P* 34:60.

Figures 2-18, 2-24, 2-25, 2-26. From *Fundamentals of Radiography*, pp. 48, 75, published by Eastman Kodak Co., Rochester, N. Y.

CHAPTER 3　How To Study a Chest Film

Hardly anyone ever reads the preface to a book, but if you did, you know that the goal of this one is twofold: to help the medical student understand x-ray shadows as an aid to learning in the other disciplines, and to equip him with a basic knowledge of the reasons for the roentgen appearance of some of the common disease conditions he will meet as a physician. It is my hope that those who study this book will develop a habit of mind in which every shadow on the radiograph arouses the responsive question, "*Why* does it look like that?", and that the student will have no hesitation about asking an answer from those who ought to know. He will find that sometimes the answer can be given quite readily. Sometimes he can reason it out himself. But occasionally no one has yet explained precisely, or understood, a particular shadow, and where this is so, one must be haunted by such a lack of comprehension until the matter is clarified. New waves of fresh information wash over old puzzlements of this sort perpetually. What escaped *us* yesterday may become clear to *you* tomorrow, and a logical approach to x-ray data will fill you with the sort of questions which inevitably turn up new ideas.

One glance at a chest film is often enough to "see" a very striking abnormality. Having seen it, the observer must reason out its structural identity, seldom quite so obvious, and attempt to deduce the nature of it in accord with his knowledge of the patient's illness. While the one-glance approach has its value, it is full of danger to the patient, because the presence of a very obvious abnormality tends to suppress, psychologically, your search for more subtle changes. The subtler changes are quite often more important to the patient than the more obvious ones.

Let us say that you correctly interpret the shadow of a large mass in the lung on Mr. B's chest film (Figure 3-2A) as being consistent with the cancer you thought he might have when you examined him. You will have failed him if you neglect a deliberate quest for any possible secondary involvement of his bones, since quite a different program of treatment may then become appropriate. Figure 3-2B illustrates the point by showing in more detail, with a more penetrating x-ray beam, the extent of his bone destruction. Although the prime responsibility is the radiologist's and not yours, of course, you are never absolved from the responsibility of considering the entire problem.

The radiologist usually gives the film an initial once-over glance, but then he studies it in a very systematic fashion. Because you have less experience than he in looking at radiographs, it takes longer to see abnormal shadows, but if you study each x-ray film, systematically as he does, you will soon find that you are repaid many times for your pains. You will have the satisfaction of putting your finger on the abnormal feature of the film. You will also have added one more survey to the list of chest films studied from which you build normal base lines about which you can feel secure. The whole procedure is rather like what you would experience if you looked at a child's map of your state. You would know that it was out of proportion, but it might take you a little while and some remembered distances before you could tell him exactly how it was inaccurate.

30

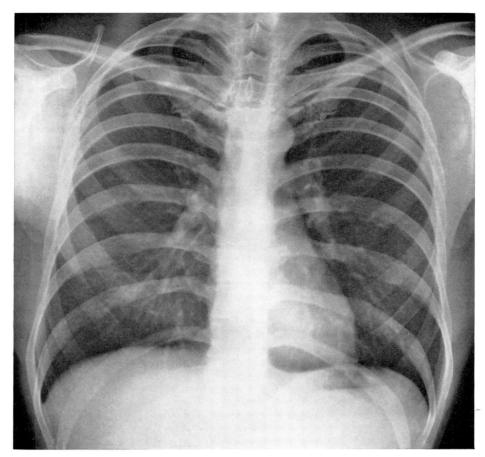

Figure 3-1 (above). Normal chest film.

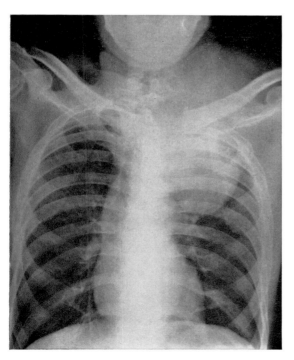

Figure 3-2. *A* (left). PA chest film of Mr. B, admitted with cough, chest pain, hoarseness, and a fist-sized mass in the left supraclavicular region. *B* (below). Detail study of the thoracic inlet made with a more penetrating beam. Left posterior first rib and parts of the first two thoracic vertebrae have been destroyed by tumor.

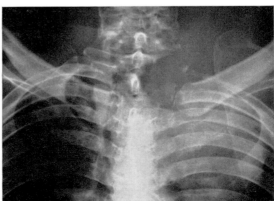

The system generally employed by the radiologist is to *look at* various structures in a deliberate order, concentrating on the anatomy of each while excluding the superimposed shadows of other structures. Even as an exercise in intellectual discipline, this is not as difficult as it sounds. Prove it to your own satisfaction by trying to *look at* one clavicle or one rib on any of the chest films in this chapter, thinking of its normal anatomic proportions and excluding other shadows overlying it which you know are not a part of the bone you are studying.

In this and succeeding chapters I propose to show you how to study the chest film systematically in order to learn from it how roentgen shadows are composed. Because a steady diet of normals can be very boring, I also propose to show you the normal by giving you interesting abnormals to contrast with it, but please remember that the idea at this point is not at all to learn the roentgen appearance of a few isolated conditions. You will gather together and review all this sort of information and reasoning later.

The best way to be systematic about studying any film is to adopt a definite order in which you look at the structures whose shadows appear there. For a chest film, you will *look at* the bony framework, and then, just as deliberately, *look through it* at lung tissue and the heart.

Begin with the scapulae. Then look at the portions of humerus and shoulder joint often visible on the chest film. Inspect the clavicles, and then finally study the ribs, quickly but in pairs from top to bottom. When you can, always compare the two sides for symmetry. The spine and sternum are, of course, superimposed upon each other and upon the dense shadows of the mediastinal structures in the PA view, so that, at the kilovoltages used for lung study, little of the beam penetrates, and the film remains unexposed down the mid-line.

Remember that the technique used for chest films has been designed for study of the lung, and what you see of the bones is incidental. Ideal techniques for studying these same bones will be quite different. In a PA chest film, for example, the scapulae and posterior ribs are as far as possible from the film. Therefore, they are enlarged and distorted to some extent. In addition, on the chest film the scapulae have been intentionally rotated as much as they can be to the sides by placing the hands on the hips, palms out, with the elbows forward. Try it. In the PA view of the chest this maneuver prevents the superimposition of the scapular shadows upon the upper lung fields, and only the medial margin of the scapula will still be seen overlapping the axillary portions of the upper ribs.

Now that I have drawn your attention to it, notice that you can see the medial margin of the left scapula in Figure 3-3 but not that of the right (patient's right, remember). A carefully repeated assay of the shadow values in symmetrical interspaces will convince you that there *is* some sort of vaguely outlined but perfectly definite *increased density* in the right upper lung field where the scapular line ought to be.

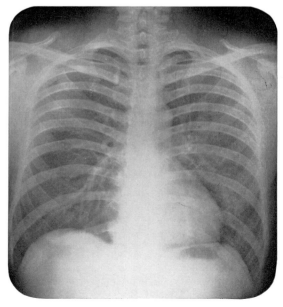

Figure 3-3

Now look at Figure 3-4, a special AP view made obliquely across the patient's *right* scapula. In this view the scapula was close to the film and can be seen in much better detail. You are complaining that you have never seen such a view of the scapula before, but look at Figure 3-6, a view of a normal *left* scapula, also taken obliquely. This placement of the figures gives you another exercise in looking back and forth at mirror images in order to use the opposite side as a norm for comparison.

You can see that the scapula in Figure 3-4 is deformed, curled around an extra piece of bone growing forward from the anterior surface of the body of the scapula. The extra bone prevents the scapula from lying slim and flat against the posterior rib cage, as you expect it to do when you examine and manipulate a normal articulated shoulder girdle. The extra bone in this patient accounts for the added density in the chest film. Now try your hand at the unknown in Figure 3-5 using Figure 3-6 as a normal to compare with it. The patient in the unknown was in great pain and lay on his back with the film cassette under him. His left arm was across his chest and he was rolled slightly to the right.

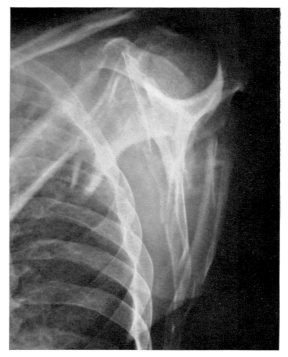

Figure 3-5 (*Unknown 3-1*). See text.

Figure 3-6. Normal for comparison.

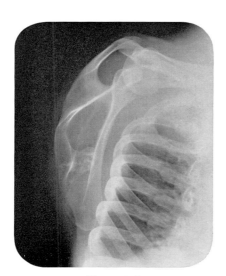

Figure 3-4

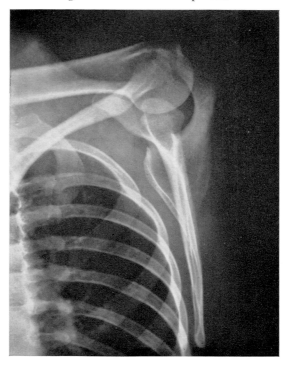

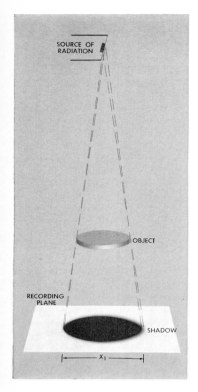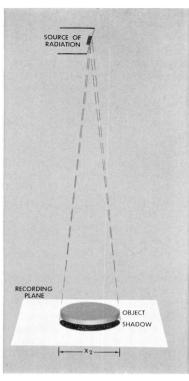

Figure 3-7. Effect of projection in enlarging the roentgen shadows of objects far away from the film.

Figure 3-8. AP view of the chest is made with the posterior ribs close to the film. The heart, far from the film, is projected and looks larger than normal.

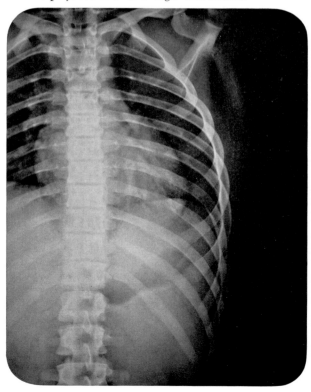

Never discount the factor of projection in altering the appearance of structures far away from the film. You need not be confused by such changes, however, once you are familiar with them. In Figure 3-7 you have a diagram illustrating the effect of projection, in which you can equate the "object" with the scapula in any AP and PA chest film. You can equate it also with the anteriorly placed heart in the AP film, Figure 3-8. Note that the heart in this film appears to be larger with less sharp margins than the hearts in the PA chest films you have seen up to now. Note the slight difference in the width and shape of the posterior interspaces compared with those on the usual PA film.

The routine chest film measures 14 by 17 inches, and its cassette film holder is placed with the long dimension vertical. In broad-chested persons little of the *shoulder girdle* and *humerus* will be seen, but in slender, smaller individuals you may actually have all of the shoulder and most of the upper arm to study. Figure 3-9 is a radiograph of the shoulder made AP. Figure 3-10, placed next to it, is a photograph of the bones of the other shoulder so that you can look back and forth as you would do with a chest film, developing a feeling for comparing mirror-image symmetries. Notice how you seem to see the coracoid *through* the spine of the scapula, because they superimpose, just as you see the head of the humerus and the acromion additively.

The man in Figure 3-11 had fallen from a horse and had his arm immobilized in plaster *(a, a)*, which you see more densely wherever the ray came through it tangentially, like the eggshell discussed in the first chapter. Since there are several fractures and several fragments, this is what is called a *comminuted* fracture. Note the folds and wrinkles in the plaster and the point in the axilla where the cast ends *(b)*.

The woman in Figure 3-12 could not comb her hair or tie her apron strings without intense pain in her shoulder. She had tenderness over the insertion of the supraspinatus tendon, and, as you see, she has *calcification* in that area and around the shoulder joint: dense white shadows not present on any of the x-rays of normal shoul-

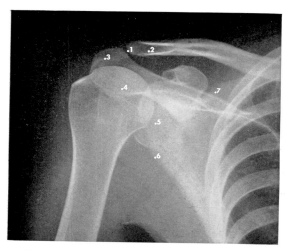

Figure 3-9. Radiograph of the right shoulder.

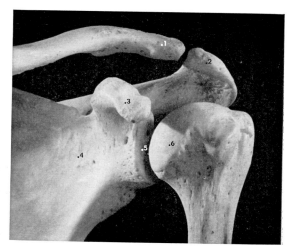

Figure 3-10. Photograph of the bones of the left shoulder. (Numbers, intended as an exercise in identifying structures, do not match.)

ders you have seen so far. These findings, *b*, are typical of "bursitis" or calcific peritendinitis of the shoulder.

Note the dense white triangular shadow medial to the mid-humerus (*a*) in Figure 3-12. It is common in radiology and is called an "overlap shadow." It is created in this instance by the *added densities* of heavy breast and soft tissues of the upper arm. The confusion arising from the unexpected density of the shadow at

a will be easy for you to resolve if you remember that *thickness* as well as *composition* determines radiodensity. Although fat, skin, and muscle ought to be less radiodense than bone, the shadow cast by a thick mass of these tissues will approach that of bone as you see it in this figure. Note, on the other hand, that a small amount of air imprisoned in the axilla is black on the film, probably because it was a long pocket of air x-rayed end-on.

Figures 3-11 (left) and 3-12 (right). Two patients with shoulder pain.

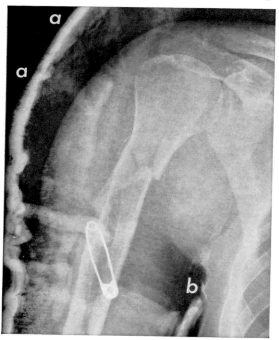

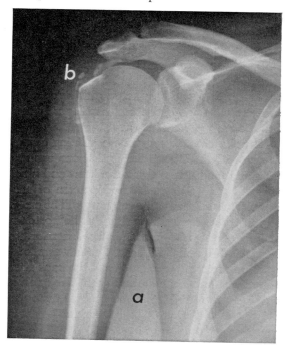

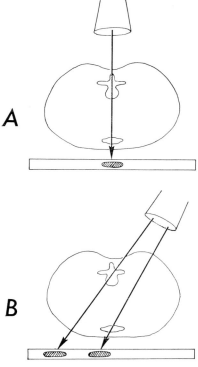

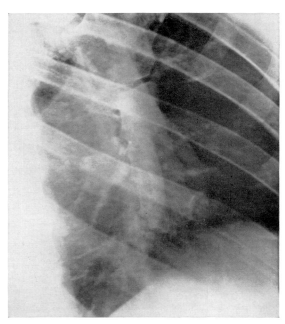

Figure 3-13

Figure 3-14. Film of the sternum made with an oblique PA beam. Note that the shadows of posterior ribs are projected across the sternum.

The *sternum*, in spite of its position, can be filmed in a nearly PA direction, as in Figure 3-13*B*, an arrangement of x-ray beam and patient that brings the sternum close to the film but not superimposed on the spine. Note that the ray is being angled in obliquely so that the sternum is thrown clear of the shadow of the spine. Figure 3-14 shows you a film produced using the opposite oblique. In Figure 3-15 a body-section technique has been used. Note how well you can see the details of structure, including the bony notches on each side for the anterior rib ends and costal cartilages, which are themselves radiolucent.

The *ribs* confuse everyone beginning to look at chest films. The miracle is that one can discern anything useful about the heart and lungs through such a cross-hatched pattern of shadows. Three-dimensional thinking will be easier if you try to concentrate first on the posterior halves of the ribs and then the anterior. In Figure 3-16*B* and *C* the same thorax was photographed from the front and from the back after the cavity had been stuffed with black velvet to give you the illusion you seek in trying to study the posterior ribs while excluding from your mind the anterior ones.

Figure 3-15. Film of the sternum made in the same way as Figure 3-14 except that now a body-section technique has been added, the pivot point calculated to lie at the level of the sternum so that the shadows of posterior ribs are also erased and the structure of the sternum is much better seen.

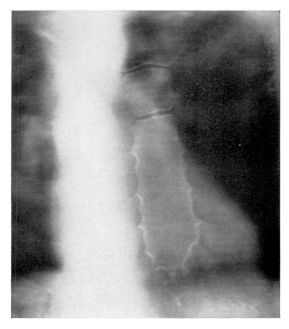

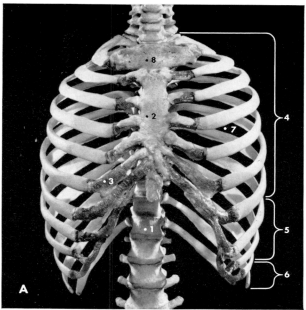

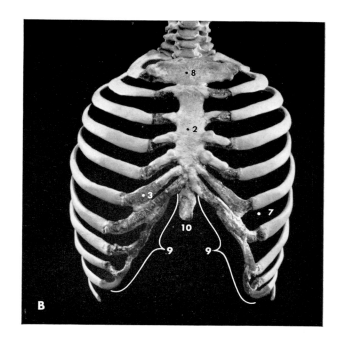

Figure 3-16. Structures identified by number:

1. Thoracic vertebrae
2. Sternum
3. Costal cartilage
4. Vertebrosternal ribs *7* { *True*
5. Vertebrochondral ribs *3*
6. Vertebral ribs *2 False*
7. Intercostal space
8. Manubrium
9. Costal arches
10. Infrasternal angle

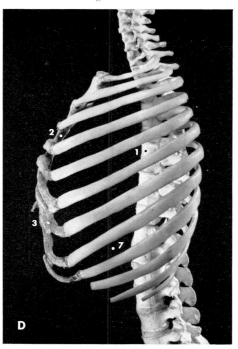

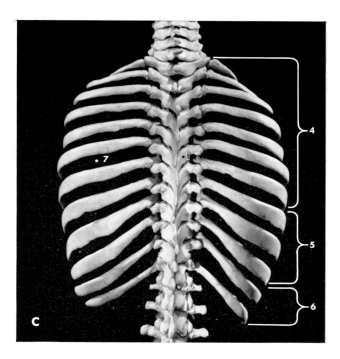

(*B*, *C*, and *D* were photographed with the thoracic cavity stuffed with black velvet.)

37

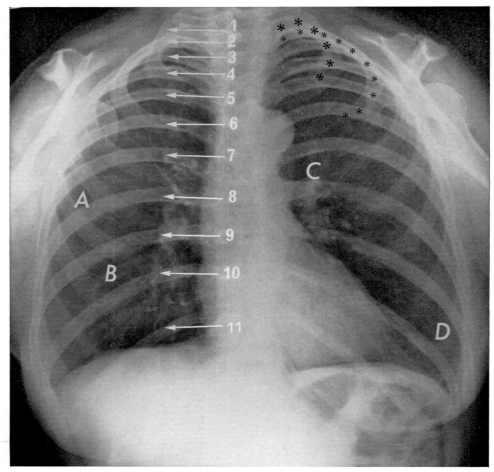

Figure 3-17. Counting and identifying ribs and rib interspaces is an important part of the systematic chest film survey. (See text for instructions.) Note, incidentally, that the breast shadows in this patient come well below the level of the diaphragm and do not obscure the lower lung field; in many female patients they do.

Using the bilateral symmetry of each pair of ribs in Figure 3-17, and beginning at the origin of the first rib at its junction with the first thoracic vertebra, trace each rib as far as you can anteriorly to the beginning of the radiolucent (and hence invisible) costal cartilage. The ribs are useful to the radiologist because he locates an abnormal shadow by its proximity to a particular rib or interspace on a particular film he is describing. Anyone reading his written report can identify in this way the precise shadow he was discussing. Thus A in Figure 3-17 could be described as lying in the seventh interspace on the right close to the axilla (that is, the outer third of the space between the posterior halves of the right seventh and eighth

ribs). If you do not locate it there, count again, for you are probably getting lost in the overlap tangle of ribs 1, 2, and 3. To avoid this, identify carefully the first rib by finding its anterior junction with the manubrium and following this rib *backward* to the spine. Then count down the posterior ribs. *B* would be said to be located in the ninth interspace on the right. Note that the word interspace always implies the space between posterior segments of adjoining ribs unless the anterior is specified. Try your hand at designating the location of *C* and *D*, covering the left half of this figure and the spine with all its numbers. (Have you noticed anything peculiar about this film?)

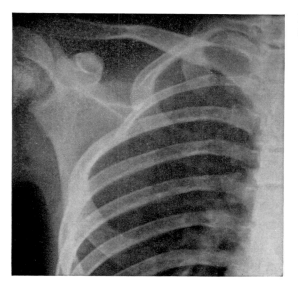

Figure 3-18 *(Unknown 3-2)* (left). Describe this radiograph over the phone to another physician.

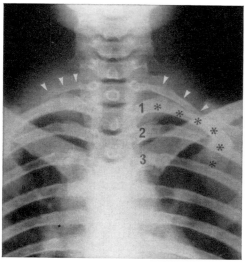

Figure 3-19 *(Unknown 3-3)* (above). Identifying the first rib accurately is always important, often difficult. If you are following the instructions in the text, you begin by finding the anterior end of the first rib, tracing it backward to its posterior end. The anterior end of the first rib should be located just below the medial end of the clavicle. Here, because you are working with an AP film, the anterior ends of the first ribs are projected so that they appear to be separated widely. This is not the way they appear on a PA film because then they lie close to the film. *If you think the ribs are correctly labeled here, how do you account for the structures indicated by white arrows?*

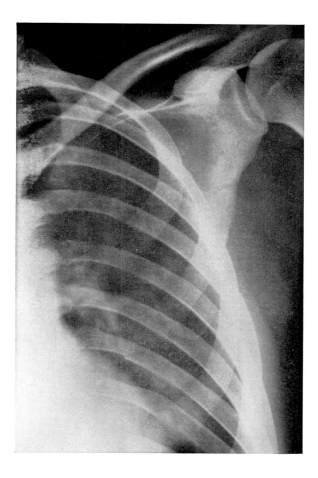

Figure 3-20 *(Unknown 3-4)* (left). This patient has been filmed after an automobile accident. Which rib is fractured?

Because of their curiously curved shape, the shadows of the two *clavicles* will appear symmetrical on the chest film only if there is no rotation of the chest. In a perfectly true PA film the beam passes straight through the mid-sagittal plane. The arms and shoulders of the patient are arranged symmetrically, and the technician checks for rotation and corrects it before making the exposure. Turned even a few degrees, the clavicles will exhibit a remarkable degree of asymmetry. This fact will prove very useful to you because a glance at the clavicles will tell you whether or not the beam has passed through the sagittal plane and whether you are therefore looking at a true PA or AP film without rotation.

Even slight rotation is undesirable in a chest film because the heart and mediastinum are then radiographed obliquely and their shadows appear enlarged and distorted. If you think of the mediastinum as a disc of denser structures flattened between the two inflated lungs and normally rayed end-on in a PA chest film, it is easy to see how rotation of this disc will produce a wider shadow. If it were a valid finding, enlargement of the heart or widening of the mediastinal shadow would be an important piece of roentgen evidence for disease. One has to be able to disregard apparent enlargement due to rotation, therefore, and the best clue to rotation is asymmetry of the shadows of the two clavicles. Learn to watch them, mentally noting their symmetry or lack of it, in your systematic survey of the chest film.

Now look back at Figure 3-17. Did you notice that there were no clavicles? The patient was born without them and makes an ideal subject on whom to learn to count ribs. Compare it with any normal chest film and observe that you can mentally subtract the shadow of the clavicle when you want to in order to study or count the first three ribs.

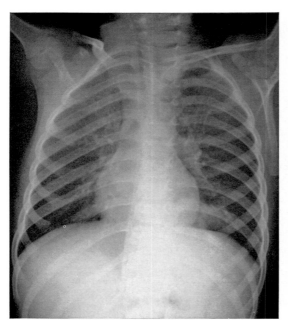

Figure 3-21. Chest film made when the patient was accidentally somewhat rotated. Note marked asymmetry of the clavicles.

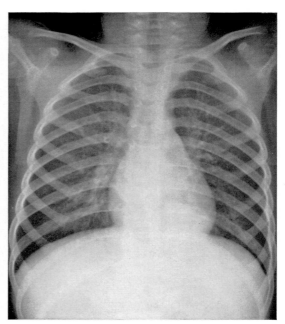

Figure 3-22. Same patient refilmed precisely PA.

40

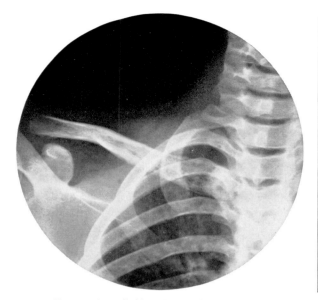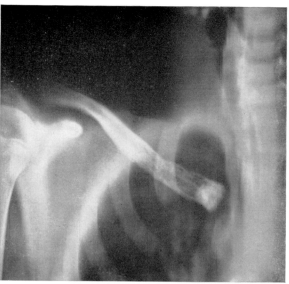

Figures 3-23 (left) and 3-24 (right). Just as the upper ribs may be obscured by the clavicle, so abnormality of the clavicle may be obscured by the overlapping ribs. Here a moth-eaten appearance of the right clavicle is difficult to study on the routine view and much easier to study by body-section technique (Figure 3-24). Erosion or invasion of the clavicle by malignant tumor (in this case sarcoma) will produce this appearance.

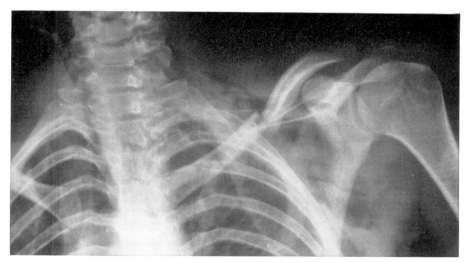

Figure 3-25 (*Unknown 3-5*). The figure is obviously not a true PA film (medial end of right clavicle seen overlying fourth interspace) for the very good reason that the patient was in a great deal of pain. Study the bones, using normals in Figure 3-22 for comparison. Then study the soft tissues outside the chest cage around the shoulder girdle, also comparing those in Figure 3-22. How do you account for the dark streaks?

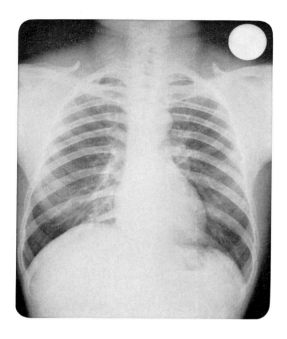

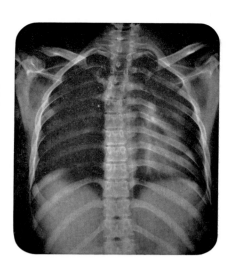

Figure 3-26 (left). Regular chest film made PA at 6 feet with the patient standing.

Figure 3-27 (right). AP film of the chest exposed for study of the spine. Patient lying down. Bucky diaphragm used.

The thoracic spine is not well seen in the chest films you have been looking at because its density added to those of the mediastinal structures and sternum together absorb all the rays, and none reach the film to blacken it. This is true of the techniques commonly used for studying the lung.

Seeing detail through very dense parts of the body requires a different technique. More penetration can be achieved in several ways. One is by increasing the exposure factors (kilovoltage, milliamperage, and time) to produce a beam of x-rays of shorter wave length, so-called harder rays. A film made in this way is often called an "overexposed film," intentionally overexposed in order to increase the penetration of dense structures.

Unfortunately, when x-rays impinge on matter of any kind, secondary x-rays are generated which radiate in all directions as from many point sources of light. This is called "scattered radiation," and is, of course, added photographically to the primary beam, additionally blackening the film. Since there are thus multiple sources of radiation, a blurred and distorted image is produced. Moreover, increasing the exposure factors to produce a harder and more penetrating beam also increases the amount of scattered radiation. Thus, a simple overexposed film will usually be lacking in contrast and sharpness.

Most of the undesirable distortion which is produced by scattered radiation can be eliminated by an ingenious device called the *Potter-Bucky diaphragm*. It is a flat grid composed of alternate very thin strips of radiolucent and radio-opaque material (wood and lead, for example). Only the most perpendicular rays pass through the lucent strips. The oblique rays, representing most of the scattered radiation, strike the sides of the lead strips and are absorbed.

If the interposed grid is motionless, of course, the lead strips will appear on the film as fine white lines. To prevent this, it is only necessary to move the grid across the film all during the exposure; no lines will appear.

You will find that in an obese patient, or in any patient whose spine, mediastinum, skull, or heavy long bones must be studied by x-ray, Bucky technique films will have been made automatically by the technician. Every film of the abdomen which you see will have been made in this way also.

The PA chest film in Figure 3-26 was made expressly for the purpose of studying the lung, and a relatively soft, nonpenetrating technique was used for it. On the other hand, the film in Figure 3-27 was made AP (so that the spine toward which the study was directed would be close to the film), and a Bucky diaphragm and the appropriate exposure technique were used to produce it. Note how well you can see the structure of the vertebrae with their interposed

42

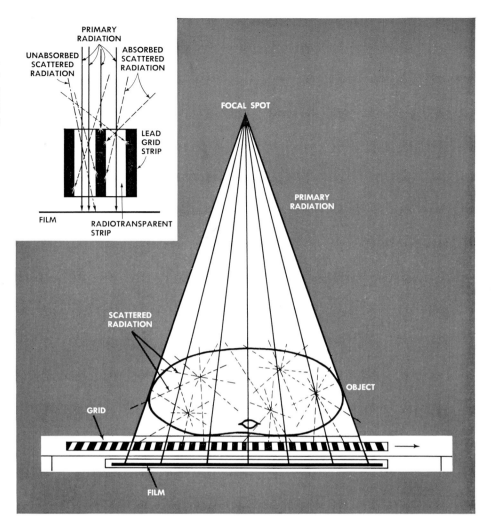

Figure 3-28. The Potter-Bucky diaphragm, plus increased kilovoltage and time, give the desired increased penetration and clearer detail to radiographs of thick parts of the body (see text).

cartilaginous discs. Note also that here you can see the ribs below the diaphragm, scarcely visible in most regular chest films. This film would be useless for studying the lung, all the delicate detail being lost, or "burned out" in radiologic parlance.

Just as the lung detail is burned out with such techniques, so also are the soft tissues of the chest lying outside the thoracic cage. Having completed your survey of the bones, you should now *look at* these soft tissues, studying breast shadows, supraclavicular areas, axillae, and the tissue along the sides of the chest. You will be able to study them in any film exposed for study of the lungs, and soft tissues often give you important information about the patient. Are his soft tissues scanty, indicating perhaps that he has lost weight? Are the normally symmetrical triangles of dark fat in the supra-

clavicular region disturbed in any way? Look back at Figure 3-2A and at Unknown 3-5. Always be sure to check whether there are two breasts; a chest film showing one missing breast often means that the patient is being studied for recurrence of cancer, and attention should be directed toward bones and lung fields for evidence of metastases. The lung field under a missing breast appears a little darker than the other lung field because of the missing breast and pectoral muscles, removed at the time of the mastectomy. The patient in Figure 3-26 was a right-handed male, and the right pectoral muscle mass is seen to be heavier than the left, a common finding.

So much, then, for the first step in studying a chest film: a systematic survey of the bones and soft tissues. You are now ready to look past the bones at the shadow of the lung itself.

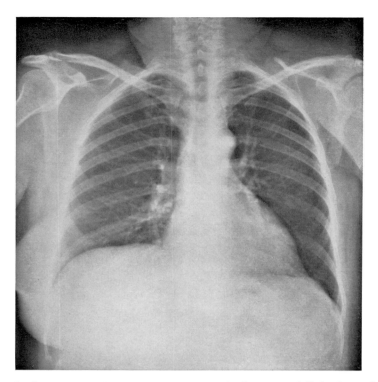

Figure 3-29 *(Unknown 3-6)* (above) and Figure 3-30 *(Unknown 3-7)* (below) are designed as exercises in the systematic survey of the chest film covered so far, that is, bones and soft tissues. In the succeeding chapters you will add gradually to this survey the hila, lung fields, diaphragms, pleural space, mediastinum, and heart, in that order.

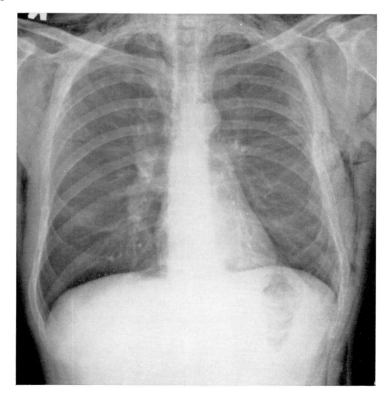

CHAPTER 4 The Lung Itself

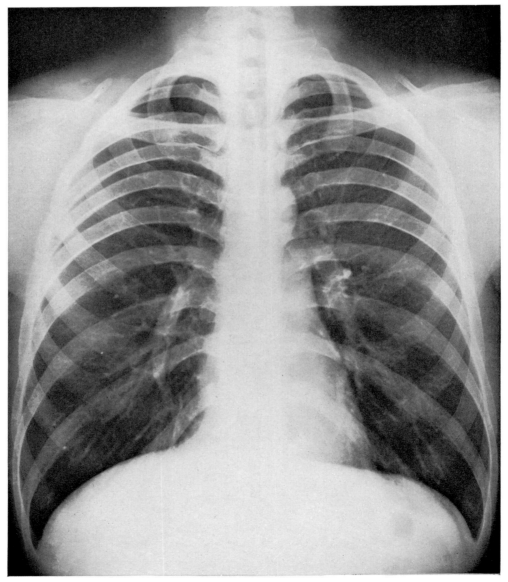

Figure 4-1

Look, now, past all those distracting shadows of the ribs and soft tissues at the roentgen images which belong to the lung itself. Because of its contained air, the normally expanded lung is largely radiolucent, as we have said, but nevertheless you do see in Figure 4-1 traceries of branching, gray, linear shadows. What precisely are they? You can reason it out.

Reflect, first, that logically any structure of greater radiodensity suspended in the middle of a radiolucent structure like the lung will absorb some of the x-rays and cast a gray shadow on the film, a patch of film where less silver has been precipitated.

If this structure is spherical and of uniform composition, it will cast a round shadow. If the surface of the mass is knobby and irregular, knobs will be present in the outline as in Figure 4-2. If the suspended dense structure is cylindrical, like a blood-filled vessel traversing the lung substance, a tapering linear gray shadow results, and if the vessel branches, the shadow will be seen to branch.

When a vessel passes through the lung in a direction roughly parallel with the film (and perpendicular to the ray), its tapering and its branching will be accurately rendered upon the PA film. But if it passes through the lung in a more nearly sagittal direction, it will then line up with the beam, absorbing more x-rays so that its shadow will appear as a dense round spot. The situation is analogous to the rose leaf on edge in the first chapter. You can find such end-on vessels in Figure 4-1. There is one overlying the right tenth rib and a smaller one in the middle of the right eighth interspace midway between the mediastinum and the lateral chest wall.

That the normal "lung markings," as the radiologist calls these linear shadows, are indeed vessels and not bronchi and bronchioles is also quite logical. The bronchial tree, being air-filled, casts little or no shadow when it is normal. It is practical, therefore, to think of the normal lung markings as wholly vascular in nature. Figure 4-3 shows the lateral radiograph of a lung the vessels of which have been injected with a radio-opaque substance.

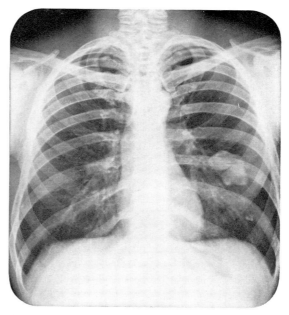

Figure 4-2. Mass suspended in air-filled lung casts a shadow recording its knobby outline.

Figure 4-3. Lateral radiograph of lung specimen which has had its arterial tree injected with a radio-opaque substance.

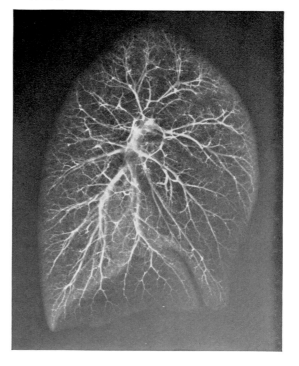

The tracheobronchial tree may be rendered *visible*, of course, with relatively harmless radio-opaque fluids instilled via a tracheal catheter into the lung of a living patient, who later coughs up or absorbs and excretes the opaque substance. This procedure, called "bronchography," is carried out under local anesthesia to depress the cough reflex and provides much important information about patients with respiratory diseases. Figure 4-4 shows the tracheal catheter lying with its tip in the left main bronchus. Note that the trachea and right main bronchus, because of the air they contain, may be seen as darker shadows within the dense mediastinum. In Figure 4-5 the catheter has been withdrawn into the trachea. This film was made after the opaque substance had been instilled into the right bronchial tree.

The *vascular tree* within the lung may also be opacified in the living patient, so that the vessels are more clearly seen than they are on the plain chest film. Radio-opaque fluid, miscible with blood, may be injected quickly into an antecubital vein or through a filament catheter, so that a particular volume of blood passing back through the right heart to the lungs

is "seen" as a series of dense white "casts" of the cardiac chambers and the pulmonary vessels in sequence. Multiple rapid-filming devices or x-ray movies are used to record the passage of the visible "bolus" of blood from heart to lungs, back to heart, and out to body tissues. Figure 4-6 shows a middle frame from such a serial *angiocardiogram*. Note that both arteries and veins in the lungs are filled. The large central white shadow is the left atrium filling from the pulmonary veins. Figure 4-7 was made 1 second later and shows the left ventricle and aorta also filled, and now, you notice, there seem to be fewer filled vessels in the lung. This is because the last of the opacified volume of blood has passed out of the arteries into the veins. The arteries themselves are filling with new blood from the right side of the heart which contains no opaque substance; they are on the film, but only as dense as ordinary blood will make them.

Much less dramatic but nonetheless important information is available from any simple PA chest film as you study the vascular shadows in the lung marked only by the blood they contain. Look back at Figure 4-1 at some details which may have escaped you earlier. No-

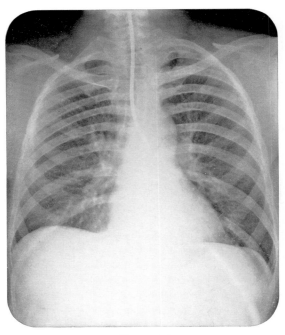

Figure 4-4

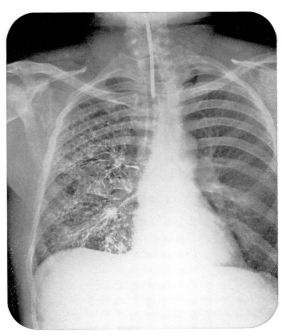

Figure 4-5

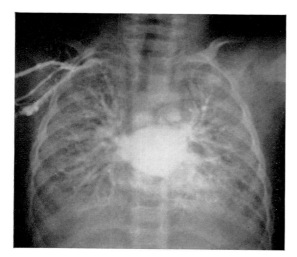

Figure 4-6

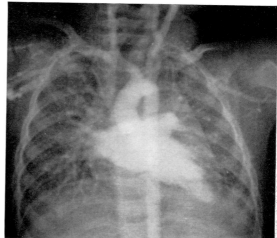

Figure 4-7

tice, first, that the largest vessels at the hilum of the lung cast the heaviest and widest shadows, just as you would expect. This Medusa-like tangle of arteries and veins on either side of the heart shadow is referred to by the radiologist as the "hilum" or "lung root" in his reports. The right hilar vessels seem to extend out farther than those on the left, but this is only because a part of the left hilum is obscured by the shadow of the more prominent left side of the heart. Measured from the center of the vertebral column, they will be found to be symmetrical except for the slightly higher take-off of the left pulmonary artery, which hooks up over the left main bronchus rather abruptly (Figure 4-8). For this reason the left hilum on any normal chest film is a little higher than the right.

Figure 4-8. The anatomical composition of the hilum. The aorta has been rendered as though transparent. Tracheobronchial tree indicated with cartilage rings; arteries light and veins dark.

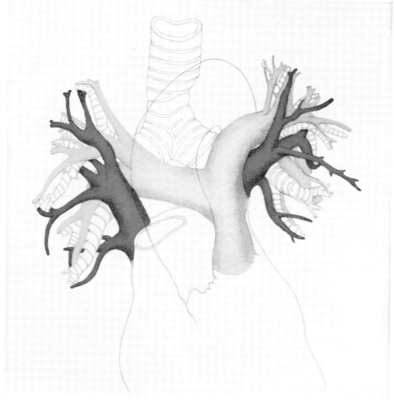

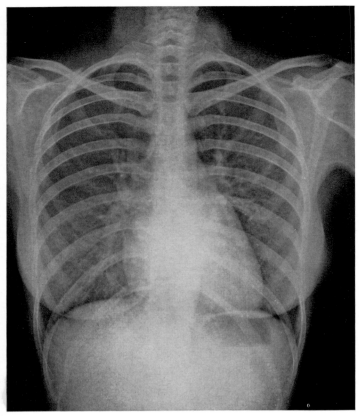

Figure 4-9. Engorged hilar root shadows in mitral stenosis.

arteriosus with a shunt of blood from the aorta to the pulmonary artery, and septal defects between the atria commonly give this picture. Figure 4-10 shows an example of the marked hilar arterial engorgement seen in congenital heart disease of this type.

There is often actually some enlargement of both veins and arteries, and it is not usually possible for you to say from the plain radiograph which vessels predominate. In judging the appearance of the hilum in the patient whose film you see for the first time, you will decide simply that you are looking at vascular trunks of normal caliber or that they are enlarged. However, it is a constantly diverting game of logic to reason out whether veins or arteries probably account for most of the enlargement of a thickened root shadow, and in any well-studied cardiac patient you will probably have no difficulty in doing so.

The vascular trunks of the hilum normally branch and taper out into the lung field in all directions. They are so fine in the far peripheral lung close to the chest wall that you can scarcely see them. If you mask off between two pieces

Compare the normal hila in Figure 4-1 with a few abnormal hilar shadows. The lung root may be enlarged because of engorgement of its *veins,* for example, in any condition in which there is obstruction to the return of oxygenated blood from the lung to the left side of the heart. Such a condition exists in acute left heart failure after a myocardial infarction. More chronically the same situation exists in rheumatic heart disease with mitral stenosis, where the gradual narrowing of the mitral valve results in back pressure in the pulmonary veins. Figure 4-9 shows the appearance of the hilum in moderately advanced mitral stenosis. Note the enlargement of the lung root and its obviously fat and tortuous branches, compared with the slim, straight vessels in Figure 4-1.

Dilatation of the *arteries* in the hilum will also become familiar to you in types of congenital heart disease in which an abnormal opening in the septum reroutes blood from the left chambers back into the right chambers and to the lesser circulation, thus overloading the right heart and pulmonary arteries. A patent ductus

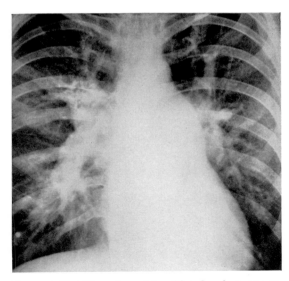

Figure 4-10. Hila enlarged by dilated pulmonary arteries in a patient with interatrial septal defect. Normal quantity of blood returning to the right atrium from the vena cava is augmented by blood shunted through the defect from the left atrium. This results in recirculation of blood through the lungs, an overload of the pulmonary circulation, and dilated arteries.

50

of paper first the hilum and medial half of the lung and then the lateral half, you will be struck by the decreased number of trunks laterally. But this will not surprise you when you recall that the lung is much thicker medially where it bounds the mediastinum than at its lateral extremity and that there are many more vessels superimposed on each other in the medial half of the lung field on the radiograph. If you similarly divide the lung field on the x-ray film into upper and lower halves, you can see at once that there are many more branching vascular trunks in the lower half of the lung than there are in the upper half. This, too, is a function of thickness, and to think three-dimensionally about the vascular tree within the lung at this point is to recall the pyramidal shape of the lung with its broad base against the diaphragm and its apex coming to a point under the arch of the first rib.

You will be disturbed from time to time by the juxtacardiac portion of the lower right lung (the right cardiophrenic angle). Many vascular trunks overlap there in the PA view because those for the anteriorly placed middle lobe are superimposed on those for the posteriorly placed lower lobe. One is easily misled into supposing there to be some increased density in this area when, in fact, none exists. You can prove this to your own satisfaction by reviewing in films on this page and preceding pages the appearance of the portion of the right lung lying just above the diaphragm and to the right of the heart. Observe that even in normal films (see Figure 4-1) the area looks more heavily traversed by vessel trunks than you expect it to be. Part of the difficulty is the visual trick your eye plays you: you are probably comparing the lung on the two sides of the heart, but, because of the shape of the heart, the lung tissue just beyond the left border of the heart is not actually comparable with the problem area on the right which we have been discussing. The point is easily proved by measuring from the mid-line: the truly comparable part of the left lung field lies closer to the mid-line obscured by the shadow of the heart itself. In Figures 4-11 and 4-12 you have two abnormal and one normal cardiophrenic angles to compare.

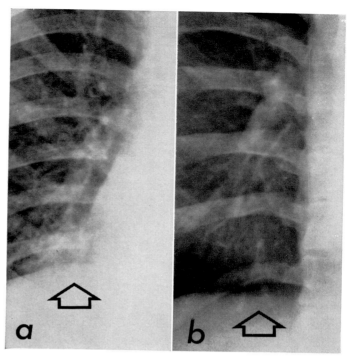

Figure 4-11. Right cardiophrenic angle, a section of the lung field often difficult to assay because of the large numbers of vessels superimposed. Here *a* shows a fluffy density filling in the area which is seen to be clear in the normal, *b*. Compare with Figure 4-12.

Figure 4-12. Cardiophrenic angle and lower right lung field in mild cardiac failure. The shadows of the engorged veins in the hilum superimposed on those of the arteries give a matted, thickened look to the hilum and lung field.

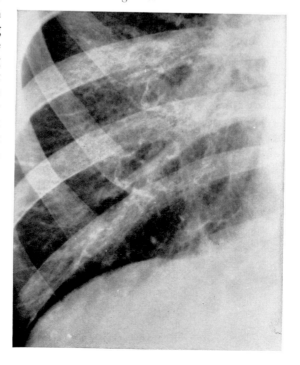

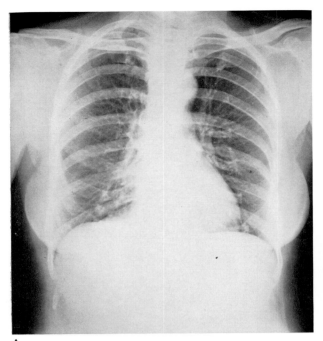
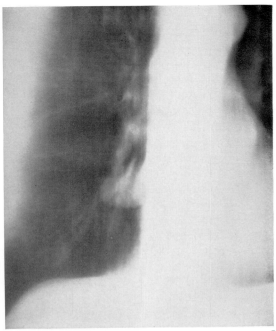

A

B

Figure 4-13A. Ill-defined thickness in the lower part of the right hilum in a patient with cough and bloody sputum, proved on body-section study, *B*, to be a smooth round mass below a clearly normal right pulmonary artery. Finding at surgery: benign adenoma.

Often enlargement of the hilum is not vascular in nature. There are many *lymph nodes* in the hilum and mediastinum, too small to be seen individually and lost among the heavier shadows of the vessels. They may enlarge, however, and become visible, either singly or in groups, when they respond to an inflammatory process in the lung, for example, or are secondarily invaded by tumor. They may be seen as overlapping round shadows, or, when they are matted together, they may cast a confluent shadow.

Primary tumor masses occurring near the hilum are common. If you are thinking three-dimensionally about the lung root on the radiograph, you will also realize that tumor masses in the peripheral lung tissue in front of or behind the hilum may cast shadows which superimpose on that of the hilum in the PA chest film. Figures 4-13 and 4-14 are examples of this sort of problem. In Figure 4-13 the mass is just below the right hilum, and in Figure 4-14 it is either behind or in front but superimposed on a true left hilar mass of tumor-invaded nodes. A variety of special procedures will help to distinguish the nature of such masses. Bronchography will determine whether they relate to the bronchus or simply displace it, and angiocardiography will give you the same information about the major vessels. Body-section studies are immensely useful as well, and you should think of those in the illustrations used here as radiographs of a slice of the patient made through the level of the hilum in the coronal plane.

Hilar enlargements due to tumor tend to be rounder and smoother in outline and are more frequently unilateral. Masses which prove to be clusters of enlarged nodes, you will find, tend to look like what you would expect if you radiographed a bunch of grapes, with many overlapping round shadows. Vascular hilar enlargements, on the other hand, taper into the lung field and are almost invariably bilateral. You are going to see exceptions, of course, but these very rough generalizations will provide you with a working rule temporarily. Remember, too, that you must expect to see hilar enlargements which are *combinations* of tumor-and-nodes (as in 4-14) or vessels-and-nodes (in pneumonia and other inflammations) and that when this happens you are not going to be sure of it from the plain chest film, though you must wonder about the matter.

52

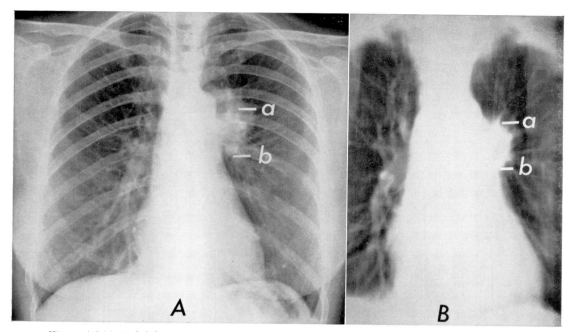

Figure 4-14A. Left hilar mass, normal right hilum. Note that a body-section study, *B*, was made through the hilum. It shows clearly a cluster of enlarged nodes in the hilum, *(a-b)*, but it excludes the upper part of the original shadow in *A*, overlapped on that of the nodes and representing the primary tumor behind or in front of the hilum. Thus the abnormal shadow on the plain film is actually two densities overlapping. A lateral film might help; additional body-section studies would show at what level the primary mass lay.

Figure 4-15 *(Unknown 4-1)*. Patient with cough and chest pain. Study the film systematically, surveying bones, soft tissues, and lung fields as outlined so far. Then come back to the legend and answer the following questions: Is it a female patient? What sorts of pathologic conditions might such a right hilar shadow represent? Is it probably vascular or not? What do you make of the left hilum? The lung fields?

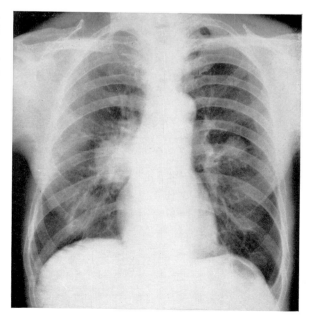

Finally, remember that sometimes a very innocent looking hilum is not actually normal and may conceal among its vascular shadows tumor-involved nodes not yet large enough to be seen on the films. Retrospective studies of the films in large groups of patients who were found to have tumor-involved hilar nodes at surgery, have shown a number of perfectly normal appearing hilar shadows. The radiologist can do nothing about this except to report that your patient seems to have normal hilar shadows, and both you and he have to be aware of the possibilities in any instance in which the presence of involved nodes would make a difference in the treatment of the patient. You will hear a good deal more in subsequent chapters about what I shall call the *fallibility of the method,* by which I mean areas in which you must anticipate some unreliability of the roentgen examination, some quite unavoidable failure of the x-ray studies to give you the information you need about your patient. You learn the limitations of other modes of inquiry constantly in medical school, and you must be aware that, despite its great usefulness, the radiographic inquiry also has some limitations, even in the hands of the most expert interpreter. When he can help you solve a specific problem, the radiologist will do so. When he knows he cannot help you, or that a simple negative report is likely to be misinterpreted as a clean bill of health for the structure in question, it is his obligation to warn you of the fact. It is this type of problem which, more than anything else, makes it imperative that you not rely entirely on the written report but supplement it with a personal conference with the radiologist while viewing the films yourself.

The first "false negative" film you see on a patient of your own will convince you that intelligent film reporting is dependent upon some knowledge of the patient's problem. Without that information the radiologist cannot truly serve the best interests of the patient, cannot offer you a written report for your records which is framed around the difficulties of a particular human being with a particular set of symptoms.

Contemporary medical practice is a collaborative affair for medical students as well as for their instructors in clinical work, and medical students must not feel hesitant about approaching someone in the department of radiology for an explanation of shadows which puzzle them or for the physiologic implications of a particular roentgen finding. A relationship of mutual trust, good-fellowship, and devotion to the evolution of new ideas must be developed and fostered between radiologist and physician-in-training. The younger men, because of their more recent study of allied fields, are often in a position to contribute to the refreshment of knowledge of the more mature.

Look, for example, at Figures 4-16, 4-17, and 4-19, which are called "wedge arteriograms" and represent an exciting approach to one aspect of pulmonary physiology, feasible in the living patient and contributing important information about his small pulmonary arteries which was once not obtainable without lung biopsy. A fine catheter is passed from an arm vein through the right chambers of the heart out along the pulmonary artery. It is wedged into one of the smaller lung vessels in a portion of the lung free of overlap from the shadows of mediastinum or scapula. Pressure readings are made, and then a small amount of radioopaque fluid is injected as the film exposure is being made. Figure 4-16 shows the normal appearance of the smallest vessels of the arterial bed in the lung periphery. Some of these are vessels too small to cast any shadow well defined enough to study on the plain film (compare Figure 4-18). Yet the pressures on the right side of the heart and in the main pulmonary arteries must reflect the status of these small vessels, the distensibility of their walls, the structure of their intima, and their characteristic branching, whether normal, decreased, or increased.

Obtaining and analyzing studies of this sort in the course of the work-up of the patient are clearly collaborative procedures between you and the specially trained men you entrust with the problem, and the same philosophy ought to apply to more routine procedures.

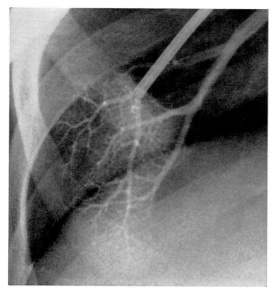

Figure 4-16. Normal wedge arteriogram showing the capillary bed in the lung.

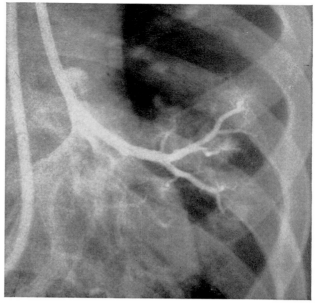

Figure 4-17. Patient with pulmonary hypertension. From the narrowing of small end-arteries and sparse branching this has been called the "pruned tree" arteriogram. Pulmonary flow is reduced 50 per cent.

Figure 4-18. The nonopacified normal peripheral lung for comparison.

Figure 4-19. Wedge arteriogram on a patient with interatrial septal defect and a left-to-right shunt so extensive that the pulmonary flow was increased to 470 per cent of the systemic flow.

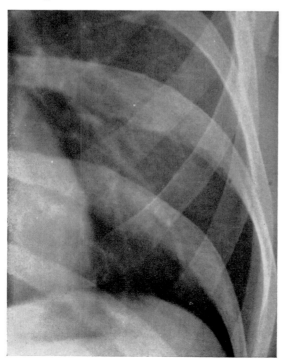

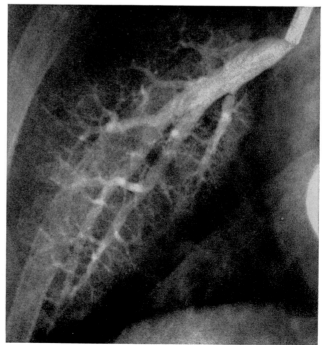

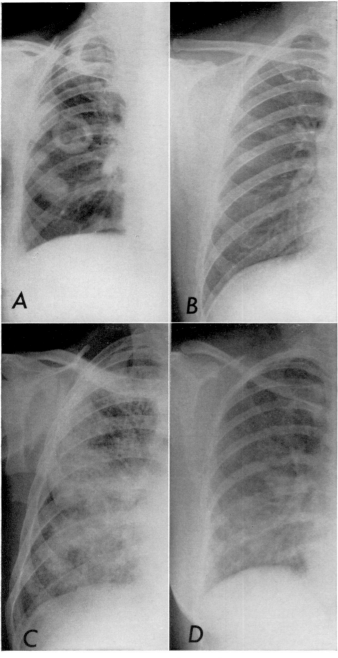

Figure 4-20. (See text.)

Imagine, now, the *alveolar portion of the lung* folded like a conical cuff around three sides of the hilum. You have looked at the peripheral lung when it was normal and seemed completely radiolucent in the lateral third of the PA film, where it is not superimposed on hilar trunks. What shadows will be added, then, if the vascular tree is normal but the alveolar lung is sprinkled with minute tumor nodules, patches of pneumonia, or small areas of collapse, or where it is threaded and reefed in by scar tissue from old infections, or flooded with interstitial fluid?

Look briefly over the eight lung fields on these two pages and then come back to the text. Are there any normals? Which ones seem to have changes so widespread in the lung that you think at once of some generalized process involving *all* lung tissue? Which show fewer than six isolated areas of abnormality?

Now consider them one by one. In <u>A</u>, several round shadows hang in an otherwise normal lung, their margins smooth and sharp, since they are surrounded by well-aerated lung tissue on all sides. One of them appears circular with a darker central area because it has a hollow, air-filled cavity inside it. (More x-rays pass through this part than through the shell tangentially.) The radiologist may not be able to tell you whether these are tumor nodules growing in the lung or granulomas expanding similarly; he *can* help you to assess the probabilities for one or the other diagnosis on the basis of their appearance, their growth rate from film to film over a period of time, and the clinical story.

<u>B</u> is normal, the right lung of the patient seen in <u>E</u>. It can be used as a norm for studying the others.

Both <u>C</u> and <u>D</u> show innumerable patches of increased density which, on the original film, involved both lungs. (<i>G</i> is the left half of <i>D</i>.) Unfortunately, at least 40 different conditions produce a picture similar to these two films. Some are common, others rare. From the film alone, without any knowledge of the acuteness of the patient's illness or of his occupational background or even the tentative clinical diagnosis, neither you nor the radiologist himself can know the nature of the disease. You can describe the abnormal shadows, no more.

However, when you know that the man in *C* had inhaled beryllium salts in a fluorescent lamp factory over a period of time, you *can* say that his chest film shows shadows just like those seen in autopsy-proved cases of berylliosis where myriads of small granulomas and a lacework of scar tissue produce such roentgen shadows in the lung. On the other hand, if you know that the woman in *D* (and *G*) was pulled out of the water several hours ago, half drowned, her film becomes intelligible because this is a picture often seen after such mishaps. Patches of bronchopneumonia and many small areas of collapse from inhaled water and bronchial secretions produce this sort of patchy density. In addition, from the violent struggle in the water, there is usually some pulmonary edema with extra fluid in the interstitium of the lung about the vessels to absorb more of the x-ray beam.

Any chest film is only a point on a curve in the course of the patient's disease. *Change* from film to film in a day or a week or a year often alters the whole spectrum of diagnostic possibilities considered on viewing the original film. You may still not be able to be sure what the patient has, but you can then be sure of a good many things that he has not. To know that the man in *C* had shown the changes you see there for several months before this film was made, and that his lung picture did not change appreciably before he died, would strongly affirm your conviction that he had a chronic lung injury, probably related to his known exposure to dust. The drowned woman got well in a few days, and you could predict she would. In fact *H* shows her left lung 2 days after *G*. Slightly enlarged vessel shadows seem the only remaining abnormality.

In case you have not been able to find anything wrong with *E,* look again at the ninth interspace. This solitary nodule had not changed since a chest film 1 year before and at surgery proved to be a benign tumor. In *F* the entire alveolar lung is sprinkled with minute areas of a density rightly suggesting calcium and representing the healed scars of an old infection, unchanged for many years. It has been estimated that such lesions must be at least 2 millimeters in size to be visible by x-ray.

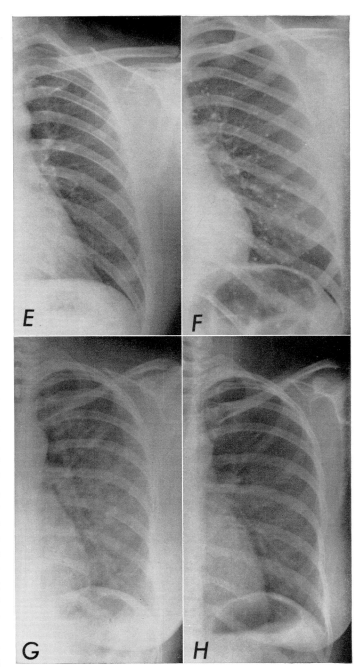

Figure 4-21. (See text.)

The preceding page spread was intended not to confuse you but to give you an idea of some of the types of *disseminated lesions* in the lung parenchyma which you will be seeing and impart a feeling for the problems you and the radiologist may have to face in interpreting the shadows cast by such lesions. To be sure, some shadows in the lung are easier to interpret than others, and it is important for you to realize early in your study of radiology that there are many times when no diagnosis can be made from the films with certainty. There are many other times when the radiologist can be definite about his diagnostic interpretation of the films and will be so with courageous insistence in the best interests of the patient. There are, in fact, some conditions in which the appearance of the radiograph is to be trusted as a diagnostic clue even more than the opinion of the pathologist based on a single biopsy specimen. A well-informed, modern pathologist will agree that his opinion is not necessarily the final answer and that his contribution to the whole-patient study must be fitted into the pattern formed by all other diagnostic evidence.

If you remember in looking at radiographs that an abnormal shadow consistently present on two or more films must have been produced by an area of abnormality in the patient's tissues, but that sometimes the form and shape of that shadow give definite clues to its nature and sometimes they do not, you will be able to keep in good focus the problems of interpreting such shadows. You will be seeing roentgen shadows of all kinds in this book, some of which can be interpreted sensibly in only one way (example: the presence of congenitally duplicate structures). Other roentgen shadows, like those on the preceding page spread, might be cast by any one of several different abnormal processes going on in the patient's tissues, and one can interpret them only up to a point.

The knowledge acquired by a man who reads films several hours a day for 10 years, who habitually checks his affirmative statements against clinical, surgical, and autopsy findings, and who regularly reads the periodicals covering new work in the field, enables him to recognize most of the types of shadows about which one may be definite. That experience also teaches him not to guess about the significance of many other types of shadows. There is absolutely no excuse for guessing at any time. On the other hand, a frank guess plainly labeled as such may be a useful device for examining the whole diagnostic problem, just as a working clinical diagnosis is a guess in the sense of a feasible possibility.

In sum, your best procedure in medicine is to assay the patient's problem on the basis of a good history and a careful physical examination, and then to order such radiographic procedures as are pertinent to your working diagnosis. If subsequently you find upon the films shadows in keeping with it, you will have affirmed to some extent your initial feeling about the patient's disease process. If no abnormal roentgen findings are present, you may have to revise your impression, or you may feel strongly enough to retain it, temporarily at least. If repeated diagnostic studies of all kinds refute your impression, you will, in time, have to renounce it.

The one thing you must not do is to attempt to make of radiology a card-sorting device on which you lean more and more in order not to have to make up your mind about a differential diagnosis on the basis of the history and physical examination alone. Nothing can take the place of a careful historical record and a thorough physical examination. Allowing yourself the slack discipline of looking at x-ray films before you have studied the patient, will create in you a sense of dependence on these procedures which is out of proportion to their importance. You cannot hope to develop the invaluable tool that a brilliantly taken history and physical can become if you use the x-ray to guide your hand instead of to check its accuracy.

On the other hand, after you have ordered and examined films on your patient in accordance with your working diagnosis, if the radiologist raises the possibility that the patient may have a condition you had not considered, he is trying to help you with a labeled guess based on his experience in viewing films. It may be a simple matter for you to refute that possibility by another procedure.

I should like to recommend that you consciously choose, in medical school and later, a realistic and mature attitude toward the art and science of radiology (for it is both science and art). Medical students are prone to adopt attitudes which do not help them to profit by the aid radiologic data can be to them in learning. One of these attitudes is expressed by the person who says, "It is all a mystery, impossible to understand; the radiologist sees things I cannot hope to see." This is patently defeatist, as I hope I have already proved to you. You may not see as much as the radiologist sees, but with his help you can indeed see the abnormal shadows which are present, and you can relate them to the patient's disease. It goes without saying that to do so is an accretional process and that the more determinedly sensible your approach is, the more you will learn.

Another dangerous attitude you should avoid is the one which demands diagnostic labels prematurely. It is rigidly unimaginative, for example, to say, "Pneumonia as a process in the lung should always look the same on the x-ray film." Of course it does not; why would it? The process the pathologist sees at autopsy varies from patient to patient, in both gross and microscopic findings, even though he labels them all "pneumonia." The disease process varies in accordance with the type of patient who is playing host to the disease, his physiologic responses, his capacity to resist, his age when he contracts the disease, the treatment which has been administered to him, the presence of coincidental disease processes. Why, then, would not the radiograph reflect such variation?

It does, indeed, and while one must remember that it does so vary, one may at the same time be comforted by the fact that it usually varies within certain fairly well-described limits. Thus the radiologist becomes accustomed to a spectrum of shadows for any given disease process, and the more experienced he becomes, the more accurately he will interpret those shadows in the light of the patient's clinical picture. For example, the radiologist recognizes the changes in a pneumonic process at various stages of healing and will often be able to advise the clinician that the process is healing at an expected rate or alert him to the fact that the healing is being unaccountably delayed and that the reason for this may be of vital importance. He recognizes the fact that pneumonia expresses itself in the lung in one way in an infant and very differently in an old man who has the leftover scar traces of many similar infections in his lung and perhaps a compromised blood supply. In general the infant recovers clinically and his chest film clears very rapidly, while the old man takes longer to throw off the process and his chest film may be expected to show changes lingering on for some time. Invariably the radiograph is recording a phase of the pathologic process, since it is a factual shadowgram, so that the very fact that "pneumonia does *not* always look the same" is of importance to you, the clinician.

In *Life on the Mississippi*, Mark Twain describes the confusion he experienced while an apprentice pilot. He endured a learning process which required him to recognize the appearance of the river bank by day and by night, with the water at different levels, at different times of the year and in different kinds of weather. As a pilot he had to know the landmarks up one side of the river and down the other, a total of several thousand miles of bends and turns to be memorized together with the soundings of a river bottom which was constantly changing. If you have not read it, do, because the contrast between the purely rote memorizing, of which it is an excellent example, and the type of rational learning you can apply to so much of medicine will give you courage. Some have felt that diagnostic radiology was a tallying process, innumerable characteristic roentgen pictures to be learned by memory. It is not, and I hope that the chapter you have just finished will have enlisted your interest in the fascinating intellectual procedure involved in putting together the story of the patient, what you hear through the stethoscope, and what you see upon the chest film.

The philosophic digression you have just read was necessary at this point in order to orient you toward the proper handling of roentgen data. Do not let it prevent your being aware of how much you already know about analyzing a chest film. You know, for example, from this chapter, that the hilum and normal lung markings are mostly vascular. You have realized that changes in the size and tortuosity of these shadows may reflect vascular changes related to either heart or lung disease. You have set up a system for studying these structures deliberately in a certain order. You recognize that vascular engorgement in the hilum may be arterial or venous or both, and that only experts can tell which. You know that when there is evidence of inflammation in the lung, hilar engorgement will probably represent both vessels and swollen lymph nodes. You are going to look very carefully at the hilar shadows of any patient who you believe has a lung tumor, but you will remember that early in the disease an innocent appearing hilum may conceal tumor-positive nodes which will become apparent only when they grow large enough.

You know that the normal lung parenchyma is very radiolucent itself and that the normal lung markings are the vessels which traverse it. You have seen a few examples of parenchymal lung disease where tumor, inflammation, scar tissue, or abnormally increased interstitial fluid increased the absorption of x-rays and cast disseminated shadows on the film, gray-white spots superimposed on the vascular tree.

You have, I hope, accepted the fact that sometimes differing conditions may cast shadows so similar that no positive diagnosis can be made from the films alone. In these patients it becomes a team effort by all the doctors concerned to fit together clinical findings of all sorts, including the radiographic evidence, in order to settle upon a working diagnosis. At other times, the experience of the radiologist in looking at similar films of patients with about the same signs and symptoms will enable him to be more definite in his interpretation. Serial films in the course of an illness ought to be reviewed constantly and should be reinterpreted if necessary in the light of new developments in the over-all clinical picture.

As opposed to the disseminated densities in the lung parenchyma which you have seen in this chapter, Chapter 5 will present you with important and easy-to-remember roentgen findings in patients in whom a whole lung (or at least a generous segment of it) has become solid, non-air-containing, radiodense, for any reason whatever. Before you go on, though, try your hand at the following unknowns.

Unknown 4-2 (no figure). It is 11 o'clock at night. You receive a telephone report that an admission chest film on a patient you have just examined shows the shadow of a straight pin overlying the dark shadow of the air-filled trachea. The patient, a woman, in for elective foot surgery tomorrow, talked comfortably when you were with her. What is your procedure?

Unknown 4-3. A 23-year-old medical student gives you a 2-week history of cough, fever, weight loss, and bloody sputum, but he was able to go to classes today. Figure 4-22 shows a detail of his right mid-lung field. He tells you that an insurance chest film was entirely negative 3 months ago. Compare what you see here with the eight lung fields you have just studied. What sorts and shapes of abnormal shadows do you see here? How would you be inclined to interpret them in terms of pathologic changes which might cast such shadows? Weighing all factors (history, possible pathologic condition, and roentgen appearance), which of the following very general categories of lung disease do you think most probable in this patient:

Acute inflammation 1-day old

No disease

Subacute inflammation 1-month old

Chronic lung insult related to employment

Metastatic tumor spread in the lung

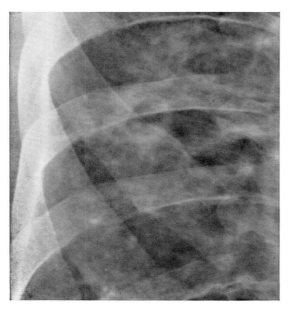

Figure 4-22

Unknown 4-4. In Figures 4-23 and 4-24 you see part of the chest film of a farmer who had inhaled nitrous dioxide produced by new ensilage in the bottom of a silo. Of the two films, which is the one made 30 days after exposure at the height of the illness, and which the one made 4 months later when the patient was greatly improved?

When you have decided which of the two goes with a sick patient and which with a patient in good health, clear your brain slate and imagine that I offer you these two films just as they are printed with no clinical information at all, telling you only that Figure 4-24 on the right was made 4 months *after* Figure 4-23. What could you say definitely then from the films alone about such a patient? What general classes of illness might you consider possible causes for the production of such a change in the shadows of hilum and lung? How far do you think you would be justified in going diagnostically if you had to give a written report on these two films without any clinical information?

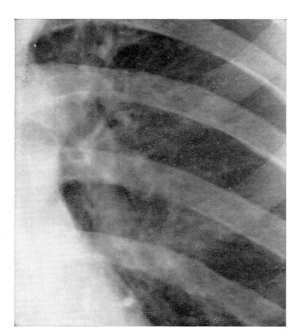

Figure 4-23

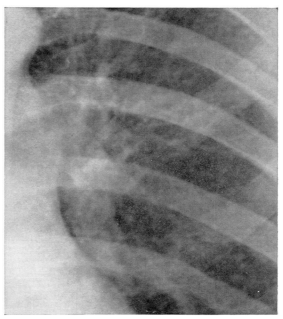

Figure 4-24

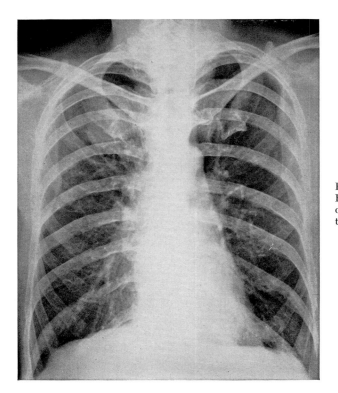

Figure 4-25 *(Unknown 4-5)*. As a review, survey Figure 4-25 systematically for bones, hilar shadows, lung markings, symmetrical interspaces, and the segments of parenchymal lung seen in each.

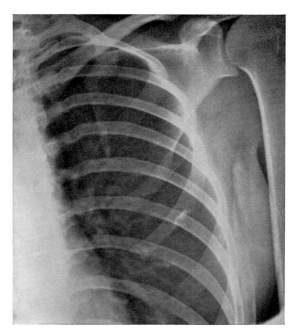

Figure 4-26 *(Unknown 4-6)*. What might be the nature, composition, and location of the structure responsible for the white shadow overlying the lateral part of the seventh rib? How would you proceed to investigate it further in an asymptomatic patient? What do you make of the vertical sharp-margined gray shadow which crosses the fourth and fifth ribs from just below the medial end of the first rib? Is it to be accounted for as an abnormality, or can you resolve it into a portion of an anatomic structure?

Figure 4-2. Courtesy Mr. R. Morrison and the publisher, *MR&P* 27:132.

Figure 4-3. Courtesy Drs. C. Tobin and M. Zariquiey, and the publisher, *MR&P* 29:10.

Figures 4-4, 4-5. Courtesy Dr. R. Janes and the publisher, *MR&P* 25:95.

Figures 4-6, 4-7. Courtesy Drs. B. Gasul, R. Arcilla, V. Vlastimil, E. Fell, M. Moreano, J. Bicoff, G. Hait, J. Lynfield, and H. Bucheleres, and the publisher, *MR&P* 35 Supplement, 1959:6.

Figures 4-10, 4-12. Courtesy Dr. B. Felson, F. Fleishner, J. McDonald and C. Rabin and the publisher, *Radiology* 73:744.

Figure 4-11. Courtesy Dr. C. Dotter and the publisher, *MR&P* 32:48, and Dr. J. Reed, Detroit, Mich.

Figures 4-13, 4-25, 4-26. Courtesy Dr. B. Epstein and the publisher, *MR&P* 34:58, 62, 66.

Figure 4-14. Courtesy Dr. B. Epstein, New Hyde Park, N. Y.

Figure 4-15. Courtesy Dr. W. Chamberlain, Washington, D. C.

Figures 4-16, 4-17, 4-19. Courtesy Drs. A. Bell, S. Shimomura, W. Guthrie, H. Hempel, H. Fitzpatrick, and C. Begg, and the publisher, *Radiology* 73:566.

Figure 4-18. Courtesy Dr. C. Dotter and the publisher, *MR&P* 32:48.

Figures 4-20*B*, 4-21*E*. Courtesy Dr. R. Sherman, New York, N. Y.

Figure 4-21*F*. Courtesy Dr. R. Weyher, Detroit, Mich.

Figure 4-22. Courtesy Dr. A. Bendick and the publisher, *MR&P* 34:76.

Figures 4-23, 4-24. Courtesy Drs. E. Cornelius and E. Betlach, and the publisher, *Radiology* 74:233.

CHAPTER 5 The Roentgen Signs of Massive Lung Consolidation

By massive lung consolidation I mean, for practical purposes, that a whole lung, a whole lobe, or at least one entire bronchopulmonary segment is solid in that it is almost entirely airless. The solid part will cast a uniformly dense shadow on the film, approximately the same density as the heart shadow, and its projection shadow will relate to the shape of the part involved. Although this sounds as though a theoretical situation were being proposed, the fact is that in everyday radiologic practice shadows of this kind are common. Hardly a day passes in a big general hospital without there turning up, for example, a radiograph in which by a logical analysis of the abnormal shadows on the chest film one can recognize a consolidated lobe in a patient with clinical lobar pneumonia. Likewise a shadow which can only represent a solid right upper lobe may be recognized in a patient already suspected of having lung cancer. To have thought through the details of the roentgen findings in such consolidations systematically is to be braced for an understandable feeling of (temporary) confusion as you view films which do not look like anything you have ever seen before.

In Figure 5-1 you have diagramed for you the roentgen findings you must anticipate when one or the other *whole lung* becomes solid. Begin by noticing that in *A* the normal heart shadow is thrown into relief by the normally aerated lung on either side of it. So also the two domed diaphragmatic shadows covering the liver and spleen are seen in relief because there is air in the lung above them. The stomach bubble under the medial half of the left diaphragm may be seen in the standing patient as the shadow of radiolucent air imprisoned in the

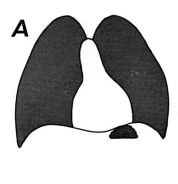

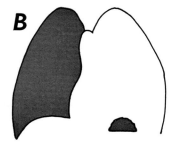

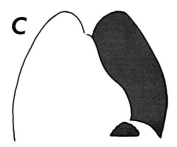

Figure 5-1

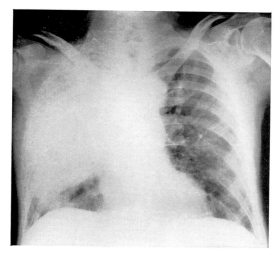

Figure 5-3

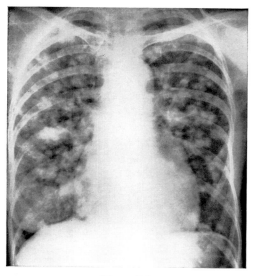

Figure 5-2

fundus of the stomach above a horizontal fluid level. When present, the stomach bubble effectively locates the level of the diaphragm for you.

Now suppose that the entire left lung becomes consolidated, as in *B*. The heart, mediastinal structures, and dense lung are all of the same density now, and their shadows merge into one, so that the left side of the heart profile disappears. They also merge with the shadows of the spleen, and the outline of the left diaphragm is therefore lost, its location indicated only by the rays which reach the film through the air in the stomach. Look back at the cadaver sections in Chapter 2 to check these relations of stomach, spleen, and diaphragm.

If the left lung remains normal and the right solidifies, the chest film will look like *C*. The liver, right lung, and heart being nearly identical in density, their shadows now merge into one.

Disappearance of profiles normally seen, then, on a chest film of this sort implies solid change in the lung next to them and is always an important roentgenographic observation. It is interesting to realize that even a lung which is riddled with small disseminated nodules of tumor will contain enough air still to behave like a well-aerated lung in respect to profiles.

The patient in Figure 5-2 proved at autopsy to have both lungs generously sprinkled with tumor nodules; yet you do see the heart shadow and both diaphragms because of the air in alveoli around the disseminated lesions.

Contrast with it Figure 5-3 in which pneumonia consolidating the entire upper part of the right lung, but sparing the lower part, results in loss of the upper part of the mediastinal and heart shadows, but preserves those of the right diaphragm and liver.

Any consolidation against the mediastinum will result in loss of a part of the mediastinal border, therefore, and any consolidation of the base of the lung will erase the shadow of the diaphragm or a segment of it. Because the heart is in the anterior half of the chest, consolidation which erases the border of the heart must, of course, be located in the anterior part of the lung; so you will not be surprised the first time you observe for yourself that, although the diaphragmatic shadow on one side is absent and the lower part of the lung on that side appears dense, the border of the heart is seen clearly through it, thrown into relief by juxtaposed air-filled anterior lung. When you see this you will reason accurately that the lower lobe, in contact with the diaphragm, is solid, while the rest of the lung is normal.

65

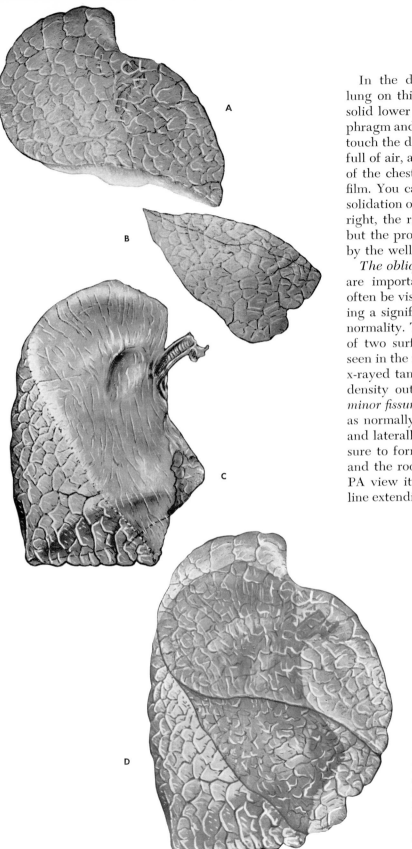

In the drawings of seemingly transparent lung on this page you can see exactly why a solid lower lobe erases the shadow of the diaphragm and how the upper lobes, which do not touch the diaphragm, would apply themselves, full of air, against the heart in the anterior part of the chest and preserve its profile in the PA film. You can also see at once how, with consolidation of the upper and middle lobes on the right, the right heart border would disappear but the profile of the diaphragm be preserved by the well-aerated lower lobe.

The oblique planes of the two major fissures are important to remember, since they will often be visible to you in the lateral view bearing a significant relationship to an area of abnormality. The fissures are normally composed of two surfaces of pleura in contact and are seen in the normal chest film only when pleura, x-rayed tangentially, appears as a thin line of density outlined on both sides by lung. The *minor fissure* on the right should be thought of as normally horizontal and extending forward and laterally from the middle of the major fissure to form the floor of the right upper lobe and the roof of the right middle lobe. On the PA view it is frequently to be seen as a thin line extending straight laterally from the hilum.

Figure 5-4. Transparent drawings of the right lung, separated into upper, middle, and lower lobes *(A, B, C)* and reassembled *(D)*. Seen from the lateral surface. The patient faces to your right. Opposite page: Lung broken down into the bronchopulmonary segments.

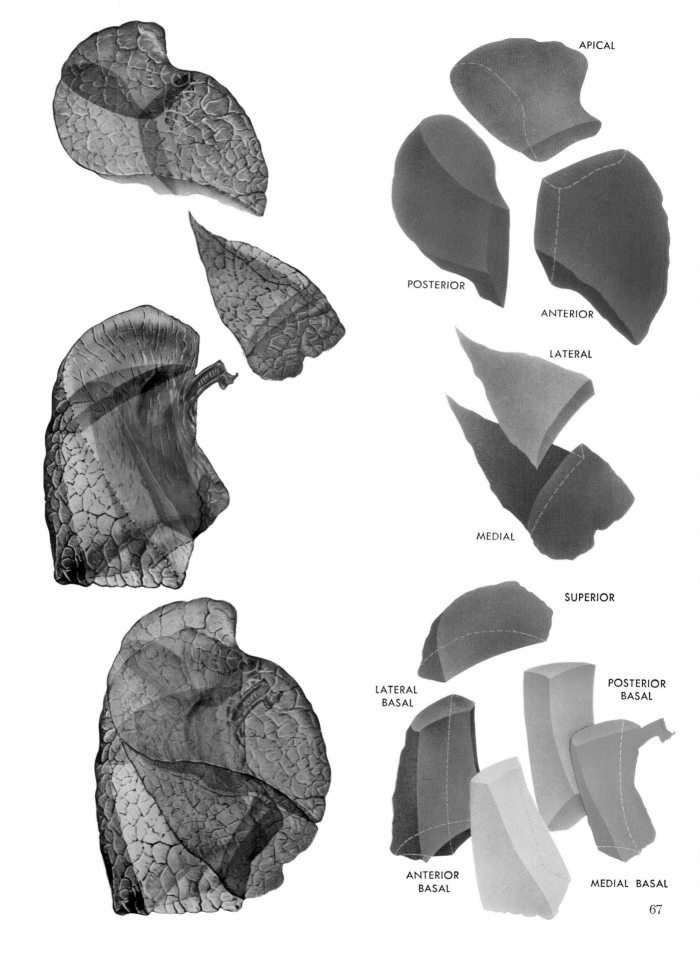

APICAL

POSTERIOR

ANTERIOR

LATERAL

MEDIAL

SUPERIOR

LATERAL
BASAL

POSTERIOR
BASAL

ANTERIOR
BASAL

MEDIAL BASAL

67

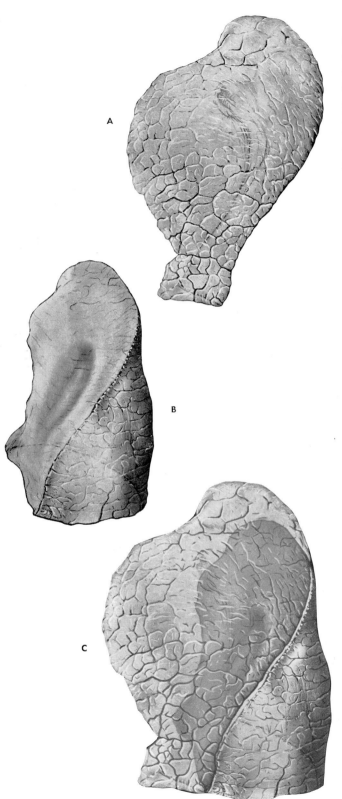

Imagine, now, and make a sketch in diagram form, predicting the block of density you would expect to see on the lateral film if each lobe of the five became consolidated in turn. Then try to predict the appearance of the block of density you will see on the PA view to go with each lateral. This will be easier if you begin with the right upper lobe, producing a density extending from the horizontal plane of the minor fissure upward to the apex. Work out for yourself these predictable shadow profiles, check them, and you will never forget them. As you reason each one, note which borders of the heart, diaphragm, and mediastinum can be expected to disappear.

Remember that a dense sphere within the lung will project as a circular shadow profile in either PA or lateral view, but that asymmetrical wedges of different sorts will project quite differently according to the direction of the ray passing through them. The middle lobe best illustrates this point, since it is a long wedge x-rayed end-on in the PA view and appears as a much smaller shadow than when its full length is seen in the lateral view of the chest. The shadow profile in each instance is to be learned as an exercise in reasoning, independent of anatomic surface markings.

Figure 5-5. Transparent drawings of the left lung, separated into upper and lower lobes (A, B) and reassembled (C). Seen from the lateral surface. The patient faces to your left. Note the similarities and differences between the middle lobe on the right and its analogue, the lingular segment of the upper lobe on the left. Density in either will obscure the lower part of the heart profile in the PA view. Opposite page: The bronchopulmonary segments.

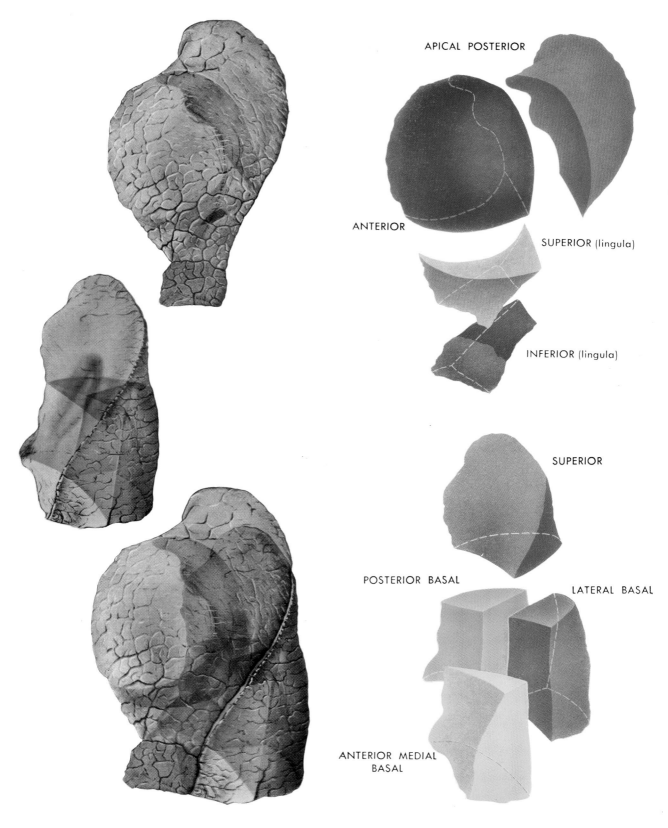

APICAL POSTERIOR

ANTERIOR

SUPERIOR (lingula)

INFERIOR (lingula)

SUPERIOR

POSTERIOR BASAL

LATERAL BASAL

ANTERIOR MEDIAL
BASAL

69

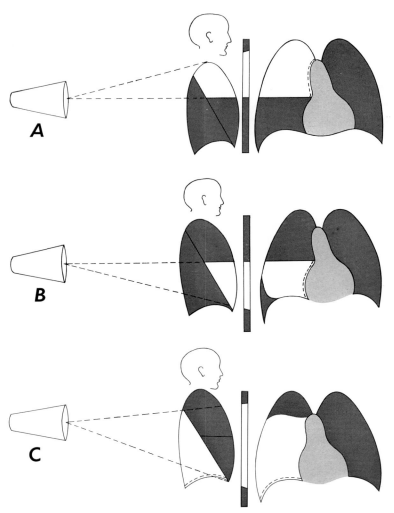

Figure 5-6. Projection shadows of each of the three lobes on the right. In *A* the right upper lobe is consolidated, its inferior margin outlined by the air-filled middle lobe lying beneath the minor septum. In *B* the middle lobe alone is dense; note that in the PA view it does not extend into the costophrenic sinus against the lateral insertion of the diaphragm. In *C*, on the contrary, the lung tissue filling the right costophrenic sinus is seen to be dense because the right lower lobe is dense. The heart shadow has been rendered in gray in these diagrams in order to clarify the shape of the lung mass shadows, but its density would merge with that of the middle lobe in *B* in an actual radiograph. Disappearing borders are outlined by dotted lines.

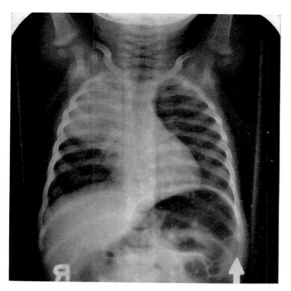
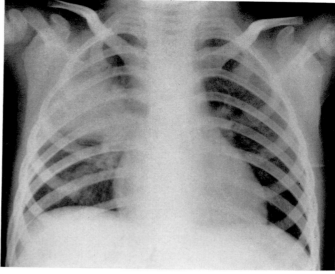

EXAMPLES OF MASSIVE DENSITIES IN THE RIGHT LUNG

Figure 5-7 (above, left). Consolidation of the entire right upper lobe in a child with clinical signs of pneumonia. If you happened to see this film before examining the patient, where would you be expecting to find the altered breath sounds? Note that the upper right border of the mediastinum is lost.

Figure 5-8 (above, right). Another child with pneumonia, but this time only part of the right upper lobe is involved. The color section on bronchopulmonary segments will help you figure out which parts of the right upper lobe are probably consolidated here, and which parts clear. Note that the mediastinal border is preserved.

Figure 5-9 (below, left). A zone of lung consolidation which is not uniformly solid and therefore casts a shadow of nonuniform density on the film. This often happens. You will see it first, very likely, in a patient with lobar pneumonia which is healing, different segments clearing at different rates and becoming normally aerated again. The well-seen smooth right border of the heart shows the process here to be in the upper part of the right lower lobe. The middle and upper lobes must be relatively clear. The base of the lower lobe is not involved. How do you know this?

Figure 5-10 (below, right). Patient with a large tumor mass involving the whole base of the right lower lobe (diaphragmatic profile missing) and most of the middle lobe (right heart profile missing).

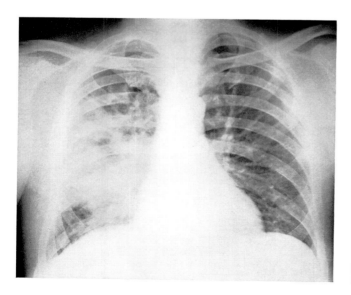
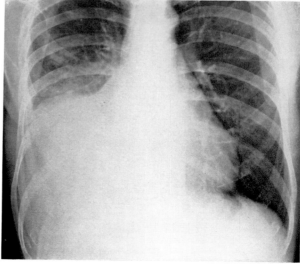

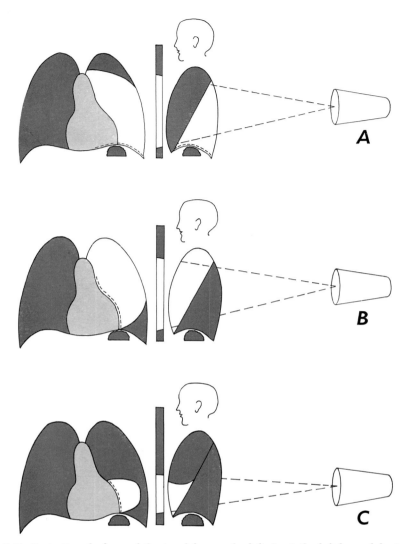

Figure 5-11. Projection shadows of the two lobes on the left. In *A* the left lower lobe is consolidated; the diaphragmatic shadow disappears (dotted lines) since the roentgen shadows of the lower lobe and spleen are merged into one; the approximate location of the left diaphragm may be indicated by the stomach bubble if one is present; the left heart border does not disappear but is seen through the dense lower lobe because air in the lingula of the left upper lobe anteriorly still throws it into relief. In *B* the entire left upper lobe is consolidated and the left heart border is lost, but the diaphragm is seen because of lower lobe air above it. In *C* only the lingular portion of the left upper lobe is solid, erasing the left heart border. Predict the radiographic appearance of the PA and lateral views in a patient with left upper lobe consolidation which *spared* the lingula.

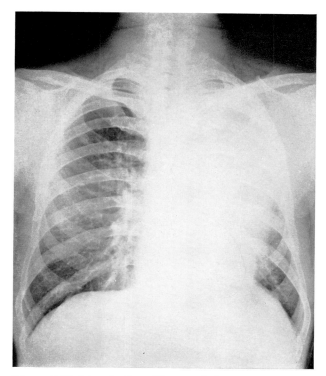

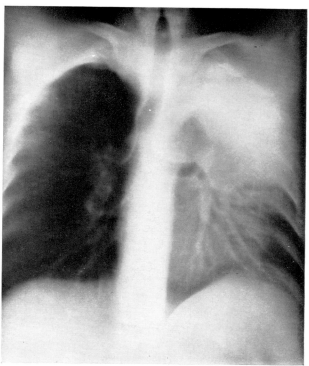

Figure 5-12 (above). Consolidation of the entire left upper lobe (distal to tumor). The lower lobe is well aerated so that you see the diaphragmatic profile, but the margins of the mediastinal structures (including much of the heart border) are lost.

Figure 5-13 (above). Body-section study through the level of the carina and main bronchi. Air is seen in trachea and both major bronchi, but the left upper lobe bronchus is amputated by tumor. Descending gray streaks are, of course, vessels in the air-filled left lower lobe (same patient as Figure 5-12).

DENSITIES IN THE LEFT LUNG

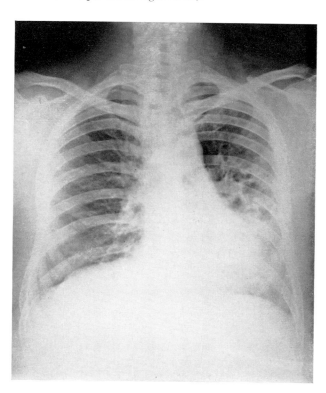

Figure 5-14 (right). Bronchiectasis with suppuration in the lingula adjacent to the heart in this 41-year-old man with a long-standing history of cough and purulent sputum renders the left cardiac border smudged and indistinct, a very common finding in lung disease of this segment. In bronchiectasis the dilated bronchi fill with secretion, displacing the air they normally contain. They become radio-opaque and appear as densities within the lung. If they were fluid-filled tubes tapering symmetrically, they ought to resemble the vascular trunks you have just seen in Figure 5-13. However, the diseased bronchus usually has saccular localized dilatations in bronchiectasis, and the density you see tends to look like a row of beads on a string. In addition, peribronchial inflammation and some collapse of poorly aerated lung between the bronchi result gradually in crowding together of these beaded trunks and over-all increase in the density of that segment of the lung.

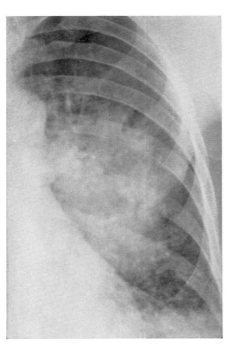

Figure 5-15 (*Unknown 5-1*). An area of patchy consolidation in a patient with fever, cough, and chest pain for 2 days, before which he was well. Clinically he has pneumonia. He is not your patient, but you have happened to see his film in the x-ray department and are asked to examine him. Where will you be expecting to hear altered breath sounds best, and why?

When massive densities involve an entire lung or an entire lobe, you have certain clues which tell you how much of the lung is consolidated, and sometimes these same clues help you to determine the location of a patch of consolidation in the lung which does not occupy an entire lobe or bronchopulmonary segment, but only a part of one. Consolidation of all the lung tissue against the diaphragm will cause the outline of the diaphragm to disappear entirely, but a patch of dense lung against the lateral half of the diaphragm will cause the disappearance of only the lateral half of its outline, leaving the medial half visible.

Tomorrow you may see a chest film in which the lower left hemithorax appears dense, but if you can nevertheless see the entire dia-phragmatic profile, you will know that there must be air filling the lower lobe. If you cannot see any part of the diaphragm, but still see the left heart border through dense lung, you will know that there must be air in the upper lobe. You will not call either picture consolidation of the entire lung.

Neither will you be prompted to call a patch of partial consolidation like that in Figure 5-15 involvement of a whole lobe, but will think of it as involving most of a bronchopulmonary segment in the posterior part of the chest, since the heart border is so well preserved.

Now that you can recognize and locate anatomically areas of massive consolidation in the lung, as contrasted with the scattered small areas of density you saw in the last chapter, you are probably somewhat impatient to know how one labels them. As I have said, pneumonia and tumor can both produce solid areas in lung giving the findings outlined above. Airless lung which has collapsed can also produce much the same appearance, often adding some deviation of the mediastinum, as you will see in the next chapters. Collections of fluid in the pleural space can also produce dense areas in the thoracic cavity, of course, obscuring the otherwise healthy lung it envelops, and causing the disappearance of the diaphragmatic outline. Moreover, in both pneumonia and tumor, some atelectasis and pleural fluid are common in addition to the primary consolidation in the lung itself. One has to remember that these processes go together pathologically and, since they may cast very similar shadows, are often impossible to differentiate from the films alone on the initial study. In the next chapters you will learn how to determine the presence of pleural effusion and how to analyze the particular signals indicating that a lobe has collapsed. Then you will add them to the signs of consolidation we have covered above and interpret chest films systematically on each level.

In Chapter 3 you set up a system for beginning to study a chest film by surveying the bony structures and the soft tissues. In Chapter 4 you added the systematic survey of the hilum and its tapering vessels and the parenchyma of the lung itself. In Chapter 5 you have added a survey to make sure that no large patches of lung appear dense and that the heart borders and both diaphragmatic outlines are present, checking for *disappearance of profiles normally seen.* You are building gradually the sort of careful analysis of a chest film that will help you now in using roentgen data and serve you all your life in understanding the films on your own patients. Do not be impatient for diagnostic labels.

Did you observe that there was only one breast in Figure 5-2?

Credits: Illustrations this chapter.

Figures 5-4, 5-5. Courtesy Dr. M. Zariquiey and the publisher, *MR&P* 33:68-76.

Figure 5-6. After Sante.

Figure 5-7. Courtesy Mr. J. Pigg, Sr., and the publisher, *MR&P* 37:13.

Figure 5-10. Courtesy Dr. B. Epstein, New Hyde Park, N. Y.

Figures 5-12, 5-13, 5-14. Courtesy Dr. B. Epstein and the publisher, *MR&P* 34:63, 66.

CHAPTER 6 The Diaphragm and The Pleural Space

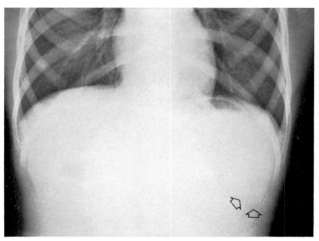

Figure 6-1. Normal diaphragms. Note stomach bubble with fluid level under the left diaphragm. Arrows mark the tip of the spleen. The spleen and the fluid-filled part of the stomach form a continuous shadow.

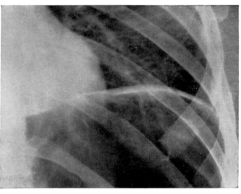

Figure 6-2. Left diaphragm filmed erect after an accident in which large amounts of air were admitted to the peritoneal space. Spleen and stomach are displaced downward and toward the mid-line.

The region of the diaphragm on the chest film affords some fine exercises in the logic of roentgen shadows. Just as you see the profile of the heart, dense between two lucent lungs, so you see the dome of the diaphragm because of a change in the sum of all superimposed densities. The sum of the shadows below the level of the dome of the diaphragm on the radiograph includes a part of the lung posteriorly and the dense liver (or spleen) solidly applied against its inferior concave surface. Above the level of the dome of the diaphragm the sum of all the densities is dominated by that of the lung, which offers little obstruction to the beam.

Hence, on the chest film the diaphragm and its subtended organs are silhouetted, white against the lucency of the lung field above, *even though their shadows are added to that of the piece of lung which dips into the posterior sulcus.*

Anatomically composed of a thin sheet of muscle attached to xiphoid, lower six costal cartilages, ribs, and upper lumbar vertebrae, the diaphragm itself contributes little to the white shadow on the chest film which we mean when we refer to the "diaphragm." If free air in the peritoneal space interposes between spleen and diaphragm, as it did in the patient in Figure 6-2, the thin sheet of muscle alone is

seen with air both above and below it. As usual
when a curved, shell-like structure is x-rayed,
what you see is that part of the diaphragm
which is traversed in tangent by the beam. Although it appears to be linear, you will think
in terms of roentgen densities and know it to
be a domed shell dividing chest from abdomen.
Under the fluoroscope it would be seen to contract downward and flatten with inspiration
and to relax upward as the patient breathed out.

On most chest films made with the patient
standing, the fundus of the stomach will be
seen high against the diaphragm, usually containing swallowed air and fluid gastric juice
(or lunch). A typical stomach bubble (Figure
6-1) shows a straight line marking the fluid
level, above which air provides a radiolucent
pocket through which more rays may pass. The
same film made with the patient lying down
and the beam still directed sagittally will show
no level because the beam will strike the fluid
level perpendicularly. Notice that in Figure 6-1
you seem to see the thickness of the diaphragm
itself because there is air above and below it,
but what you are actually looking at is the diaphragm plus the wall of the stomach under it.

A potentially hollow viscus which is completely filled with fluid and surrounded by
dense viscera will not be distinguishable radiographically, but any viscus which contains air
will appear on the film as a dark shadow. While
you are about it, take time to consider what
you can do with air and a fluid level in radiography. Any hollow structure, normal or abnormal, which contains or can safely be made to
contain both a gas and a fluid will show a fluid
level provided the beam crosses the plane of
that level. Thus, by tilting the patient in several
directions and always projecting the beam hori-
zontally across the surface of the air-fluid interface, the entire inside of a cavity can be visualized piece by piece. This can apply to the inside
of the stomach, the inside of an abscess cavity,
the inside of the ventricles of the brain or of the
urinary bladder. Air thus becomes a useful *contrast substance,* forming a radiolucent cast of
the hollow structure containing it, just as barium sulfate and other safely inert substances
form radio-opaque casts of the hollow structures into which they are introduced.

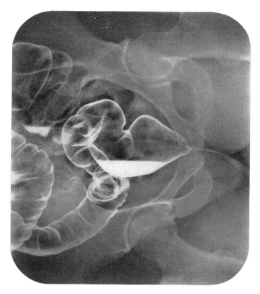

Figure 6-3 (above). The inside of the empty colon has
been coated with a fluid opaque substance and inflated
with air. You are looking through the patient from behind as he lies on his left side. The opaque material has
formed a pool against the dependent left wall of the
rectum.

Figure 6-4 (below). Just the reverse is seen here, with
the patient lying on his right side; you are looking
through him from the front. The sigmoid rises up out of
the pelvis to the patient's left. A pool of opaque material with a fluid level is seen against the now dependent
right wall of the rectum. In both instances the beam
has passed through the patient sagittally. This is known
as a "double contrast study" because both air and an
opaque substance are being employed.

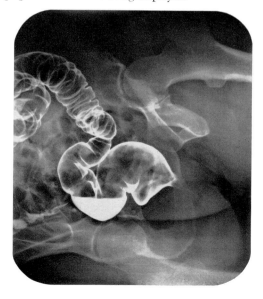

Because the stomach bubble (present only if there is air in the stomach) normally lies close against the under surface of the left diaphragm, it should be included in your systematic survey of a chest film. The interposition of anything between diaphragm and fundus of stomach will displace the bubble downward. It may be deformed by the presence of tumor in the stomach. Both its appearance and its location are of importance.

For example, when any massive density in the chest just above the left diaphragm causes the disappearance of the normal diaphragmatic outline, as you have seen in the last chapter, the location of the stomach bubble may tell you where the diaphragm is. In the lateral chest film the presence of the stomach bubble close under one diaphragmatic shadow determines which is the left diaphragm.

Although the anatomist thinks of and sees the diaphragm as a single sheet of muscle and tendon, dividing chest from abdomen, the radiologist sees it on the PA chest film and at fluoroscopy as two curved shadows on either side of the heart. He speaks of the "left and right diaphragms," in spite of the fact that he knows that usage to be anatomically and semantically not precise. It is convenient to refer to the two halves of the diaphragm in this way because they often respond independently to unilateral disease in the chest above or in the abdomen below.

The two diaphragms, then, as seen on the PA chest film, are normally smooth curves taking off from the mid-line at the origin of the tenth or eleventh ribs. You should make a practice of counting down the posterior ribs close to the spine to determine the level of the diaphragm. Try it on a few of the chest films you have seen (being sure to identify the first rib by tracing it backward from the sternoclavicular junction).

If you do this a few times on actual films you see in the course of your clinical day, you will find that hospitalized patients tend to show a considerable variation in the level of their diaphragms. The well person who is having a check-up obeys efficiently the request of the technician to "take a deep breath"; but the anxious, tired, pain-beset hospital patient may

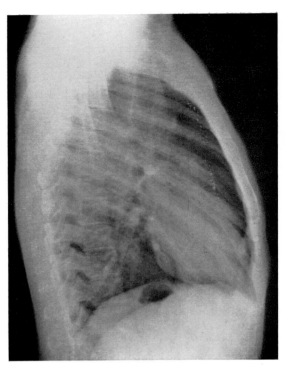

Figure 6-5. Normal right lateral chest film. Note the two diaphragmatic shadows curving down posteriorly. Which is the left diaphragm?

fail to do so, even though he has a fractured ankle to be set and nothing at all wrong with his chest or abdomen. The result is, of course, that the lower part of his lung close to the diaphragm will be poorly inflated with air and consequently more dense on the chest film, giving an appearance of abnormality where, in fact, none exists.

In Figures 6-6 and 6-7 the arterial tree of a dog's lung has been injected with opaque fluid and sealed off, inflation and deflation of the lung being carried out through a tube tied into the bronchus. In Figure 6-6 you see the lung collapsed around its arterial tree in just about the same degree of hypoaeration which would exist near the diaphragm at full expiration. In Figure 6-7 the specimen has been inflated to approximate the lung near the diaphragm at deep inspiration.

Figure 6-6

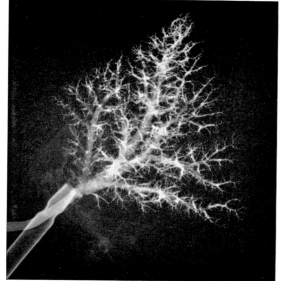

Figure 6-7

Compare a chest film made at expiration (Figure 6-8) and one made when the same patient had taken a deep breath (Figure 6-9). Poorly aerated alveoli and crowded-together vessels naturally decrease the radiolucency of the lung to some extent. Note, too, that the flexible mediastinum and fluid-filled heart have been compressed upward by the high diaphragms in Figure 6-8, so that they cast an appreciably wider shadow and appear to be en- larged. This will be true of any film made at expiration and is an additional reason why it is important for you to determine the level of the diaphragm in the course of your survey of any chest film. The patient must be cajoled into taking a deep breath if he is at all capable of it, and before you attempt to draw any conclusions from his chest film, you must check the position of his diaphragm and decide whether he has done so.

Figure 6-8

Figure 6-9

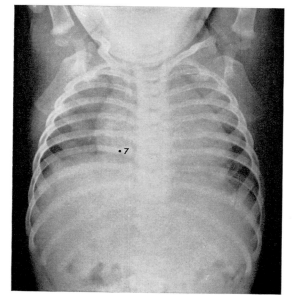

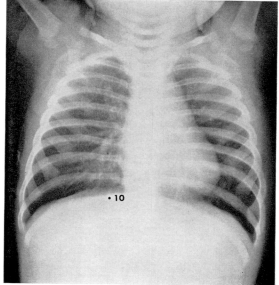

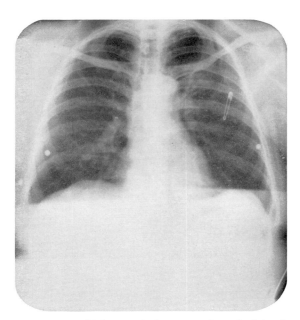

Figure 6-10 *(Unknown 6-1)*. Locate these fluid levels anatomically.

The motion of the diaphragm may be studied under the fluoroscope. When chest films are difficult to interpret and there is some question of abnormality in the lung close to the diaphragm, a fluoroscopic study of the area in question often contributes vital information. A small amount of fluid in the pleural space may not be visible in the PA chest film, for example, but may be seen during various maneuvers under the fluoroscope. The fluoroscopist tilts and turns the patient as he watches the motion of the diaphragm. That motion will be inhibited when there is inflammation near the diaphragm, and the presence of a subdiaphragmatic abscess may first be suspected when the motion is found to be limited at fluoroscopy.

So far you have seen the two diaphragms elevated only because the patient failed to take a deep breath; but if on a film made at full inspiration his diaphragms are still high, one must account for their position. Obese and sthenic persons often have high diaphragms. The two diaphragms may be elevated by large collections of fluid in the peritoneal space, as in the patient with heart failure or cirrhosis of the liver. With distension of many loops of large or small bowel in intestinal obstruction, the diaphragms are usually high and may also be limited in their downward motion, responding reflexly to abdominal pain. For the same reason they are normally high and "splinted" in their motion for a few days after abdominal surgery. You would expect them to be high in the third trimester of pregnancy and they are.

On the other hand the diaphragms may be depressed and flattened in any condition which greatly increases the volume of the structures within the thoracic cage. Thus, in emphysema, with irreversible trapping of air in the lung and gradually increasing overexpansion, the diaphragms are low and flat. They may show serrated margins because then the insertions into the lower ribs become visible. Likewise with the added volume of large collections of pleural fluid or of tumor masses in the lung, the diaphragm may be depressed. Remember that if the diaphragm is obscured by the density of tumor or fluid above it, its depressed position or immobilization may not be suspected from the films alone.

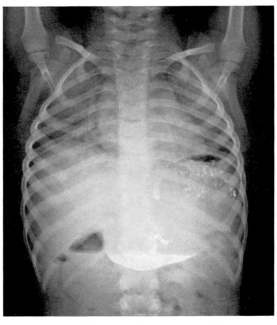

Figure 6-11 *(Unknown 6-2)*. Systematic chest survey.

80

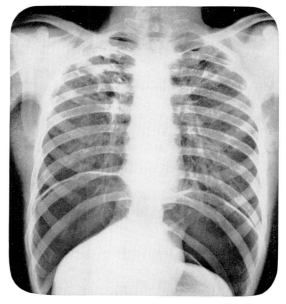

Figure 6-12 (*Unknown 6-3*). Determine the level of the diaphragms in this patient with bilateral upper lobe tuberculosis. Did the patient take a deep breath?

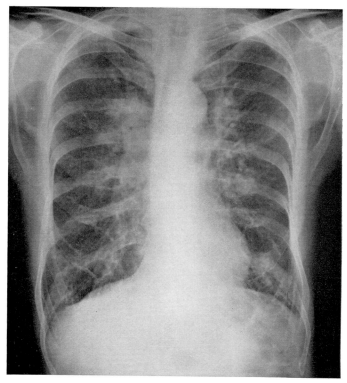

Figure 6-14. Both diaphragms depressed and flattened by permanent overinflation of the lungs in emphysema in an old man.

Figure 6-13

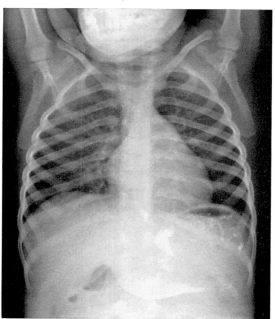

Figure 6-15. A low, flattened, serrated diaphragm is often seen in older patients, most of whom do have some degree of emphysema. This diaphragm did not move at fluoroscopy.

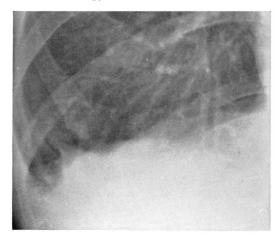

81

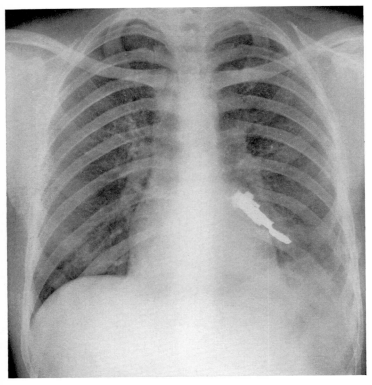

Figure 6-16

The man in Figures 6-16 and 6-17 was injured when a metallic fragment entered his chest. At fluoroscopy the radiologist found the left diaphragm fixed and motionless. Scar tissue and adhesions, formed above it by the time this study was made, obscure the profile as seen in the PA view. Figure 6-18 is a normal lateral view for comparison with Figure 6-17. The smooth outlines of the two diaphragmatic shadows are seen curving down posteriorly, parallel with each other. The barium-filled esophagus bisects the chest and enters the abdomen at about the mid-point of the diaphragm just above the faintly seen stomach bubble. Now compare the two diaphragmatic outlines in Figure 6-17. The right diaphragm (black-outlined arrows) is normal. The left (marked with white arrows) comes to a peak behind the heart near the foreign body. Some air in the stomach may be seen under it. The anterior segment of the left diaphragm appears denser because it overlaps the heart shadow.

Figure 6-17

Figure 6-18

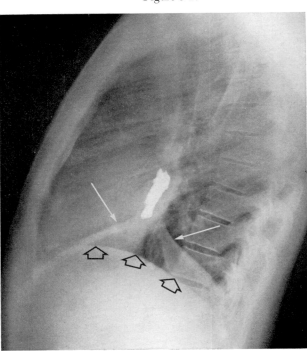

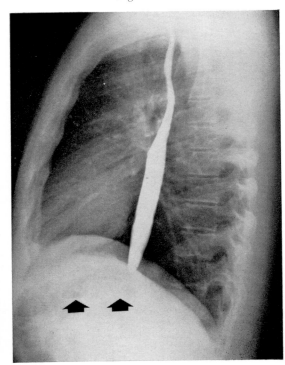

Elevation of one diaphragm is not infrequently seen when there is apparently nothing wrong with the patient ("eventration"), and although the muscular structure or the innervation of the diaphragm may be faulty, there are usually no symptoms. That was not the case with the 3-year-old boy in Figure 6-19, who was entirely healthy until about 3 hours before this film was made, when he was knocked down by a wave at the seashore. He had severe pain in the left side, developed a gasping respiration, and vomited dark, bloody fluid.

As you look at this film you know that it has been made upright because there is a fluid level present. It is hard for you to believe that the thin white line in the left fifth interspace could represent the diaphragm. There appears to be a much distended hollow viscus below it containing both air and fluid, and no lung markings are seen in the lower left interspaces. The heart is displaced to the right.

Exploratory surgery was undertaken, but the child did not survive. A congenitally defective part of his left diaphragm had been ruptured by the blow to the abdomen and the entire stomach forced into his chest through the rent. Figure 6-20 shows the open chest at autopsy. Clamps hold up the thin diaphragm, the hole in it visible as a dark opening; the stomach has been drawn back into the abdomen. Abnormal tears in the diaphragm, whether caused by trauma alone or by trauma to a congenitally defective muscle, may result in herniation of various organs including the liver, spleen, and even the kidneys upward into the chest.

Small herniations of a part of the stomach through the esophageal hiatus are very common, and are referred to as "hiatus hernias," although herniations may take place through any of the diaphragmatic openings, often without causing any symptoms. Congenital diaphragmatic hernias are common, and the entire stomach and colon have been found in the left chest in a patient with no complaints. The identity of the herniated structures may be established by barium studies. Barium given to the patient in Figure 6-19 would have been seen to pass down the esophagus through the diaphragm and return into the chest through the abnormal opening. That thin white line in

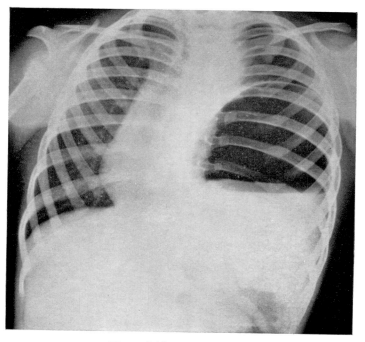

Figure 6-19

Figure 6-20

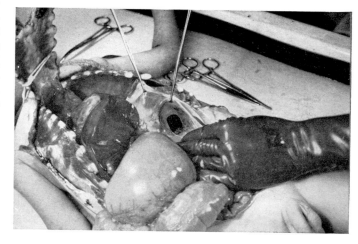

the fifth interspace is not the diaphragm, therefore, but the fundus of the stomach, and the fluid-air level is in the herniated part of the stomach above the diaphragm.

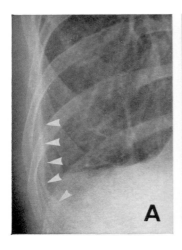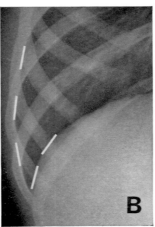

Figure 6-21 (left). *A.* The old, thickened pleura, caught tangentially by the beam of x-rays here, is actually a cuff of scarred tissue curving away from you and toward you over the surface of the lung and represents parietal and visceral pleura densely adherent to each other. The pleural space in this area is entirely obliterated, and with it the costophrenic sinus. (Compare *B*, a normal costophrenic sinus.) This is not to be confused with a small pleural effusion: remember that thickened pleura will not change from film to film or with tilting of the patient as free fluid does.

Figure 6-22 (below). Calcification of an extensive plaque of thickened pleura. Note obliterated costophrenic sinus.

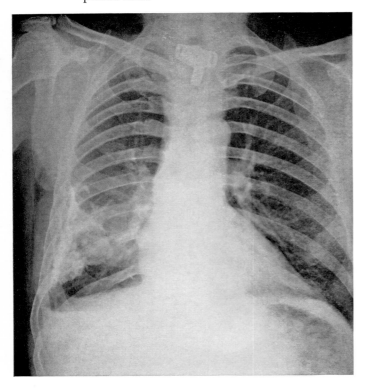

The *pleura* is a closed envelope which on one side invests the surface of the lung, dipping into its fissures, and on the other side is applied against the inner surface of the thoracic cage. Too delicate to be seen radiographically under normal circumstances, it may become visible when it has been thickened by inflammation and catches the beam of x-rays tangentially against the chest wall. The two thicknesses of pleura in the minor fissure may frequently be seen as a thin white line extending straight laterally from the right hilum, because the minor fissure is normally horizontal. Both the left and right major fissures and the minor fissure on the right may be seen on the lateral chest film whenever they happen to line up with the beam.

The pleural space, although normally empty and collapsed, *may come to contain either fluid or air or both,* any of which will alter strikingly the appearance of the chest film. A massive collection of fluid on one side can displace the mediastinum toward the opposite side, depress the diaphragm, partially collapse the lung, and render the entire hemithorax dense and white. Air in large or small amounts may gain access to the pleural space by rupture through the pleural surface of the lung or after trauma when the lung is punctured by the ends of fractured ribs. Air may be introduced into the pleural space intentionally for diagnostic purposes following a pleural tap. If the amount of pleural air is large, the lung will be seen partly collapsed against the mediastinum. Any amount of air in the pleural space allows you to see

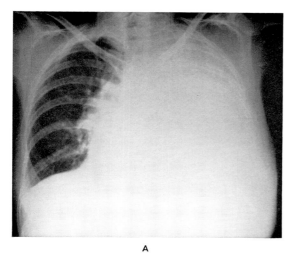

A

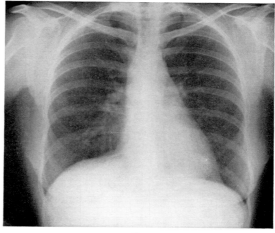

B

some part of the surface of the lung, which you do not see in the normal chest film because it lies closely in contact with the chest wall. Detection of a small pneumothorax depends on seeing the veil-like pleural margin of the lung beyond which no lung markings extend.

Large amounts of pleural air or fluid are easy to visualize; small amounts are much more difficult. If you will look again at any normal diaphragm shadow in the PA projection, you will see that it dips laterally to form a sharp angle with the chest wall. The base of the lower lobe, cupped convexly over the diaphragm, dips into this recess at the sides and deep posteriorly. *The costophrenic sinus (or sulcus)*, then, of which only the lateral part appears in the PA chest film, is a continuous ditch formed between the chest wall and the diaphragm at its insertion. The lowest part of this ditch, when the patient sits or stands, is located far posteriorly on either side of the spine, as you have already appreciated from the lateral chest film. Into this ditch extends the base of each lower lobe against the posterior insertion of the diaphragm, and pleural fluid gravitates into it. Thus the first several hundred milliliters of pleural fluid which accumulates will not be visible in the lateral costophrenic sinus on the PA chest film but would be seen in the lateral chest film obscuring the posterior portion of the diaphragm. It would also be appreciated at fluoroscopy, coming into view as the radiologist turns and tilts the patient.

Figure 6-23 (above). *A.* Massive left pleural effusion. The trachea and heart are markedly displaced to the right by the accumulation of fluid in the left pleural space. *B* shows the patient after recovery. Note the sharp, clear costophrenic sinuses.

Figure 6-24 (below). Massive pneumothorax. The right lung is only partly collapsed because of dense pleural adhesions (larger arrows). Smaller arrows indicate cavities within the diseased lung. Note that you can see the three lobes collapsing separately in the pleural air. Note small amount of pleural fluid in the costophrenic sinus.

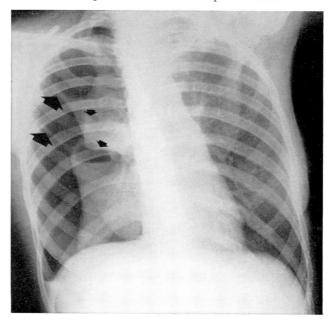

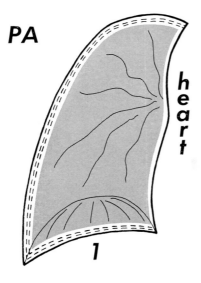

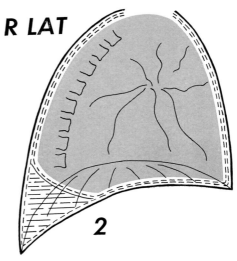

Figure 6-25. *1* and *2*. Small hydrothorax not seen in the PA view. Short broken lines indicate pleura. *3*. Large hydropneumothorax.

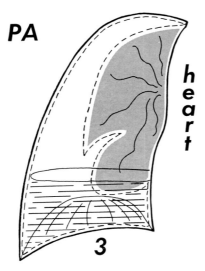

shadow against the chest wall (Figure 6-27). It never forms a horizontal fluid level unless there is also air present opening up the superior portion of the pleural space.

Whereas small amounts of pleural fluid collect far posteriorly against the diaphragm, small amounts of pleural air collect high over the cupola of the lung apex and against the upper lateral chest wall. They may be very difficult to see there because of the overlapping tangle of bones, and minimal pneumothorax is quite often missed unless you are looking carefully for it. It is more obvious when the lung is less well aerated, so that a film made at full expiration may show clearly the margin of slightly denser lung outlined by darker pleural air against the chest wall. Again, a fluoroscopic study will help, or a film may be made PA with the patient lying on his good side, when the air in the pleural space will collect over the lower ribs where it is easy to see. This is called a "lateral decubitus film" (Figure 6-28).

[Problem: What happens to the fluid in Figure 6-25, *1* and *2*, if, in preparing for a diagnostic tap posteriorly, the patient sits on a chair and leans forward?]

When enough fluid is present to fill up the posterior sulcus, the lateral part of the sulcus begins to fill, and this will be noted on the PA chest film as a blunting or obliteration of the costophrenic sinus on that side. (A similar but permanent blunting of the sinus is seen after purulent pleurisy or long-standing inflammatory effusions: Figure 6-21.) As a greater amount of fluid collects, the density of it obscures the rounded shadow of the diaphragm entirely and will be seen as an upward-curving

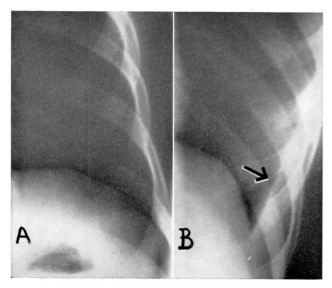

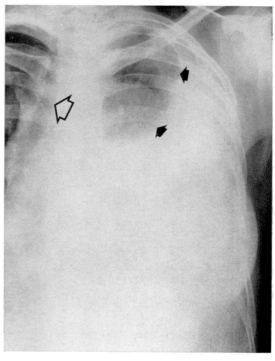

Figure 6-26 (above). Fluid which is free in the pleural space may generally be dumped into the lateral costo-phrenic sinus, where it is easy to see, if the fluoroscopist tilts the patient sharply to that side, as in *B*.

Figure 6-27 (above). Large accumulations of fluid show a crescentic line ascending along the lateral chest wall (black arrows). Note the displacement of the trachea to the opposite side (mediastinal shift).

Figure 6-28 (below). Pneumothorax. Margin of the lung outlined by air. PA lateral decubitus film. Patient lying on his side.

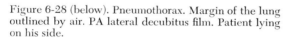

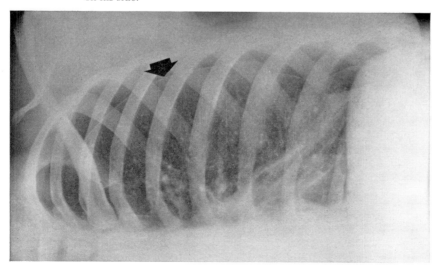

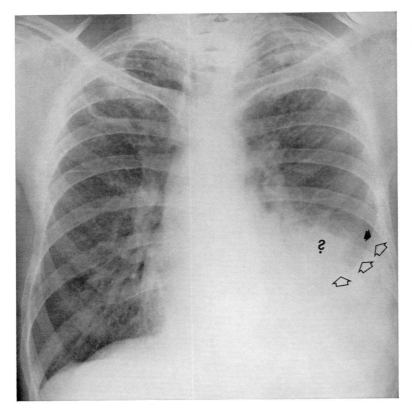

Figure 6-29. Pleural effusion (boxed arrows mark the fluid margin crossing the sixth rib, black arrow) partly conceals density in the lower part of the left lung in this patient with known bilateral upper lobe tuberculosis. There is nothing distinctive about the density, which could represent tumor, tuberculous pneumonia, or some other pathologic pulmonary condition.

Sizable collections of fluid often mask disease in the lower part of the lung, and since common lung diseases like pneumonia, tuberculosis, and tumor are frequently accompanied by pleural effusion, it may be very important to be able to visualize what is under the fluid density on the chest film. In Figure 6-29 there is certainly pleural fluid present, but there also seems to be more density in the lower lung field than can be accounted for by fluid alone. This density rises up out of the fluid and hides the heart border, and one must suspect disease in the lower part of the lung in this patient with known tuberculosis in both upper lobes. The usual clinical procedure is, of course, thoracentesis and withdrawal of most of the fluid, more films being made immediately afterward before fluid can reaccumulate.

Investigation of the concealed lung or diaphragm is often possible without thoracentesis by making decubitus films of various sorts, causing the fluid to shift its position so that the lower lung becomes visible. In Figure 6-30A

pleural fluid had collected under the base of the right lung against the diaphragm, lifting up the lung but remaining imprisoned beneath it. The costophrenic angle is sharp, and you note that the diaphragm-plus-fluid forms a high shadow which suggests an abnormally elevated right diaphragm. A decubitus film (C), made with the patient lying on his affected side, shifts the fluid into the lateral part of the pleural space against the chest wall where its volume can be estimated and the diaphragm and lower lung may be seen to better advantage.

Deliberate shifts of the fluid during diagnostic procedures will be limited, naturally, by any pleural adhesions which have formed. Collections of fluid within parts of the pleural space bound round by such adhesions sometimes cast very confusing shadows indeed. Loculated fluid of this sort may occur anywhere against the outer surface of the lung and be seen on the chest film as a shadow, the shape of which will be determined by the way it lines up with the x-ray beam. A pillow-shaped pocket of pus lo-

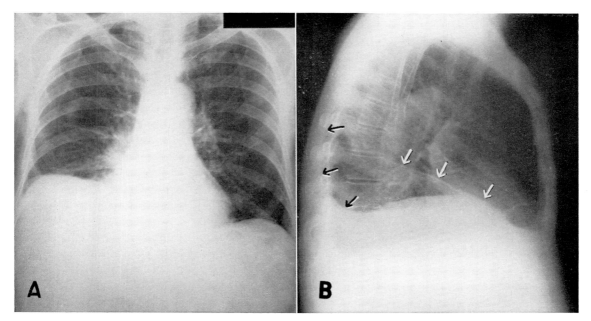

Figure 6-30. A. Subpulmonary collection of pleural fluid imitates a high right diaphragm. B. Lateral film shows fluid curving up along the posterior chest wall (black arrows) and dipping into the major fissure. C. Decubitus film shifts the fluid against the lateral chest wall, where it is seen to dip into the minor fissure.

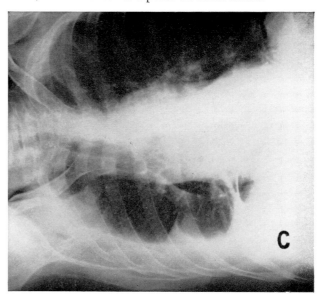

cated posteriorly halfway up the chest, for example, will appear on the PA film as a rounded density very like a patch of pneumonia in the mid-lung field. Only a lateral or oblique film can demonstrate that it is against the chest wall and not in the lung. It is to be remembered that viscous fluid or thick pus will not shift as described above. The possibility of shifting fluid should be taken into account when planning a thoracentesis.

Fluid may also become imprisoned in the fissures, and when it does, fluoroscopy and films made at the direction of the radiologist will be able to show that the fluid lies in the known anatomic plane of one of the fissures. Remember that the planes of the two major fissures descend obliquely from high against the posterior chest wall to a point low against the anterior chest wall. Similarly the plane of the minor fissure on the right is normally horizontal, extending forward and laterally from the middle of the major fissure at a level opposite the right hilum. Collections of fluid within these fissures will lie in the same planes, and you can look for them there. Frequently you can see free fluid dipping into both major and minor fissures when enough has accumulated, as you do in Figure 6-30B and C.

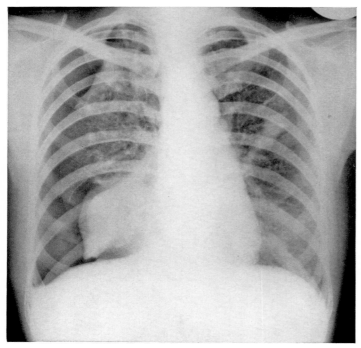

Figure 6-31 (*Unknown 6-4*)

Whenever you see an obscured diaphragm which does not curve downward to the lateral costophrenic sinus, you must wonder whether there is fluid above it and look closely for an upward curve of density against the lateral chest wall or for a fluid level. Whenever you see a fluid level, you must look closely for the margin of lung which is certainly present with pneumothorax, and always visible somewhere. Whichever you see, you must not forget to wonder what may be going on in that part of the lung which is concealed by the fluid shadow and to plan its better visualization.

You have now added to your systematic chest survey a careful inspection of the diaphragms and the costophrenic sinuses as well as of the pleural space when it becomes visible. You should make a deliberate attempt to see a chest fluoroscopy being done on a patient with hydropneumothorax, because you will derive from it an unforgettable three-dimensional feeling about every patient with pleural fluid, whether he also has air in his pleural space or not.

Figure 6-32 (*Unknown 6-5*)

Figure 6-31 (*Unknown 6-4*), Figure 6-32 (*Unknown 6-5*), and Figure 6-33 (*Unknown 6-6*) are to be analyzed via a systematic chest survey using roentgen signs alone without any clinical information in order to prove how much you have learned thus far. Of course, you could go much farther toward a diagnosis with some clinical information, but before you turn to the answers, try deciding just how much you could tell someone about these films before you knew anything about the patient.

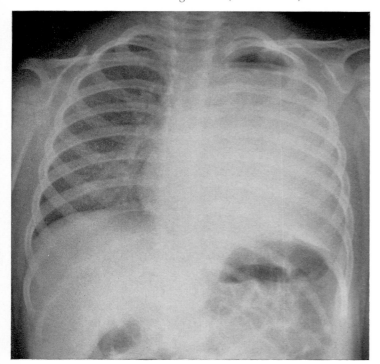

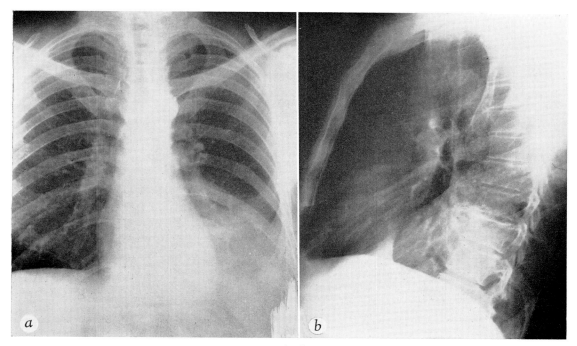

Figure 6-33 *(Unknown 6-6)*

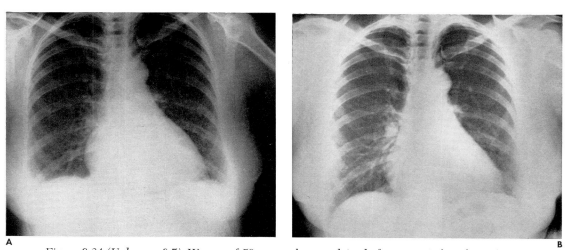

Figure 6-34 *(Unknown 6-7)*. Woman of 59 years who complained of soreness in her chest. *A* was made on admission; *B,* made 5 months later with the patient restored to good health, should help you to analyze *A.*

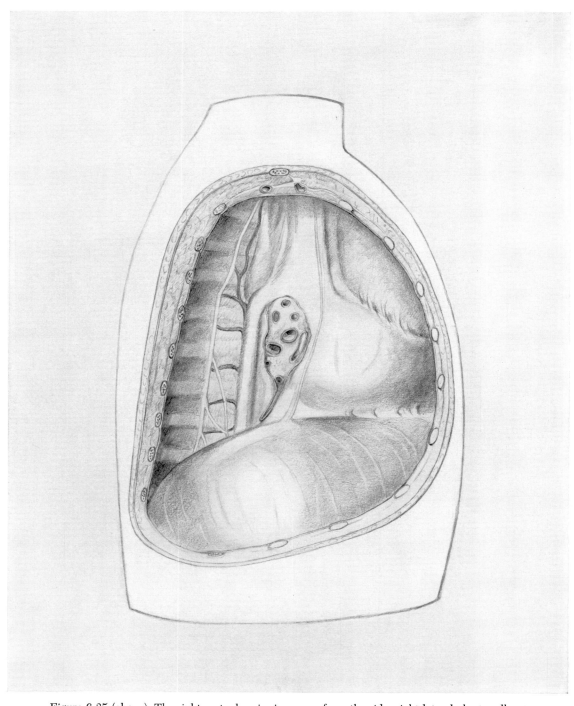

Figure 6-35 (above). The right costophrenic sinus seen from the side, right lateral chest wall cut away. Fluid collecting posteriorly on one side would look like Figure 6-36A.

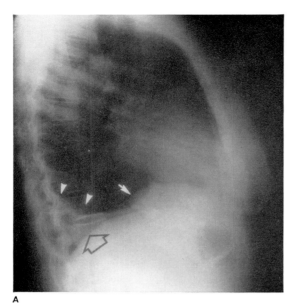 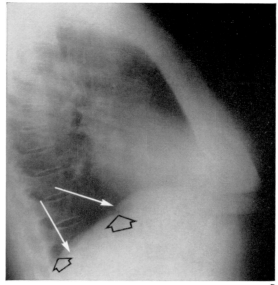

A   B

Figure 6-36. The related lateral films of the patient in Figure 6-34. *A*, made the same day as Figure 6-34*A*; *B*, made the same day as Figure 6-34*B*. Note reappearance of the two sharp posterior angles in *B* when the fluid has disappeared. (White arrows indicate right diaphragm and curving fluid line in the posterior sulcus. Black boxed arrow indicates left diaphragm.)

Credits: Illustrations this chapter.

Figure 6-2. Courtesy Dr. M. Strahl, Brooklyn, N. Y.

Figures 6-3, 6-4. Courtesy Dr. E. Ahern and the publisher, *MR&P* 30:9.

Figure 6-5. Courtesy Dr. C. Dotter, Portland, Ore.

Figures 6-6, 6-7, 6-8, 6-9, 6-11, 6-13. Courtesy Dr. J. Hope et al., and the publisher, *MR&P* 33:26, 28.

Figure 6-10. Courtesy Dr. H. Forsyth, Jr., and the publisher, *MR&P* 31:129.

Figure 6-12. Courtesy Mr. C. Brownell and the publisher, *MR&P* 27:114.

Figures 6-16, 6-17. Courtesy Dr. G. Wyatt, Iowa City, Iowa.

Figures 6-19, 6-20. Courtesy Drs. L. Adelson and A. Peacock, and the publisher, *MR&P* 25:111, 112.

Figure 6-21*A*. Courtesy Dr. W. Brosius, Detroit, Mich.

Figure 6-21*B*. Courtesy Drs. A. Fine and T. Steinhausen, and the publisher, *MR&P* 23:54-56.

Figure 6-22. Courtesy Drs. W. Tuddenham, G. McDonnel, T. Tristan, H. Pendergrass, and L. Stanton, and the publisher, *MR&P* 33:60.

Figures 6-23, 6-34, 6-36. Courtesy Dr. J. Mokrohisky and the publisher, *Radiology* 70:578-580.

Figures 6-26, 6-30. Courtesy Dr. J. Petersen and the publisher, *Radiology* 74:36, 40.

Figure 6-28. Courtesy Dr. E. Carpenter, Superior, Wis.

Figure 6-31. Courtesy Dr. G. Schwalbach, Rochester, N. Y.

Figure 6-33. Courtesy Drs. R. Belgrad, C. Good, and L. Woolner, and the publisher, *Radiology* 79:795.

Figure 6-35. Adapted from Sobotta-Uhlenhuth; *Atlas of Descriptive Human Anatomy*, 7th Ed., 1957, Hafner Publishing Co., New York, N. Y.

CHAPTER 7

Mediastinal Shift, Atelectasis
and Emphysema

Anatomists describe the mediastinum as a mass of tissue. I prefer to think of it as a bundle of structures sandwiched between the two inflated lungs. With the exception of the air-filled trachea, all these structures have the same radiodensity and merge into a homogeneous shadow superimposed upon that of the spine in the PA projection. Thus, the shadows of the mediastinal structures cannot be separated from each other except by a variety of special procedures employing contrast substances. Only the lateral margins, which are outlined by air in the lungs on either side, can be identified without such procedures.

Figure 7-1. Three tag points to be used in checking the mid-line position of the mediastinum. (See text.)

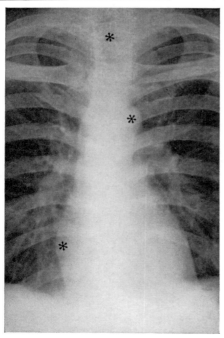

With important changes in the air content of either lung, or with large accumulations of pleural air or fluid, the mediastinum will bow to one side like an elastic diaphragm. You will need to identify a few anatomic points along the margins of the mediastinal shadow and to know their normal locations if you are to be able to recognize mediastinal displacement. There are three of these signal points which ought to be included in your systematic chest survey.

The first is the column of air in the trachea visible as a dark vertical shadow on the PA chest film, normally a little to the right of the mid-line as it approaches the carina. The second is the white knob you see to the left of the spine at about the fifth rib posteriorly. This knob is the shadow margin created by the arch of the aorta as it swings posteriorly and turns downward to become the descending aorta. You see it, of course, only because there is radiolucent lung tissue abutted against it, and it will disappear if that lung tissue becomes airless or if a dense mass lies against its lateral margin.

Finding the trachea and the aortic knob in their usual locations, then, will tell you that the upper mediastinum is where it ought to be. When there is a marked decrease in the amount of air in the right upper lobe, for example, the trachea will be found shifted toward that side. The knob of the aorta will be pulled with it toward the mid-line, its shadow disappearing as it becomes superimposed upon that of the spine. In just the same way the trachea and the aortic knob may be displaced to the left when there is decrease in the air content of the left upper lobe. If you review the anatomic relations of the aortic arch you will find that nor-

~

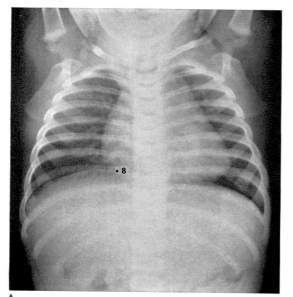 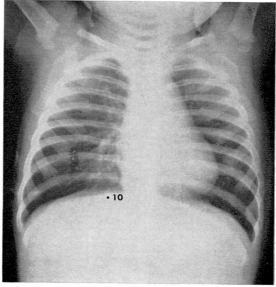

Figure 7-2A. The right border of the heart, exaggerated by the high diaphragm at expiration, returns to normal position with good inspiration (B). The heart in this patient was abnormal, and is slightly enlarged to the left.

mally both upper and lower lobes adjoin it. For this reason, if there is no air at all in the left upper lobe it will lie, dense and much decreased in size, against the anterior mediastinum, and you may actually still see the aorta through it, illuminated by the overexpanded lower lobe. Check the position of trachea and aortic knob on some of the chest films you have seen so far.

The third tag point in determining the position of the mediastinum is the shadow of the right heart border. Major changes in the size of either lower lobe will swing the heart to one side, and it will look displaced to you. You may think that since we have not yet discussed the heart and cardiac enlargement, you will not yet be able to use the right heart border with much sense of security, but be reassured. Up to now I have shown you very few abnormal hearts and a good many normal chest films. Look back over some of them at the right border of the heart as it curves down toward the diaphragm. By the time you have looked at a dozen or so, you should be convinced that the border of the normal right heart shadow is generally about a fingerbreadth beyond the right border of the spine on a full 14- by 17-inch chest film and proportionately less on these engraved reductions. Of course, this is a very rough working rule, and you will learn how to modify it as you look at more and more films.

Obviously, elevation of the diaphragms compressing the liquid-filled heart from below will exaggerate the lateral projection of both heart borders. Therefore, accuracy about mediastinal position will depend on your having counted down the ribs so that you are sure the diaphragms are drawn down well. Obviously, too, if the right middle lobe lying against the right heart is consolidated, that border will disappear and cannot be used in tagging the position of the lower mediastinum.

If, however, you are satisfied that the diaphragms are well down, that the clavicles and ribs are symmetrical and show no rotation, and that the right heart border appears to be in about its usual position, you can say then that the lower mediastinum is not appreciably displaced, or at least was not when the film was made.

95

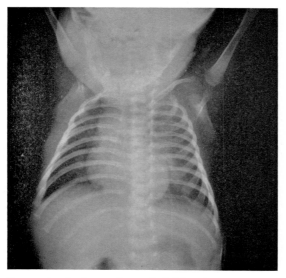

Figure 7-3. Is this mediastinal shift? Before you go on, analyze this film according to every kind of basic information you now possess.

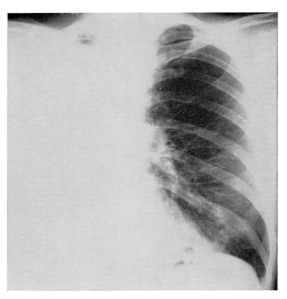

Figure 7-4. Have you evidence here for mediastinal shift? (Answered in the text.)

If the whole lung on one side collapses, then all three tag points will usually show a shift in position, since the whole mediastinum swings to that side. If only an upper lobe is involved, you may find that the trachea and aortic knob are shifted, while the right heart border is not. On the other hand, collapse of only a lower lobe may cause a definite shift of the position of the heart, although that of the trachea and aorta remains normal. Less massive changes such as collapse of the right middle lobe or of one bronchopulmonary segment will usually not be enough to displace the mediastinum at all and are readily compensated for by slight overexpansion of adjoining lung tissue.

If you analyzed Figure 7-3 correctly, you realized that the patient was markedly rotated so that the right ribs appear much longer than those on the left. The straight PA film made a few minutes later is seen in Figure 7-5, in which a slightly better inspiration has also been taken. Aortic knob and right heart border are now normal (for an infant with his diaphragms at the middle of the ninth interspace), and the mediastinum is clearly in mid-position. The child has a patchy pneumonitis in mid-lung on the right, a density appreciable by comparing the two sides, interspace for interspace.

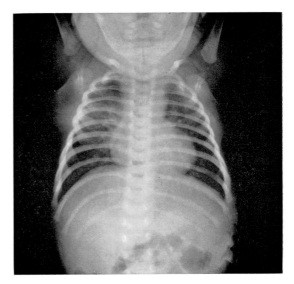

Figure 7-5

96

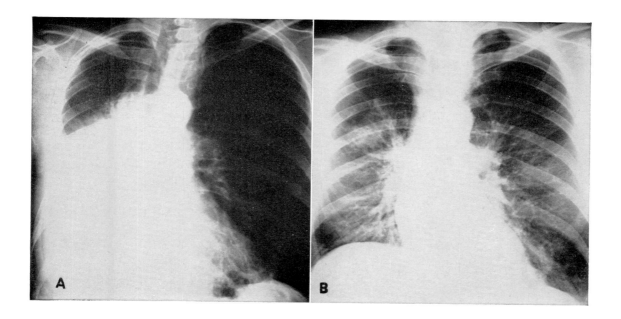

The patient in Figure 7-4 has a massive collapse of the right lung. The heart shadow is shifted to the right and merged with that of the atelectatic right lung. The trachea is not seen on this film, but there is no aortic knob visible to the left of the spine. The right heart border can be of no use to you here because of the density of the lung against it.

The presence of lung carcinoma with atelectasis was established, and the patient in Figure 7-4 received a course of radiation therapy. The three parts of Figure 7-6 are a series of subsequent studies made during that treatment and at 3 months after it had been completed. In *A* part of the right upper lobe has re-expanded but not enough to allow the trachea, now clearly seen, to return to mid-line. However, the aortic knob is now well seen. The right heart border and diaphragmatic profiles are still absent. In *B* they have reappeared with the re-expansion of the entire lung. The primary lung tumor mass may now be seen in the mid-lung field overlying the right seventh rib, and both hila are seen enlarged with tumor-invaded nodes. In *C*, made 3 months after the completion of treatment, there is further regression, and the mediastinum is clearly in normal position.

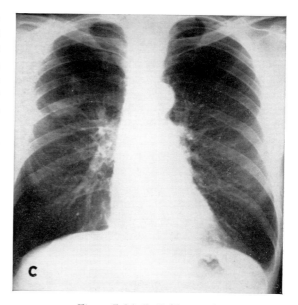

Figure 7-6*A, B, C.* (See text.)

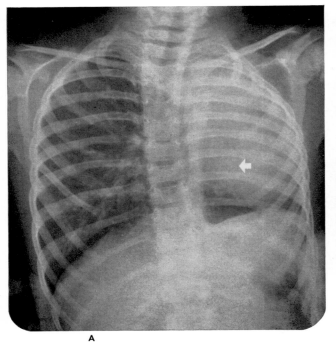

A

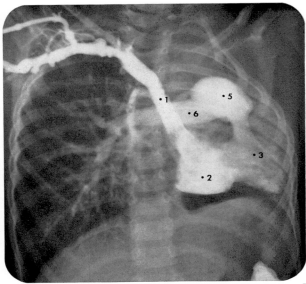

B

Figure 7-7A. Permanently displaced mediastinum in a 4-year-old who had hypoplasia of the left lung and compensatory overexpansion of the right lung coming across the mid-line (arrow). The dense mass in the left hemithorax is the heart, as proved by angiography (B). Note absence of left pulmonary artery.

The mediastinum may be displaced _permanently_ (for example, by scar tissue in the lung retracting it to one side, or by surgical removal of one lobe or the whole lung); _temporarily_ (as when a major lobe collapses postoperatively); or _transiently_ (as when a foreign body in one major bronchus interferes with the inflation or deflation of that part of the lung during each inspiration). Permanent and temporary displacements of the mediastinum will usually be appreciable from the PA chest film, and you will be looking for them every time you check the three tag points in your systematic chest survey.

Transient shifts, however, are often first recognized only at fluoroscopy when the radiologist employs one of the many maneuvers he has developed to demonstrate such findings. One of these is to ask the patient to sniff suddenly with one border of the mediastinum held in view under the fluoroscope. The sudden inspiratory sniff will cause the mediastinum to jump slightly to one side if inequality of aeration is present.

Because any single chest film only represents the state of affairs in your patient's chest at one particular fraction of a second in time, it is quite possible to expose the film when the mediastinum is in mid-position, even though there is a definite mediastinal shift during some other phase of respiration. The film you hold in your hand later that day thus may give no indication at all that there is a transient shift of the mediastinum. If you suspect there may be one, you ought to ask for a fluoroscopic study or for films made at inspiration and expiration, a commonly used device for recording transient mediastinal shift.

The mediastinum may also be pushed to one side by pressure from an overexpanded lung, as in obstructive emphysema when air is drawn into that part of the lung with every breath but incompletely expelled. A ball-valve foreign body may do this. The same dynamics exist when faulty bronchi with inadequate cartilaginous support collapse with each attempted expiration. Obstructive emphysema probably also exists at some point in the natural history of any endobronchial tumor, although soon the obstruction is completed as the tumor grows, and the lung beyond it collapses as its air is absorbed or escapes to other segments. On serial films one would be able to observe the mediastinum at first displaced away from the side of the lesion by the overexpanded lung and later displaced toward the side of the lesion as the affected lobe collapses, another illustration of the value of serial films and the proper evaluation of changing roentgen signs.

The mediastinum is, of course, shifted away from the side on which any massive pleural effusion accumulates, as you have seen in Chapter 6. Will it be similarly shifted with pneumothorax?

The mediastinum may become fixed as a result of adhesions subsequent to inflammation, or by tumor invasion. It may also be checked in its displacement by pleural adhesions which prevent the full collapse of one lung.

When lung tissue is inflated with more than its normal content of air, it becomes more radiolucent than normal. No matter how clearly radiolucent the normal lung tissue on a chest film now looks to you, remember that it is quite logical that a cube of air should be more radiolucent than the same cube of air traversed by blood-filled capillaries. As you would expect, then, the roentgen appearance of overexpanded lung will be an over-all increased radiolucency, the affected lung appearing too dark with the exposures used for chest work routinely. In addition, the lung markings will be spread apart as the vessels are separated farther and farther by the ballooned alveoli. In obstructive emphysema localized to one segment of lung, as you see it in the man in Figure 7-9, this appearance may be so exaggerated as to be confused with pneumothorax. The true state of affairs may generally be determined by a careful fluoroscopic study. Injudicious exploratory needling is very dangerous, since it may convert well-contained emphysema into tension pneumothorax, a potential disaster for the patient.

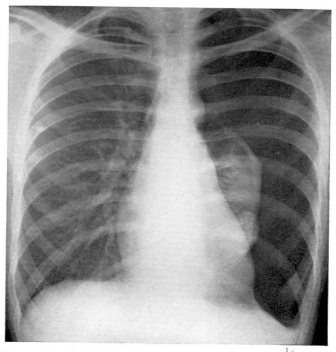

Figure 7-8 (above). Pneumothorax with the mediastinum in the mid-line. The volume of pleural air is compensated for here by the degree of collapse of the left lung.

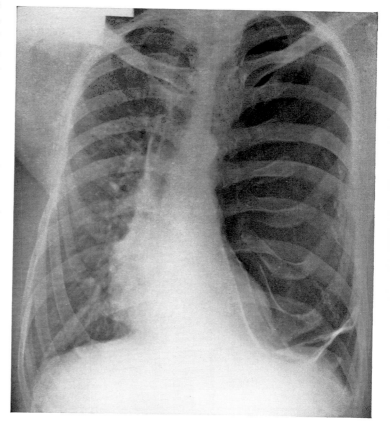

Figure 7-9 (right). Obstructive emphysema of part of the left lung, causing shift of the mediastinum to the right. No pneumothorax was present.

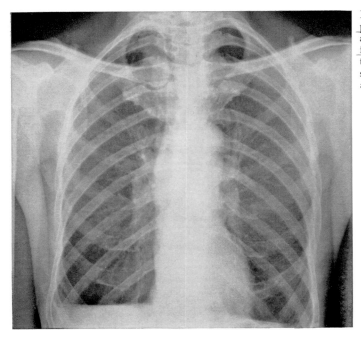

Figure 7-10 (left). Older man with emphysema. Note low, flattened diaphragms at the level of the twelfth rib. Diffuse fibrosis throughout the lung detracts from the increased radiolucency you expect to see. These diaphragms moved very little at fluoroscopy.

⋇ With the chronic emphysema of old age, the lungs are both generally overexpanded, the diaphragms low, flattened, and often serrated. Many cases will be obvious to you by these tokens, together with the increased radiolucency you will see at the usual roentgen exposures for chest work. Lesser degrees of generalized emphysema may be much less obvious. In those patients the fluoroscopic finding of diaphragms which move down slightly with inspiration and return only very slowly on forced expiration will help to establish a diagnosis of emphysema. In many patients with emphysema the concomitant development of pulmonary fibrosis adds to the increased radiolucency the shadow of a web of filamentous strands of increased density. These radiate outward from the hilum through the entire lung. Localized emphysematous bullae may be seen anywhere in the lung, like huge air cysts bordered by dense thin walls which enclose them. Rupture of such bullae, producing a spontaneous pneumothorax, is not unusual.

Figure 7-11 (below). Low diaphragms in a patient with chronic asthma moved very slowly upward during forced expiration, and the motion was quite limited.

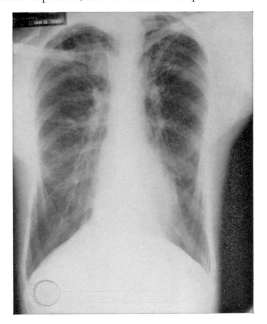

100

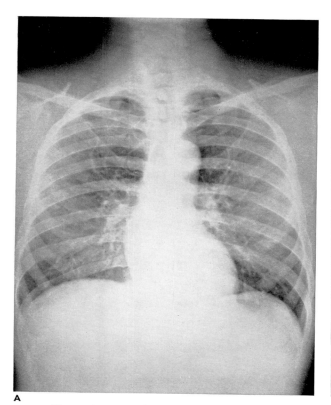

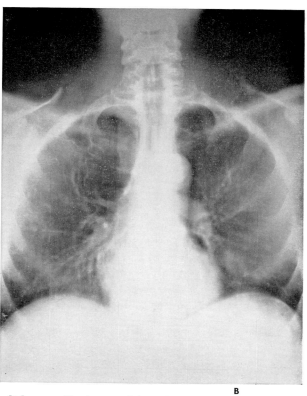

A

B

Figure 7-12. Patient with <u>localized emphysema</u> in the medial parts of both upper lobes. *A.* Note increased lucency just to the left of the aortic knob. Bullae are better seen in *B* and *C,* body-section studies.

C

Figure 7-13 (below). Microradiograph of a slice of lung with apical bullous emphysema.

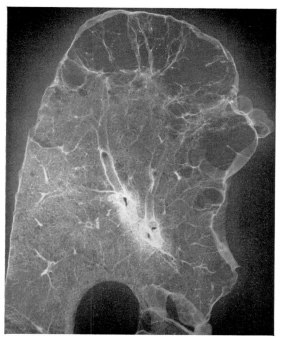

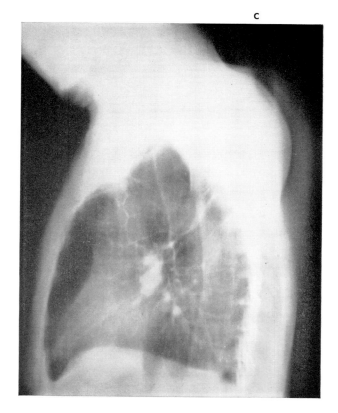

101

Atelectasis, on the other hand, causes the lung to appear less radiolucent than normal, and atelectasis of one lobe will be seen first as a difference in density between the two sides. Thus you will be looking for an unaccountably dense area in the lung.

You have already seen diffusely increased density due to the high position of both diaphragms in a film made at peak expiration, and you realize that that amount of decreased radiolucency at some phase of his respiratory cycle goes with every breath your patient takes (Figure 7-14). By the same token, you can imagine the chest film of a stillborn infant who has never breathed at all or swallowed air. His lungs and bony thorax would be collapsed about the heart and mediastinal structures as one uniformly dense shadow within the rib cage and would blend continuously with those of the dense abdominal structures (Figure 7-15).

The collapsing lung or lobe tends to fold up fan-wise against the mediastinum in a characteristic manner (Figure 7-16), and a dynamic concept of these collapse patterns and the roentgen signs by which they are to be recognized is, again, nothing more than an exercise in the logic of radiodensities applied anatomically. You would anticipate, for example, that with atelectasis of the *right upper lobe* the location of the minor fissure dividing it from the middle lobe could be seen increasingly well as the contrast increased between the poorly aerated lung tissue above it and the well-aerated lung tissue below it. Moreover, since the fissure is fixed at the hilum, it is natural that it would be seen to tilt upward from that fixed point as the upper lobe collapsed. At 50 per cent collapse, the line of the fissure limiting the lobe inferiorly would extend from the hilum outward and upward toward the axilla. When further collapsed, the shadow of the pancake-flat upper lobe would apply itself against the upper mediastinum and merge with its shadow. At the same time the middle and lower lobes would compensate by overexpanding and would show increased radiolucency compared with those on the opposite side. The shadow of the trachea would be drawn to the right, and the aortic knob would be drawn with it, disappearing into the shadow of the spine. The right hilum would appear to be drawn upward slightly.

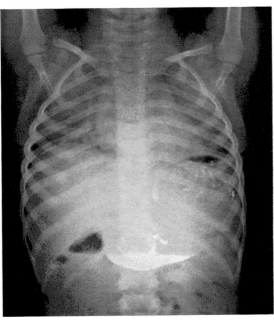

Figure 7-14. Diffuse bilateral hypoaeration occurring at peak expiration normally in a child.

Figure 7-15. Stillborn twins, one dead at 3 months, one born dead at term. Note that lungs, heart, and abdominal structures blend into one uniform shadow.

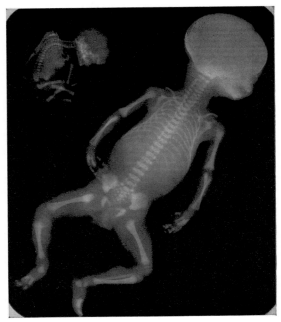

102

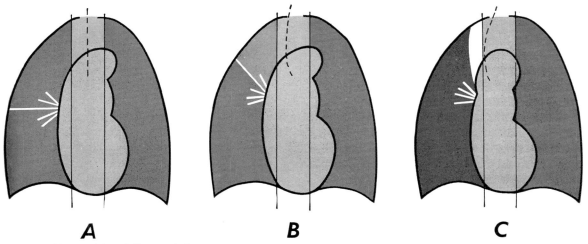

A   **B**   **C**

Figure 7-16. <u>Collapse of the right upper lobe</u>. *A.* Normal chest with normal position of minor fissure, right hilum, trachea, aortic knob, and right heart border, and equal aeration of all lobes. *B.* Right upper lobe collapsed 50 per cent. Minor fissure deflected upward, trachea pulled slightly to the right. No change in the right heart border. Changes in aortic knob and hilum equivocal. *C.* Major collapse of the right upper lobe, which is now a flat wedge of density against the superior mediastinum. Trachea and aortic knob deflected to the right. Right hilum drawn upward. Overaeration (hyper-radiance) of lower and middle lobes. No change in the right heart border. (Hilar displacement upward or downward is sometimes the first evidence of a collapsed lobe to be noticed.)

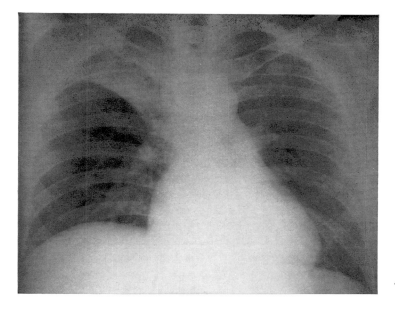

Figure 7-17. <u>Partial atelectasis, right upper lobe</u>, cleared 24 hours after intratracheal suction.

103

Now put together the signs of *left lower lobe* collapse in just the same deliberately logical way. Since the major fissure on the left lines up with the beam of x-rays only in the lateral view, and is always quite oblique to the ray in the PA view, no clear-cut margin between normal and atelectatic lung tissue is to be seen in the PA film as the left lower lobe begins to collapse. However, the heart gradually shifts toward the left so that you see less and less of the heart border to the right of the spine. You watch the left diaphragm become slightly more elevated and less and less clearly seen medially, although the lateral half of its shadow profile remains clear because of the compensatory expansion of the lingula of the left upper lobe now touching it. The left hilum is depressed, gradually disappearing behind the left border of the heart, an important and often missed roentgen sign of left lower lobe collapse. The

lung markings of the left upper lobe appear spread apart and the lung tissue more lucent than that in comparable interspaces on the right. The totally collapsed lobe appears, finally, as a wedge-shaped shadow against the mediastinum posteriorly. Its outer margin is to be seen through the heart shadow, thrown into contrast by air in the normal lung tissue against it laterally, that is, in the overexpanded upper lobe.

Re-expansion of the lower lobe could be expected to reverse all the findings. The wedge of density would disappear. The medial half of the left diaphragm would be visible again, and the left hilum would return upward to its normal position a little higher than the right. The radiolucency of the two lungs would be the same, and the mediastinum would return to the mid-line, showing the expected curve of the heart to the right of the spine.

Figure 7-18. Collapse of the left lower lobe. *A.* Normal profiles and mediastinal tag points. *B.* Early signs of left lower lobe collapse. Less of the heart is seen to the right of the spine. Vague decrease in lucency of lower left lung field with preservation of the diaphragmatic profile, which becomes slightly elevated and less sharp medially. *C.* Massive collapse of the left lower lobe. Little or no heart profile seen to the right of the spine. Medial half of the left diaphragm profile missing. Left lower lobe seen as a wedge of density through the heart shadow. Left hilum depressed. Increased radiolucency of the left upper lobe.

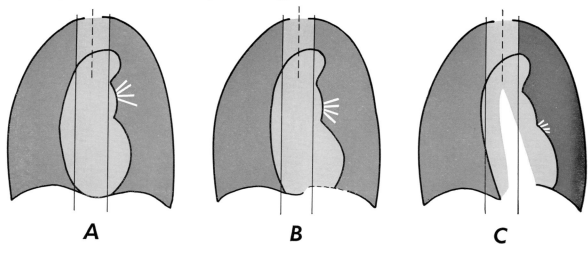

A **B** **C**

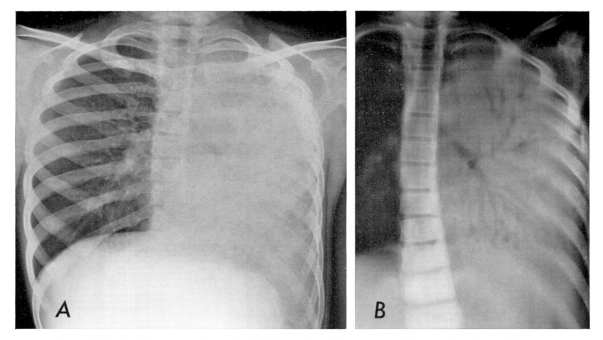

Figure 7-19. *A.* <u>Collapse of the entire left lung.</u> Here the signs are different from lower lobe collapse. The trachea is shifted, the right heart border is not seen at all, the left heart profile is entirely obscured by collapsed lung lying next to it, and the profile of the diaphragm is not seen. The mottled areas of radiolucency represent air in bronchi surrounded by dense lung. This is often called an "<u>air bronchogram.</u>" *B.* Body-section study shows even more clearly the air-filled, crowded-together bronchial trunks. Compare with the same type of crowding in the lower lobe collapse in Figure 7-20. The air bronchogram also effectively excludes the possibility of a large pleural effusion because it indicates the location of lung tissue.

Figure 7-20. *a.* <u>Collapsed left lower lobe.</u> Note depressed hilum, wedge of atelectatic lung seen through the heart shadow, and increased radiolucency of the left upper lobe. *b.* Same patient with opaque substance instilled into bronchial tree shows crowded bronchiectatic lower lobe trunks and slender, spread-apart upper lobe trunks.

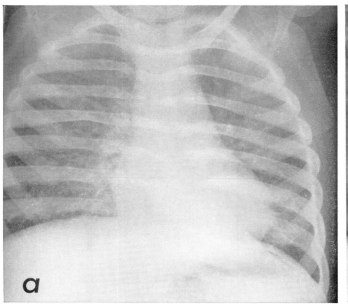
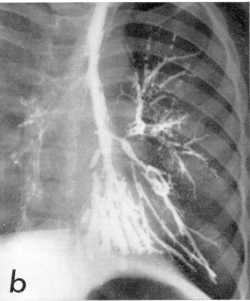

105

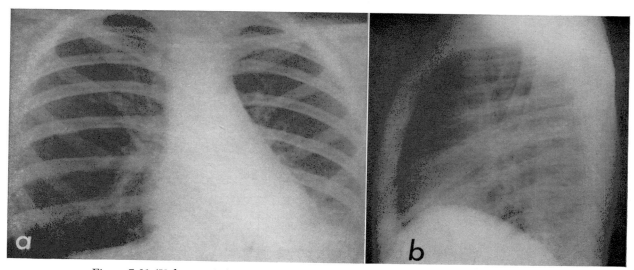

Figure 7-21 (*Unknown 7-1*). Which of the findings we have been discussing are present in this patient?

No matter how subtle the findings may be radiologically, if you are making a practice of going over each chest film in a systematic fashion, one day soon you will discover suddenly that the mediastinum you are looking at is shifted or that the medial half of one diaphragmatic shadow is missing. Any such finding must be accounted for, and it is then that you will begin to look more closely at the relative position of the two hila, compare the radiolucency of lung tissue on the two sides, and check for the presence of slim wedges of density against the mediastinum. In the next patient in whom you suspect atelectasis of a lobe, you ought to arrange to be present when the radiologist carries out the indicated fluoroscopy. There you will watch the mediastinum shift conspicuously and observe inequality of aeration to be exaggerated at some phase of respiration.

Although collapse of any of the four major lobes will generally result in the findings outlined for you above, collapse of the right middle lobe or of a single bronchopulmonary segment will be too minor a change to cause mediastinal displacement, hilar shift, or much variation in lung markings. Collapse of these smaller structures must be diagnosed from their appearance and anatomic location, with heavy reliance on

the history and change from film to film.

For example, when the middle lobe collapses, it will appear as a peaked smudge of white shadow against the heart in the PA view. The lateral view will be most helpful because in it a long wedge of increased density will slope downward across the heart shadow. This wedge will be more slender than that seen in simple pneumonia of the middle lobe, and its upper border will be the depressed minor fissure, its lower border the elevated anterior portion of the major fissure. It is the location of the density in the two views, then, and the deflection of the neighboring fissures which suggest atelectasis of the middle lobe, and there will be no mediastinal or hilar shift present. On routine PA views, unless one is checking the clarity and sharpness of the right heart border with care, it is easy to miss a right middle lobe collapse. A lordotic view is helpful because it tilts the middle lobe on end and concentrates its density.

Slender areas of density due to the collapse of smaller segments of lung may often be seen lying parallel to the surface of an elevated diaphragm after abdominal surgery. Radiologists refer to them as "plate-like areas of atelectasis." They disappear with better aeration of the lung base as the patient recovers and moves his diaphragm better.

106

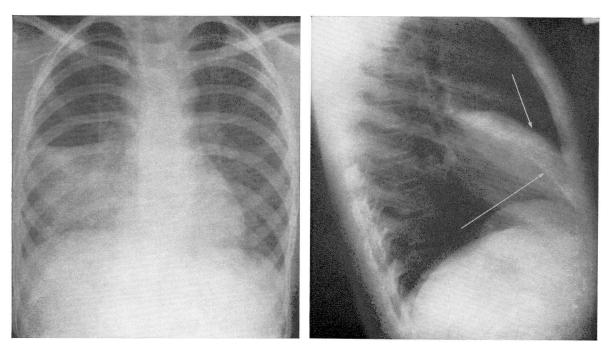

Figure 7-22 *(Unknown 7-2)*. Your patient has clinical signs of pneumonia. What part of the lung is involved here and how do you know?

Figure 7-23 *(Unknown 7-3)*. Analyze these films, locating anatomically any abnormalities.

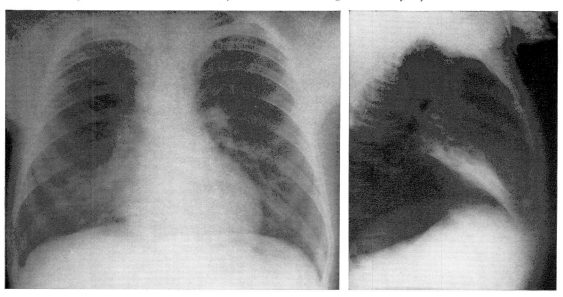

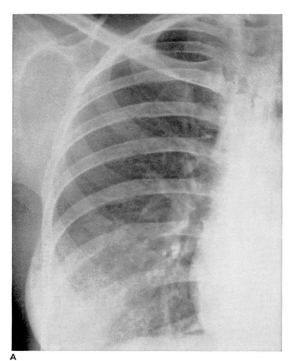
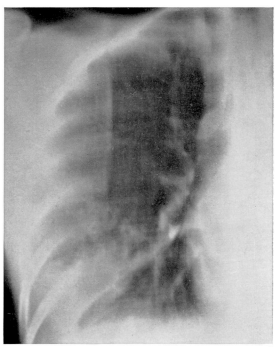

A   B

Figure 7-24 *(Unknown 7-4)*. A 26-year-old woman had a tooth extracted under anesthesia. Part of the tooth was found to be missing. *A* is a plain film made 5 days later, when she developed fever and cough. *B* is a body-section study. Admission film had been normal.

Figure 7-25 *(Unknown 7-5)*. *A.* Admission film on a patient with a 2-week history of fever and cough. Would atelectasis explain all the roentgen findings? *B.* Body-section study of the same patient.

A   B

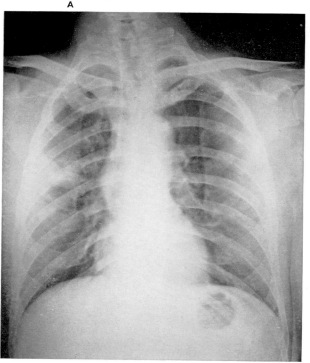
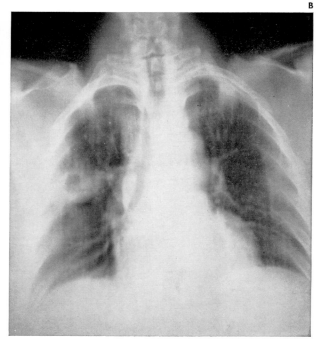

Roentgen observations which imply the presence of extensive emphysema or massive atelectasis will serve to remind you of distortions in architecture and aberrations of function which you might otherwise forget to consider in a particular patient. The old man with chronic emphysema is most concerned with his respiratory difficulties, but you will not be able to look at those overexpanded lungs and fibrous traceries of shadow without thinking of the increased work being done by the right side of his heart. In the same way, the signs of a collapsed lung must remind you that its vessels are crowded together, that the pulmonary circulation of blood is greatly decreased, and that the functioning of the heart must be embarrassed.

Finally, you must not forget, in looking at such films, that changes in volume within the thorax may compensate for other changes and obscure them. If the mediastinum seems in its normal mid-line position in spite of the fact that one entire lung field is dense, you can know only that the volumes of the two hemithoraces are equal. Underneath that white density there may be just enough collapse to compensate for the added volume of tumor or pleural effusion.

Remember that the radiograph is a shadowgram. Although you know that inflammation and tumor both render the lung dense, you must anticipate, for example, that in either condition some atelectasis is likely to be present as well, adding to the density of the already involved lung. Tumor or inflammation may cause collapse of a lobe even though the entire lobe is not actually involved in the primary process.

The consolidated pneumonic lobe often remains normal in size, as you saw it in Chapter 5, but equally often such a lobe will be distinctly decreased in size. In a good many patients with the clinical signs of pneumonia, therefore, you must expect to find some additional roentgen indications of atelectasis. As you expand your knowledge of medicine, you will learn to evaluate the roentgen signs of lobar collapse according to whether, for example, your patient was admitted with clear-cut pneumonia or has only a minor degree of

fever and cough the day following surgery. In the former you must think in terms of pneumonia-plus-atelectasis and treat accordingly. In the latter you must think in terms of atelectasis primarily and of the possibility of inflammation developing in the collapsed lobe. That they may look the same, or very nearly so, on the films should not disturb you, since you are using the radiographic findings as part of the entire clinical analysis rather than as oracular information.

In just the same way, bronchogenic carcinoma quite often presents itself initially as atelectasis, that is, as a lobe which has gradually collapsed beyond the invisible, obstructing bronchial tumor. Indeed, all three explanations for increased density may be present together in a patient who develops pneumonia in a partly collapsed lobe beyond a tumor of the bronchus. A respectable percentage of lung cancers are at first thought to be pneumonia with atelectasis, and only the unaccountable failure of the atelectasis to resolve and the lungs to re-expand fully with proper treatment eventually raises the question of tumor.

Up to this point in the book I have avoided giving you diagnostic labels. It is immensely important for you to realize that the type of analysis of roentgen findings you have been learning offers you an improved understanding of the dynamic pathologic changes within the thoracic cage of your patient. As such it is much more useful to you than any collection of diagnostic tags and labels. When you see mediastinal shift on a chest film or appreciate exaggerated radiolucency or the disappearance of normal profiles, you are recognizing roentgen findings rather than diagnoses. Such findings are heavy with implication as to what is going on inside your patient. Their presence will often go a long way toward confirming, expanding, or exploding an original working diagnosis based on the history and physical examination. The trained radiologist's daily experience with roentgen shadows increases his capacity for similar but more sophisticated deductions, and some of these permit him to conclude that a specific condition must be present beyond all reasonable doubt. Be satisfied with recognizing roentgen signs yourself, still a bit longer.

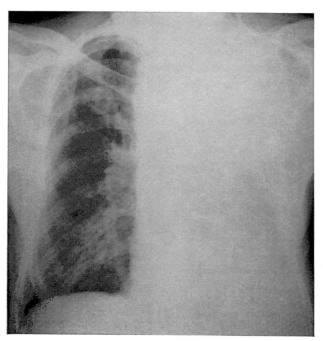

Figure 7-26

Unknown 7-6 (Figure 7-26). Mr. W, 58, has had a cough for 3 months and has been losing weight. He is no sicker than he was yesterday or last week, but sick people tend to lose their courage when the sun goes down, and you admit him, as is the common lot of interns, in the middle of the night.

On physical examination you find dullness to percussion present over the entire left chest, more marked in the upper half where the breath sounds are decreased and distant. There is bronchial breathing anteriorly over the upper left chest. The right side of the chest is normal. How much does this admission PA film help you? If this is all you are going to see on a plain film made with the conventional chest techniques, what other films are you likely to need? Predict what they will show for each of your differential possibilities.

Figure 7-27

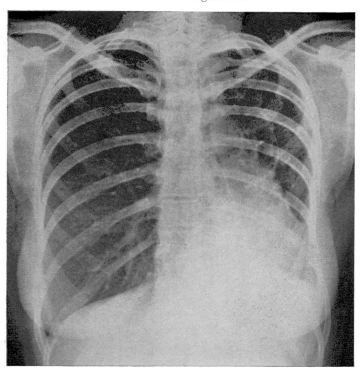

Unknown 7-7 (Figure 7-27). Mrs. D, 26, had an appendectomy a week ago without incident or complication. She has been running a low-grade fever for 2 days, but wants to go home. You order a chest film, tell her she can go home that evening, and go off duty yourself, stopping in the x-ray department on your way out of the hospital to look at her film.

Credits: Illustrations this chapter.

Figures 7-2, 7-3, 7-5, 7-14. Courtesy Dr. J. Hope et al., and the publisher, *MR&P* 33:27, 28, 30.

Figures 7-4, 7-6. Courtesy Drs. E. Uhlmann and J. Ovadia, and the publisher, *Radiology* 74:263, 269.

Figure 7-7. Courtesy Dr. H. Fulton and the publisher, *MR&P* 30:81, 82.

Figure 7-9. Courtesy Dr. W. Crandall, Sulphur, Okla.

Figure 7-10. Courtesy Dr. W. Tuddenham et al., and the publisher, *MR&P* 33:60.

Figure 7-11. Courtesy Dr. E. Lasser and the publisher, *Radiology* 77:441.

Figures 7-12, 7-24, 7-25. Courtesy Dr. B. Epstein and the publisher, *MR&P* 34:63-65.

Figure 7-13. Courtesy Drs. C. Oderr, P. Pizzolato, J. Ziskind, and the publisher, *Radiology* 71:242.

Figure 7-15. Courtesy Drs. I. Harris and M. Stuecheli, and the publisher, *MR&P* 28:29.

Figure 7-17. Courtesy Dr. E. Phillips, El Paso, Texas.

Figure 7-19. Courtesy Dr. B. Epstein, New Hyde Park, N. Y.

Figure 7-20. Courtesy Dr. H. White and the publisher, *Radiology* 71:820.

Figures 7-21, 7-22, 7-23. Courtesy Drs. V. Condon and E. Phillips, and the publisher, *Am. J. Roentgenol.* 88:548-550.

111

CHAPTER 8

Study of the Mediastinal Structures

The heart is the largest of the mediastinal structures, and all of the profiles which bulge beyond the shadow of the spine on both sides represent parts of the heart or of its great vessels. You can think of these profiles as nine intersecting arcs. Justify their identity on the basis of the angiocardiograms on the opposite page. Remember that some of the structures producing these shadows are more posterior in the chest (8, 9) and others far anterior (2, 7). Remember, too, that when an opaque substance mixed with blood fills a particular chamber of the heart its shadow may seem to you quite different in shape from what you have learned about that chamber based on a gross examination of the heart and its surface markings. Where a chamber is thickest its shadow will be most dense in the angiogram, and where it tapers off and becomes very thin a much less dense shadow is produced. Look at the shadow of the right ventricle, for example, in Figure 8-3. The slender, flattened part of the chamber

Figure 8-1 (left). The normal mediastinal profiles are all vascular and resolve into a series of nine intersecting arcs, as shown in Figure 8-2 (right). (1) superior vena cava; (2) ascending aorta; (3) right atrium; (4) inferior vena cava and cardiac fat pad; (5) left subclavian vein and artery, left common carotid artery; (6) aortic arch; (7) pulmonary artery; (8) left atrium; (9) left ventricle.

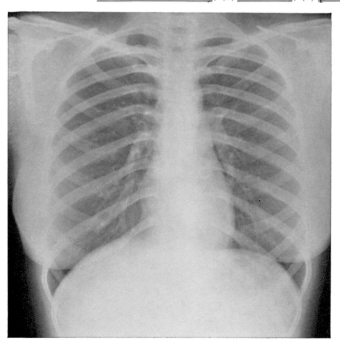

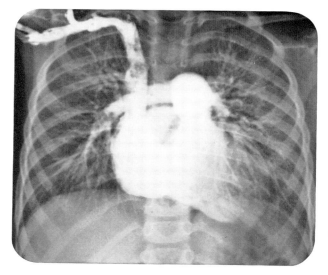

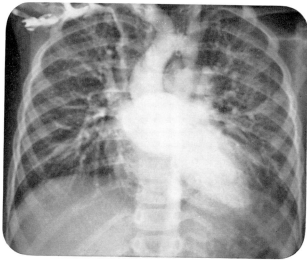

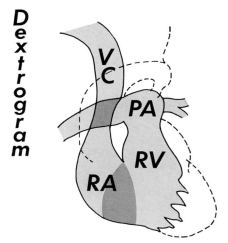

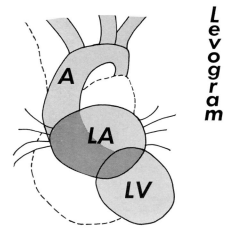

Dextrogram

VC

PA

RV

RA

Levogram

A

LA

LV

Figure 8-3 (left, above, with diagram below). *Dextrogram*, taken from a series of films made as the opaque-loaded bolus of blood passed through the heart. You see only the right chambers and great vessels. The branches of the pulmonary arteries are about to fill with opaque fluid.

Figure 8-4 (right, above, with diagram below). *Levogram*, taken 3 seconds later when the right side of the heart had been cleared of opaque-containing blood. You see only the shadows of the left chambers and great vessels. This child had coarctation of the aorta (indentation below the arch of the aorta).

which extends far to the left against the interventricular septum in the PA view hardly seems to belong to the dense massive shadow of the rest of the ventricle. Note also that you appreciate only vaguely the location of the tricuspid valve in this view, because the dense shadows of the right atrium and right ventricle are partly superimposed. In the levogram notice that you

see the dense upper margin of the crab-shaped left atrium through the shadow of the ascending aorta, in spite of the fact that you know the left atrium is on the posterior surface of the heart and that the ascending aorta arises anteriorly. Their opaque-filled cavities have cast separate shadows outlining them for you, and the two shadows overlap in this view.

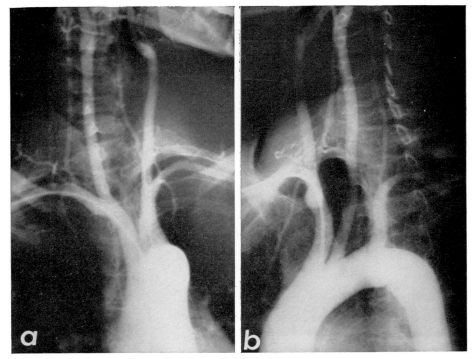

Figure 8-5. The normal aortic arch and brachiocephalic arteries. Opaque fluid was injected through a catheter in the brachial artery. *a* is almost PA (very slightly rotated to the left). In *b* the patient has been sharply rotated to his right, unrolling the aortic arch so that its branches no longer overlap. Remember that both venous and arterial shadows account for arcs 1 and 5 in Figure 8-1.

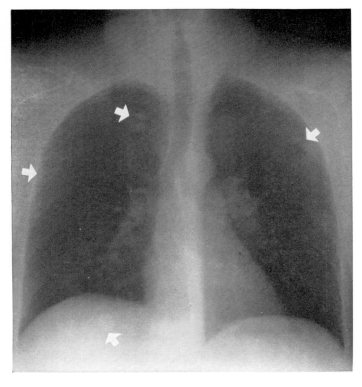

Figure 8-6 (left). Supervoltage PA radiograph of the chest, made with machines ordinarily employed in radiotherapy, may be used in studying the soft tissue structures of the mediastinum without any contrast medium. Note the dark tracheal air column. Arrows indicate metastatic tumor nodules in the lung, the lowest located far posteriorly.

The plain film of the chest made PA, then, shows you a number of mediastinal bulges seen in profile against the radiolucent lung on either side of the spine, all of them vascular shadows. In addition, you can usually see air in the trachea, but beyond this all other mediastinal organs merge with one another, and their shadows are superimposed upon those of the spine and the heart. You cannot account for the shadow of the esophagus or distinguish lymph nodes, thymus, or nerves; the thoracic duct merges with the shadows of other soft tissues and fluid-carrying vessels. Except for their mar-

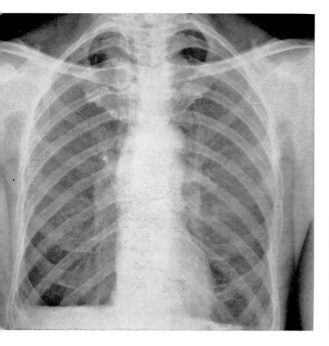

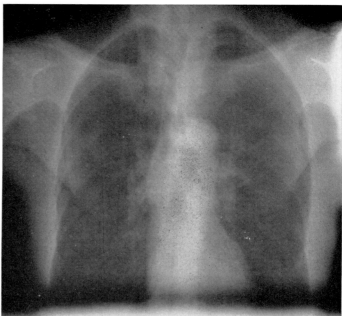

ginal profiles and their branches entering the lucent lungs, even the great vessels are merged with other shadows.

Fortunately most of the mediastinal structures can be visualized safely in one way or another by the use of specialized techniques. The vascular structures, of course, have been studied in the past two decades in an impressive variety of ways. In Figure 8-5, the aortic arch and its branches in the superior mediastinum are seen studied in two projections after a radio-opaque contrast material has been injected via a catheter placed into the right brachial artery. The coronary arteries may be visualized by injecting close to the coronary ostia. The chambers of the heart are studied by injecting an opaque substance through a catheter placed in the antecubital vein and observing the bolus of radiodense blood as it passes through the heart. Angiocardiograms will be discussed further in subsequent chapters.

Much information may be obtained by study of the radiolucent column of air in the trachea. The compression or displacement of the trachea or major bronchi is often not apparent on the plain PA chest film, but is well seen on Bucky films, films made with supervoltage techniques, or in body-section studies.

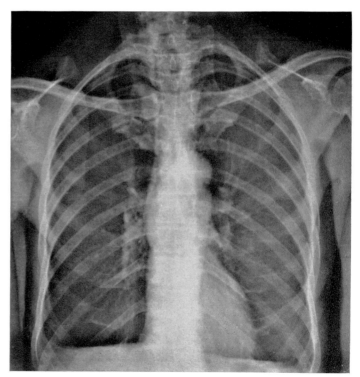

Figure 8-7. *A* (above, left). Conventional PA plain film of the chest. A subcarinal mass was not suspected until the supervoltage film (*B* above, right) was made. Note the round mass below the carina which narrows the right main bronchus and which proved to be malignant. It causes only a slight fullness through the middle of the mediastinal shadow but no abnormal bulge along either margin. *C* (immediately above). Bucky film for comparison.

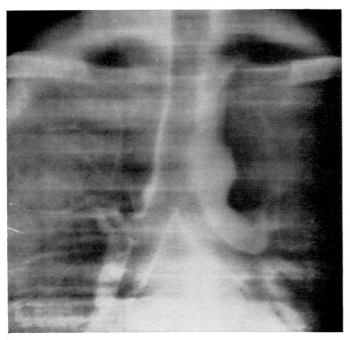

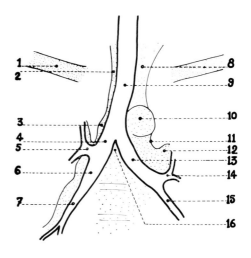

Figure 8-8. *A* (above, left). Body-section study of the normal tracheobronchial tree. *B* (above, right). Diagram:

1. Clavicle
2. Normal opacity of great vessels and tracheal wall
3. Azygos vein
4. Right main stem bronchus
5. Right upper lobe bronchus
6. Site of origin of right middle lobe bronchus
7. Right lower lobe bronchus
8. Normal opacity of vessels and tracheal wall
9. Trachea
10. Aortic arch
11. Concave profile between aortic knob and left pulmonary pedicle
12. Left pulmonary pedicle
13. Left main stem bronchus
14. Left upper lobe bronchus
15. Left lower lobe bronchus
16. Carina

On these pages you are employing as a contrast medium the normally present air within the bronchial tree. While it is perfectly feasible also to instill opaque fluid into the trachea, coating the inner surface of the structures to be studied, as in bronchography, films which depend on air alone for contrast may be very informative. The air column will be seen well in Bucky films and supervoltage studies, as you have observed on the preceding page. It is visualized in even better detail in body-section studies, such as those in Figures 8-8 and 8-9. Body-section studies here give you more precise details because the confusing superimposed shadows of structures in front of or behind the tracheobronchial tree have been eliminated. Note the row of white dots down the right wall of the trachea in Figure 8-8A. These are the tracheal cartilages seen in cross section as each one curves around to support the trachea anteriorly. Because they are C-shaped and open behind, the cartilages will cause a disc-shaped foreign body (like a coin) to orient sagittally. Thus, if a child has "choked" on a penny, and you find a metallic shadow which

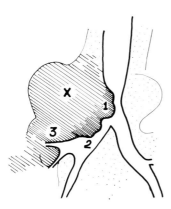

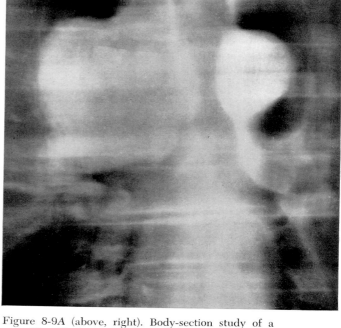

Figure 8-9A (above, right). Body-section study of a man, 65, with dyspnea and weight loss. Note irregular narrowing of the trachea (1) in diagram, above, left (8-9B), and right main stem bronchus (2). The mass (x) would appear on the regular chest film as an abnormal bulge on the right, opposite the aortic knob. Note downward deflection of a branch of the upper lobe bronchus (3). Biopsy showed bronchogenic carcinoma.

lies on edge in the PA view, you will probably be right if you guess that it is in the trachea rather than in the esophagus, where it is much more likely to lie in the coronal plane.

Note the slight normal deflection of the trachea to the right at the level of the aortic knob in Figure 8-8A. This will be exaggerated by any increase in size of the aorta at the arch. A deflected tracheal shadow on a chest film may not always signify mediastinal shift due to lung disease, therefore. The deflection of the shadow of any structure from its normal position is invariably meaningful, however, so that appreciation of the normal radiographic relationships of neighboring and superimposed structures is important. Not every radiology department is equipped to make supervoltage films and body-section studies. I have shown them here because so much normal anatomy can be learned and remembered from them. If you have once seen them, you will be able to make a more intelligent appraisal of their shadows on the simple overpenetrated Bucky film of the chest that is used everywhere.

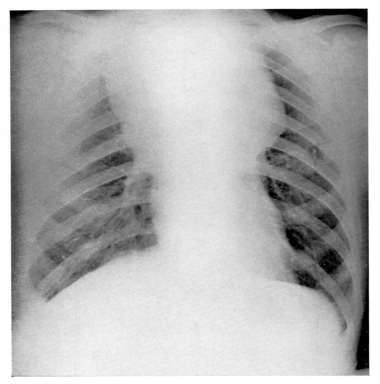

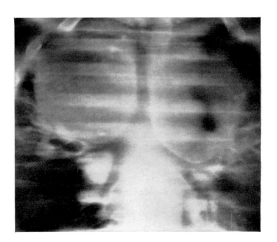

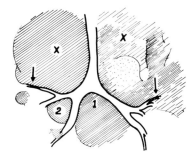

Figure 8-10 (above). Abnormal profiles due to a large mediastinal mass projecting to both sides. With this type of malignant mass, most commonly produced by lymphoma, there is tracheal compression and dyspnea. Note the decrease in size after radiation therapy (Figure 8-11, below).

Figure 8-12 (above, with diagram). Body-section study of a large upper mediastinal mass very similar to that in Figure 8-10. This one was due to malignant lymphoma in a man 27 years old with dyspnea. Note additional subcarinal and interbronchial masses (1 and 2).

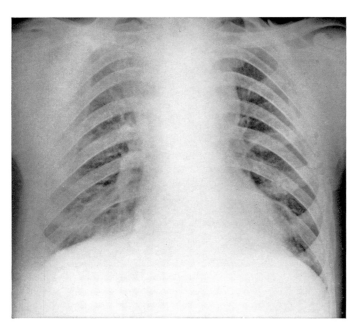

Here you can study the abnormal soft tissue profiles produced by mediastinal masses of various sorts and compare them with the normal arc profiles identified in Figure 8-2. In all these patients the initial plain film of the chest showed a mediastinal bulge or fullness. In some of them the radiologist would be able to weight his interpretation very heavily in favor of a particular type of pathologic condition (as in the patients with mediastinal lymphoma in Figures 8-10 and 8-12). In other types of soft tissue mediastinal bulges the list of differential possibilities may be very long indeed, and one can only note the presence of a mass and describe it.

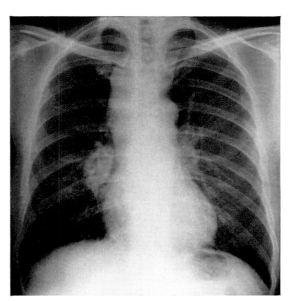

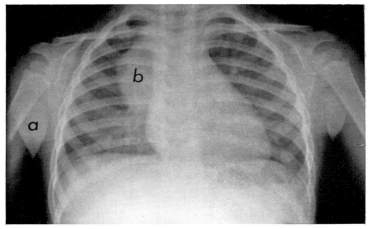

Figure 8-14 (*Unknown 8-1*). (1) Is the patient a child or an adult? (2) Explain the white shadow at *a* as a normal roentgenographic finding. (3) The mass at *b* is obvious, but does the fact that you can see the margin of the heart so clearly through it help you in determining its location in the chest? Why?

Figure 8-13A (above). Widening of the superior mediastinal shadow produced by a malignant paratracheal mass. In Figure 8-13B (below), the mass and trachea at postmortem. Note in the radiograph that the trachea is deflected to the left. There is also a rounded mass in the right hilum, likewise confirmed at autopsy.

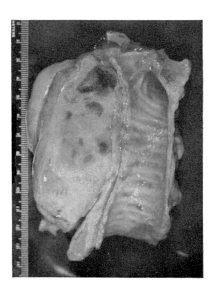

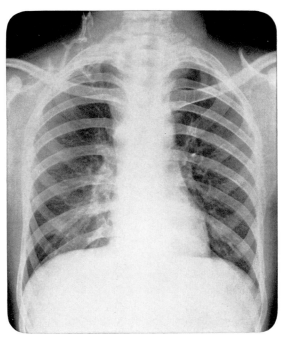

Figure 8-15 (*Unknown 8-2*). If you knew that the patient whose PA chest film you see above had distended veins over his neck and arms, what clinical possibilities would you consider?

119

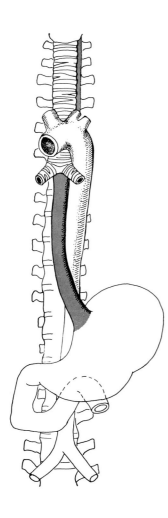

Figure 8-16. Relationships of the trachea, esophagus, and aorta.

The normal relationships of trachea, aorta, and esophagus to each other and to the vertebral column behind them may be reviewed from the diagrams on this page. Deflections of any of these structures as seen on the chest film become more comprehensible, and the origin of abnormal masses more easily remembered, if you can readily recall the normal relationships. It would be possible, although rather strenuous for the patient, to have contrast substances outlining all three of these tubular organs at once, but one can do almost as well by making a habit of relating the air in the trachea to the aorta or esophagus when either one contains a contrast substance.

Figure 8-17. Mediastinal relationships in cross section. Tr, trachea; IV, innominate vein; AV, azygos vein; A, aorta; SVC, superior vena cava; Br, bronchus; PA, pulmonary artery; heavy lines, pleural reflections.

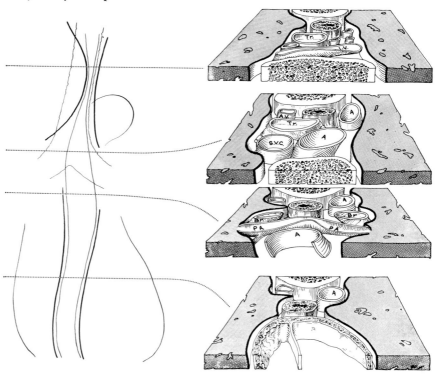

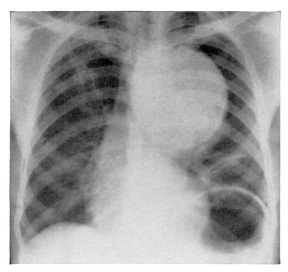

Figure 8-18. *A* (above). Aneurysm of the aortic arch. *B* (right, above). Findings at autopsy 1 year later. *C* (right, below). Admission chest film a few days before death.

Figure 8-18*C* (*Unknown 8-3*). The patient has been readmitted, afebrile but with increased dyspnea, chest pain, and hoarseness. You have a chest film on him from the first admission a year before (8-18*A*). Can you account for the change in the roentgen findings?

Observe, for example, in Figure 8-18*A* that the large round mass on the left looks like a concentric expansion of arc 6, the aortic arch, and as expected, it proved to be a large aneurysm of the arch. Figure 8-18*B* is a coronal section through the heart and lungs at autopsy. The aneurysm contains a large laminated thrombus, and although the trachea lies behind the ascending aorta, its deflected position can be seen on the x-ray film. Note, too, that the left main bronchus is compressed. Predict the effect of the aortic mass on the barium-filled esophagus.

The pronounced elevation of the left diaphragm seen in Figure 8-18*A* became even more striking at fluoroscopy when the diaphragm moved upward on deep inspiration. The man also had a brassy cough and was hoarse. One can reasonably suppose, then, that both his left phrenic and recurrent laryngeal nerves were being subjected to pressure. Elevation of one diaphragm with paralysis (indicated at fluoroscopy) must always make one think of the possibility of a mediastinal mass, perhaps not so obvious as this one.

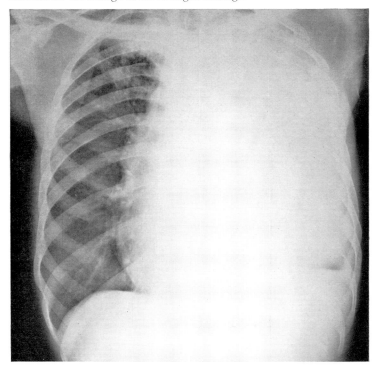

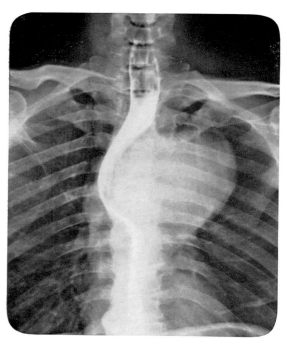

Figure 8-19. Another patient with an aortic aneurysm shows you the deflection of the barium-filled esophagus you predicted for the patient in Figure 8-18.

This man, 53, was admitted to the hospital with dyspnea, cough and wheezing, occasional hemoptysis, and dysphagia. He also had pain of 3 years' duration in his thoracic spine and left chest which had grown progressively worse. A chest film 3 years before admission had shown normal heart and lungs.

On physical examination the patient was slightly cyanotic, dyspneic, and anxious, with a hacking cough. He was afebrile, had a rapid regular pulse, and his heart sounds were of poor quality throughout the anterior part of the chest with no murmurs. There was a downward tugging movement of the trachea. Percussion showed dullness in the first and second intercostal spaces for a distance of 2 inches to the left of the sternal border. Serology was positive.

What additional films might you order?

Deflection of either the trachea or the esophagus to one side can be appreciated readily in the PA view and may indicate significant mediastinal abnormality. Such deflections are very common, and you will probably see one in the near future. When you do, be sure to note whether you are looking at a whole mediastinal shift, or at the deflection of only certain of its structures, as in Figure 8-19. You can see the trachea on most conventional and on all Bucky PA films of the chest. Barium paste is often given to a patient to swallow during chest fluoroscopy and leaves a streak of barium caught in the mucosal folds of the esophagus for a few minutes after the main bolus has passed into the stomach. You may, therefore, be able to see the position of the esophagus now and then on a PA chest film. The first chance you have, notice that the normal esophagus deviates slightly to the right at the level of the arch of the aorta.

When you see the barium-filled esophagus in the lateral view, on the other hand, notice that it bisects the chest cavity, reaching the diaphragm at about its mid-point (Figure 8-21). It lies close against the posterior surface of the heart. One could anticipate from this relationship that the esophagus would be displaced backward by the enlargement of the left atrium.

The lateral chest film offers you an excellent view of the anterior mediastinum. Note the radiolucent area in front of the heart shadow (Figure 8-20A). Many types of tumor masses occur here. The thyroid gland may extend downward into the anterior mediastinum. Thymic masses as well as certain teratomas may be found there. When such anterior mediastinal masses are viewed laterally, they fill in the normal anterior clear space and merge their shadows with that of the heart.

Masses of many kinds occur in the posterior mediastinum, those of neurogenic origin being found there commonly. Such masses will fill in the normal radiolucent area behind the heart in the lateral view (Figure 8-20A) and may obscure part of the diaphragmatic profile. They may erode bone, and so may aortic aneurysms. Films of the thoracic spine of the man in Figure 8-19 might have shown that erosion of several vertebrae accounted for his back pain.

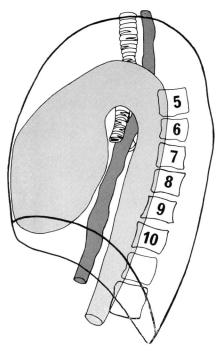

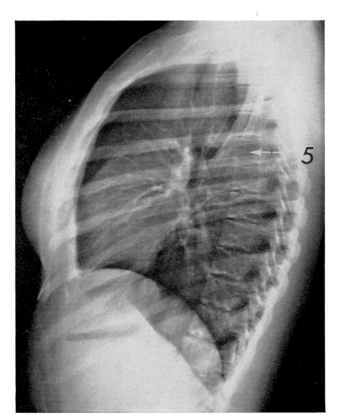

Figure 8-20. *A* (right, above). Left lateral radiograph of the normal chest. *B* (above) is a tracing of the outline of the chest from *A*. The heart outline and vertebrae have also been traced. Arrow indicates T5. The outlines of the approximate positions of trachea, esophagus, and aorta have been added.

Note that on the radiograph you locate the hilum precisely by the white spot representing the density of the left pulmonary artery coming toward you and x-rayed end-on. The vascular branches radiating in all directions also help pinpoint the location of the hilum. Two vertical crenelated white lines bound the dark column of the trachea and represent its cartilaginous walls. Note the two dark areas where the lungs come close together, one in front of and above the heart and one behind and below the heart.

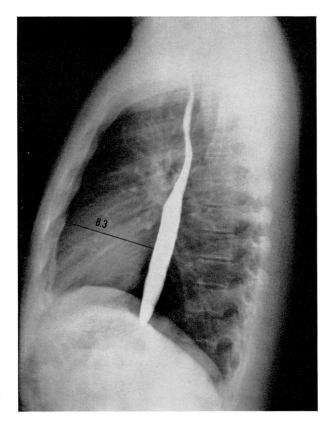

Figure 8-21 (right). Another patient with the esophagus full of barium. Note that although it lies close to the spine, it could be said to bisect the chest in this view.

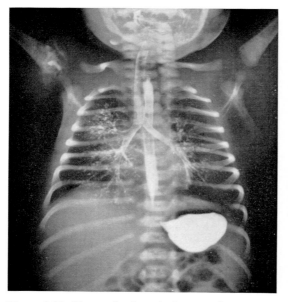

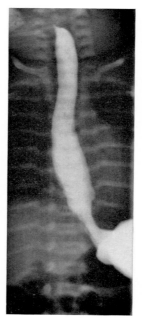

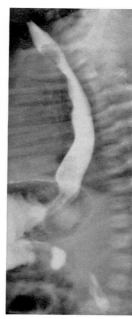

Figure 8-22. The tracheobronchial tree and esophagus in an infant, simultaneously visualized with opaque fluid. (The opaque substance given here by mouth was coughed up and aspirated.)

Figure 8-23. AP and lateral esophagus filled with water-barium mix, also in an infant. (Note ovoid radiolucent air bubble in upper esophagus, lateral view.)

Figure 8-24. PA and lateral views of a patient who proved to have a teratoma, probably arising in the anterior mediastinum but projecting to the right. In the lateral view its shadow can be seen as a dense shadow superimposed on that of the heart.

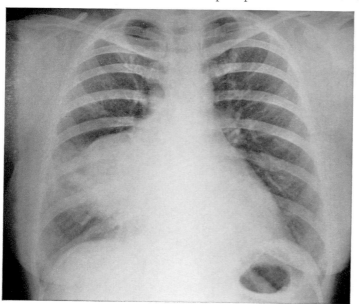

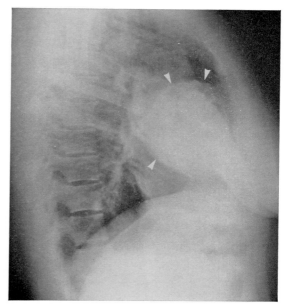

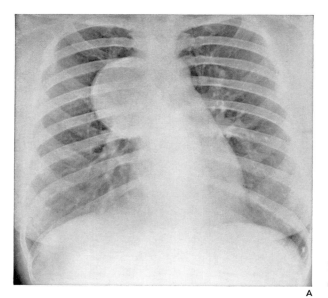
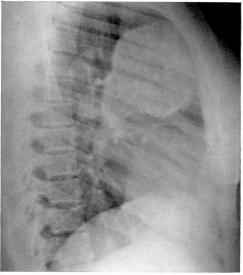

A B

Figure 8-25 (above and right). A large, spherical anterior mediastinal mass protrudes to the right of the spine and shows a shell of calcification. Note high anterior location in the lateral view. Small cut shows radiograph of the surgical specimen, an Echinococcus cyst.

MEDIASTINAL MASSES WITH CALCIFICATION

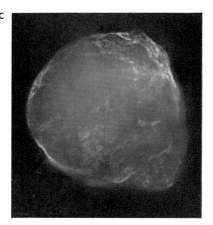

C

Figure 8-26 (below). Plain film (A) shows a bulge in the right mediastinal profile
near the intersection of arcs 1 and 2, the paratracheal area. A suggestion of calcification in the plain film is confirmed in the body-section study (B). The mass was
probably of inflammatory origin. Clusters of dense calcium nuggets like these in
the paratracheal region are frequently old healed tuberculous nodes.

A

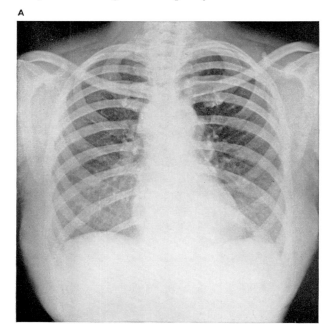

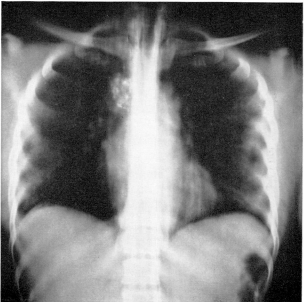

B

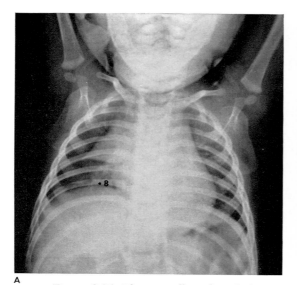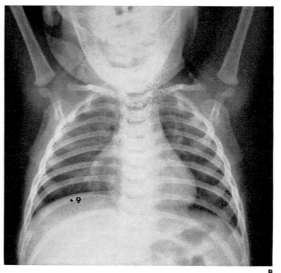

Figure 8-27. The normally enlarged thymus of an infant, seen as a triangular, sail-shaped shadow overlapping the hilum as it projects laterally from the anterior mediastinum. It will be better visualized at expiration (A) than at inspiration (B).

Few mediastinal masses have anything distinctive about their outline. One which does is the normally enlarged infant thymus, which will be seen to project from the mediastinal margin like a triangular sail, often bilateral, but usually more prominent on the right. The projection will be exaggerated at full expiration, as in Figure 8-27A. Note the diminution in the size of the mass in Figure 8-27B, a film made at inspiration on the same patient. The mediastinum is much more difficult to appraise in the infant and young child than it is in the adult, since the proportionately greater flexibility of the structures involved tends to produce buckling, folding, and compression, which will give an appearance of widening when no abnormality exists.

You will find that some abnormal mediastinal profiles seem to you to be quite clearly neither cardiac nor pulmonary. Unfortunately, it will not be so easy to make this distinction with others. Look, for example, at Figures 8-28 and 8-29. In many ways they are quite similar. Each

has a dense rounded mass in the left upper chest which seems to protrude from the upper mediastinum. Both men were dyspneic, had chest pain and cough. Yet the man in Figure 8-28 was found to have a large left upper lobe bronchogenic carcinoma, which obscured his normal left mediastinal profile, and the man in Figure 8-29 had a large aortic aneurysm. Either mass could have resulted in enough phrenic nerve pressure to paralyze the left diaphragm. Either could have involved the vertebrae, destroying bone and causing back pain. Of course, supplementary procedures would have given the important additional information needed to make a diagnosis in each case. The aneurysm might have been seen to be clearly a part of the aorta at fluoroscopy or on oblique films, while the lung tumor might have shown an abnormal air bronchogram on a Bucky film and would probably have been diagnosed at bronchoscopy. The inconclusiveness of initial chest films should not discourage you, for they are not very often diagnostic.

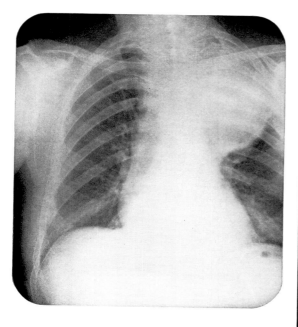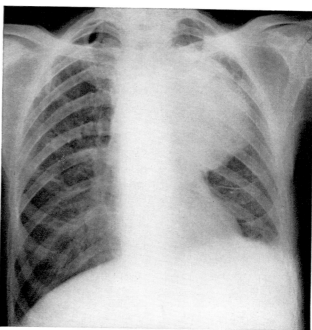

Figures 8-28 and 8-29. Two patients with almost identical histories. Are these both mediastinal masses?

Figure 8-30. *A* (below, left). Initial film on a patient with cough. It is not easy to say whether the bulge adjacent to the heart (at arc 3) is a part of the heart, a density in the right middle lobe, or a mediastinal mass. However, a body-section study (*B*, below, right) showed it to be a part of a much larger lobulated mass in the anterior mediastinum, and at necropsy it proved to be a malignant thymoma extending from the suprasternal notch in front of the trachea to the right of the heart, overlying the right atrium and invading the right lung by direct extension. (This mass would be seen to fill in the clear space in front of the heart if you had a lateral film.)

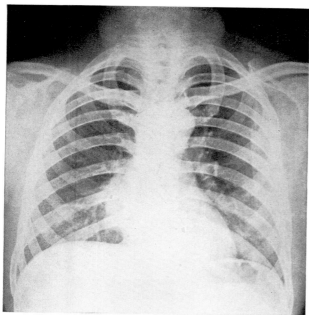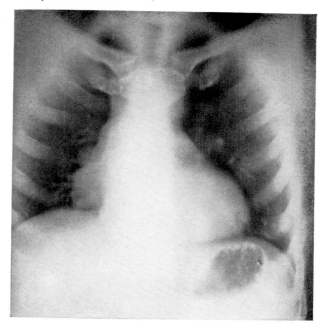

Many an ambitious radiology resident has assigned himself the mediastinum as a subject for a seminar presentation, only to discover that even the most superficial discussion of the subject would take him weeks to prepare and many hours to deliver. Radiography of the mediastinum is interesting, complex, and still far from completely investigated. Like the lung or the heart it deserves several chapters here, but I hope that with this slight introduction you will be able to add gradually, and with confidence and clarity, to your concept of its anatomy and of the radiographic means which are available for studying its structures.

There follow a few review unknowns on which to try out your increasing visual skills. As you study them (and reach the correct conclusions), be sure to realize how much you have learned about analyzing chest films.

Unknown 8-4 (Figure 8-31). Deflection of the cervical trachea may also be a helpful finding. The child whose lateral film you see in Figure 8-31 was admitted with a high fever, pain, difficulty in swallowing, and a markedly elevated white blood cell count. With the radiographic findings and the history, you should be able to make a diagnosis and proceed to treat this child. The normal position of the tracheal air column and its distance from the vertebrae are shown in Figure 8-32, a child hospitalized for a tonsillectomy. (Adenoids, *A*, and tonsils, *B*, may be seen outlined by air.)

Figure 8-31

Figure 8-32

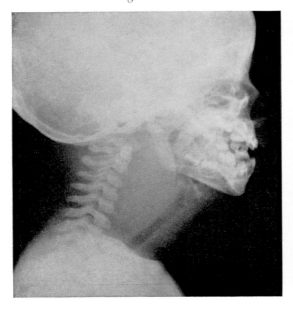

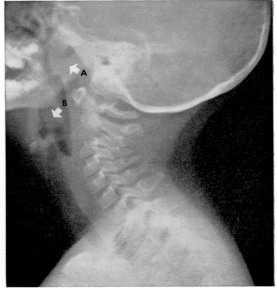

128

Unknown 8-5 (Figure 8-33). Patient with no chest symptoms, an enlarged spleen, and a white blood cell count of 27,000, predominantly lymphocytes. Analyze the film. What does it contribute toward a diagnosis?

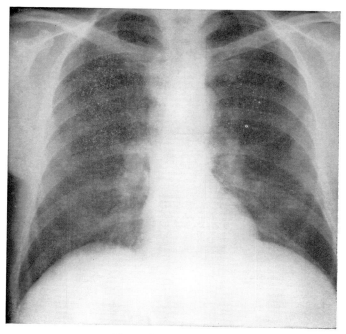

Figure 8-33

Unknown 8-6 (Figure 8-34). Asymptomatic Negro patient, 27. Physical examination was entirely normal (including the blood count and other laboratory work made the first day of admission). What possible diagnoses would you consider in the light of these films and this history?

Figure 8-34

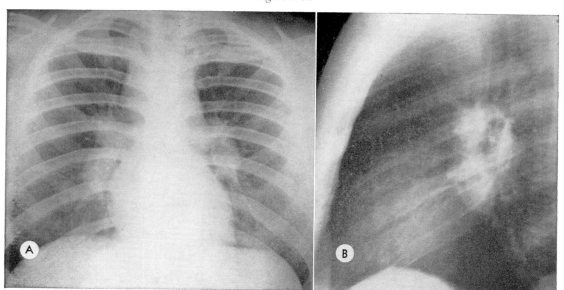

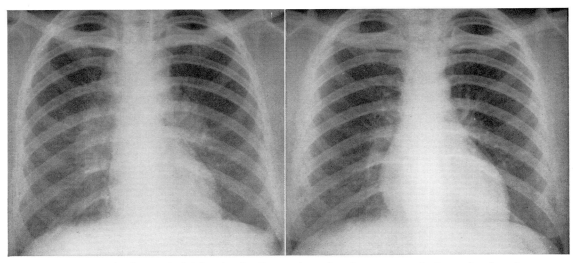

Figure 8-35 *(Unknown 8-7)* (above). The film on the right, above, was made 6 months after the one on the left. The patient received no treatment. From the roentgen findings alone what has happened?

Figure 8-36 *(Unknown 8-8)* (below). The patient whose chest film you see below had no symptoms, had not been ill, and was afebrile. Analyze the film and the detail of part of the lung parenchyma (right). Now suppose someone finds a film made a year earlier which looks exactly like the film on the left above in Unknown 8-7. What can you say about the changes which have occurred regardless of what the disease is?

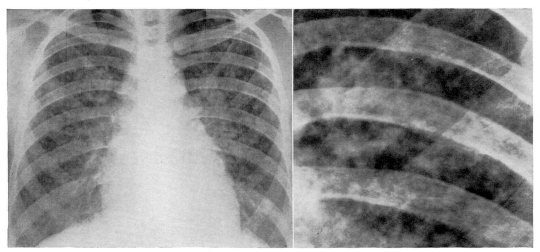

Figure 8-37 (*Unknown 8-9*). A child with a mild upper respiratory infection. What structures do you think are abnormal? Have you ever seen a film anything like this one before?

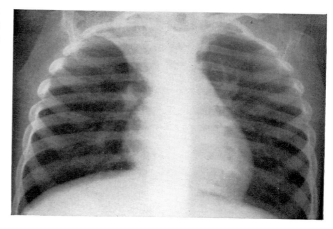

Credits: Illustrations this chapter.

CHAPTER 9 How To Gather and Use Roentgen Data

You already know that this book is not at all intended to be a reference book in radiology but rather an instruction in how to look at films, how to recognize important roentgen changes when they are present, and how to confer intelligently with the radiologist in the whole-patient study. The importance for all graduating physicians of knowing some radiology has been increasing steadily, and no medical student should allow himself a defeatist attitude about his chances of learning a good deal about radiology while he is in school. You have learned some basic radiology in the preceding chapters, perhaps more than you realize.

On the other hand, the field of diagnostic roentgenology has expanded so much and in so many detailed ways that you should not expect to learn to interpret films regularly and with confidence in a 4- or 5-year period of initiation. You can and should learn to study the films on your own patients, using them to check your clinical impressions, and to appreciate the magnitude of any changes which may be present.

The preceding chapters will have given you some idea how to go about analyzing chest films, but I am sure you feel less self-confidence about approaching actual films than you would like to feel. How to proceed to build your own store of roentgen knowledge on this admittedly sketchy beginning should be your next concern. Almost everyone does this after a fashion: some build at random and without much sense of organization or satisfaction; some do it systematically and deliberately. Those who do usually find that roentgen facts which are gathered together in clumps and groups are considerably easier to remember.

Now suppose you say to yourself, "I have learned how to look at the bony thorax, the lungs, diaphragm, pleural space, and mediastinum . . . but I don't feel that I know anything about diagnosing tuberculosis, for example. Of what use is it just to be able to recognize a pleural effusion?" There, indeed, you can begin.

Stop and list for yourself the ways in which you know that tuberculosis can manifest itself on the chest film, and you will see that you already have some idea about the radiologic spectrum of the disease. Tuberculosis can, of course, be manifest initially as a simple pleural effusion, the organism being recoverable from the tapped fluid, even when there are no visible abnormalities in the lung by x-ray. It can be discovered on a routine check film in an asymptomatic patient as a shadowy infiltration in the infraclavicular area of one lung, visible to you when you compare the interspaces carefully. It can show itself as a more extensive infiltration with or without cavitation, all of which you have seen in the preceding chapters and would be able to recognize. You have been shown enlarged hilar and paratracheal lymph nodes, which are seen in childhood tuberculosis, and you know that clusters of calcifications in these areas remain in adult chest films to indicate where such nodes have healed.

Tuberculosis can cause pneumothorax, with or without pleural effusion, and you know where to look for small amounts of air or fluid in the pleural space. Miliary tuberculosis will result in the appearance of innumerable tiny densities scattered throughout both parenchymal lung fields, as you would expect. Endobronchial tuberculosis may cause scarring, bronchial obstruction, and atelectasis.

In more advanced chronic cases, tuberculosis produces extensive scar tissue formation and cavitation in the lung, distorting its structure and altering the position of the hilum or of the mediastinum. You need not be told that Bucky films, body-section studies, or special apical views may be needed in order to discover an open cavity in a mass of scar tissue behind a heavy overlap of bony rib cage and clavicle. Solitary tuberculous granulomas in the lung may closely resemble solitary tumor nodules, and you saw one in Chapter 4. You are certainly anticipating my reminder that serial studies made at intervals will afford information as to the progress or control of the disease which cannot be obtained in any other way. In sum, you already *have* a good deal of knowledge about the roentgen shadows which this single disease might be expected to produce in the lung.

Remember, however, that these are roentgen findings and not diagnoses, both for you and for the radiologist. In the new patient being studied medically for the first time, the finding of a fluffy, infiltrative shadow in the lung does not make a diagnosis of tuberculosis. In fact, the diagnosis of tuberculosis is never a matter for the radiologist to settle. If he phrases his report rather positively in the direction of that disease as a most probable explanation for the shadows he sees, he does so with the certainty that you, the clinician, will not consider the diagnosis established without bacteriologic confirmation.

Thus, certain diseases ought never to be "diagnosed" in written roentgen reports. Others show an almost pathognomonic roentgen appearance, and then time is saved for everyone if the radiologist simply states that the findings are that of such and such a condition. Remember that the more expert and knowledgeable the radiologist becomes, the more confidently he will undertake to help direct your thinking, and the more reliance you may place on his diagnostic suggestions. He can also do your patient as much service by ruling out as "very unlikely from the roentgen appearance" some items included in your differential slate as he can by making diagnostic suggestions of his own.

The roentgen literature is full of well-researched and well-written articles reporting the statistical incidence of this or that roentgen finding in this or that disease condition. Familiarity with such studies helps the radiologist in advising you. He knows, for example, that patients with bacterial pneumonias of the lobar type usually show beginning density in the lung by x-ray between 5 and 10 hours after the onset of symptoms, while those with viral or atypical pneumonias frequently show no changes for 20 to 40 hours. Patients with pulmonary tuberculosis may not show any demonstrable roentgen shadow for 4 or 5 months after exposure. The radiologist must always interpret the shadows he sees in the light of such considerations.

Never forget, however, that your patient is not a statistic. The radiologist may interpret his findings in the light of statistical probabilities, but you are treating one human being. No matter how well informed and experienced a radiologist may be, he is not an oracle, and his advice and interpretations of shadows must always be fitted into the clinical picture and weighed against conflicting evidence. A good many radiologists prefer to study the films at first with no knowledge of the clinical story, purely as an exercise in roentgen interpretation, and then to reconsider their own ideas about the shadows in the light of the clinical findings. Their report to you often does not include, therefore, all the possibilities they considered on first looking at the film, and it is a short cut in the press of work to suggest in writing only those disease entities which are still believed possible at the time the first film studies are being reported. Subsequent film studies and subsequent clinical findings will narrow the list of possibilities until a diagnosis is made.

Some disease conditions, of course, produce no roentgen changes whatever. For example, the usual course of typhoid fever is not accompanied by any useful radiologic findings, but when the organism invades bone, an osteomyelitis differing somewhat roentgenologically from more common forms of bone inflammation will be visible in the film. In the course of your training in medical school you will learn in which of the common disease conditions you can or cannot expect roentgen help.

A negative roentgen examination in the patient with a compelling story and clinical findings in whom radiologic changes *are* to be expected, on the other hand, is one of the most constant and disturbing problems the radiologist has to face. He has to be familiar with, and remind you constantly about, the occasional fallibility of the roentgen method and also about the point in any disease at which roentgen changes may be expected to be present. The patient with miliary tuberculosis, for example, febrile and very ill, may show minute miliary densities in the parenchyma of the lung in the chest film relatively late in the illness, several weeks after a presumptive clinical diagnosis will have been made and therapy begun. The patient with a history suggestive of gallbladder disease may have negative x-ray studies for years before he finally shows positive roentgen evidence for chronic cholecystitis and stones. In the patient with enough scarring from duodenal ulcer it may be impossible to demonstrate a newly recurrent crater by barium study, and much more reliance must be placed on this patient's own evaluation of his worsening condition than on the fact that the roentgen study reports no change.

You have, thus, two types of roentgen data to accumulate and to clump together. You must have a clear visual image of the various sorts of informative roentgen changes a particular disease *may* produce, like the spectrum of changes in the chest film in pulmonary sarcoidosis which you saw in the series of unknowns in the last chapter. You must, at the same time in another compartment of your mind, gradually accumulate information as to the fallibilities of the roentgen method *in that same disease.* You must be prepared for the negative examination and wise enough to discount it in the patient about whom you are justly worried. In general, positive roentgen findings are helpful, but a negative study is not a clear slate.

Your procedure, then, from this point on in extending your knowledge of radiologic diagnosis should be to become a collector. Reasoning always from your increasing knowledge of pathophysiology, you will add, day by day, to each group of visual images representing the roentgen changes which may be produced by

a disease entity. You will discover that as you collect visual images, each one serves as a review of the pathophysiology involved. It is unquestionably in this way that you will find them most useful in medical school, since they provide a visual device for remembering data which seem much more complex when learned first from the printed page.

Gradually building in your own mind a familiarity with the varied roentgen appearances of a particular disease is somewhat the same procedure most radiologists carry out when they build what is affectionately referred to as "The Teaching Collection," a tangible accumulation of roentgen data, arranged and categorized for their own reference use. Few such collections are really complete, any more than your mental collection will be, but they are added to and reworked and improved constantly, just as your own set of intellectual images will be. If you approach in a deliberate way the collection of grouped roentgen images representing gross pathologic changes, I believe you will find that you do indeed have a fair grasp of diagnostic roentgenology when you are ready to assume postdoctorate responsibilities. It will not stop there, of course, because you will have developed the habit of adding to the catalogue of images from daily experience.

You will also be making a practice of filing away learned instances in which the roentgen examination was negative in the face of clinical evidence *for* a disease process. To be sure, this is a more sophisticated procedure, but just as important and just as much a question of collecting. Remember that candor between you and the radiologist is to be recommended strongly. You must be able to say to him, "How sure are you?" and he must be able to reply, "I am not sure at all, but I believe it is the most probable explanation." At other times he must be able to say to you, "I can't, of course, guarantee what the microscopic study will show, but I, personally, have no doubts whatever." Occasionally he must say to you, "I have little experience with this disease. The literature describes the changes we have here, but let's get another opinion." You must be accomplished enough in time to say, on receiving a negative report, "That's all very well, but I feel strongly that my patient has the disease. I will inquire how soon the radiologist feels re-examination might show changes without wasting the patient's funds." You must also *listen* to the radiologist when he feels strongly about a diagnosis and insists that no other should be entertained. Argue with him, if you like, but listen.

Figures 9-1 and 9-2. An example of *minimal apical tuberculosis* in details from two chest films made on the same patient. Figure 9-1, a routine film made in September, is normal. Figure 9-2, made 5 months later, shows numerous small, fluffy shadows in the lung tissue at the left apex, in the second and third interspaces, and superimposed on the first three ribs. Compare the interspaces. Up to this point in the book you have seen a number of instances of the roentgen shadows which may be produced in the chest film by tuberculosis (Figures 2-12, 2-13, 4-22, 6-12, 6-24, 6-27, and 6-31). Add to them now the cases of tuberculosis which follow, and you will have a nucleus of images to start your collection.

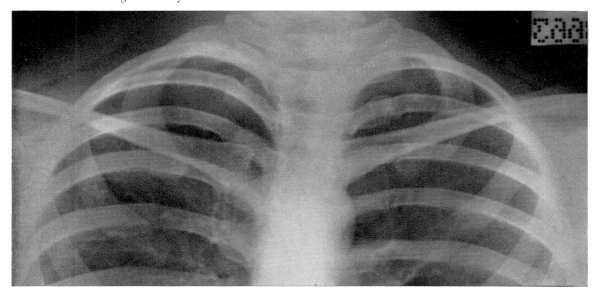

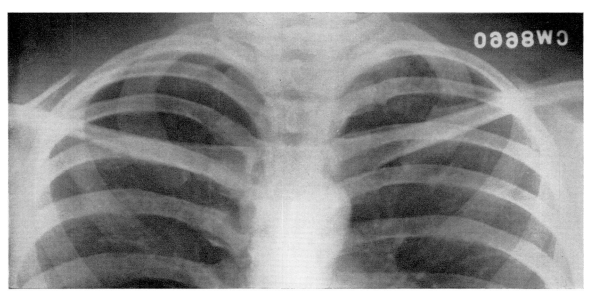

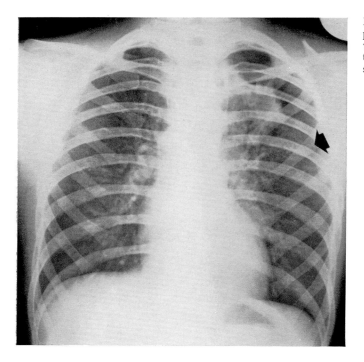

Figure 9-3 (left). *More extensive tuberculosis,* left upper lobe, with small pneumothorax (arrow indicates visible margin of lung). Strands of shadow extending to the chest wall are pleural adhesions over the apex restricting the degree of collapse.

A

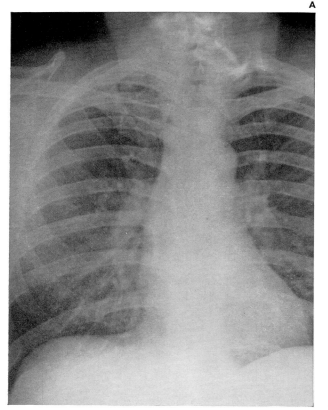

Figure 9-4. *Cavitation in an apical lesion.* A (left) shows cloudy infiltration in the right apical region in a patient with positive sputum, but overlapping bones obscure the cavities later seen in the body-section study, B (below).

B

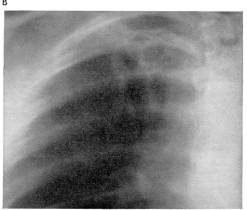

136

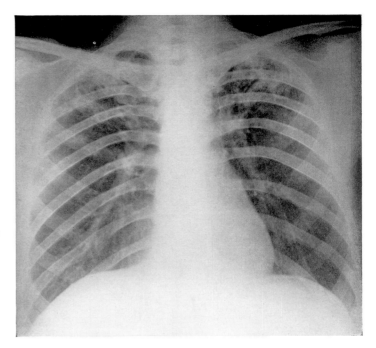

Figure 9-5. *Bilateral chronic upper lobe tuberculosis.* Note that, in addition to the obvious infiltrative parenchymal streaks in both upper lobes, there are large ring-like cavities present. The one on the right can be seen rising above the medial end of the right clavicle, and that on the left overlies the fourth rib near the lateral chest wall. Note also the very characteristic vascular lung markings extending down into the lower lung fields from the hila. These are longer, straighter, and more vertical than the normal lower lung markings and may be likened to the taut guy ropes of a tent. Their appearance is easy to remember when you realize that in this type of upper lobe tuberculosis there is so much scarring and retraction that the upper lobes are markedly reduced in size, and both hila are drawn upward, stretching the vessels to the lower lobes.

Figure 9-6. *Cavitation in a relatively new tuberculous lesion.* Considering the size of the cavity here, there is less extensive parenchymal density than might be expected in chronic involvement. When you compare carefully the lung seen in the seventh, eighth, and ninth interspaces on the two sides, those on the left appear normal, while those on the right show scattered soft shadows.

Think, now, of the pathologic process which is going on rather than of the roentgen shadows. Consider that the balance between the resistance of the patient and the virulence of the disease must determine the rate of tissue breakdown. This being so, it must follow that the relationship of the size of the cavity to the type of inflammatory density in the involved lung around it, as you see them in the x-ray, provides an index to the state of the host-disease balance. In a portion of lung showing many soft, fluffy shadows, the sudden appearance of a large, thin-walled cavity probably means rapid tissue breakdown in a poorly resisting lung. A similar cavity in a segment of lung known to have been diseased for a long time, and showing instead the dense, discrete, and stringy shadows of healing fibrotic lesions, would not carry the same implications. Just so, the progress of changes in a series of films made at intervals provides a useful index to the patient-disease relationship and all the factors which may influence it.

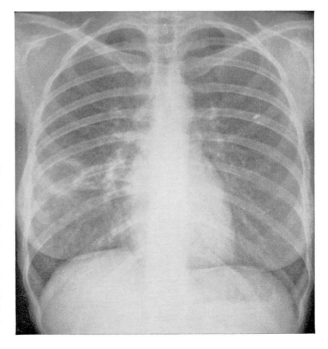

137

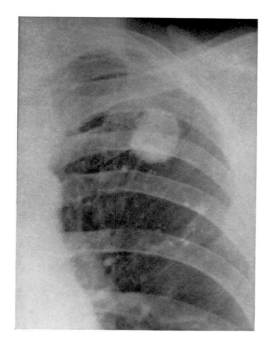

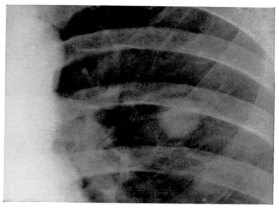

Figures 9-7 (left) and 9-8 (above). *Tuberculous granulomas* in the lung may closely simulate solitary tumors, either primary or metastatic. Some granulomas contain no calcium, others calcify centrally (or expand around and engulf an earlier calcific focus). Still others calcify peripherally and appear to have a shell.

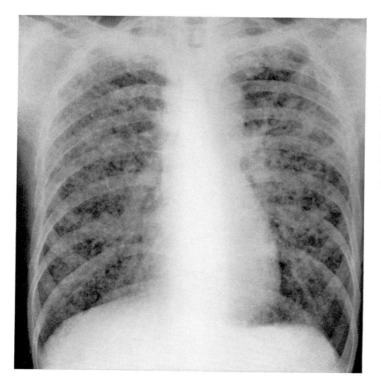

Figure 9-9 (left). *Miliary tuberculosis.* The innumerable lesions scattered throughout the parenchyma here, and probably resulting from hematogenous spread, have been engrafted upon a lung field in which there was already some tuberculous infiltration in the upper lobes. In looking at any film, you have to consider that the shadows you see may represent acute changes superimposed on chronic ones.

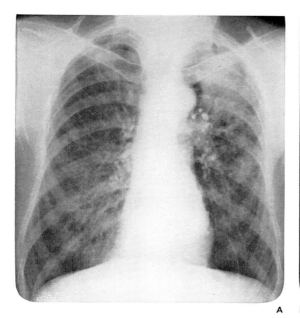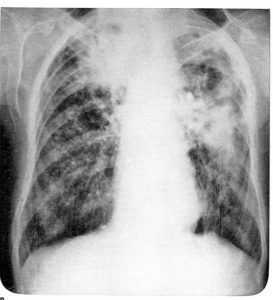

A   B

Figure 9-10. *Silicotuberculosis.* A stonemason, 61, admitted with a productive cough *(A)*, showed extensive calcification in both hila and an infiltrative density in the left upper lobe. Sputum was positive for tubercle bacilli. Patient was discharged after 2½ years of hospital care, went back to work for 4 months, and was readmitted *(B)* with extension of involvement and cavitation. He died 2 months later. *C,* photograph, and *D,* radiograph of lung specimen. *E,* air-inflated specimen radiographed after vessels were injected with radio-opaque material. Note striking diminution of vascularity in diseased areas.

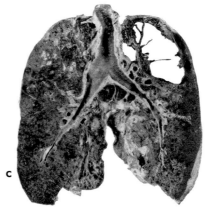

C

D   E

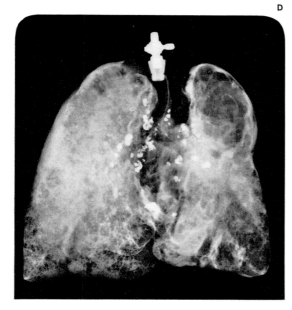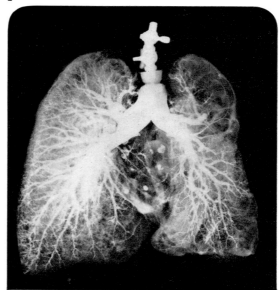

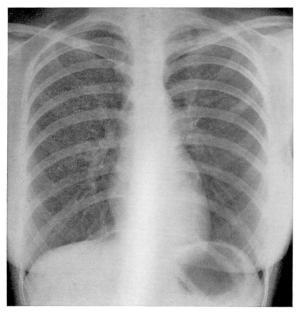
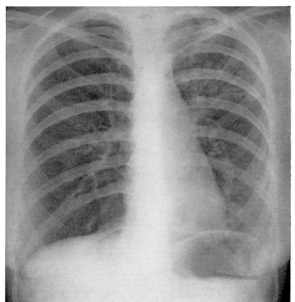

A. December 1943   B. August 1944

Figure 9-11. *Serial films over a period of 3 years in a patient with tuberculosis.* In *A* she has a soft infiltrative lesion extending upward from the left hilum to the apex. Compare carefully the fourth interspaces on the two sides. (Caution: in this patient the first, second, and third ribs overlap very closely high over the apex. The fourth rib is the one crossing the medial part of the clavicle, and the fourth interspace below it on the left shows infiltration. There is also early infiltrative density in the left sixth interspace.) In *B*, made 8 months later, there is progressive involvement of the left upper lobe and new areas of density extending downward toward the left diaphragm, which may be either in the lingular segment of the upper lobe or in the lower lobe. In *C*, made 6 months later, involvement throughout the left lung, but with the development of scar tissue, the patches of shadow have taken on a harder, denser, and more discrete appearance. *D*, a year later, gives you radiographic indications that there is much more scar tissue retraction than on the earlier films. Note that the trachea and the heart have been drawn over to the left. Cavitation is obvious in the upper lobe. You see the profile of the diaphragm still. In *E*, there appears to be an immense cavitation replacing the upper lobe (absence of lung markings). The left diaphragmatic profile and that of the left heart border have disappeared, indicating consolidation, and there is new spread of the disease to the right lung. Some pleural effusion on the left cannot be excluded. *F* is a radiograph of the postmortem specimen of the two air-inflated lungs, the vessels of which have been injected with an opaque substance. Note the striking change in the vascular supply to the destroyed lung.

140

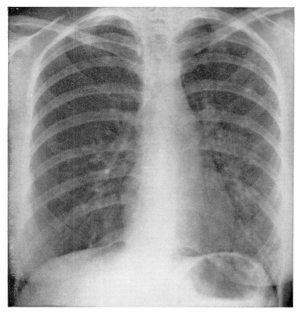

C. February 1945

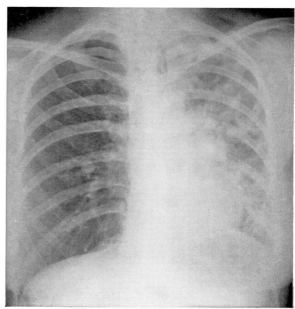

D. February 1946

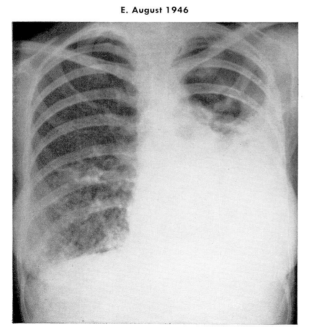

E. August 1946

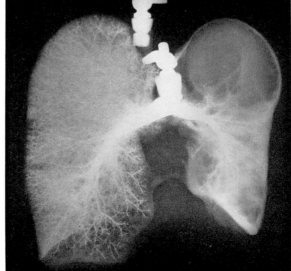

F. October 1946

141

You can understand now why I have deferred so long giving you illustrations clearly labeled as a particular disease entity. To do so, without first showing you how to make roentgen findings serve you, would have been to invite the card-sorting approach to radiologic diagnosis. From this point on you will become a collector of all the roentgen images which can be produced by a particular disease, but I hope you will always do so by relating the shadows to the pathologic condition.

As an unknown for this chapter try listing all the roentgen changes which could be produced by bronchogenic carcinoma. You have already seen a number of them in the course of the preceding chapters, but you will be able to imagine others. As an embellishment for this exercise, think of each one as belonging to a patient who presents himself in your office for the first time today, so that, in addition to going over all the types of shadows caused by lung cancer, you will also be preparing yourself for the modes in which patients with the disease may first be encountered. If you make the effort of writing down your list, you will be able to tick it off against the one in the Answer Appendix (which is admittedly incomplete).

Credits: Illustrations this chapter.

Figure 9-3. Courtesy Dr. G. Schwalbach, Rochester, N. Y.

Figure 9-4. Courtesy Dr. H. Maier and the publisher, Eastman Kodak Co.

Figure 9-6. Courtesy Mr. R. Bottin, Indianapolis, Ind.

Figure 9-9. Courtesy Dr. G. Baron, Rochester, N. Y.

Figure 9-10. Courtesy Dr. W. Brosius and the publisher, *MR&P* 30:85, 86.

Figure 9-11. Courtesy Dr. W. Brosius, Detroit, Mich.

CHAPTER 10 The Heart

We are a race of measurers, partly perhaps because it is easier to measure than to think. The inviting, flat surface of the illuminated radiograph has stimulated its viewers to accumulate volumes of measurements, documenting the distance between almost any two structures you can name. Some of these dimensions are important and useful, having proved in the course of time that they can serve reliably in the whole-patient study. Others are window dressing, not sufficiently reliable to be worth recording, and have largely been abandoned. For example, the measured deflection from its normal position of the calcified pineal gland is a practical and useful sign of the presence of an expanding mass in one cerebral hemisphere. All radiologists use it. Its normal variation in position is well documented and is available in charted form for daily consultation in borderline cases. On the other hand, the precise measurement of the maternal pelvis and its proportionate relationship to the size of the fetal head near term has been studied roentgenologically in many ingenious ways; yet, other factors related to soft tissue pliability and to physiologic variations in efficiency from one woman to another have so often disproved the predictions of the radiologist that x-ray pelvimetry has only a limited use in most obstetric practice today.

It will come as no great surprise to you then, that the shadow of the heart on the chest film struck early observers as a plausible index to cardiac enlargement and that systems for measuring that shadow abound. Before angiocardiography was developed, making possible the study of the individual cardiac chambers, the over-all size of the heart was measured in its every dimension, and some of these measure-ments proved useful. Since heart catheterization and angiocardiography have come into wide use, however, much less reliance is placed on plain film measurements in the cardiac patient, and the attention of clinicians is directed toward a variety of more precisely meaningful procedures, many of them not radiographic at all.

Nevertheless, in the day-to-day routine sorting of patient problems, the shadow of the heart on the plain film of the chest will prove invaluable to you. Detailed studies in cardiac evaluation you will relegate to experts, of course, but you can develop for your own daily use a rough estimate of the size of the heart, using only the measurement you make on a 6-foot PA film (which enlarges the heart by projection less than 5 per cent). If you know one easy-to-carry-out measuring system and employ it on every PA chest film you study, you will soon develop an ability to estimate heart size with reasonable accuracy.

You must add to this mode of assaying the status of the heart an awareness of the ways in which cardiac enlargement may be simulated or masked (and be able to discount them). Even more important, you must have some familiarity with changes in the *shape* of the heart due to specific chamber enlargements. A change in shape, either with or without enlargement, may indicate the type of heart disease which is present more clearly than any other single clinical sign.

In sum, then, you must be able to estimate over-all cardiac size, to discount conditions which may simulate enlargement, and to recognize some of the common kinds of heart disease as indicated by changes in the shape of the heart shadow. These three things every physician ought to know comfortably.

The simplest method of measuring the heart is to determine its relationship to the width of the chest at its widest point near the level of the diaphragms. This is called the "cardiothoracic ratio," and is carried out on the PA 6-foot chest film only. Measure between two vertical lines drawn tangential to the most prominent point on the right and left cardiac profiles. The prominence of the bulge on the right is usually a little higher than the apex of the left profile. In adults the width of the heart should be less than half the widest thoracic diameter, measured from inside the rib cage.

No ruler is necessary for this measurement, nor do you need to remember anything more than the 50 per cent figure. Using any handy piece of paper with a straight edge (the handiest will often be the margin of the patient's own film envelope), determine the width of the heart. Then decide whether this width exceeds the distance from the mid-point (spine) to the inside of the rib cage (half the transthoracic diameter).

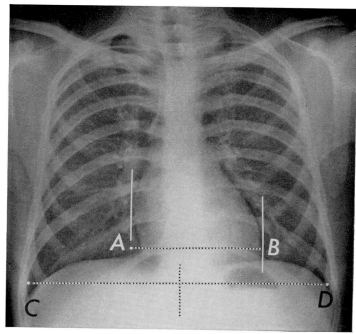

Figure 10-2 (above). This young man was told after an insurance examination that he had a heart murmur. Is his heart enlarged? (No, it measures well within 50 per cent of the thoracic diameter.) Enlargement, when present, helps to measure heart disease, but note that disease may be present without any enlargement. Here the radiologist would tell you that the flat, almost absent aortic knuckle together with the presence of saucered erosions on the under surface of the ribs (see detail, Figure 10-3, below), suggest strongly coarctation of the aorta. He would probably ask you if the patient had femoral pulses. Rib erosions reflect the collateral pathways developed via the intercostal arteries.

Figure 10-1

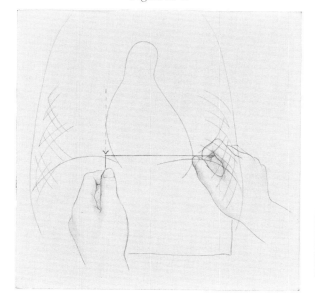

Figure 10-3

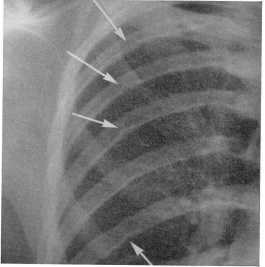

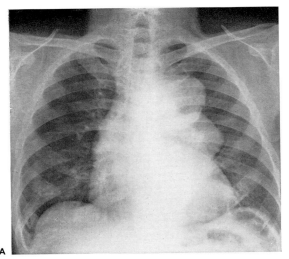

A

Figure 10-4. Is this heart enlarged? *A* (above) is the PA view, *B* (below) and *C* (bottom) are oblique views. Figure out how the patient is being turned (clavicles, ribs, apex of left ventricle). (See text.)

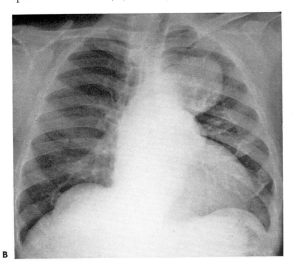

B

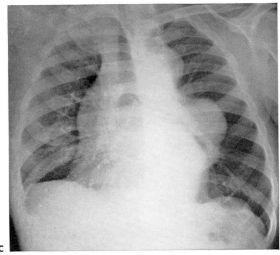

C

As you have seen from the preceding page, hearts may be detectably abnormal without being measurably enlarged. They may also be measurably enlarged and obviously also abnormal as to shape, like that of the patient in Figure 10-4. He was a clerical worker of 51, admitted because of 2 days of severe chest pain and a 4-year history of cardiovascular disease with two myocardial infarctions and a blood pressure of 240/140. Note that his heart is measurably enlarged in the PA view (as well as in both obliques), that the prominent bulge in the region of the aortic knob is exaggerated in *B* as he is turned so that his right shoulder is closer to you. A second abnormal bulge in the descending aorta just below the aortic knob in *A*, on the other hand, is exaggerated when he is turned in the opposite direction, so that his left shoulder is toward you (*C*). He died very suddenly a month later, and although no postmortem was obtained, the films and clinical story provide clear-cut evidence that he had extensive hypertensive cardiovascular disease with aneurysmal dilatations of both the arch and the descending portion of the aorta, with probable dissection.

Hearts may also be only *apparently enlarged* for a variety of reasons which you must be able to discount. You already know some of the ways in which cardiac enlargement may be simulated. You have seen it in chest films not made at inspiration, and it is logical to expect that a high diaphragm will tilt the heart upward bringing its apex closer to the lateral chest wall. In addition to this, the flare of the ribs is greater at inspiration and decreases at expiration, further altering the apparent cardiothoracic ratio. In any patient in whom you would have reason to expect the diaphragm to be high, you will be anticipating an apparently enlarged heart shadow. With any kind of abdominal distension (late pregnancy, ascites, intestinal obstruction) you may not be able to estimate heart size for this reason.

Remember, too, that portable bedside chest films are usually made AP and result in an appreciable enlargement of the heart shadow by projection, since the heart is farther away from the film. The factor of projection may be further exaggerated if, because of awkward arrangements of furniture in small, crowded hospital rooms, the technician must make the film at a distance much less than 6 feet. Important and valuable information may be obtained in the very sick patient from bedside films, but an estimation of heart size is not one of them.

The next point to be checked, after you have counted down the ribs to determine the level of the diaphragms and made sure you are looking at a 6-foot PA film, is that there is no rotation off the sagittal plane. You have already seen in an earlier chapter the degree to which rotation may produce an appearance of widening of the heart and mediastinal shadows, and you know that symmetry of the clavicles and ribs gives you your assurance that no rotation is present. We will be discussing the intentionally rotated oblique films in more detail, and there you will be able to study the precise effect of rotation on the cardiac shadow more closely.

Deformity of the thoracic cage will, of course, often render impossible any attempt to measure the size of the heart, and you would not expect to be able to do so in severe scoliosis, for example. The solitary (but symmetrical) deformity of a depressed sternum usually displaces the heart to the left, and your suspicions will be aroused when you find no right heart border from which to measure. A lateral film will settle the matter. In severe cases the posterior surface of the sternum is only a few centimeters from the anterior margins of the vertebral bodies, so that mediastinal shift and cardiac displacement simulating enlargement are inevitable.

You might wonder whether the size of the heart shadow would be increased if the film happened to be taken at full diastole, and decreased if it were made at the end of systole. The shadow *is* slightly different at the extremes of the cardiac cycle, as you see in Figure 10-5, but the difference is not usually enough to matter in using a rough estimate like the cardiothoracic ratio, at least in adults.

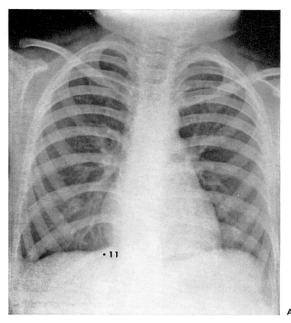

A

Figure 10-5. The heart, *A* (above) at diastole and *B* (below) at systole. Neither is measurably enlarged, but the hearts are different sizes due to different degrees of filling, not due to respiration (check by counting ribs).

B

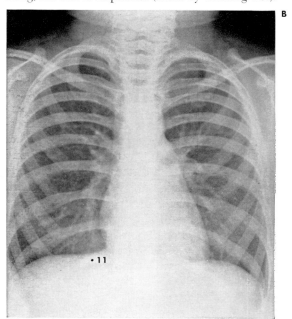

147

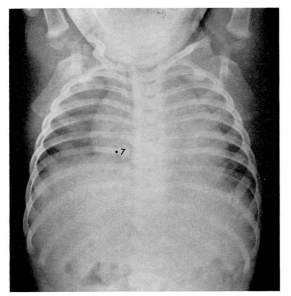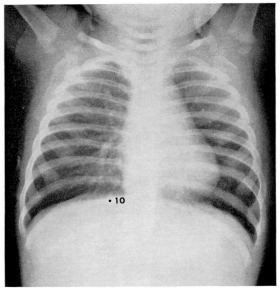

Figure 10-6. Seven-month-old infant examined because of cough and upper respiratory infection appears to have cardiac enlargement until high diaphragms and hazy lung fields are noted (A). When a second film is made at full inspiration (B), the heart is not enlarged to measurement.

It is important for you to develop an immense degree of caution with regard to making pronouncements about the size of the infant heart as you see it on chest films. This is particularly true in the infant under 1 year of age. Because of the greater flexibility of all the structures, and because of the basic difference in proportion of abdominal size to thoracic size, the normal diaphragmatic level in the infant is higher than in the adult. He is usually filmed AP and supine (although at a distance proportionate to 6 feet in the adult). He wiggles and is hard to immobilize, which produces rotation. He has not yet developed the proportion of lung size to heart size characteristic of the adult and present already in the older child. Beware of x-ray appearances suggesting cardiac enlargement under 1 year, therefore, without supporting clinical evidence.

On the other hand, always remember that overdistension of the lungs for any reason compresses the heart and mediastinal structures from both sides and narrows their PA shadow. Therefore, in the dyspneic patient with low diaphragms and in the emphysematous patient, the heart size as measured on the PA chest film may be deceptively small, not informing you reliably about the cardiac status at all. In patients with chronic emphysema, the heart is often found at autopsy to be enlarged by weight as a result of right ventricular hypertrophy (cor pulmonale), although no cardiac enlargement had ever been noted roentgenologically.

Noncardiac disease may mask true cardiac enlargement. If you think back through the earlier chapters, you will have no difficulty in appreciating the degree to which mediastinal or pulmonary disease may render the dimensions of the heart unobtainable. Any density which obscures one cardiac profile makes it futile to try to estimate heart size. Thus, neither the size nor the shape of the heart can be studied from plain films in the patient who has a massive pleural effusion, consolidation in the anterior part of either lung, or a large anterior mediastinal mass.

True mediastinal shift is usually the result of some important change in intrathoracic dynamics and may so alter the position of the heart that measurements are meaningless.

148

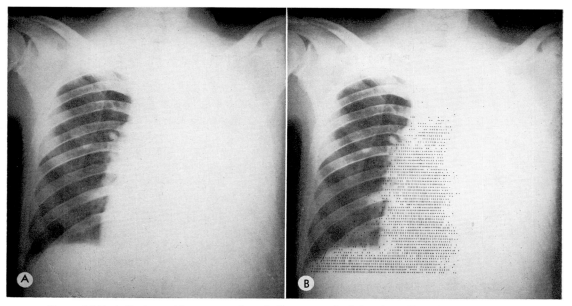

Figure 10-7. *A.* Patient with massive pleural effusion on the left. Chest film affords no information whatever about the heart, which might be very much enlarged. *B.* Visualization of the heart is effected by scintillation scanner technique, the blood contained in the heart having been rendered radioactive by an intravenous injection of radio-iodinated serum albumin. Heart is small and displaced slightly to the right by the effusion.

Figure 10-8. Normal heart *(A)* and cardioscan *(B)* for comparison. Note that the heart here measures more than half the thoracic diameter, undoubtedly because both the chest films and the cardioscans superimposed on them had to be made AP and with the patient recumbent for technical reasons.

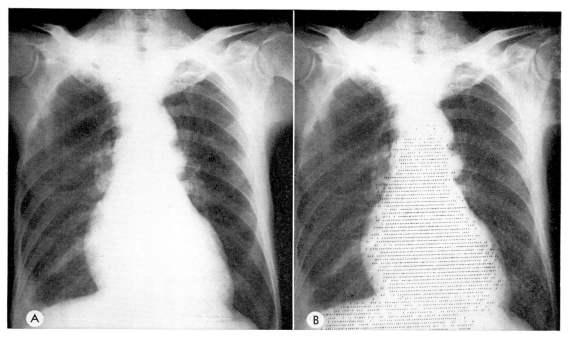

149

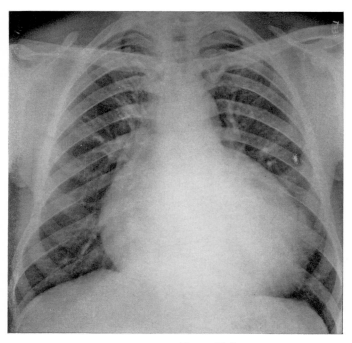

Figure 10-9

Consider, now, a chest film in which, after checking out all misleading factors, you find that the measured heart shadow exceeds its allowed 50 per cent of the transthoracic diameter. How can you distinguish between cardiac hypertrophy, cardiac dilatation, and the shadow cast by a pericardial effusion around the heart?

This problem is a very real one. The heart muscle, the blood contained within the cardiac chambers, and any fluid encasing it in the pericardial sac all have about the same roentgen density and will be quite indistinguishable on a chest film.

Figure 10-9 gives you an example. A patient with acute rheumatic fever and pancarditis shows obvious enlargement of the heart shadow. From similar cases which you have seen at autopsy, you know as you look at this film that there may well be valvular involvement, myocardial damage, and pericarditis with effusion. The heart disease is properly termed "pancarditis," and dilatation of the chambers due to poorly functioning valves and an inflamed, inefficient myocardium, as well as the pericardial fluid, all could contribute to the production of

a large shadow. The obvious advantage to you of thinking in terms of gross pathology as you look at the film can scarcely be overemphasized.

There are some roentgen details which will help you in distinguishing between hypertrophy and dilatation. The well-compensated, hypertrophied heart tends to have sharply outlined, firmly rounded contours for its measurably enlarged shadow, just as you would expect with good myocardial tone. Left ventricular hypertrophy, when it predominates as it so commonly does in the hypertensive or older patient, produces relatively more enlargement to the left and an alteration in shape like the one you see in Figure 10-10. When this heart goes into failure, decompensates, and dilates, it will lose to some extent its well-rounded contours, the shadow increasing in width by projection both to the left and to the right.

Additional important indications of the physiologic state of the failing heart will be found on studying the hilar shadows and lung fields carefully (Figures 10-11 and 10-12). In acute left ventricular failure which develops very rapidly, fluffy increased densities about both hila may indicate pulmonary edema (Figure

Figure 10-10. Hypertrophy of the heart in hypertension. Normal hilar shadows and pulmonary vessel markings. No evidence of decompensation.

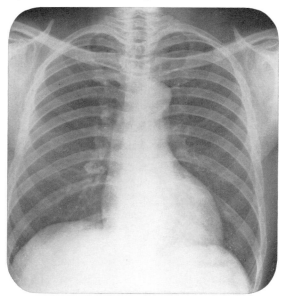

150

10-13). In failure developing more gradually, the hilar vessels (pulmonary veins) will appear enlarged and tortuous and will be seen to extend farther out into the lung fields than they do normally at that caliber. With longstanding failure, very informative changes appear in the lung fields. The lungs as a whole appear hazy and less radiolucent than normal. Short, parallel horizontal lines of increased density at the lung bases close to the costophrenic angle, which have been identified as distended lymphatics of the interlobular septa, become visible as interstitial edema increases. A subpleural accumulation of fluid seen tangentially just inside the rib cage close to the costophrenic angle should also be looked for and will generally precede the appearance of frank pleural effusion.

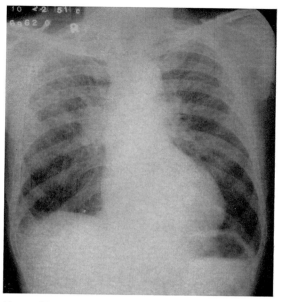

Figure 10-11. Man with severe exertional dyspnea and electrocardiographic evidence of myocardial damage shows hilar engorgement, distended pulmonary vessels, and fluid in the right costophrenic angle indicating failure.

Figure 10-12. Signs of chronic or repeated failure. Haziness of the lung field, horizontal linear densities (Kerley's B-Lines), and subpleural fluid in four patients with mitral valvular disease. Patient 9, seen on 11-11 after 12 days of medical management, shows clearing.

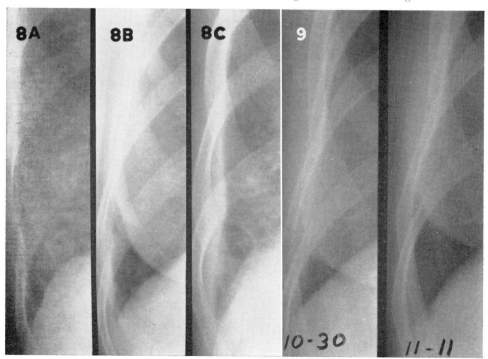

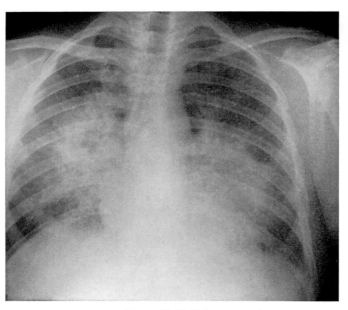

Figure 10-13. Pulmonary edema.

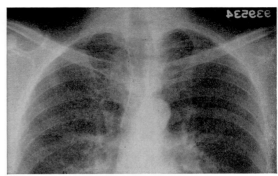

Figure 10-14. The hila in a patient with left ventricular failure due to aortic stenosis.

The patient at the left above in Figure 10-13 has the peculiar densities about both hila which the radiologist would unhesitatingly label pulmonary edema. It looks much the same whether resulting from sudden left ventricular failure, as after a myocardial infarction, or accompanying uremia and kidney failure.

The patient in Figure 10-14 had aortic stenosis and failure of the left ventricle with distended pulmonary veins. Note that here the hila of left-sided cardiac failure are dominated by engorged vessels although there is added a homogeneous density between the great trunks close to the lung root which undoubtedly represents an increase in interstitial fluid close to the hilum. Thus you may at first have some difficulty in distinguishing between the lung fields of failure and those of acute pulmonary edema. In general, the perihilar densities of edema are whiter and more homogeneous, and often extend about halfway out toward the chest wall. You are struck by the density and the fluffiness of the bilateral shadows, whereas in failure you can usually see the lung root well enough to say that the vessels are engorged; the density provided by interstitial fluid is less impressive.

In advanced cardiac failure you will be seeing bilateral pleural effusion commonly, and many instances of heart failure in which the fluid is seen only on the right. Fluid occurring only on the left side, with a clear costophrenic angle on the right, is so rarely due to cardiac failure that you should think of other possible explanations when you see it.

Thus the diagnosis of cardiac failure is made from the enlargement of the heart shadow together with its tendency toward shapelessness, plus the confirmation provided by secondary signs in the hila and lung fields. The tendency to lose its former distinctive shape is not easy to assay if you are seeing the patient for the first time when he is in pronounced failure. It may be impossible at times to determine anything at all about the probable shape of the heart before it decompensated. In other patients, like the one in Figure 10-11, the degree of failure, although pronounced as indicated by the hila, has not as yet altered the pre-existing shape of the heart with its relatively greater left ventricular hypertrophy.

After response to treatment and with improvement of the physiologic state of the heart, the signs of failure which are reflected in the lungs, pleurae, and hila are seen to gradually diminish as the tone of the heart improves and its size decreases. Serial roentgenograms provide an excellent means of following the progress of the cardiac patient through an episode of failure, and you will find that they tally well with other clinical signs available to you.

Distinguishing between cardiac dilatation and an enlargement due to pericardial effusion

152

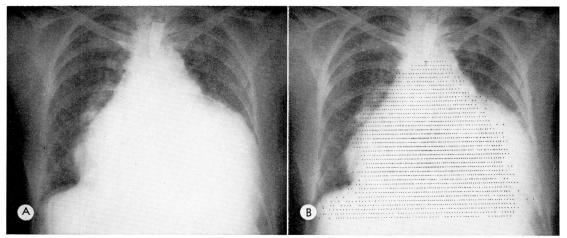

Figure 10-15. Markedly enlarged heart. Clinically there is some question whether this shapeless shadow represents a massive pericardial effusion. Radiologically either diagnosis is tenable. The heart is so large that it partly conceals the hila, although that on the right is definitely engorged. The diminution of pulsations remarked at fluoroscopy would still be compatible with either diagnosis. One ought to be reluctant to tap this heart. In *B* a cardioscan establishes the presence of a very large heart. (Note that the discrepancy along the left border is technical and cannot be taken here as an indication of the presence of pericardial fluid.)

can be an extraordinarily difficult matter. If clear-cut signs of failure are present in the hila and lungs, dilatation is the more probable explanation statistically, but the presence of some pericardial fluid as well certainly cannot be excluded.

Pure pericardial effusion without failure tends to show a cardiac shadow resembling a bag of water set down upon the diaphragm with marked and equal enlargement both to left and to right. So large and formless a shadow as the one you see in Figure 10-15A might well be due either to a much enlarged heart or to a pericardial effusion. Few care to risk further damage to an already flabby myocardium by irresponsibly tapping a dilated heart in an attempt to determine whether pericardial fluid might be present.

Much has been written about the damping of cardiac pulsations as visible under the fluoroscope in pericardial effusion, but a diagnosis is seldom quite so simple as that. It is true that with massive collections of fluid the cardiac pulsations are strikingly diminished in amplitude, but they are also diminished in myocardial failure severe enough to produce the same large heart shadow.

The radiologist is experienced in judging heart pulsations, and his fluoroscopic opinion is worth having on any patient in whom you suspect pericarditis. Do not anticipate that even the most experienced radiologist will always be able to decide the matter, however; some cases will be easy, others very difficult. Obviously, in a patient without any signs of failure, the quality and amplitude of whose normal cardiac pulsations are already known to the radiologist (who has fluoroscoped him before), the sudden development of a wide, boggy cardiac shadow suggesting effusion and the finding of pulsations which are markedly diminished at fluoroscopy will clearly indicate that pericarditis is the diagnosis of choice. Conversely, in the patient with known heart disease who has been in and out of failure and whose pulsations are never of good quality, the presence of pericardial fluid is unlikely to be determined fluoroscopically. Sudden increase in heart size to both sides without evidence of failure is probably the most reliable signal that pericardial fluid is present. The presence of small amounts of pericardial fluid is usually unsuspected radiologically and very difficult to establish.

153

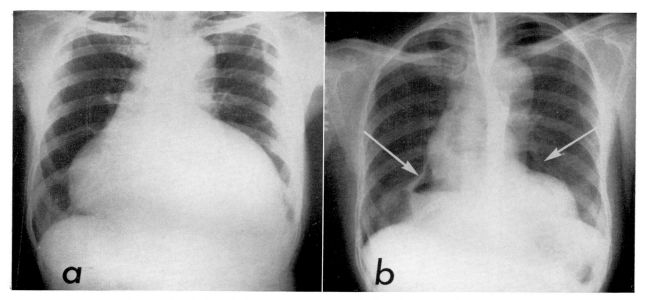

Figure 10-16. *A.* An elderly woman, who had had a bowel resection for carcinoma 1 year before, entered the hospital because of anemia and weakness. The chest film was interpreted as strongly suggestive of pericardial effusion. There were no clinical or electrocardiographic signs to support the diagnosis. However, because there was no evidence of failure and because at fluoroscopy complete damping of cardiac pulsations anteriorly was noted, a pericardial tap was performed. *B* shows the appearance of the chest following the removal of 700 cubic centimeters of fluid and the introduction of air. Note decrease in size of the cardiac shadow and fluid level on the right. Arrows mark the elevated pericardium outlined by air. Malignant cells were found in the pericardial fluid.

Figure 10-17 *(Unknown 10-1)*

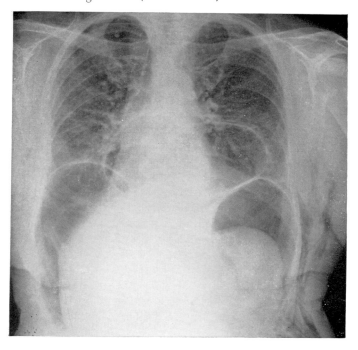

Analyze the film. Today patients in whom the question of pericardial effusion arises are often studied by a special procedure in which a small volume of CO_2 is injected into an antecubital vein with the patient positioned on his left side. He is radiographed in the PA sagittal projection to show the relationship of gas-filled superior vena cava and right atrium to the right margin of the cardiac profile. In cardiac dilatation without pericardial effusion, only a thin gray shadow will intervene between air-in-lung and gas-inside-heart. With pericarditis the effusion will cast a thicker shadow. The gas is rapidly absorbed and does not reach the lungs because of the left decubitus positioning.

154

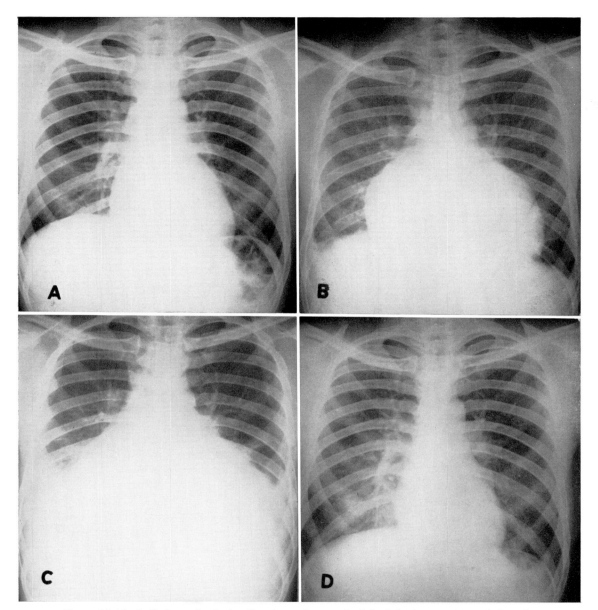

Figure 10-18. A. Patient who had suffered a stab wound of the left chest 24 hours before this film was made. B. Appearance on the sixteenth day when 250 cubic centimeters of old blood was removed by pericardial tap. Note fluid in right pleural space. C. Film made the twenty-fourth day after injury shows further increase in the size of the heart shadow to both sides and increase in the pleural effusion. D. This film was made 9 weeks after injury. The patient was asymptomatic. Note that final heart shadow is smaller than that in A, when there was probably already some blood in the pericardial space.

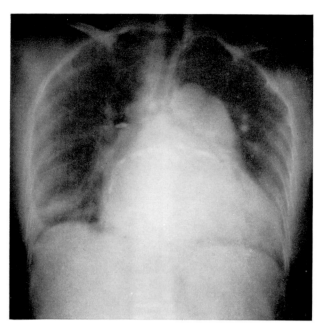

Figure 10-19 (above). Body-section radiograph shows extensive calcification of the right lateral and superior walls of the left atrium in a patient with mitral insufficiency.

Figure 10-20 (below). Pericardial calcification clearly seen in the lateral body-section study.

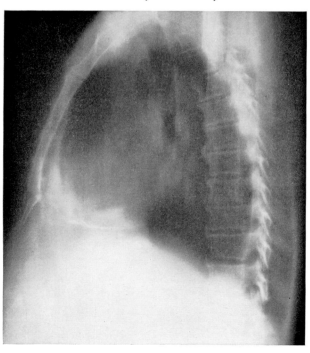

Constrictive pericarditis is particularly interesting roentgenologically because signs of *right* heart failure may appear clinically although the heart is not enlarged and the lungs and hila remain clear. The "small, still heart" of constrictive pericarditis was described by early fluoroscopic observers and is seen in patients with advanced and uniform constriction. Most patients with early obliterative or partially constricting pericarditis do not have such dramatic findings. For example, the heart *may* be enlarged, especially if it was already enlarged before the episode of pericarditis. Pulsations may be diminished on the right or at the base of the heart while those at the apex on the left remain normal or are even exaggerated. This probably occurs because the base of the heart moves least and the apex most during normal cardiac pulsation, so that it would be logical to expect early obliteration at the base while the apex behaved like a tambour at the end of a rigid cylinder.

When the process is long standing, pericardial calcification may be present. Such calcification is only one of several types which can be detected by x-ray procedures, and which offer diagnostic help. Calcification of the valves in both rheumatic and arteriosclerotic heart disease has been studied at fluoroscopy for many years. The location of the valves in all conventional projections has been carefully described and is well known. Where only one valve is calcified and there is any question as to which one it is, fluoroscopy, oblique studies, overpenetrated films, or body-section studies will usually determine its identity.

Calcification of the coronary arteries may be seen at fluoroscopy and identified on cinefluorograms. Calcification of the aorta is commonly seen in advanced arteriosclerosis, and the calcified intima of the arch in many persons past middle life may be seen as a shell just inside the margin of the aortic knob. Calcification of the ascending aorta is often syphilitic in origin, and the walls of aneurysms, etiologically either arteriosclerotic or luetic, may show calcium. Calcification of the wall of the distended left atrium in mitral valvular disease with insufficiency may often be seen on Bucky films or on body-section studies (Figure 10-19).

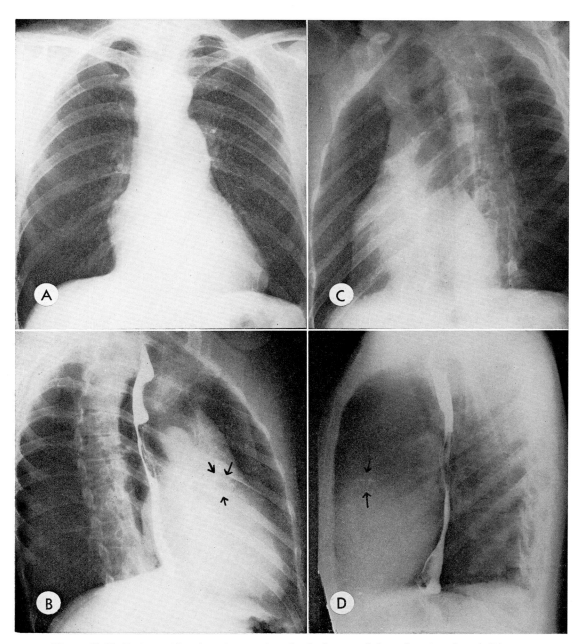

Figure 10-21. Patient with pulmonic stenosis and calcification of the pulmonic valve. *A*, PA projection shows the heart to be somewhat enlarged with a prominent right atrial border and a full pulmonary artery (arc 7 along the left border). *B*, right anterior oblique projection. The enlarged right ventricle rounds out the anterior profile. Valvular calcification is marked with arrows. *C*, left anterior oblique projection. Right ventricular enlargement produces a rounded anterior profile. *D*, left lateral projection. Note location of the well seen valvular calcification which could not possibly be in aortic or mitral valves, neither being located so far anteriorly.

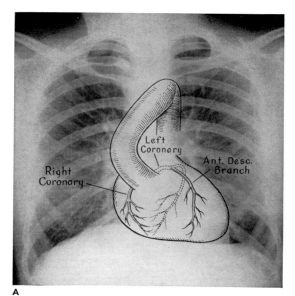 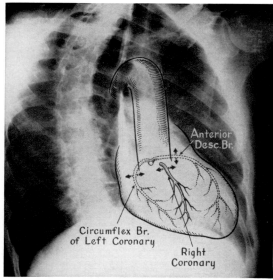

A

B

Figure 10-22A. In learning to recognize the two commonly used oblique views, you can help orient the degree of rotation if you review the position of the branches of the coronary arteries. The heart pictured here, although not enlarged to measurement, shows left ventricular prominence and a rather wide-swinging ascending aorta.

Figure 10-22B. *The right anterior oblique view.* Made technically as pictured below with the right anterior axillary line against the cassette holder. This view roughly superimposes the two ventricles upon each other, and the ascending and descending limbs of the aorta on each other. Note that the right coronary artery bisects the heart shadow in this projection. The posterior surface of the normal heart in this view looks flat and parallel with the spine. Note the resulting triangular shape of the heart shadow.

Figure 10-24

Figure 10-23

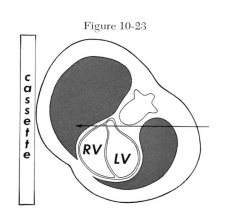

158

Figure 10-22C. *The left anterior oblique view.* Made technically as pictured below with the left anterior axillary line against the cassette holder. This view separates the two ventricles, the left ventricle lying posterior to the descending branch of the left coronary which bisects the shadow of the heart and marks the position of the interventricular septum. Anterior to this point lies the mass of the right ventricle, on the anterior and inferior surface of the heart. Note that this view also unrolls the aorta, and its ascending and descending limbs are seen enclosing the "aortic window." This produces a quite different shape for the heart shadow roentgenologically, which can be likened to a goosenecked flask. Note that as the mass of the left ventricle enlarges, the characteristic shape in this projection will be exaggerated because the left ventricle will project further back, overlapping the vertebrae. Note also the position of the left atrium on the posterior surface of the heart. Enlargement of the left atrium could be expected to fill in the aortic window and elevate the bronchi (particularly the left), producing a splaying of the carina, as you will see in the next few pages.

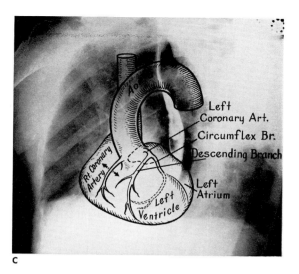

(Note: This page spread and the next two are arranged with right oblique views, diagrams, and angiocardiograms on the left page, and left oblique views, diagrams, and angiocardiograms on the right page. This is done so that you can easily tip and fold the pages into the middle in order to study various left and right views together.)

Figure 10-25

Figure 10-26

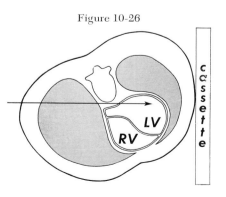

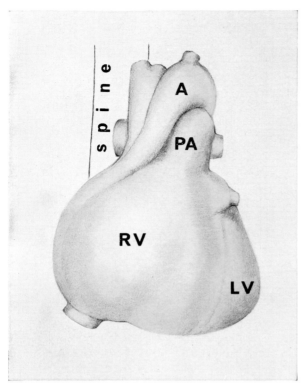

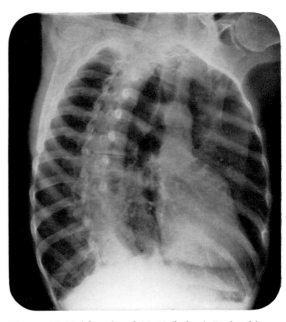

Figures 10-27 (above) and 10-28 (below). Anterior surface and right anterior oblique surface views of the heart with chambers and great vessels labeled.

Figures 10-29 (above) and 10-30 (below). Right oblique radiographs of two patients with normal hearts. Note the generally triangular shape of the heart shadow and its flat posterior surface, which will help you to distinguish this view from the left oblique.

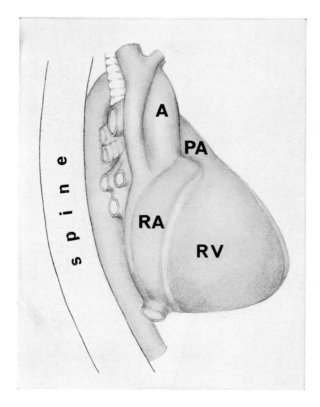

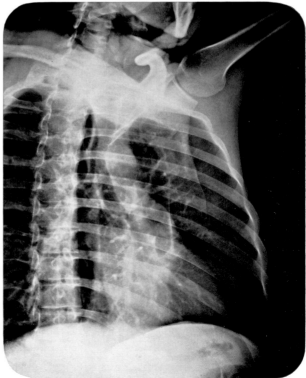

Your initial difficulty in distinguishing the right from the left oblique radiographs may be solved if you learn to study the shape of the heart rather than the various confusing labels on the films. Take the two oblique films in your hands, reversing each until you have a *right* oblique in which the heart is to the right of the spine (your right) and looks triangular with a flat posterior surface, and a *left* oblique in which the heart lies to the left of the spine and is much more bulbous in shape with a rounded posterior surface. You will then be looking through the two films in the correct way (that is, with the patient facing you but turned a little to each side). Note that when you reverse a left anterior oblique film and look through it the wrong way, it will *look* wrong to you. This is because it presents the mass of the heart to the right of the spine (as you expect to see it in the right oblique), but its posterior surface is not flat as you know it ought to be in a right oblique. Watch out for oblique films placed on the view boxes reversed in this fashion, becoming of course, therefore, unreadable paradoxes. You may recognize this situation in one of the cuts in this chapter.

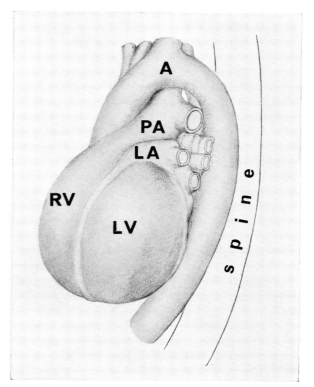

Figure 10-31 (above). Left anterior oblique surface view of the heart with chambers and vessels labeled.

Figure 10-32 (below, left). Left oblique radiograph of a patient during a bronchogram. Note close relationship of left main bronchus (arrow) to left atrium.

Figure 10-33 (below, right). Left oblique radiograph with the somewhat elongated and tortuous aorta well unrolled. Note rounded posterior surface of the heart and shape differing markedly from that seen in the right oblique.

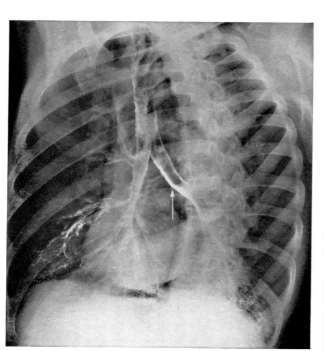

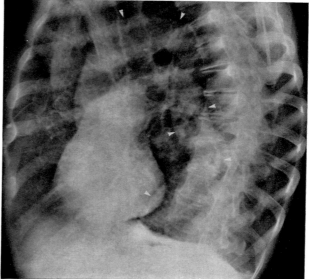

Figure 10-34. *Serial angiocardiogram:* **RIGHT ANTERIOR OBLIQUE PROJECTION**

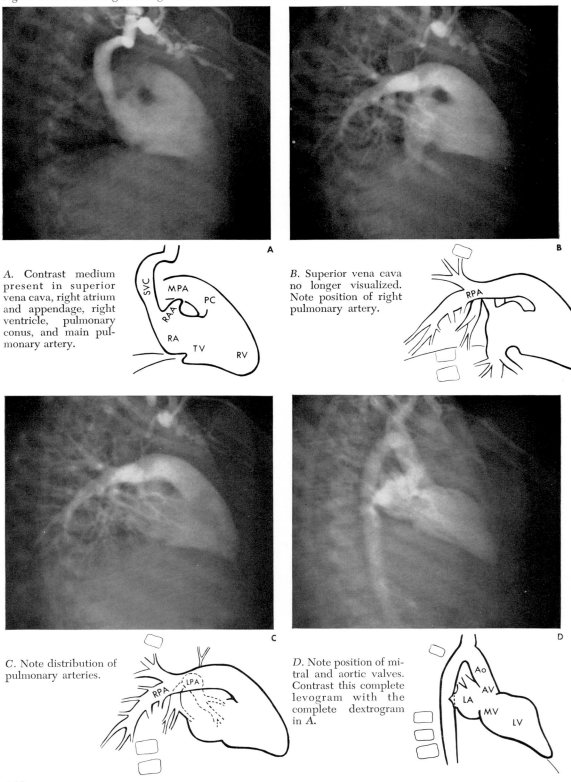

A. Contrast medium present in superior vena cava, right atrium and appendage, right ventricle, pulmonary conus, and main pulmonary artery.

B. Superior vena cava no longer visualized. Note position of right pulmonary artery.

C. Note distribution of pulmonary arteries.

D. Note position of mitral and aortic valves. Contrast this complete levogram with the complete dextrogram in *A.*

Figure 10-35. *Serial angiocardiogram:* **LEFT ANTERIOR OBLIQUE PROJECTION**

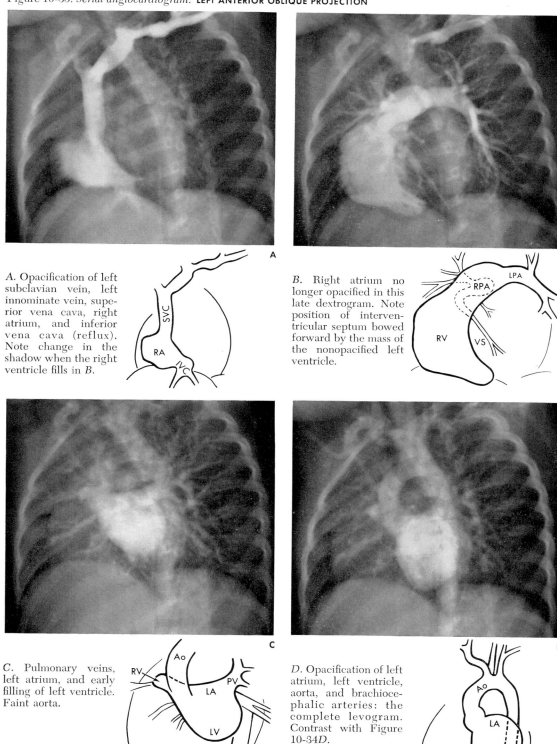

A. Opacification of left subclavian vein, left innominate vein, superior vena cava, right atrium, and inferior vena cava (reflux). Note change in the shadow when the right ventricle fills in *B.*

B. Right atrium no longer opacified in this late dextrogram. Note position of interventricular septum bowed forward by the mass of the nonopacified left ventricle.

C. Pulmonary veins, left atrium, and early filling of left ventricle. Faint aorta.

D. Opacification of left atrium, left ventricle, aorta, and brachiocephalic arteries: the complete levogram. Contrast with Figure 10-34*D.*

163

Figure 10-36. *Serial Angiocardiogram:* **ANTERO-POSTERIOR PROJECTION**

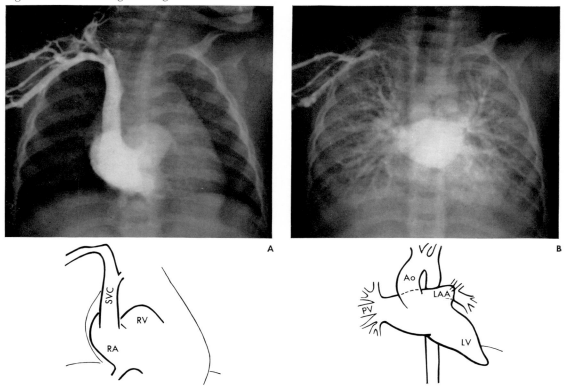

The angiocardiograms presented on this and the preceding pages differ in the projection used. On the preceding page spread, the beam of x-rays is traversing the chest, first as it does for the right oblique film, and then as it does for the left oblique film. On this page the beam passes through the chest in an antero-posterior direction. In all three series you watch the bolus of opaque-loaded blood pass successively through the right chambers to the lung and back through the left chambers. (The right oblique and left oblique projection series were printed first so that you could compare them with the right and left views of all sorts on the pages which preceded them.)

You should study them in two ways, first by following the bolus through the heart in each view, identifying the outline and position of each chamber within the heart shadow, and then by comparing the projection shadow of a given chamber in the three views. The three series represent selected frames, of course, and in each phase they differ very slightly with regard to the precise structures which are opacified. In other words, in *A* of Figure 10-36, above, you see the right atrium and the right

ventricle filled, but as yet no part of the pulmonary outflow tract; in *A* of Figure 10-34 you see the two right chambers and the pulmonary conus and main pulmonary artery; and in *A* of Figure 10-35 you see only the venae cavae and right atrium, the right ventricle filling only in frame *B*.

Now, as you look at the size and shape of the projection shadow of opaque material filling the left ventricle in Figure 10-36C, try to predict what you might expect to happen to the shape of the ventricle (and consequently to the heart shadow itself) with increasing degrees of left ventricular hypertrophy and subsequent dilatation. Imagine that this normal child's heart responds to years of hypertension, and predict its change in shape and the change in the angiocardiogram which could be anticipated. As you do this you will comprehend better the shape of the adult hearts with left ventricular hypertrophy and failure which you saw several pages back. You will also understand that, in a plain film made in the left oblique projection, the posterior surface of the heart becomes increasingly round in hypertensive heart disease and projects farther and far-

164

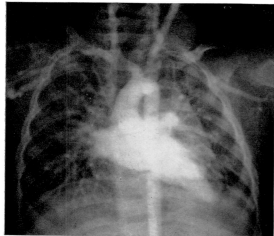

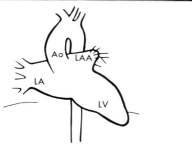

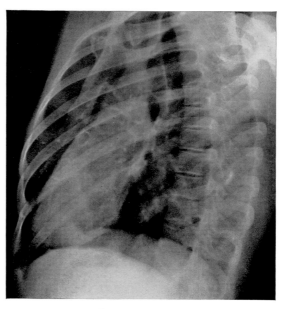

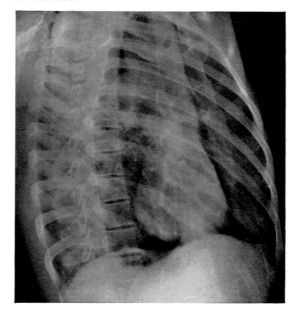

Figure 10-37 *(Unknown 10-2)* (above), and Figure 10-38 *(Unknown 10-3)* (below). Identify the projection in each case.

ther posteriorly to the left. Its surface in the left oblique should normally clear the anterior margin of the spine, but in hypertensive cardiovascular disease the left ventricle commonly overlaps the spine and is seen superimposed upon it.

Now imagine as you look at the shadow of the left atrium in Figure 10-36*B* that *it* gradually dilates, as it would in a patient with mitral valvular disease with insufficiency. What would you expect that to do to the heart shadow on the PA plain film? You would anticipate an increase in the width of the heart through the base, in the PA, and in both the other views you would expect to see the result of crowding upon the structures which are in close relationship posteriorly with the enlarging left atrium. Thus the left main bronchus would be elevated and the carina splayed. The esophagus may be displaced to either side and is generally bowed backward as seen in the oblique views. In the left oblique the aortic window may disappear, filled in by the fluid-filled atrium of about the same radiodensity as the aorta itself. In the next few pages you will be able to study actual examples and to confirm these predictions.

165

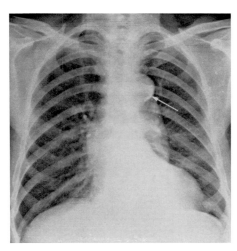

Figure 10-39. *A* (above). PA radiograph of a patient with arteriosclerotic heart disease. Note calcification at the arch of the aorta, wide swinging ascending and descending limbs due to elongation. Is *B* (below) a right oblique as it is printed?

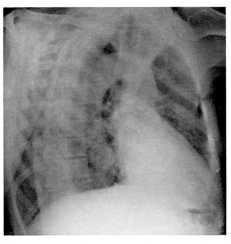

Yes, this is a right oblique and viewed correctly. Note flat posterior surface of the heart and triangular shape. Note also that, because of its elongation, the two limbs of the aorta are not seen superimposed as you expect in a normal right oblique. The aorta is more dense than normal because of its calcified intima and appears to be partly unrolled in this view, although its arched curve would be much wider if you had the left oblique to look at.

It would be unfortunate to have to qualify so soon my too-neat pronouncement with regard to your always being able to recognize the obliques and identify them correctly from the shape of the heart. Figure 10-39 has shown you one minor qualification, and others do exist with various heart abnormalities.

Obviously the shape of the heart in the two obliques will be much easier for you to recognize when the heart is, in fact, normal. With pathologic changes in shape, referable to the relative enlargement of one chamber, the shape will change also in the oblique views. Nevertheless, you will certainly find that you are helped to recognize the obliques even in the presence of many types of cardiac pathology, if you pay attention to the shape of the heart shadow.

For example, in the obliques of a hypertensive heart enlarged by a left ventricle relatively much larger than normal, such as the one in Figure 10-39, the posterior surface of the heart remains flat in the right oblique and will be increasingly rounded in the left oblique. Accordingly, you will still be sure which oblique is the left and which the right, and will be able to put them on the view boxes correctly and not reversed.

On the other hand, the abnormal heart shadow of mitral valvular disease, thickened through the base with fullness high on its posterior surface will no longer show a flat posterior surface in the right oblique. However, when you look at the left oblique of this heart, its lower posterior surface will still be rounded where the margin of the left ventricle approaches the spine.

If you imagine a heart in which both the left atrium and the left ventricle are relatively enlarged, you will construct a PA heart shadow which combines the shape you have learned to expect with hypertension with the one you have been anticipating for mitral valvular disease, a situation which prevails in combined mitral and aortic valvular lesions in rheumatic heart disease. The obliques will show you both the more rounded left ventricle and the bulging left atrium, rendering recognition of the obliques somewhat more difficult.

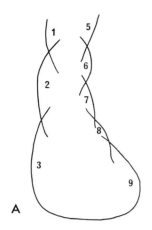

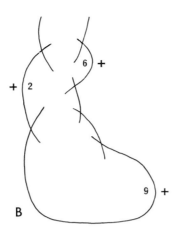

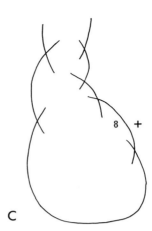

A B C

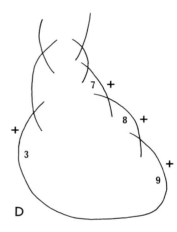

D

Figure 10-40. Changes in the shape of the heart with specific chamber enlargements, expressed in terms of alteration in the nine intersecting arcs responsible for the PA heart profile. (See text.)

Based on the series of nine intersecting arcs discussed at the beginning of Chapter 8, you see here the effect of specific chamber enlargement. The arcs, as they are seen to compose the profiles of the normal heart, are reproduced for you in *A*. In *B*, with the enlargement of the left ventricle in hypertensive or arteriosclerotic heart disease, arc 9 is markedly increased to the left. The accompanying elongation of the aorta which is to be expected will additionally expand arcs 2 and 6.

In *C* you see straightening of the left border of the heart so that its normal waistline becomes convex rather than concave, a change to be expected in minimal-to-moderate mitral valvular disease in which there is still only moderate enlargement of the left atrium. This straightening of the left heart border in early mitral disease can be shown to be due to the shadow of the auricular appendage when films are compared before and after amputation of the appendage during mitral commissurotomy (Figure 10-41).

In *D* you see the cardiac shape you might expect in advanced mitral valvular disease with marked insufficiency resulting in so much enlargement of the left atrium that it even pro-

jects beyond the shadow of the right atrium on the right border of the heart at arc 3. In addition, there is fullness of arc 7, the pulmonary outflow tract, because of chronic obstruction to the lesser circulation. There is also left ventricular enlargement resulting from aortic valvular disease with stenosis, expanding arc 9.

In combined mitral and aortic valvular lesions, the cardiac shape which evolves will depend on the lesion which effectively dominates, arc 9 becoming more prominent in hearts in which there is relatively more aortic valve involvement, and fullness of arcs 7 and 8 prevailing when the degree of mitral insufficiency is relatively greater than the aortic valvular disease.

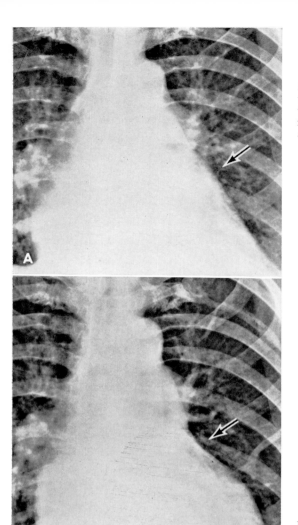

Figure 10-41 (left). *A*. Straightened left heart border in a patient with mitral stenosis. That the fullness is largely due to dilatation of the left auricular appendage is demonstrated by comparing with *B* made after mitral commissurotomy, the appendage having been amputated during surgery.

Figure 10-42 (below). Two patients with minimal to mild mitral stenosis and mitral insufficiency. Note absence of normal waistline and straightening with slight convexity of the left heart border.

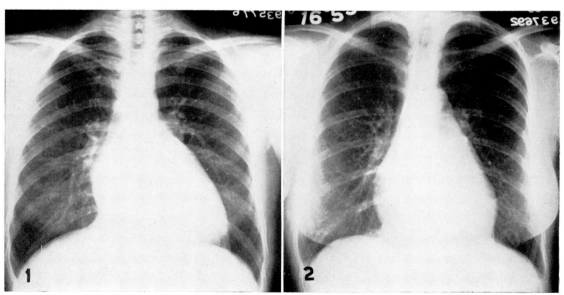

168

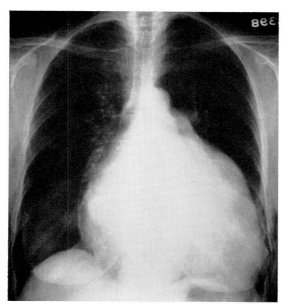

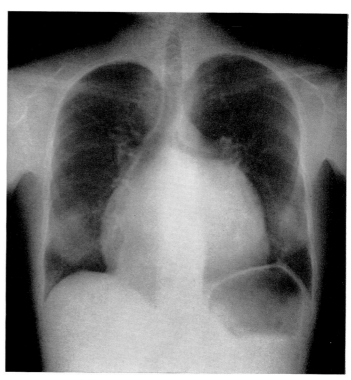

Figure 10-43 (above). Patient, 65, with advanced mitral valvular disease and mitral insufficiency. Note elevation of left main bronchus and shadow of large left atrium seen through the heart shadow.

Figure 10-44 (above). Supervoltage technique on a similar patient shows even better the left bronchial elevation and the splaying of the subcarinal angle.

Figure 10-45 (right). Right oblique in a patient with mitral valvular disease and insufficiency, showing posterior displacement of the barium-filled esophagus by the dilated left atrium. Asterisks indicate normal course of the esophagus.

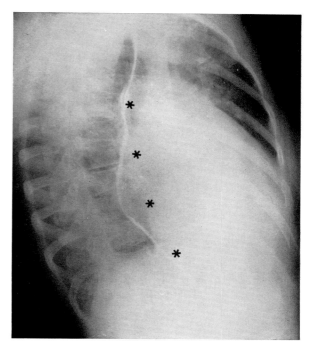

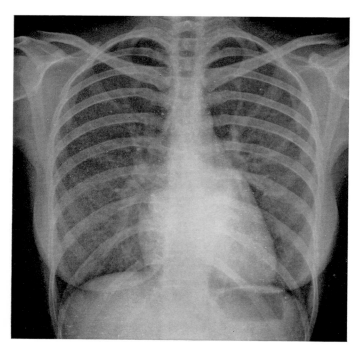

Figure 10-46 *(Unknown 10-4)* (above), and Figure 10-47 *(Unknown 10-5)* (below). Analyze these two hearts. Both young women were short of breath on admission to the hospital.

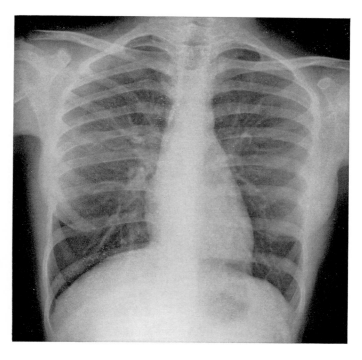

You begin now to have a feeling for the basic differences in shape between the heart shadow with predominantly left ventricular enlargement and the heart in which the left atrium is dilated. They are the most important specific chamber enlargements for you to be able to recognize. Whenever you suspect either you will try to confirm your impression by examining the obliques.

With left ventricular enlargement, the left oblique will be helpful, showing you rounding and extension of the left ventricle posteriorly overlapping the spine, and possibly some elongation of the aorta if the basic disease is arteriosclerotic. With left atrial dilatation, the left oblique may show you filling in of the aortic window, and the right oblique, posterior displacement of the barium-filled esophagus, but both obliques will show you the same thickening of the heart shadow through the base which you are beginning to recognize as the "mitral heart" in the PA chest film.

Change in the shape of the heart resulting from enlargement of the right chambers is more difficult to recognize, even for the expert radiologist. The right atrium is to be found immensely dilated, of course, in tricuspid atresia, which is so rare you may never see a case of it, and if you do you will have the impression, more than likely, that you are looking at something you have not seen before. Right ventricular hypertrophy and eventual dilatation are not at all uncommon, but because the right ventricle lies against the diaphragm and the anterior chest wall, juxtaposed to structures of equal density, enlargement of this chamber may be very difficult to recognize, even for the experts. There are one or two points to be remembered about it, however.

Hypertrophy of the right ventricle often displaces a normal-sized left ventricle to the left, so that such a heart shadow may occasionally suggest left ventricular hypertrophy at first glance at the PA. Examination of the two obliques, however, will show the right ventricle (along the anterior profile of the heart shadow) to be rounded and full, and careful correlation with the clinical findings will usually prevent misinterpretation. Remember that in judging the heart x-ray, the PA view is only a beginning and has limitations which must be kept in mind. You will *expect* to find right ventricular enlargement (cor pulmonale) in many types of chronic lung disease. The right ventricle is hypertrophied in pulmonic stenosis and in several other types of congenital heart disease. Few of these are analyzed from their plain film studies alone today, inasmuch as surgical correction can be planned only after a meticulous and precise delineation of the abnormalities which are present. Though one may suspect such changes from the shape of the heart, this type of cardiac patient is invariably studied by specialists, in the cardiopulmonary laboratory, and by either serial angiocardiograms or cineangiocardiography.

One more point to remember: in young girls the left border is often straight without any demonstrable evidence of heart disease. This may be because at that age in young women the left ventricle has not yet assumed its normal slight dominance. The two patients in Figures 10-46 and 10-47 will have puzzled you in this regard. Both show slightly convex left borders. Only the patient in 10-46 has measurable cardiac enlargement, and she had all the classic murmurs of mitral stenosis with minimal insufficiency. Her left bronchus is slightly elevated, to confirm our impression from this film alone that a slightly dilated left atrium accounts for the fullness of the left border. The girl in Figure 10-47 has no cardiac enlargement, nor had she any cardiac symptoms. Her dyspnea was due to an incipient attack of asthma. She had a history of one or two attacks a month for several years, and on fluoroscopy her straightening of the left border was easily shown to be due to slight fullness of the pulmonary outflow tract, or, in other words, arc 7. In the original PA chest film her left main bronchus could be seen to form a perfectly normal angle at the carina, and there was nothing in the oblique views to suggest atrial abnormality. Thus the straightened left border in 10-46 is due to posterior fullness, while that in 10-47 is due to fullness of an entirely different structure located anteriorly.

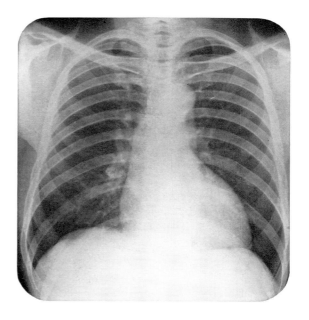

Figure 10-48 *(Unknown 10-6)* (above), and Figure 10-49 *(Unknown 10-7)* (below). Analyze the two hearts on this page with regard to specific chamber enlargement. If you now learn that they belong to two young men in their mid-thirties, would the information strengthen your tentative impression or weaken it? Compare the two aortic shadows. Does the aorta contribute to your analysis?

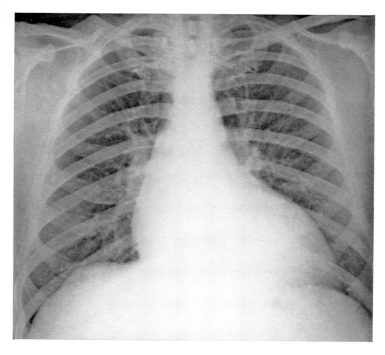

By the time you have studied the films of 50 heart patients in addition to the introductory grounding I have tried to give you in this chapter, you ought to feel fairly secure about the following decisions: (1) you ought to be able to measure heart shadows on the 6-foot PA chest film, checking the factors which might be producing spurious changes, and deciding whether there is true enlargement; (2) you ought to be able to recognize alteration in shape referable to left ventricular hypertrophy or left atrial dilatation and to check your PA impression on the two obliques; (3) you should be able to place the obliques on the viewing boxes correctly most of the time; (4) you will be beginning to know where to look for fullness in the profiles with any particular chamber or great vessel enlargement; (5) you ought to be able to decide whether a shapeless enlarged heart is in failure and (6) to have some idea as to what help you can expect from the roentgen examination and the radiologist in various sorts of cardiac disease. Try your hand at the following unknowns before you go on to the abdomen.

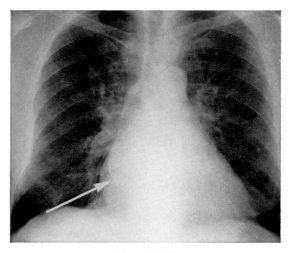

Figure 10-51

Unknown 10-9 (Figure 10-51). Do you think this patient's heart is enlarged? Do you think it has a normal left border? What is the shadow margin indicated by the arrow?

Figure 10-50

Unknown 10-8 (Figure 10-50). Analyze the film and make decisions about enlargements, shape, specific chamber size, supporting roentgen details, and (?) failure.

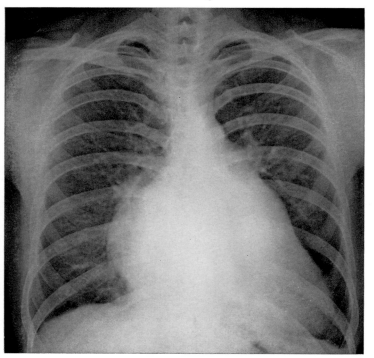

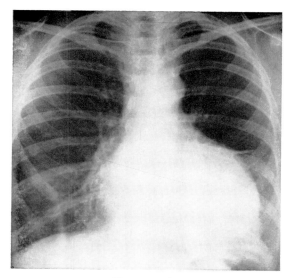

Figure 10-52

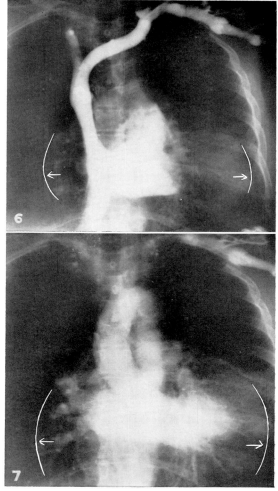

Unknown 10-10 (Figure 10-52). A 56-year-old woman with hypertension and angina pectoris had had a myocardial infarction 4 years before these films were made. She also had had known myxedema for 8 years, and it had frequently been necessary to discontinue the administration of thyroid extract because of exacerbations of chest pain. What is your general impression when you look at the PA film? What do you know about the type of heart disease usually associated with myxedema? The angiocardiograms in 6 and 7 contribute what information to the whole-patient study in this case?

Figure 10-53

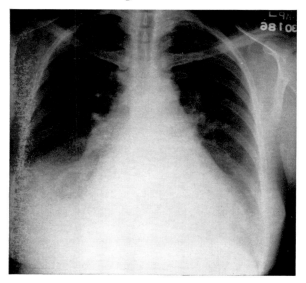

Unknown 10-11 (Figure 10-53). Is there cardiac enlargement? Any suggestion from the shape as to specific chamber enlargement? Failure?

173

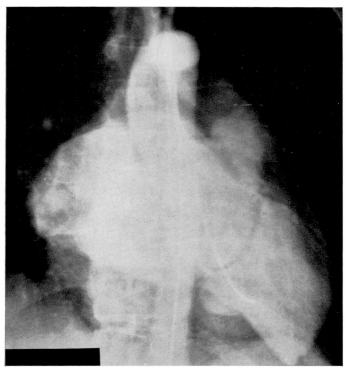

Figure 10-54

Unknown 10-14 (no figure). It is probably not important for you to be able to remember the angiocardiographic findings in the various kinds of congenital heart disease. Nevertheless, you ought to be able to reason out the general findings in some of the less complex conditions. What would you expect the serial frames of the angiocardiogram to show, for example, in co-arctation of the aorta?

Unknown 10-15 (no figure). And in interventricular septal defect when the shunt is from left to right?

Unknown 10-16 (no figure). And in patent ductus arteriosus when the shunt is from the aorta through the ductus into the pulmonary artery?

Figure 10-55

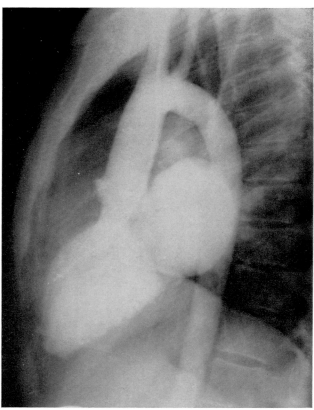

Unknown 10-12 (Figure 10-54). AP angiocardiogram with the opaque substance introduced via a catheter passed backward along the aorta and through the aortic valve. Its tip is in the ventricle. What chambers are opacified and what does their opacification imply?

Unknown 10-13 (Figure 10-55). Angiocardiogram with the opaque substance introduced via a catheter passed into the brachial artery and through the aortic valve into the ventricle. What chambers are opacified in this lateral view (compares most closely with the left obliques you have seen)? What abnormality is implied?

174

Credits: Illustrations this chapter.

Figures 10-2, 10-3. Courtesy Dr. H. Forsyth, Jr., Rochester, N. Y.

Figure 10-4. Courtesy Dr. R. Tugenhaft and the publisher, *MR&P* 35:52.

Figures 10-5, 10-6. Courtesy Dr. J. Hope et al., and the publisher, *MR&P* 33:26, 28.

Figures 10-7, 10-8, 10-15. Courtesy Drs. W. MacIntyre, G. Crespo and J. Christie, and the publisher, *Am. J. Roentgenol.* 89:317, 318.

Figures 10-10, 10-48. Courtesy Dr. S. Barton and the publisher, *MR&P* 28:109.

Figure 10-11. Courtesy Drs. M. Klein and E. Walsh, and the publisher, *Radiology* 70:674.

Figures 10-12, 10-14, 10-42, 10-43. Courtesy Drs. R. Ormond and W. Eyler, and the publisher, *Radiology* 79:378, 379, 381, 382.

Figure 10-13. Courtesy Dr. R. Barden and the publisher, *Radiology* 75:454.

Figure 10-16. Courtesy Drs. H. Mellins, P. Kottmeier and B. Keily, and the publisher, *Radiology* 73:15.

Figure 10-17. Courtesy Dr. N. Finby, New York, N. Y.

Figure 10-18. Courtesy Dr. L. Doubleday and the publisher, *Radiology* 74:28.

Figures 10-19, 10-20. Courtesy Dr. B. Epstein and the publisher, *MR&P* 34:68, 69.

Figure 10-21. Courtesy Drs. W. Northway and H. Abrams, and the publisher, *Am. J. Roentgenol.* 89:324.

Figure 10-22. Courtesy Drs. A. Lieber and J. Jorgens, and the publisher, *Am. J. Roentgenol.* 86:1069-1070.

Figure 10-29. Courtesy Mr. H. Gibson and the publisher, *MR&P* 27:126.

Figure 10-30. Courtesy Mr. C. Bridgman, Mr. E. Holly, Dr. M. Zariquiey, and the publisher, *MR&P* 32:56.

Figure 10-33. Courtesy Dr. L. Cole, Blossburg, Pa.

Figures 10-34, 10-35, 10-36. Courtesy Dr. B. Gasul et al., and the publisher, *MR&P* 35 Supplement, 1959:6, 7, 9, 10.

Figures 10-37, 10-38. Courtesy Dr. C. Dotter, Portland, Ore.

Figure 10-39. Courtesy Dr. M. Higgins, Coeur d'Alene, Idaho.

Figure 10-41. Courtesy Drs. G. Jacobson and W. Weidner, and the publisher, *Radiology* 79:275.

Figure 10-44. Courtesy Dr. W. Tuddenham et al., and the publisher, *MR&P* 33:61.

Figures 10-51, 10-53. Courtesy Drs. R. Ormond and A. Poznanski, and the publisher, *Radiology* 74:548.

Figure 10-52. Courtesy Drs. R. Kittredge, E. Arida and N. Finby, and the publisher, *Radiology* 80:432.

Figure 10-54. Courtesy Drs. K. Amplatz, R. Lester, R. Ernst and C. Lillehei, and the publisher, *Radiology* 76:396.

Figure 10-55. Courtesy Drs. J. Lehman, J. Debbas and J. Boyle, Jr., and the publisher, *Am. J. Roentgenol.* 89:305.

CHAPTER 11 The Abdomen: Study of the Plain Film

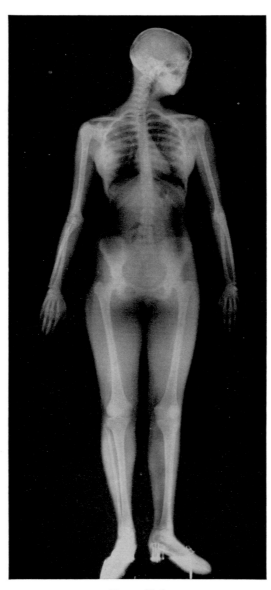

Figure 11-1

Radiographic study of the region of the abdomen is, in its way, a little more difficult and a little more subtle than that of the chest, perhaps, but it is equally interesting from the standpoint of the opportunity it affords you, the student, to discover how much of roentgen data can be learned through reasoning. Material learned by appreciating the logic of its appearance is much more easily retained because it can be reasoned out again if it is forgotten. Roentgen study of the abdomen is largely reasoning.

The wide differences in radiodensity of the chest structures provide profiles and margins which are easy to see and to interpret as you first begin to look at x-ray films. In the abdomen, however, organ masses and great vessels merge into a confluent gray shadow so that their borders and profiles vanish. Only when some structure of differing density lies against one you wish to know about can you see its boundary — often only a small segment of that boundary — from which you may be able to construe something about the size and shape of the organ in question.

The striking decrease in density of air within the gut will occur to you at once as providing the sort of boundaries and outline segments you need. You will use this kind of information constantly in assaying the size and shape of organs and masses within the abdomen from plain films.

Thus, for example, all air-containing gut may be swept into the left side of the abdomen by a grossly enlarged liver whose mass is seen as a large gray shadow, but whose margin is often only visible to you as a border outlined by air in colon. The stomach, when filled with fluid, lies against the spleen and blends with its shadow invisibly, giving no information as to its size; but if the stomach is inflated with air, it may be seen to be clearly indented from the left and displaced medially by an enlarged spleen. All air-containing structures may be displaced upward out of the pelvis by a large ovarian cyst, and individual large and small bowel loops, like a circle of dark beads, outline the cyst's upper surface.

Variable as the actual content of air in the gut certainly is, it will prove immensely useful to you in tagging abnormalities in the size and shape of other organs, and you will soon form a visual base line with regard to the amount and location of air-in-gut which you can expect to see. There is normally at least a little air in the stomach and a fair amount distributed throughout the colon. In the healthy, ambulatory adult, the small bowel usually contains little or no air, but normal infants and bedridden adults often show considerable amounts of small bowel air without any abdominal pathology to account for it.

By definition a "plain film" is a film made without any artificially introduced contrast substance.* Although we must in this chapter discuss first the plain film of the abdomen, you will find that you will anticipate better the location and appearance of the air-outlined gut after you have seen all parts of the gastrointestinal tract filled with barium. In barium studies the entire gastrointestinal tract is rendered visible, but in the plain film you will be depending on transient air content alone for information, and you will realize that many parts of the gut are ordinarily invisible because they contain fluid feces or are collapsed. Sometimes parts of the colon will be outlined by their content of semisolid feces with which bubbles of air have been mixed. This casts a distinctive speckled shadow and may be just as useful as air-filled gut in indicating the position of neighboring structures or locating parts of the colon itself. Such speckled fecal shadows always identify colon and are not seen in the small bowel.

*For this reason you should call it a *plain film* rather than a "flat plate," a meaningless term. The so-called "K.U.B." is a plain film.

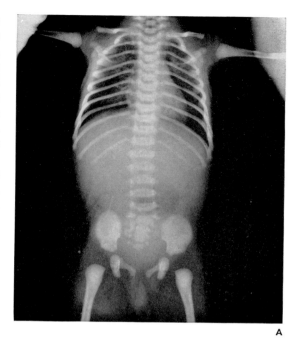

A

Figure 11-2. *A* (above). Airless abdomen in a 4-day-old girl who had been vomiting since birth. All organs blend together as one confluent gray shadow. *B* (below). Same patient, stomach inflated with air. Note density of catheter. Upper margin of the antrum of the stomach lies against the margin of the liver.

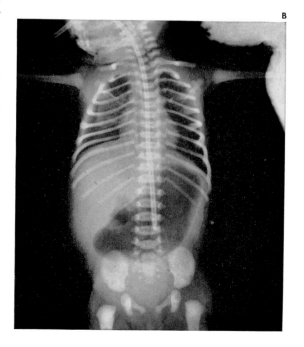

B

177

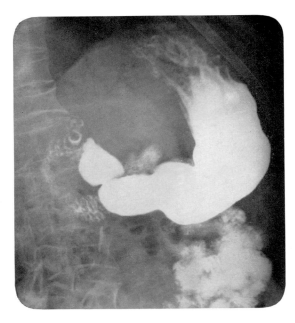

Figure 11-3 (left). The stomach is visible here because it is filled with barium sulfate. This film was made with the patient lying prone and rolled up slightly on his right side so that the pylorus and duodenal bulb, or cap, are seen (the right anterior oblique projection). The fundus of the stomach in this position is the highest part of that organ and, consequently, contains more air and less barium. A scattering of barium indicates the position of the duodenal loop, and barium-filled loops of small bowel are seen below the stomach.

Figure 11-4. The position of the stomach indicated by its accidental content of hardware. Shortly after a mental patient was admitted to the hospital she complained that she had swallowed an open safety pin and that it had stuck in her throat. Radiographs of the neck proved this to be true, and the pin was removed. Within a month it was noted that the patient's appetite was poor and she was losing weight. She also complained of abdominal distress. The left upper quadrant of her abdomen was tender and rigid on examination. A plain film of the abdomen (*A*, below, left) revealed the presence of a tangled mass of metallic foreign bodies within the stomach and a dozen others scattered throughout the intestinal tract. A gastrotomy was performed and 287 metal and glass objects removed (*B*, below).

A

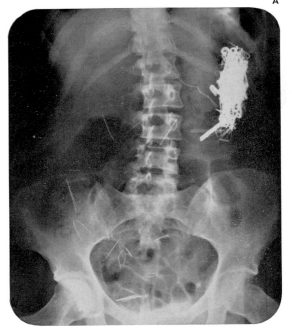

B

178

Figure 11-5 (right). The margin of the liver outlined by
air in the gut. You know the film to have been made
with the patient standing because of the fluid level in
the fundal stomach bubble. The liver in this small boy
was immensely enlarged by tumor.

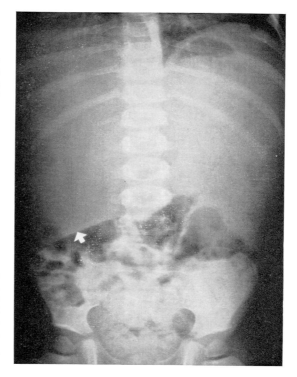

Figure 11-6 (below). Borders of a large round mid-abdominal mass are outlined by air-filled gut. The patient,
a 10-year-old girl, had been admitted because of acute
abdominal pain. At first the mass you see was thought
to represent a distended bladder, but it failed to disappear after catheterization and on exploration proved
to be an ovarian cyst twisted on its pedicle. The haustrated descending colon encircles it to the left, clearly
outlining its round border.

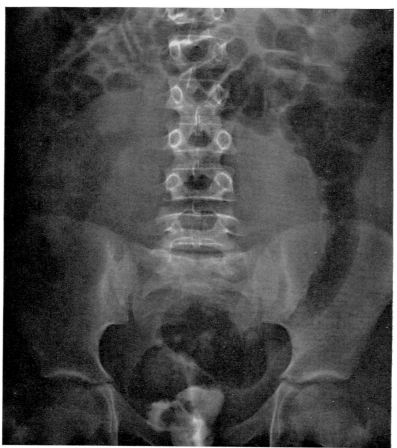

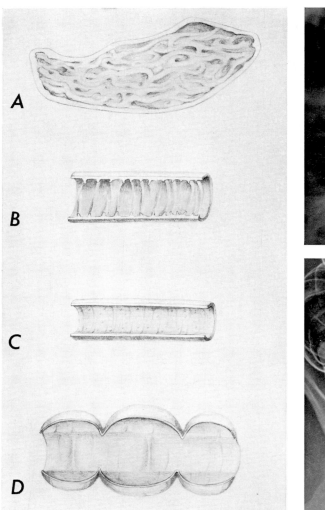

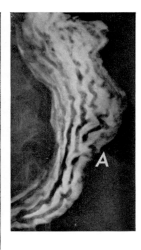

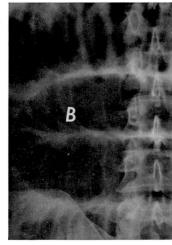

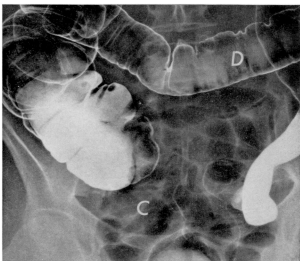

Figure 11-7 (immediately above). The mucosal linings of stomach *(A)*, jejunum *(B)*, ileum *(C)*, and colon *(D)* differ anatomically enough to be identified from the appearance of their respective air shadows.

Figure 11-8 (above, right). Examples to help you. *A.* The rugae of the stomach are seen as black wavy shadows. These radiolucent soft-tissue ridges are visible because opaque barium lies in the valleys between them. The reverse is seen often when the stomach contains only air, that is, soft-tissue ridges with more radiolucent air in the valleys between them. (See Figure 11-11.) *B.* The distinctive plical folds inside the jejunum appear as transverse, denser ridges with air between in the distended small bowel of intestinal obstruction. *C.* Air-filled loops of ileum, filled from the colon during a barium enema, overlap their shadows in the pelvis and lower abdomen. *D.* The colon with its characteristic serosal indentations, or haustra, barium- and air-filled. Reason out why the transverse colon appears to be outlined in white while the descending colon is uniformly opaque.

Because of the structural differences in the mucosa of various parts of the gut, barium casts of these structures produce white shadows on the film, the margins of which distinctively reproduce the character of the mucosal pattern. The rugae of the stomach are quite different from the plicae of the small intestine and from the smoother, more widely spaced plicae of the colon with their serosal indentations, or haustra. To distinguish their barium casts is to anticipate differences in their dark air shadows on the plain film.

The distribution throughout the abdomen of air in the gut is determined to some extent by the degree of fixation of the various structures. The stomach may alter widely in size, but it *is* fixed at the diaphragm and to the retroperi-

180

toneal part of the duodenum. The small bowel enjoys the liberty of its ample mesentery, folded into the mid-abdomen. The transverse colon varies widely in position, too, but the ascending and descending portions of the large bowel are normally retained in the lateral gutters by their shorter mesocolons. Within this degree of latitude you will learn to identify different parts of the air-filled gut by their locations as well as by their distinctive mucosal patterns.

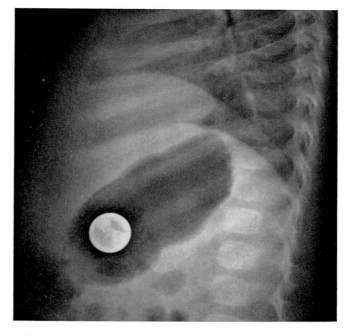

Figure 11-9 (right, above). Lateral view of the air-filled stomach containing a Lincoln-head penny. Would you be likely to be able to identify the coin if the stomach were filled with (1) barium, (2) lunch?

Figure 11-10 (right, below). Normal distribution of the colon. (a) cecum, (b) ascending colon, (c) hepatic flexure, (d) transverse colon, (e) splenic flexure, (f) descending colon, (g) sigmoid, and (h) rectum. Note overlap at flexures. Small white arrow points to terminal ileum, which often fills during the barium enema.

Figure 11-11 (below). The rugae thrown into contrast by air in the stomach.

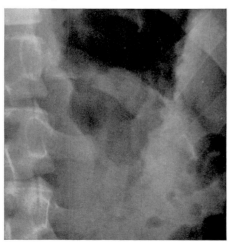

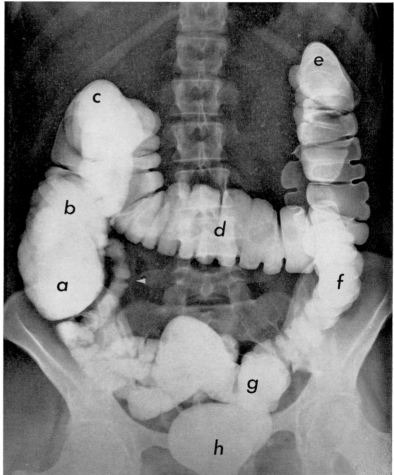

181

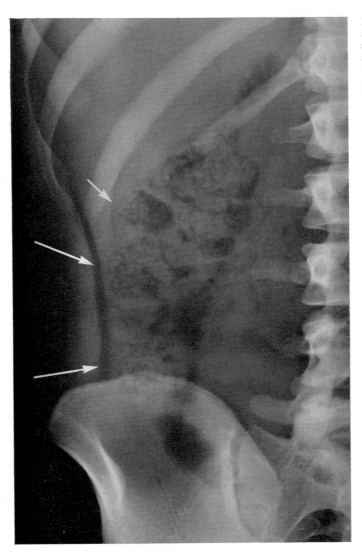

Figure 11-12. Right flank stripe (long arrows) close against which lies the ascending colon, indicated, as it so often is on the plain film, by the characteristic speckled shadow of feces mixed with air. Note margin of the liver above. Dark shadow overlying the wing of the ilium is air in cecum or terminal ileum. Short arrow indicates fat outlining margin of kidney.

Fat distributions within the abdomen also help you to make certain decisions about the structures they invest. The wide apron of the omentum will not help you because it is distributed across the abdomen and never seen cleanly in tangent. The perirenal envelope of fat, however, provides a tangential radiolucent layer outlining the kidney mass with a dark line where more x-rays reach the film to blacken it.

In the same way precisely, the fatty layer next to the peritoneum in the abdominal wall is not seen where the sagittally directed ray of a supine plain film strikes it *en face* anteriorly. At each side, however, where the fat layer turns downward toward the patient's back, the beam catches it tangentially, and the dark line so produced on the film is called the "flank stripe."*

The flank stripe disappears when the flank itself becomes edematous. This is perfectly logical: fluid infiltrating the fat renders it as dense to the x-ray beam as the largely fluid muscle which adjoins it. With inflammation near the flank, as in appendiceal abscess, for example, the flank stripe on that side may disappear, while the opposite one remains normal. In exactly the same fashion, perirenal inflammation erases the perirenal fat line.

The subcutaneous fat of a fetus near term may be traversed tangentially by the ray, outlining a leg or arm or the buttocks against the inside of the uterine wall. Concentrated accumulations of fat, such as may be present within a dermoid cyst, produce localized round radiolucent shadows on the film, appreciable to the eye because of their juxtaposition to surrounding structures of greater density.

*You will also hear it referred to as the "preperitoneal" or even "pro-peritoneal" fat line, both of which seem to me semantically poor terms. I advise you to stick to "flank stripe," which is short and direct and does not involve abused word root derivations.

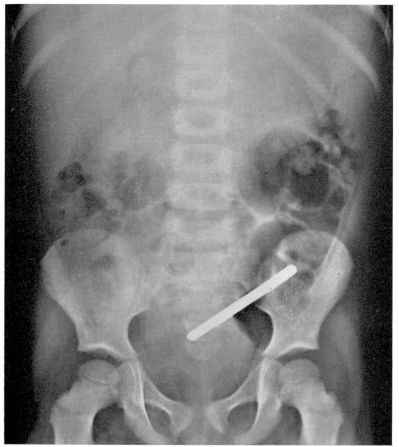

Figure 11-13. Plain film of the abdomen of a child showing a broken off rectal thermometer which proved to be in the sigmoid. Note well seen flank stripe. The close juxtaposition of the haustrated descending colon to the flank stripe on the left is normal.

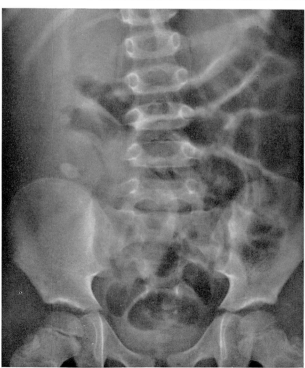

Figure 11-14. Abdomen of a 5½-year-old boy. Air-filled gut is seen displaced to the left away from the right flank where a soft tissue mass can be seen, in the middle of which there is an oval dense shadow suggesting calcium. This proved to be a <u>fecalith within a large</u> <u>appendiceal abscess.</u>

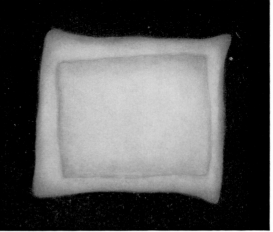

Figure 11-15 (above). *A* (left). Clay tablets from the ancient Sumerian city of Ur. Records of business transactions were recorded in this way, and, because the tablets were fragile and the records precious, an outer envelope of clay was added bearing the same information in duplicate. *B* (right). The "envelope" of air between the inner and outer layers of clay is well shown in this radiograph of the intact clay tablet. The parallel between this and any fat- or gas-encased anatomic structure of greater density is obvious.

Figure 11-16 (below). Quantities of retroperitoneal gas have infiltrated the psoas sheath and the perirenal envelope of fat in this patient, outlining the kidney even more strikingly than you can expect to see it outlined with its own fat on the plain film. (Detail on right.)

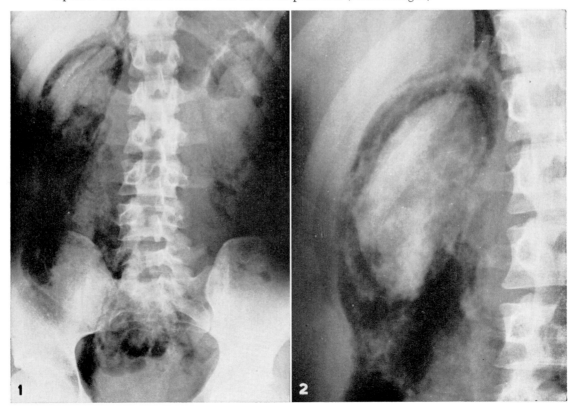

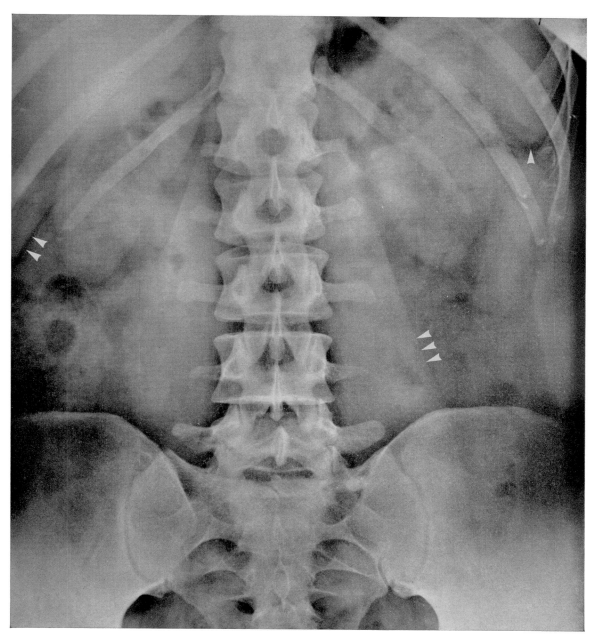

Figure 11-17. Soft-tissue outlines unusually well seen on the abdominal plain film. Single arrow indicates tip of the spleen. Double arrow marks the lower margin of the liver, which you can follow obliquely upward across the shadow of the kidney. Triple arrow indicates the left psoas margin. The psoas shadows are generally symmetrical. Here the lower part of the right is obscured by something of equal density lying against it. Note dark air in stomach overlying the upper pole of the left kidney and two haustrated, air-filled shadows representing distal transverse colon lying across the middle of the left kidney. The entire outline of the right kidney is seen but not that of the left. The left kidney is a little larger than the right. Note speckled fecal shadows in the right colon and excellent flank stripe on the left.

"placenta"

Figure 11-18

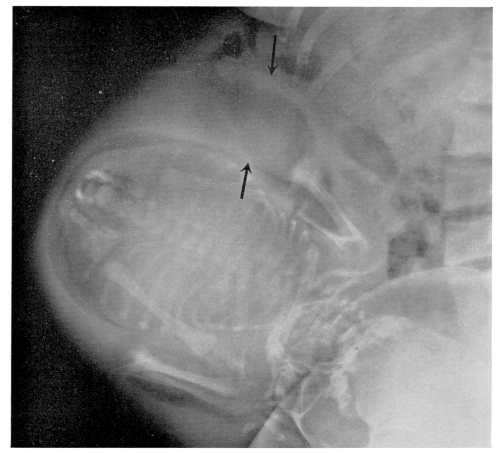

Figure 11-19

A   B

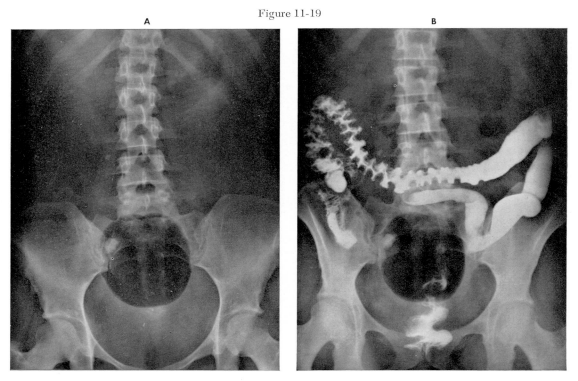

186

With the contribution of fat lines and fat accumulations still in mind, analyze the two unknowns on the opposite page.

Unknown 11-1 (Figure 11-18). This lateral view of the abdomen of a pregnant woman near term shows displacement of air-in-gut upward and backward by the uterine mass so that the wall of the uterus is bounded by air bubbles scattered at intervals along its surface. What parts of the fetus can you envision better because they are outlined by dark subcutaneous fat? What is the crescentic shadow between the two black arrows?

Unknown 11-2 (Figure 11-19). Plain film (left) and film made after barium enema (right) on a female patient with a nontender, mid-line abdominal mass. This was discovered to fill the posterior cul-de-sac on vaginal examination, the uterus being normal in size. Menses had been normal and the patient was not pregnant. The correct diagnosis was suggested by the radiologist from the plain film.

Abnormal radiodensities are provided by any area of calcification sufficiently large to absorb some of the beam. Calcified thrombi will be seen as dense white nuggets. Kidney stones and gallstones will have a characteristic location and may often show a distinctive radiographic structure in their shadows as well: gallstones are frequently laminated and faceted. If you stop to think for a moment, both the lamination and the faceting are to be expected. Gallstones, more often than kidney stones, form over a long period of time in a pool of fluid of slowly changing metabolic composition; hence the lamination seen in the radiograph. They are also more often multiple and are made to rub against each other with the contractions of the gallbladder; hence the faceting. Laminations and facets occur in kidney stones, as you could predict, when they form in a chronically obstructed renal pelvis. Kidney calculi are not very often laminated, however, and rarely develop facets. The very characteristic stag-horn calculi fill up the entire pelvis and calices, closely resembling the shadow of opaque fluid you see on a pyelogram.

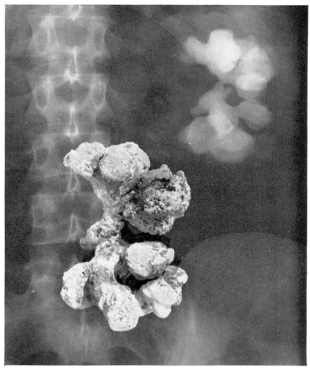

Figure 11-20 (above). Stag-horn calculus in the left kidney. The photograph of the surgical specimen has been superimposed on the radiograph (plain film) for comparison.

Figure 11-21 (below). Cluster of faceted calculi in the gallbladder. Note that these have formed in such a way that their outer surfaces seem to contain more calcium. Now look closely. The large square uppermost calculus shows a distinct new layer of *lesser* density. This illustrates the process of the development of lamination.

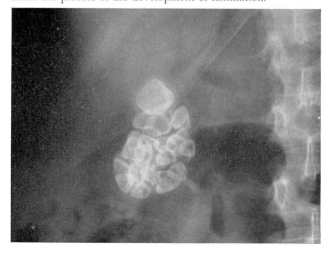

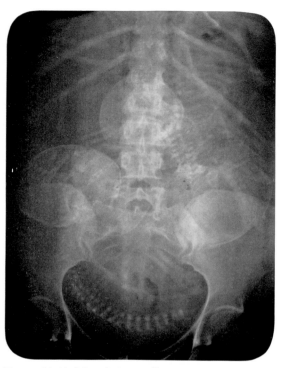

Figure 11-22 (above). Naturally occurring radiodensities. (Quadruplets were delivered. Four vertebral columns can be discerned easily from this engraving. The shell-like skulls are harder to see.)

Calcification within the capsule of any organ will resemble the radiograph of an eggshell, more dense peripherally where it is caught tangentially by the ray. Calcification in the wall of a hollow organ will look very similar, and you will often see this type of calcification in the aorta in older patients. Sometimes it will bound an aneurysm of that great vessel (Figure 11-25). Plaques of calcium scattered throughout the wall and caught by the ray in tangent will provide an interrupted white outline, as you would expect. A vessel of smaller caliber, when its wall becomes calcified, will show linear white margins like the rose stem in the first chapter, and they will be serpiginous and parallel if the vessel describes a tortuous course. You will recognize them as characteristic for a hollow cylinder of dense material about a more radiolucent core, x-rayed from the side.

In sum, then, as you look at plain films of the abdomen, you will be making interpretive deductions from profile margins and shadow differences produced by differences in radiodensities. The basic roentgen facts are unchanged, but interpretation must be within a somewhat narrower range.

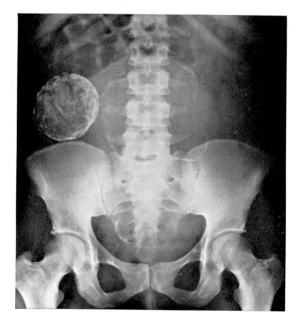

Figure 11-23 (left). Multiple uterine leiomyomata in a 42-year-old woman complaining of constipation and dysuria. The patient had lived all her life in a remote rural area and had never consulted a physician before. There had been a large painless lower abdominal mass present for 10 years, the top of which was palpable 28 centimeters above the pubic symphysis. The specimen removed at surgery showed many intramural, pedunculated, and submucous fibroids, with varying degrees of calcification.

188

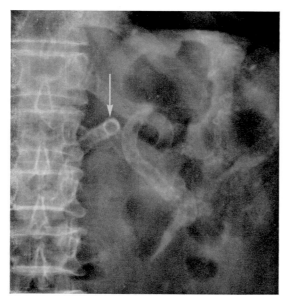

Figure 11-24. Calcified, tortuous splenic artery. Note parallel winding white lines. Arrow indicates segment passing sagittally and, hence, filmed end-on, appearing as a white ring.

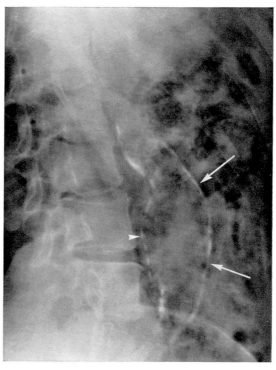

Figure 11-25. Lateral abdominal plain film showing plaques of calcium in wall of an abdominal aortic aneurysm.

Figure 11-26. Calcifications in the liver, probably representing healed abscesses in a patient with amebic dysentery. Long arrow indicates the tip of the spleen, which is not enlarged. Short arrow points to abscess in left lobe of the liver.

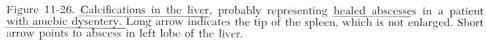

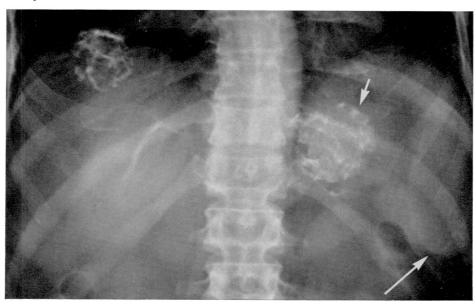

189

The plain film of the abdomen is important because it is so simple to obtain, involves almost no discomfort for the patient, and can be immensely informative without complex procedures. So much can be learned, in fact, from plain films of the abdomen in so many different conditions, that every physician should be familiar enough with them to study intelligently those on his own patients and be able to recognize some of the common aberrations.

There are many subtleties in the interpretation of abdominal plain films, to be sure, and it is easy to feel, when you first begin to look at them, that you are missing important and obvious changes. The process by which we observe visually is immensely complex. For the retina to receive, the optic tracts to transmit, and the cortex of the brain to register and record variations in the intensity and shape of gray shadows is so remarkable a process that one can only wonder at its occurring at all. Though it still wants much more complete investigation, the visual learning process has begun to be studied in many different ways. There is evidence that some persons "see" and remember shadows with more facility than others, just as some can recall maps from memory while others cannot. Most of us, however, can *learn* to see and remember shapes and variations in density, and when the learning process is reinforced by reasoning, it is still more surely within the grasp of any observer, whatever his particular gifts may be.

The most informed and experienced workers in the field of visual observation and learning processes believe that the *expert* makes most of his observations at random rather than as a result of any systematic search pattern. Clues to meaning in a radiograph appear to be much more nearly a question of knowing what to look *for* rather than what to look *at*, implying a rapid intellectualization of observations as fast as they are made. This is still very incompletely understood and need not concern you, except to explain to you why you will find the radiologist sometimes making a correct diagnosis almost before he has had time to glance at a film. Much more often he, too, must study and restudy a radiograph before he can understand what is implied by the shadows he sees.

At your stage of learning, however, an orderly manner of approaching the analysis of an abdominal plain film can be strongly recommended. I would suggest that you make a practice of looking first at the bones on a plain film of the abdomen (lower ribs, vertebral column, pelvis), excluding from your mind's eye all other structures. (If you do not look at the bones first, you will almost certainly forget them later.) Then examine carefully the soft tissues of a series of smaller areas to include the left upper quadrant, right upper quadrant, both flanks, mid-abdomen, and pelvis, in that order. In each soft-tissue zone you will be checking border indicators, organ masses, and fat lines, looking for calcification and for any shift in position or change in shape of the structures you can see and identify.

Although in the final chapter you will be directing a closer scrutiny to the radiographically rendered structure of bones in general, you must include here a survey of the bones seen on the usual plain film of the abdomen. Nearly all the abdominal films you see will have been made with the Bucky diaphragm, and you will observe that you can see the ribs below the diaphragm much better than you do in chest films. The last two ribs arise from their vertebral articulations and extend laterally without being joined to the costal cartilages.

Calcifications in the costal cartilages (which are normally radiolucent and invisible) may offer some confusion when they are seen superimposed on intra-abdominal calcifications within the gallbladder, kidney, or adrenal gland. Rib cartilage calcifications can usually be distinguished by tracing the expected course of the rib anteriorly. Lateral films and body-section studies will afford help when there is reasonable doubt as to the location of such upper abdominal calcifications.

Examine the plain film on the opposite page. Can you identify any organ masses? Are there any unexpected soft-tissue masses? Is air-in-gut displaced from any part of the abdomen? Are the psoas shadows symmetrical? Look for unexpected areas of calcium density. Is the sacroiliac joint visible? What do you make of the small dark shadows in the right iliac wing? Analyze the shadows of the vertebrae.

Figure 11-27 *(Unknown 11-3)*. (See text.)

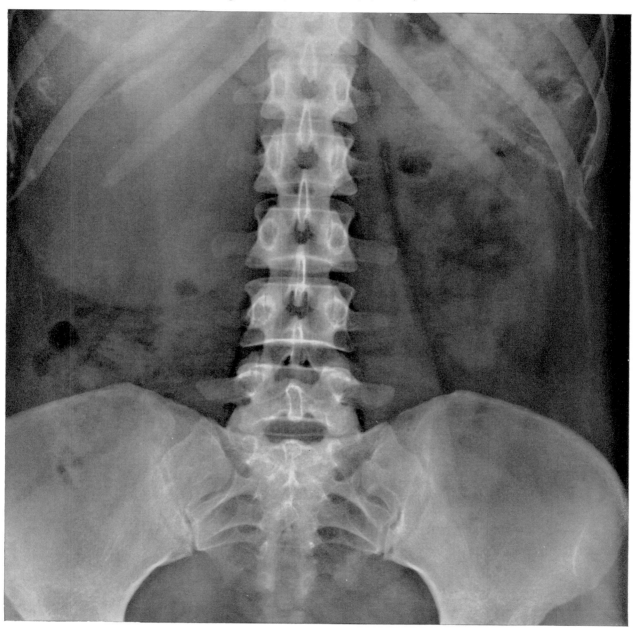

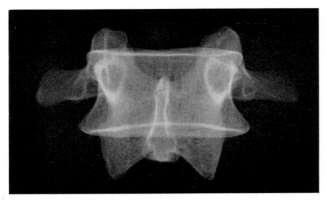

Figure 11-28. Radiograph of a single disarticulated vertebra.

Figure 11-29 (right).

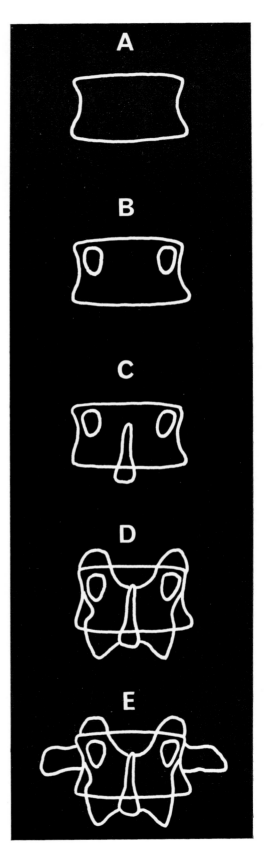

The shadows of the *lumbar vertebrae* may appear very confusing when you first look at them, but they will be easy to comprehend and remember once you have analyzed them part for part. To begin with, the box-like body of a vertebra, extending anteriorly, would have a very simple roentgen structure if it could be seen by itself and not superimposed on the complex posterior articulating processes. Because it is literally a flat cylindrical box of dense cortical bone filled with spongy bone, you would expect it to radiograph with a shell of tangentially seen (and therefore denser) bone outlining it and an interior of many superimposed slender white trabeculae with dark marrow spaces between.

Add to this box outline, now in the PA projection, the two pedicles, cylinders of cortical bone extending straight backward on either side of the spinal canal. Because they, too, are filled with spongy bone, they will radiograph as cylinders seen end-on and, as you can predict, will appear on the film as two white circles. Now as you look at the vertebrae on any plain film of the abdomen, you can account for the two "eyes" which you see superimposed on the upper part of each vertebral body.

The centrally placed white teardrop is, of course, the cortical bone investing the spinous process, also filled with spongy bone. The pairs of superior and inferior articulating processes are also to be seen as wings of bone extending upward and downward from each vertebral body to create a butterfly-like shadow behind the vertebral body. Finally, the transverse processes extend out to each side, varying slightly in shape from level to level.

192

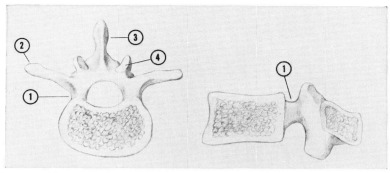

Figure 11-30. Vertebra seen from above and from the side.

1. Pedicle
2. Transverse process
3. Spinous process
4. Superior articulating process

If you always think first of the outline of the vertebral body as you look at the spine on an abdominal film, and then add the posterior structures one by one, you will not be confused by the jumble of overlapping bony parts. Realize, too, that a pathologic process which destroys any part of these bony structures will cause the disappearance of a shadow you are now expecting to see and can usually trace because of its symmetry with the same structure on the other side, or above or below at a different level. Thus, if an aneurysm erodes the left lateral surface of the first and second lumbar vertebrae where the aorta lies closely against them, you will see that the cortex on one side is missing, interrupting the smooth squared outline of the body. In the lateral projection, some part of the anterior surface of the body will also be missing, the intervertebral discs being better preserved than the bone because they resist pressure erosion better.

By the same token, when an expanding intraspinal tumor destroys the medial bony wall of the pedicles, the radiologist observes that the medial sides of one or more pairs of "eyes" are flattened and farther apart than those above and below them.

The bilateral symmetry of the posterior structures superimposed upon the vertebral body will be useful to you in another way, because it tells you that the film was made AP or PA with the ray passing sagittally through the patient. Routinely, plain films of the abdomen are made AP with the patient supine, but some barium studies and all gallbladder studies are made PA with the patient prone. (Why?) Many types of special procedures are made in conventional degrees of obliquity, and you will find that the appearance of the vertebrae indicates the direction of the ray.

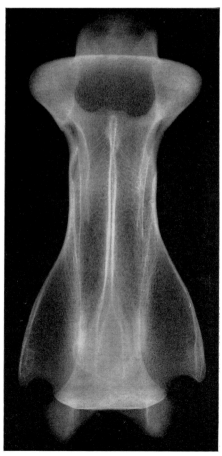

Figure 11-31 (*Unknown 11-4*). Identify. The object radiographed was 9 inches long.

193

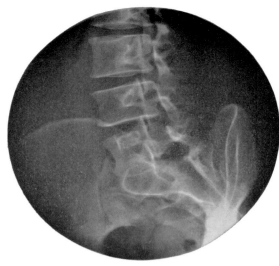

Figure 11-32. Oblique view of the lumbar vertebrae.

Thus if you see the boxy bodies of the vertebrae cleanly separated from their posterior structures, you will know that you are looking at a lateral film, but if the bodies and posterior structures are precisely superimposed and bilaterally symmetrical, you are looking at a film made with a sagittal ray. Obliques will show you the vertebrae about as you see them in Figure 11-32, and note that now you can see through the obliquely directed posterior articulations. All this will have prepared you for the partial obliquity you will often be seeing with scoliosis of the spine, no matter how carefully the technician has tried to position the patient prone or supine.

Figure 11-33. AP and lateral views of disarticulated specimen of lumbar vertebrae. Identify the various parts without turning back to page 192.

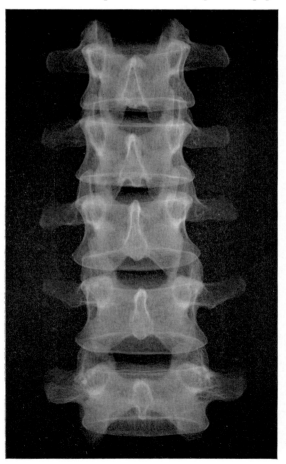
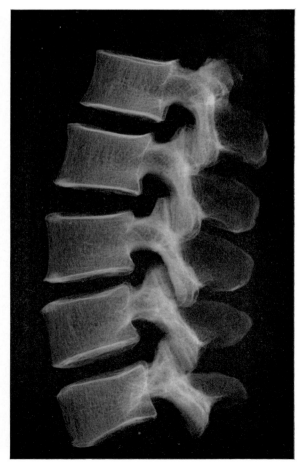

194

Two patients complaining of back pain.

Unknown 11-5 (Figure 11-34) (right). Plain film of the abdomen cropped in such a way that you will focus your attention on the bones rather than on the soft tissues (which are also interesting). Describe any abnormalities.

Unknown 11-6 (Figure 11-35) (below). Analyze the vertebral shadows, determine any abnormalities, and suggest a diagnosis from the films.

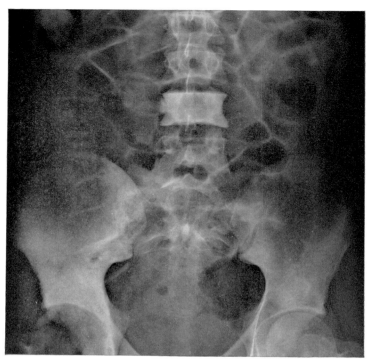

Figure 11-34 *(Unknown 11-5)*

Figure 11-35 *(Unknown 11-6)*

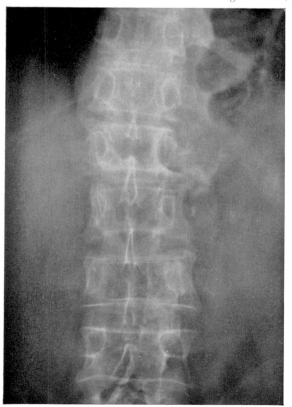

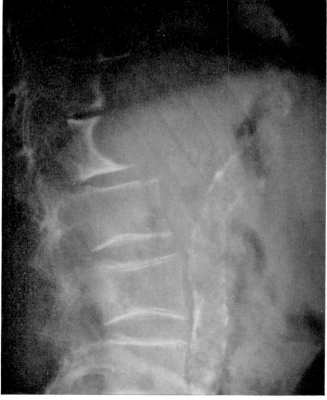

195

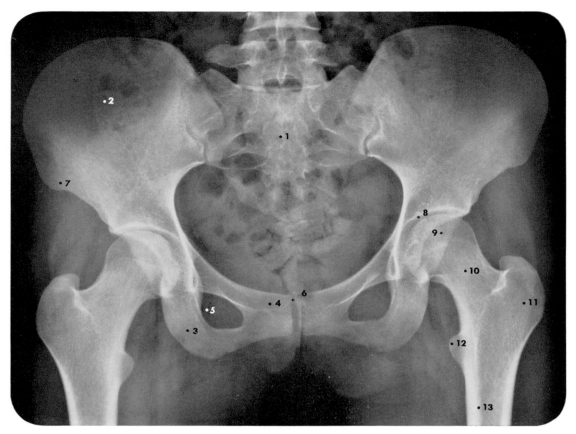

Figure 11-36. Anteroposterior radiograph of the pelvis and upper femora.

1. Sacrum
2. Ilium
3. Ischium
4. Pubis
5. Obturator foramen
6. Symphysis pubis
7. Anterior superior iliac spine
8. Acetabulum
9. Femoral head
10. Femoral neck
11. Greater trochanter
12. Lesser trochanter
13. Femoral shaft

The bones of the pelvis differ in the shape of their shadows when the ray passes through PA and AP, as you can anticipate if you think of the structure of the flared and tilted wings of the ilium. These are "flattened out against the film," appearing round and wide on a supine plain film but narrow and more vertical on barium enema films made with the patient prone. This is because the ray which passes through the patient PA is much more nearly tangential to the surface of the iliac wings, so that they are more approximately filmed on edge.

The ray is usually centered on the umbilicus in making a plain film of the abdomen, and therefore roughly half the air-in-gut shadows will be below this point. You will therefore expect to see superimposed on the bones of the pelvis and sacrum the air in cecum, sigmoid, and rectum, as well as in small bowel loops when they do contain air. A loop of air-containing bowel overlying the iliac wing on a supine plain film is often very difficult to differentiate from a round area of bone destruction, and the procedure is to look over several films of the area: small bowel air changes in shape and location from film to film, but an area of bone destruction will remain in exactly the same relation with the margins of the bone in which it is present.

Note that you see through the cartilaginous part of the anterior portion of the sacroiliac joint and through the symphysis pubis. Identify the spines and tuberosities of the ischia, and note that the hip joint is "seen" because it is bounded on both sides by the cortical bone of acetabulum and femoral head, seen in tangent. Later, when you have read the section on bone, you will look at the bones on a plain film of the abdomen with a more precise eye for abnormalities, but for now leave them and go on to a study of the series of soft-tissue zones.

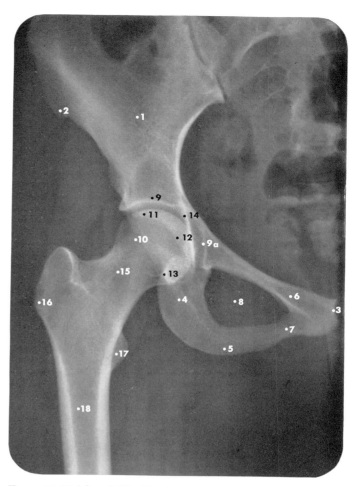

Figure 11-37 (above). The hip joint.

1. Ilium
2. Anterior superior iliac spine
3. Symphysis pubis
4. Superior ischial ramus
5. Inferior ischial ramus
6. Superior pubic ramus
7. Inferior pubic ramus
8. Obturator foramen
9-9a. Portion of acetabular roof tangential to ray
10. Posterior portion of acetabular rim
11. Anterior superior portion of acetabular rim
12. Anterior inferior portion of acetabular rim
13. Posterior end of facies lunata
14. Wall of pelvic cavity
15. Femoral neck
16. Greater trochanter
17. Lesser trochanter
18. Marrow cavity, femoral shaft

Figure 11-38 (below). Radiolucent area of bone destruction indicated by arrows did not change in relation to the margin of the sacroiliac joint from film to film. The darker air shadows lateral to it did.

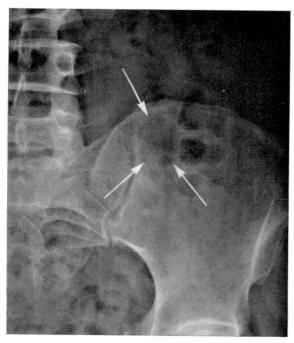

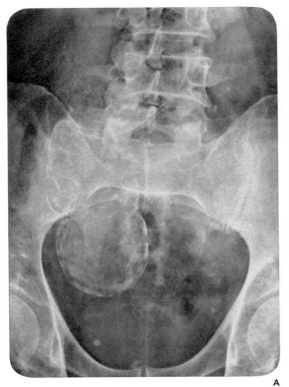

A

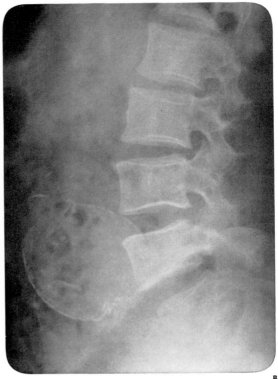

B

Figure 11-39 *(Unknown 11-7)* (above, left and right). From the type of calcification here, what can you say in a very general way about the distribution of radiodense material? What anatomic structures might be identified with the calcified mass? The small round calcification near the brim of the pelvis is a phlebolith about which you will read more in the next chapter.

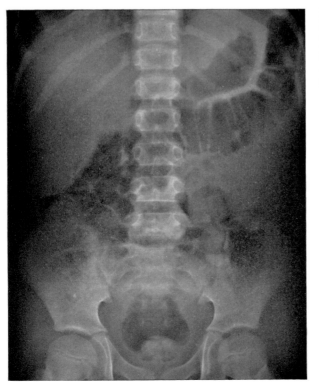

Figure 11-40 *(Unknown 11-8)* (left). Plain film of the abdomen. Identify the following: stomach, transverse colon, splenic flexure, liver margin, hepatic flexure, rectum.

Credits: Illustrations this chapter.

Figure 11-2. Courtesy Dr. J. Hope et al., and the publisher, *MR&P* 33:37.

Figure 11-3. Courtesy Drs. B. Kalayjian and M. Sapula, and the publisher, *MR&P* 30:57.

Figure 11-4. Courtesy Dr. J. McGillivray and the publisher, *MR&P* 30:27.

Figures 11-5, 11-6, 11-14. Courtesy Drs. J. Hope and C. Koop, and the publisher, *MR&P* 38:31, 45, 49.

Figure 11-8C. Courtesy Dr. C. Stevenson, Spokane, Wash.

Figure 11-11. Courtesy Dr. R. Alexander, Rochester, N. Y.

Figure 11-15. Courtesy Messrs. G. Thompson and W. Cornwell, and the publisher, *MR&P* 25:43.

Figure 11-16. Courtesy Drs. R. Gould and W. Thorwarth, and the publisher, *Radiology* 80:744.

Figure 11-18. Courtesy Mr. J. Cahoon, Jr., Durham, N. C.

Figure 11-19. Courtesy Drs. S. Larson and W. Madden, and the publisher, *MR&P* 24:27.

Figure 11-20. Courtesy Mr. V. Yamamoto and the publisher, *MR&P* 26:121.

Figure 11-23. Courtesy Drs. R. Salb and G. Burton, and the publisher, *MR&P* 33:106.

Figure 11-24. Courtesy Dr. F. Nelans, Wagner, Okla.

Figure 11-25. Courtesy Dr. J. Jiminez and the publisher, *MR&P* 25:53.

Figure 11-26. Courtesy Dr. L. Cole, Blossburg, Pa.

Figure 11-27. Courtesy Dr. J. Pepe, Brooklyn, N. Y.

Figure 11-32. Courtesy Messrs. E. Holly and G. Weingartner, and the publisher, *MR&P* 29:91.

Figure 11-34. Courtesy Dr. J. Tollman, Omaha, Neb.

Figure 11-35. Courtesy Dr. G. Hutto, Columbus, Ga.

Figures 11-36, 11-37. Courtesy Mr. C. Bridgman and the publisher, *MR&P* 26:12, 15.

Figure 11-38. Courtesy Dr. W. Tuddenham and the publisher, *Radiology* 78:697.*

Figure 11-39. Courtesy the late Dr. J. Morton, Dr. N. Gehringer, and the publisher, *MR&P* 30:88.

*The student will be interested in reading "Problems of Perception in Chest Roentgenology: Facts and Fallacies" by William J. Tuddenham, M.D., published in *The Radiologic Clinics of North America*, Vol. 1, No. 2, August 1963, (Saunders).

CHAPTER 12

The Abdomen: Examination of Soft
Tissue Zones on the Plain Film

The first soft-tissue zone, that of the *left upper quadrant,* contains the spleen, stomach, left kidney and adrenal, the splenic flexure of the colon, and the tail of the pancreas. Some of these structures will be outlined for you on the plain film by air, which they normally contain; others are seen whenever fat or air is juxtaposed to one of their margins; still others are only visible as the result of special procedures; and at least one, the left part of the pancreas, is never visible normally and has been visualized artificially only by isotope scanning.

The *spleen,* when normal in size, applies itself neatly against the under surface of the left diaphragm, above, lateral and posterior to the stomach. Its upper surface conforms to the lateral part of the left diaphragmatic outline as you have seen it on the chest film, and its inferior tip may be visible outlined against fatty omentum or abutted against air-filled colon. The *splenic flexure* is quite variable in position. It may be indented by the tip of the spleen, overlap it partly, or extend over it as high as the diaphragm. It should not be hard for you to identify in such cases, since it will have the characteristic smooth haustral indentations of colon as opposed to the crinkled margin of the stomach shadow.

The *stomach* itself is almost never difficult to identify. In the supine plain film the air in the stomach will rise into its more anteriorly placed antrum, outlining the heavy rugal folds of gastric mucosa. In the prone position, whatever air is present will rise into the posteriorly placed fundus, so that on a prone plain film made with a sagittal ray the air bubble of the stomach ap-

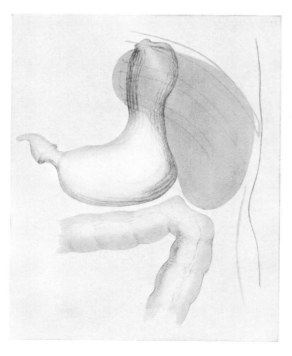

Figure 12-1. The normal stomach indented by an enlarged spleen which depresses the splenic flexure. Shown as it would look if you could see all three structures.

pears as a round dark shadow with a wrinkled margin nearer the diaphragm. These differences, in fact, will also help you to decide whether a film has been made supine or prone. The same principles apply to barium studies of the stomach, as you will see later.

The *left kidney,* located far posteriorly in the hollow lateral to the vertebral column, is often visible because of its perirenal envelope of fatty tissue. At nephrectomy most of this fat is left in place and retains its general distribution, while the space vacated by the kidney is filled with clots and gradually fibroses. As a result you may *seem* to see the outline of a kidney you know to have been removed surgically. The left kidney lies a little higher than the right, its superior pole tilted medially against the origin of the psoas muscle, but the tricorne-shaped *adrenal gland* which caps it is not visible except after a special procedure in which gas is injected retroperitoneally. The gas dissects between structures whose shadows are normally confluent, and may be seen to lift the outlined adrenal slightly away from the kidney, rendering all its margins visible.

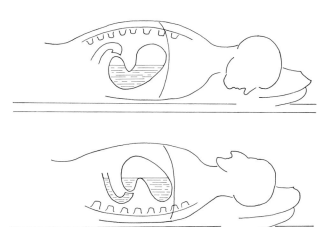

Figure 12-3. Explanation for difference in the stomach air bubble on plain films made with the patient prone (above) and supine (below).

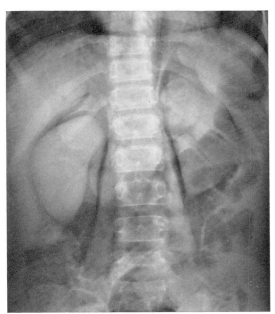

Figure 12-4 (above). Kidneys and adrenals visible in detail because they have been studied radiographically after retroperitoneal injection of gas. The enlarged right adrenal is well seen as a round soft-tissue mass superimposed on the upper pole of the right kidney. It was caused by a large pheochromocytoma successfully removed from this 12-year-old boy.

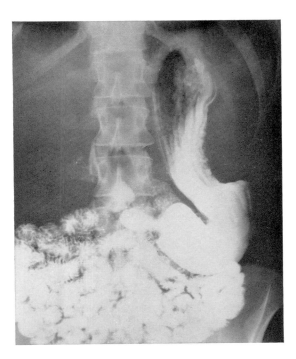

Figure 12-2 (left). The normal stomach filled with barium and indented by an enlarged spleen.

201

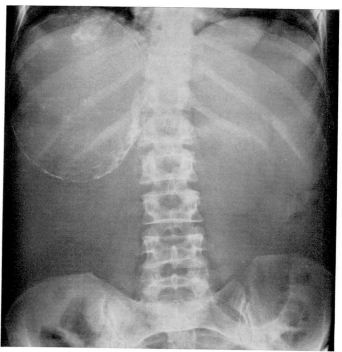

Figure 12-5. Large echinococcus cyst in the liver, calcified peripherally. Tip of spleen and outline of lower pole of left kidney are clearly seen.

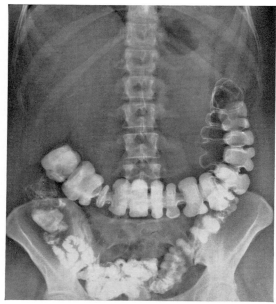

Figure 12-6 (*Unknown 12-1*). Identify splenic and hepatic flexures and tip of liver (not felt on physical examination). Judging from the stomach bubble, was this film made prone or supine?

The structures of the *right upper quadrant* include the liver, gallbladder, right kidney, adrenal gland, and hepatic flexure of the colon. The *liver*, so much larger than the spleen, normally tends to depress the organs in this quadrant. Its margin may be seen either as the inferior limit of a gray mass or as a boundary outlined by air in the transverse colon and hepatic flexure. The *hepatic flexure* is usually lower than the splenic flexure, but may occasionally overlap a part of the liver shadow. Radioisotope scanning techniques are becoming increasingly practicable for routine use in studying the liver, and metastatic lesions may be localized readily within the liver parenchyma. No secretory roentgenographic opacification technique is available at present.

The shadow of the *gallbladder* may occasionally be seen on the plain film as a rounded shadow superimposed over the liver margin and right kidney. It has for many years been successfully rendered visible by administering (by mouth or by vein) radio-opaque compounds which are excreted by the liver. These materials do not concentrate sufficiently within the liver cells to visualize them, but the common duct and ultimately the gallbladder are well visualized. With the administration of a fatty meal (or cholecystokinin) the gallbladder is made to contract, affording a second opportunity to visualize the cystic and common bile ducts.

The *right kidney*, like the left applied against the upper psoas shadow and tilted inward at its upper pole, lies a little lower than the left in most patients, displaced by the mass of the liver. Stones present in the gallbladder may be superimposed upon the shadow of the kidney or vice versa. One of the organs lies far posteriorly and the other against the anterior abdominal wall. Consequently, films intended for study of the kidney are usually made supine, with the kidneys as close as possible to the film, while gallbladder studies are made with the patient prone. The location of stones in either can usually be determined by making both prone and supine films, but where there is any question, lateral films and body-section studies may be employed. Supine oblique films are also very helpful.

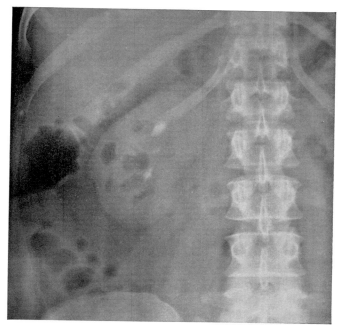

Figure 12-7. The right kidney unusually well seen and apparently containing several stones. Could these possibly be in the gallbladder?

Figure 12-8. The normal gallbladder filled with physiologically concentrated opaque material (cholecystogram). A fatty meal has just been given, and the gallbladder is contracting so that the cystic duct, common bile duct, and, by reflux, a part of the hepatic duct are outlined with contrast material. Scattered flecks of dense white are leftover orally administered opaque material in the gut.

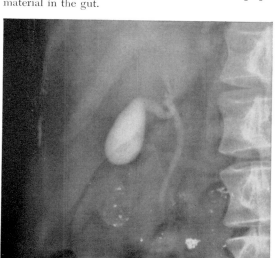

Figure 12-9. Cholangiogram, a visualization of the common bile duct in a patient whose gallbladder has been removed. Contrast substance administered intravenously.

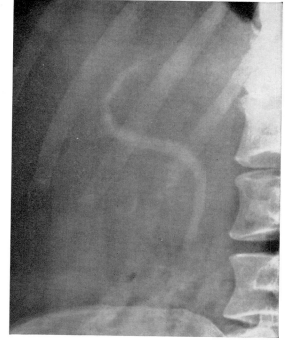

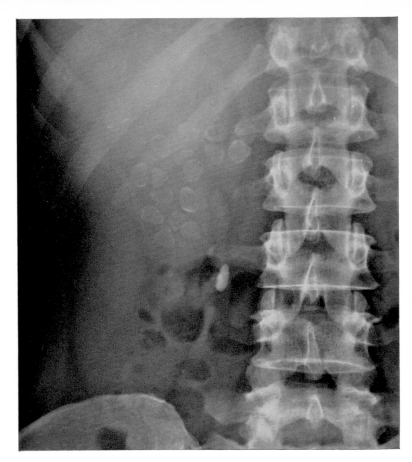

Figure 12-10 (left). Plain film showing gallstones and a solitary kidney stone in the same patient.

Figure 12-11 (below, left). Cholecystogram with faint visualization of the gallbladder (between lower two arrows at left) and three stones in the common duct (arrows at right). Do not misread the tear-shaped shadow above the lowest arrow, an overlap between gallbladder and kidney.

Figure 12-12 (immediately below). Poor function in a diseased gallbladder which fails to concentrate the radio-opaque material excreted by the liver. Arrows indicate faceted stones in the gallbladder and two stones in the common duct.

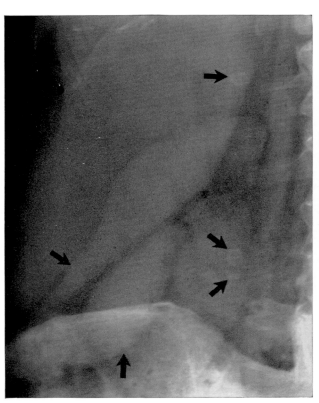

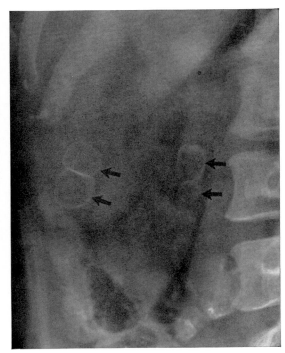

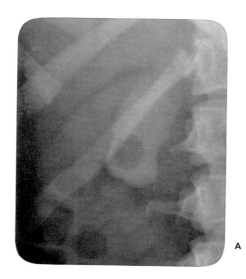

A

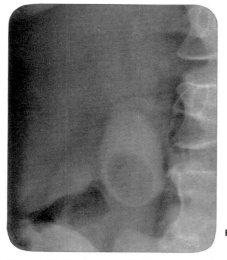

B

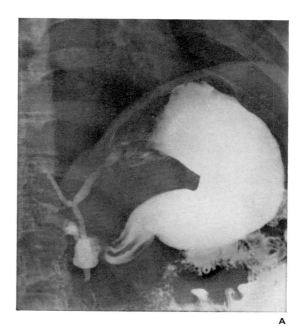

A

Figure 12-14. Sometimes barium administered for a gastrointestinal series demonstrates a fistulous communication between gallbladder and duodenum. As you see in *A* (above), there is barium in what can only be the biliary tree. In *B* (below), made later the same day, barium and air are seen in the ducts.

Figure 12-13. *A* (top). Cholecystogram shows concentration of opaque material and an entirely radiolucent stone composed of materials which rendered it invisible on the plain film. *B* (immediately above). The same stone is larger after 14 years. *C* (below). Postoperative specimen.

C

B

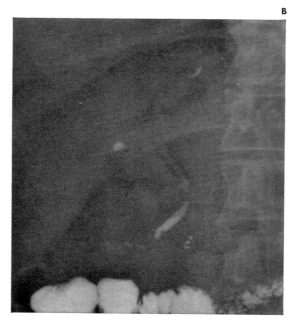

Examine the *flanks* next, on both sides of the abdomen. The flank stripes may be obscured by the intense black of this area which is often "burned out" at exposures calculated to penetrate the bones of the pelvis. Flank stripes may often be seen well in spite of this by placing the film against a bright light, kept handy by radiologists for the illumination of dark areas on films. The flank stripes will usually be symmetrical bilaterally in thin patients who have been positioned carefully. The dark haustrated colon should be seen lying close against the flank stripe. Free peritoneal fluid will bulge out the flank and separate the colon appreciably from the flank stripe. In the presence of inflammation nearby, the flank stripe on that side will be seen to be smudged.

Your special survey of the upper *mid-abdomen* includes some structures which you have "looked for" already, since only an arbitrary division can separate those structures which lie in the upper right and left quadrants from those which, like the pancreas, lie partly also in the mid-abdomen. Think of the mid-abdominal structures three-dimensionally, beginning with those most anteriorly placed. The body of the *stomach,* with its J-shaped streak of air in the supine patient, lies anteriorly against the abdominal wall and just above the curve of the air-containing *transverse colon.* The antrum and *duodenal bulb* (or cap) turn and point posteriorly so that they are best seen in the lateral view. The bulb and descending limb of the *duodenal loop,* which is partly retroperitoneal, turn downward, passing around the head of the *pancreas,* to the left and upward again toward the ligament of Treitz to join the *jejunum.* The duodenum is generally fluid-filled and invisibly merged on the plain film with the shadows and other solid or fluid-containing structures near it, although you will see the duodenal loop regularly on barium studies and from it construe the position of the always invisible pancreas.

The *gallbladder* usually lies close against the lateral surface of the duodenal bulb and descending duodenum, the latter receiving on its medial surface the common bile duct which empties through the ampulla of Vater after having traversed the substance of the head of the pancreas. The gallbladder and ducts are not visible without contrast substances unless they happen to contain stones or air.

The *pancreas,* its head encircled by the loop of the duodenum, lies below and behind the antrum and body of the stomach and against the bodies of the upper lumbar vertebrae as they project forward into the abdomen. The pancreas is invisible unless it contains calcifications and stones scattered through it which outline and mark its position. It may be indirectly bounded by organs which normally lie close to it, and a large mass in the head of the pancreas, for example, may expand the duodenal loop and displace the antrum of the stomach forward. As yet, no radiographic means of studying the pancreas functionally has been developed, the problem being to discover a safely administered radio-opaque chemical which is selectively secreted with the pancreatic juices. The pancreas may be "seen" with isotope scanning techniques.

Further posteriorly on either side of the spine are situated the *kidneys,* the left a little higher than the right in most patients, the upper poles of both tilted toward the mid-line. You should trace their outlines as completely as possible. You will have some difficulty outlining the kidneys on a good many plain films because they are nearly always partly obscured by varying amounts of gas in the gut. Make a practice of searching the area for the kidney outline or *any part of it* from which you may be able to resolve the whole shadow. Sometimes you can see the upper and lower poles on one film and the lateral surface on another. If you see no kidney shadow at all on a single film of good quality, it may mean that the kidney is very small with little or no perirenal fat, or that the kidney is ptosed or located ectopically in the pelvis or on the opposite side.

The kidneys are studied specifically by the use of renally excreted radio-opaque chemicals (the intravenous urogram), or by injecting similar contrast substances through catheters placed in the ureters during cystoscopy (the retrograde pyelogram). Either procedure results in visualization of the draining structures of the kidney: the calices, pelvis, ureters and bladder.

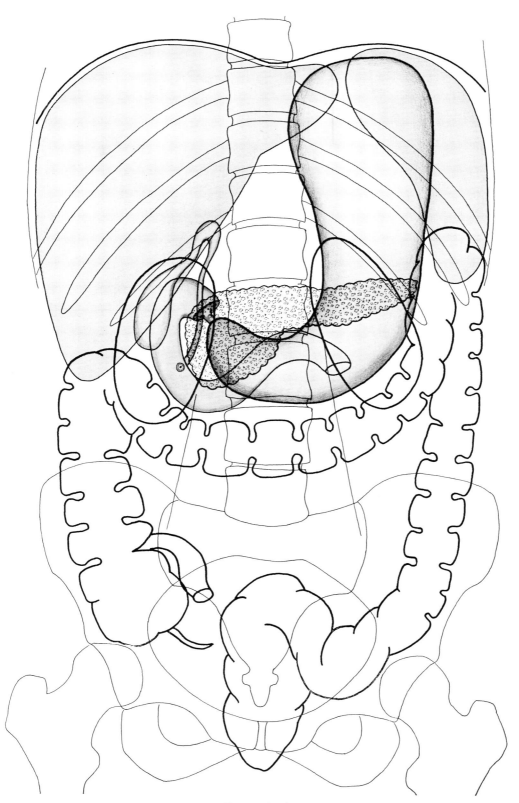

Figure 12-15

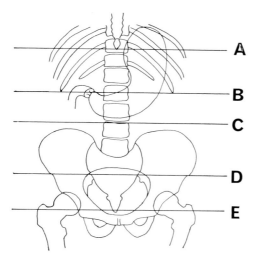

Figure 12-16

Figures 12-16 through 12-21. Schema and cross-section diagrams at indicated levels to help you think three-dimensionally about the abdomen. Remember that all such general diagrams as these will vary slightly for the individual you are examining.

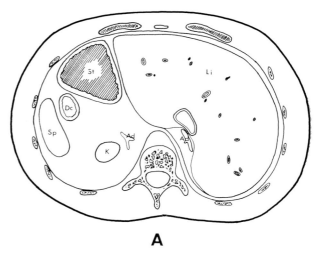

A

Figure 12-17

Figure 12-18

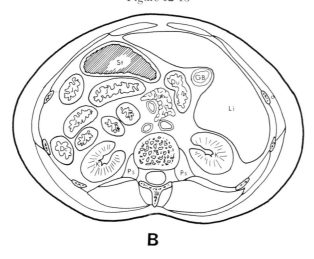

B

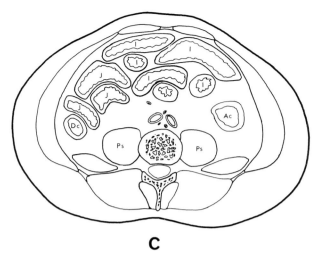

C

Figure 12-19

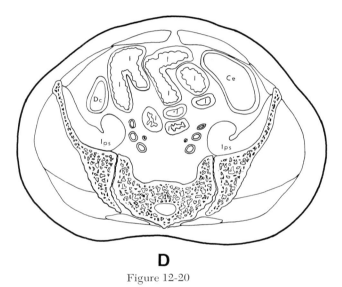

D

Figure 12-20

Figure 12-21

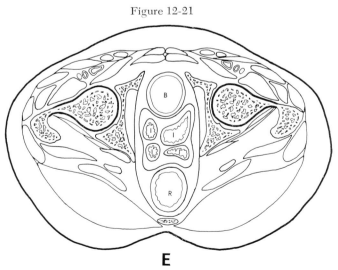

E

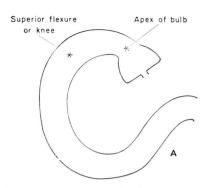

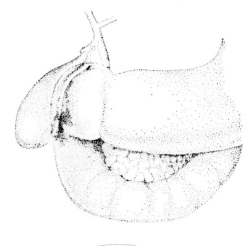

Figure 12-22. *A* (above). The duodenal loop, seen diagrammatically. *B* (right, above). Antrum of the stomach, duodenal bulb and loop in relation to the stomach and the gallbladder. *C* (right). Cross-sectional diagram through the middle of the duodenal bulb.

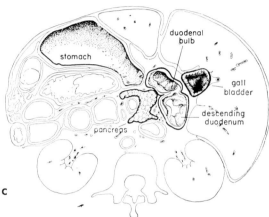

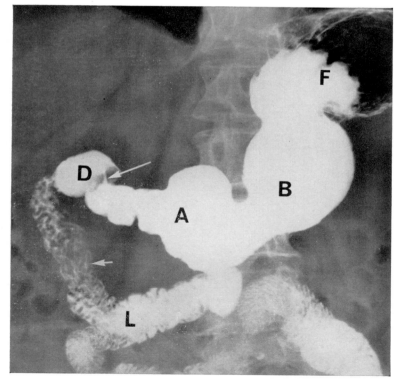

Figure 12-23 (left). Radiograph showing the stomach and duodenal loop. Deep indentations in the stomach are peristaltic waves. *F*, fundus; *B*, body; *A*, antrum; *D*, duodenal bulb or cap. Long arrow indicates pylorus, visualized here as a stream of barium passes through it, although it is not usually seen so well. Short arrow indicates the site of the ampulla of Vater on the medial surface of the descending limb of the loop. *L*, ascending limb of the duodenal loop which passes left to the ligament of Treitz and joins the jejunum.

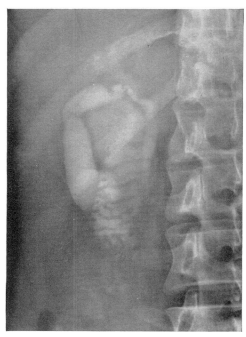

Figure 12-24 (above). The characteristic mucosal markings of the duodenum identify that structure as it fills with contrast substance from the gallbladder and common duct via the ampulla of Vater immediately after a fatty meal. Note that there is even reflux of opaque fluid into the duodenal bulb.

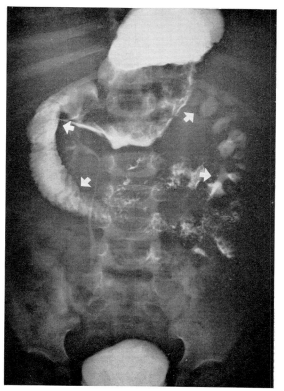

Figure 12-25 (above). A large malignant mass in the head of the pancreas expands the duodenal loop, here, compresses and elevates the antrum of the stomach, and obstructs and displaces the left kidney to the left. Film was made with barium in the upper gastrointestinal tract during pyelography, about half an hour after intravenous administration of renally excreted contrast substance.

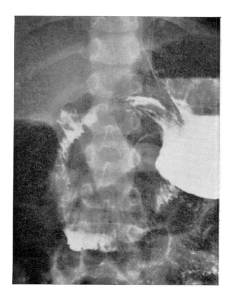

Figure 12-26 (right). The duodenal loop expanded by a pseudo cyst in the head of the pancreas resulting from trauma to the epigastrium when this 7-year-old boy fell off his bicycle.

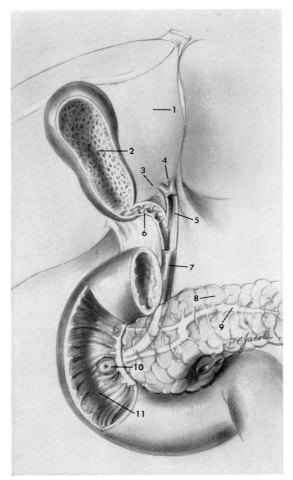

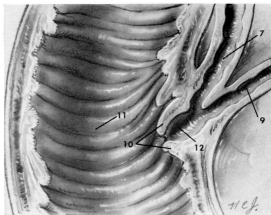

Figure 12-27 (left and above). Anatomy of the biliary tract:

1. Liver
2. Gallbladder, reflected upward
3. Right hepatic duct
4. Left hepatic duct
5. Common hepatic duct
6. Cystic duct
7. Common bile duct
8. Pancreas
9. Pancreatic duct
10. Duodenal papilla
11. Descending limb of the duodenal loop
12. Ampulla of Vater

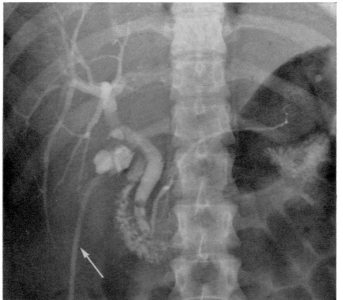

Figure 12-28 (left). Operative cholangiogram, a procedure which has been used following cholecystectomy to visualize the biliary tree and determine whether there is free emptying of bile into the small bowel. Arrow indicates the catheter through which the contrast substance is being injected. It is attached to a T-tube placed within the common duct. There is some reflux into the bed of the gallbladder. The tree of hepatic radicles is visible as well as the common duct, and there is reflux filling of the pancreatic duct behind the dark, air-filled stomach. The duodenal loop is beginning to fill. Round radiolucencies in the lower part of the common duct could represent retained calculi. A better procedure, preferred by some surgeons, is *primary cholangiography,* in which the injection of contrast substance is made before cholecystectomy is carried out. The abdomen is opened, a cannula tied into the cystic duct, and the common duct and hepatic tree opacified. This procedure differentiates calculi from air bubbles.

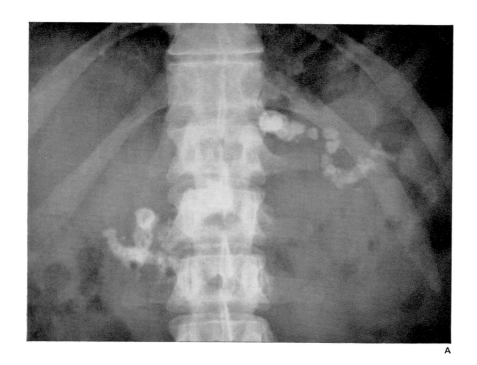

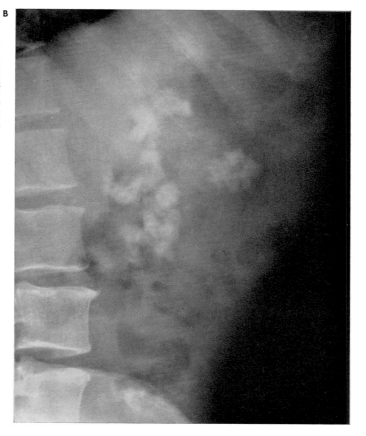

Figure 12-29. Plain film of the upper mid-abdomen showing many calcium-containing concretions in the pancreas, outlining its entire structure. Lateral view, *B* (right), confirms their presence in the location of the pancreas close to the anterior surface of the lumbar vertebrae. This occurs in some cases of chronic pancreatitis and is frequently associated with alcoholism.

Study the lower mid-abdomen next; follow the known course of the ureters along the psoas shadows down to the bladder, looking for any shadow which could represent a calculus. The ureters are invisible on the plain film, but their shadows outlined with contrast material on pyelograms will help you to learn the variations in their position. Many plain films show small, round, calcium-dense shadows just inside the brim of the bony pelvis. These are calcified thrombi in the pelvic veins, or *phleboliths*, and generally lie closer to the margin of the bowl of the pelvis than any part of the ureter. Their position, then, will help you to distinguish them from calculi, and you will also be helped by the fact that calculi may be any shape at all and often have jagged points in their shadow profiles, whereas phleboliths are invariably smooth and round, and sometimes show a central radiolucency, like a bead ready for stringing, where they have been recanalized.

The lower mid-abdomen is a common location for calcified mesenteric nodes, and they will not usually be mistaken for ureteral stones because they tend to look like clusters of smaller concretions and are somewhat denser than most stones. They vary widely in position from film to film as a rule because of the mobility of the small bowel mesentery. They often overlap the bony structures of the vertebral column and sacrum.

The many loops of small bowel are contained for the most part in the lower mid-abdomen and pelvis. In the normal ambulatory adult, as we have said, they contain fluid and little or no air, but as you will be seeing plain films mostly on patients sick enough to be hospitalized, you will become accustomed to seeing some air-outlined loops of small bowel overlying the lower lumbar vertebrae, sacrum, and pelvis. You will learn to distinguish them from the sigmoid colon in the same location because the latter has haustrations and contains solid fecal boluses. These relationships will all be much easier after you have seen a few barium studies.

The soft tissues within the bowl of the pelvis, finally, include the urinary bladder and lower ureters, the sigmoid and rectum, the uterus and adnexa in the female, and the prostate and seminal vesicles in the male. The bladder is commonly visible on the plain film as a somewhat flattened oval shadow within the pelvis when it contains a moderate amount of urine. When it is greatly distended, it may rise up to the umbilicus as a uniformly gray, rounded shadow, not infrequently mistaken for a pathologic mass. The rectum will generally be visible superimposed on the shadow of the bladder and outlined with contained air or feces. The uterus, adnexa, seminal vesicles, and prostate are not visible except by special procedures of various sorts. All may be visualized and studied with injected opaque material, however, and interesting studies have also been made of the female genital organs by introducing free gas into the peritoneal space and studying the outlines of the pelvic organs thrown into contrast by this means.

Figure 12-31 (opposite page). Plain film of the bowl of the pelvis, showing clusters of phleboliths on both sides. The one indicated by the arrow shows recanalization. Note solid fecal scybala within the air shadow of the rectum.

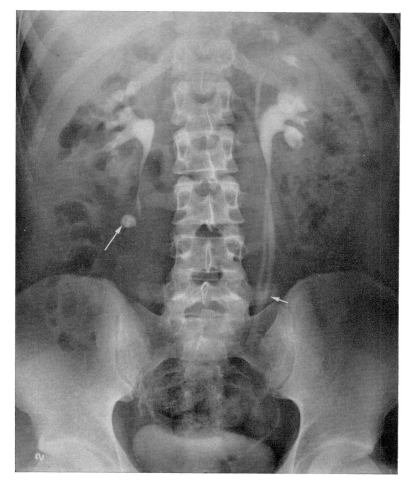

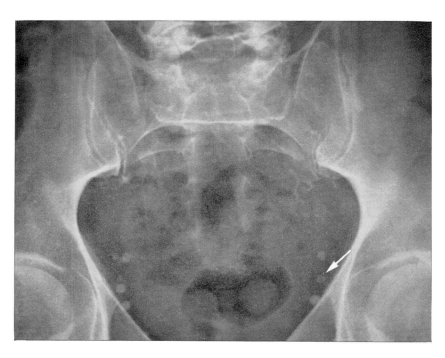

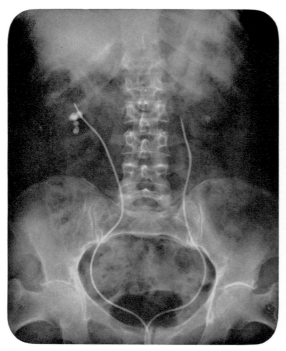

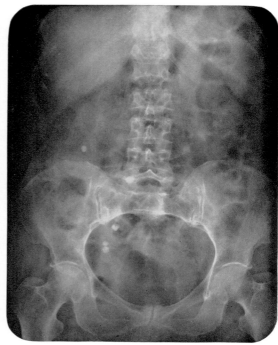

A

B

Figure 12-32. Plain films showing the progress of several calculi down the ureter. *A* (above). The day after admission for hematuria, cystoscopy and retrograde pyelography were performed. This film, made after the initial plain film and before the injection of opaque substance, shows the tips of the catheters in the kidney pelves. Five irregularly round densities overlie the right kidney. *B* (right, above). A month later a plain film shows one stone remaining in the kidney. The other four are in the ureter. No surgical procedure had been undertaken because of the patient's advanced age. All five stones were passed within 10 days.

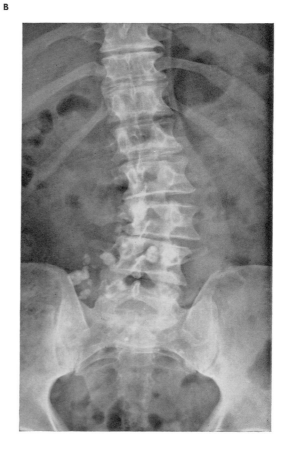

Figure 12-33 (right). A cluster of calcified mesenteric lymph nodes overlie the course of the right ureter near the upper border of the sacroiliac joint. This patient was positioned as straight as possible in the supine position. Note the obliquity produced in the mid-lumbar spine by his degree of scoliosis. The psoas shadows are asymmetrical, as you would expect.

216

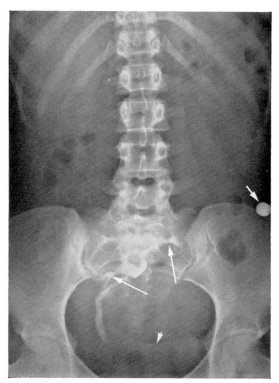

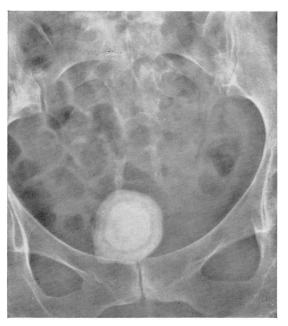

Figure 12-35 (above). Bladder calculus, later removed via the suprapubic route.

Figure 12-34 (above). Solitary ectopic pelvic kidney overlying the sacrum (arrows) visualized by urography after the plain film failed to reveal any kidney shadow on either side in the usual location. Note the short ureter. Shortest pointer indicates the top of the urinary bladder. Pointer in the flank indicates the artifactual shadow cast by a metallic snap fastener in the patient's clothing. *Anything which is perfectly geometric is apt to be an artifact.*

Figure 12-36 (below). Contrast material filling the urinary bladder will help you to recognize the shadow cast by the urine-filled bladder on plain films.

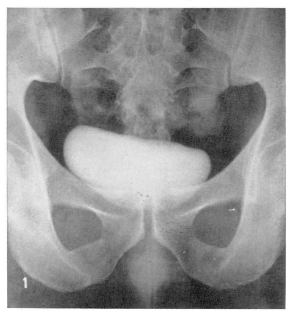

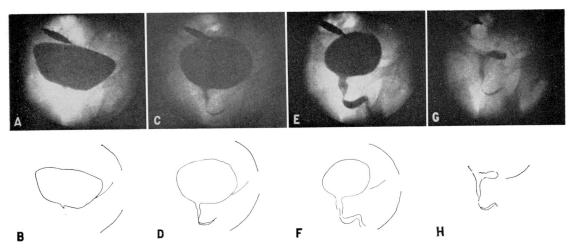

Figure 12-37. The normal urinary bladder during cystourethrography. Here you see a newer clinical technique employing cinefluorography, in which rapid photography of an intensified fluoroscopic image of the bladder enables one to record and study its manner of contraction. The bladder contracts differently in patients with neurogenic (upper and lower motor neuron) disturbances of micturition.

Figure 12-38. The opaque-filled urinary bladder (cystogram) in a patient with prostatic hypertrophy. The filling defect elevating the floor of the bladder is the enlarged prostate gland. Arrows indicate thickened bladder wall.

Figure 12-39. Cystogram shows many radiolucencies outlined by the opaque material within the bladder. These represented malignant tumor nodules.

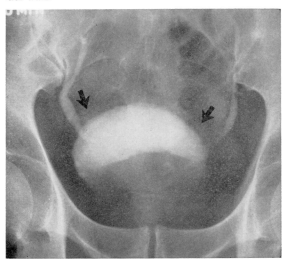

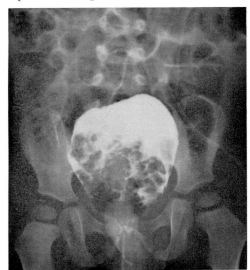

Figure 12-40 (right). The bladder filled with air and used as a means of helping to diagnose placenta praevia. The patient is standing, and normally the fetal head would lie in the mid-line much closer to the top of the bladder. The bladder is seen indented by a soft-tissue mass the thickness of the space between the arrows, which, in a patient with unexplained bleeding near term, strongly suggests a low-lying placenta.

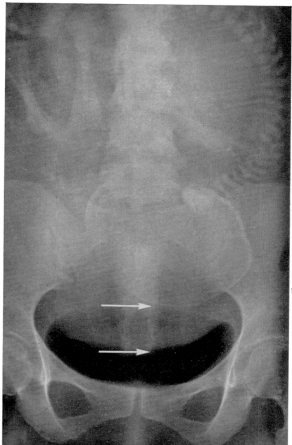

"placenta praevia"

Figure 12-41 (below). A uterosalpingogram. The uterus and fallopian tubes have been filled with a contrast substance as a part of a sterility study. There should be a spill of opaque material from fallopian tubes into the peritoneal cavity, normally.

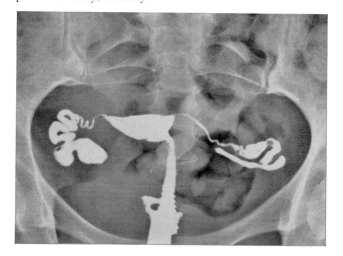

Figure 12-42 (below). Uterosalpingogram showing a double uterine cavity with no filling of the tubes.

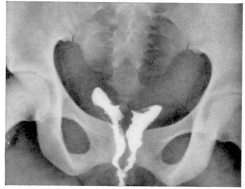

219

Up to this point, then, your survey of the abdominal plain film consists of a systematic study of the bones, soft-tissue structures in the left upper quadrant, right upper quadrant, flanks, upper mid-abdomen, lower mid-abdomen, and pelvis. You are beginning to recognize various anatomic structures in various ways and to draw conclusions about them. You have been helped in this recognition by seeing a few contrast studies, both normal and abnormal. The next step logically is to appreciate abnormality when it exists in the structures you can now identify. Begin by determining what shadow profiles and margins are present on a given plain film, and then try to decide *whether they outline structures which are within the normal range as to size, or too large, or too small, or displaced from their normal position, or abnormal in shape.* To be sure, the refinements of such determinations belong to the expert, but there is no reason why you cannot learn to recognize a good many of the modes in which such determinations are made. Here are a few pointers.

The roentgen investigation of masses whose presence is indicated only by the *displacement of organs which are themselves not abnormal* is something like detective work and entails the visualization by special procedure of every other structure in the region which might possibly identify or help to define the mass in question. Thus you may observe that the stomach itself seems normal enough but that in the lateral view it is seen to be strikingly displaced anteriorly, implying the presence of a space-taking mass behind the stomach which is not visible at all on the plain film.

The displacement of normal organs often follows a pattern which you can learn to predict. A large liver usually displaces stomach, colon, and small bowel down and to the left, and the right kidney downward. The liver border will be seen crossing the abdomen obliquely from left to right outlined by air in the gut which is pushed before it.

A very large spleen always looks as though it were suspended from the left upper quadrant and distinctively displaces the stomach to the right and the colon downward. It displaces the left kidney less regularly, probably because,

as the spleen enlarges, it is received against and supported by the surface of the left iliac wing, so that it is essentially held forward in the abdomen, sparing the kidney. The liver, on the other hand, enlarging as a whole, must usually displace the right kidney downward with its massive under surface. In either case the gastrointestinal structures, although normal themselves, help to outline and identify the organ which is enlarged.

In the same way the anatomic structure of the kidney may appear quite normal, although its *manner* of displacement affords helpful information. It is displaced downward by masses originating in the adrenal gland, as you would expect. It will be displaced laterally with its ureter by an abscess of the psoas sheath. The left kidney will be pushed outward toward the flank by an aneurysm of the abdominal aorta.

Figure 12-43. Large liver displacing gut and right kidney down and to the left. Draining structures of the right kidney are seen filled with opaque substance and overlie the fourth and fifth lumbar vertebrae.

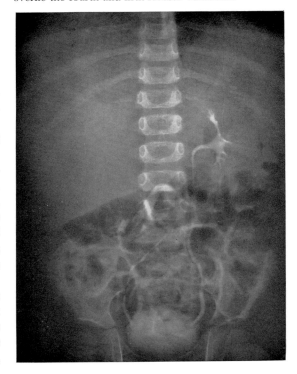

Figure 12-44 (right). A 7-year-old boy, admitted because of crampy abdominal pain and vomiting, showed displacement of barium-filled small bowel from around three soft-tissue masses which were not easy to feel by palpation and at surgery proved to be friable lymphosarcomas in the mesentery.

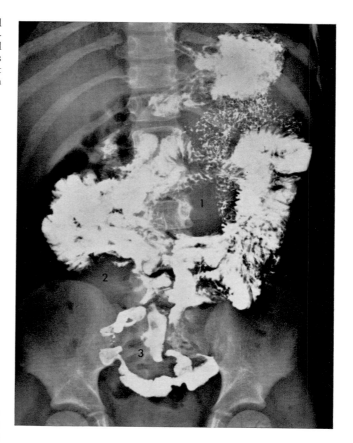

Figure 12-45 (below). Bilateral, old, well-calcified psoas abscesses displacing the kidneys laterally. Note calcified flecks in the dependent portion of each abscess.

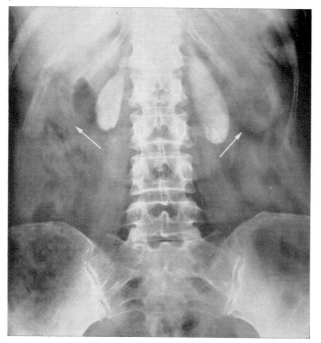

Figure 12-46. The right kidney displaced downward by a mass which proved to be a pheochromocytoma of the right adrenal.

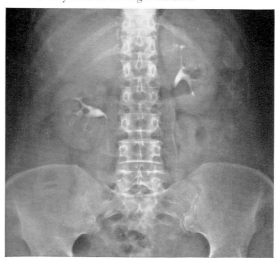

221

Abnormality in size or shape of an organ is frequently appreciable from the plain film alone, but there are some differences in the degree of accuracy with which size may be judged by x-ray. The shadow of the liver is very misleading as an index to its size, for example, and it must be grossly enlarged before one can assume hepatomegaly from the plain film. Partly because of its shape and partly because of variation in the tilted position of the liver within the abdomen, pronouncements with regard to liver enlargement based on the plain film are risky. You will find that as an assay of the liver size, old-fashioned palpation of the liver is a more reliable method.

The spleen, on the contrary, may cast a shadow on the plain film which is unquestionably increased in size, although it is not felt on bimanual examination. In such cases, the roentgen method is often vindicated at surgery or postmortem when the spleen is shown to be, in fact, enlarged. You should learn to place a good deal of reliance on a roentgen impression of splenomegaly. A very large spleen is not difficult to recognize and may reach well below the iliac crest and across the mid-line. When it has been traumatized and its capsule distended with blood, or ruptured with escape of blood into the left gutter, there will be additional roentgen changes present. The radiologist recognizes these as a coarsening of rugal folds in the displaced stomach shadow and a separation of the air-filled colon from the flank stripe. Such findings together with a history of trauma help to place the correct emphasis on the spleen in the whole-patient study. The shape of the spleen may be altered in the presence of splenic cysts, and a bulbous enlargement of its lower margin will be apparent. This localized change differs from that seen in a spleen symmetrically enlarged by pathologic change affecting the entire organ.

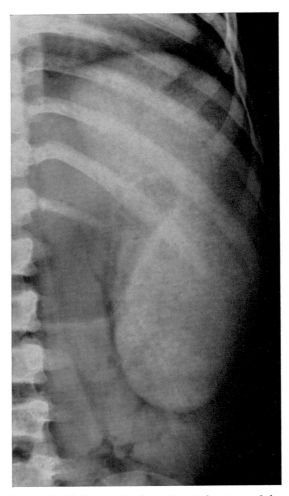

Figure 12-47. Enlarged spleen. Note indentation of the stomach shadow.

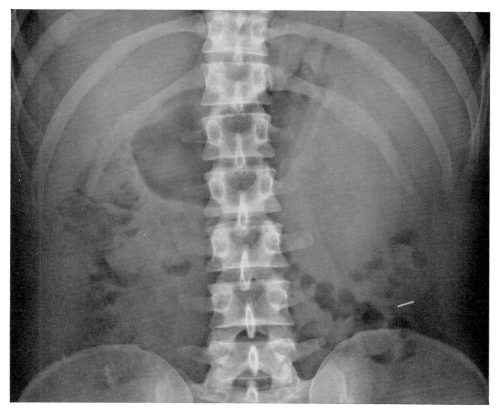

Figure 12-48 (above). Ruptured spleen, thickened through its base, displacing the normal stomach to the right and extending down as far as the white line in the left flank. Note coarse edematous rugal folds of the stomach, which probably shared in the trauma.

Figure 12-49 (below). Liver rupture with blood in the flank following an automobile accident. Note that the colon is displaced medially away from the flank stripe by the distance between the points of the arrows. At surgery a tear was found in the dome of the liver and free blood throughout the abdomen.

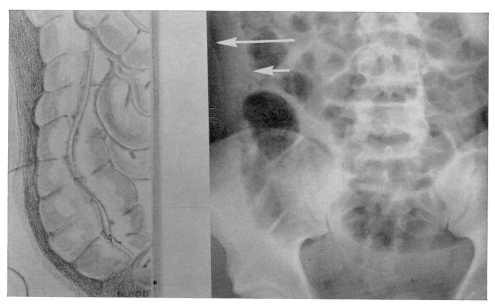

The kidneys, close to the film and outlined by fat, are much better described by the plain film evidence than they can ever be on physical examination, and you will discover that a difference in size of the two kidneys, for example, or a bulge in the kidney outline is repeatedly brought to your attention first by the radiologist. A difference in length may have significance as an indication of disparity in function. A parenchymal renal cyst or tumor will balloon out the pole in which it is present, pushing the perirenal fat before it, so that the change in the dark fat border is perfectly definite from your scrutiny of the plain film.

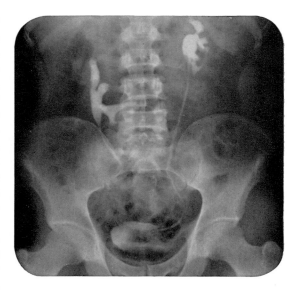

Ptosis is common and easily recognized when you find the kidney farther down the psoas shadow than normal. Any rotation of the kidney about its long axis will alter the shadow it casts, and this will be apparent to you in the first instance you see of horseshoe, or fused, kidneys. In that anomaly the lower poles of the two kidneys are fused across the mid-line, and rotation must result from the forward tilting of the lower poles. The kidney shadows will be seen to incline inward at their inferior extremities, then, and no well-defined lower poles will be visible. A soft-tissue mass may sometimes be seen across the mid-line, and the distortion of the draining structures, which becomes inevitable, produces varying degrees of obstruction.

The presence of polycystic kidneys may also be suspected from the plain film because of the large size of the kidney shadows. Their presence is confirmed by pyelograms, which show a characteristic distortion of the calices, stretched around the many retention cysts.

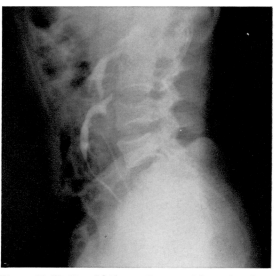

The kidney is to be discussed in a little more detail in Chapter 15. You are concerned here with learning to interpret changes in size, shape, and position of organs you can identify. Thus the kidneys in polycystic disease or fused into a single horseshoe-shaped mass lying across the bodies of the vertebrae exemplify such changes.

In the next chapter, distention of bowel shadows and the diagnosis of free peritoneal air and fluid will be discussed, since these are roentgenologically appreciable and of great practical importance.

Figure 12-50. Fused kidneys. Suspected from the plain film and from urographic and pyelographic studies. (You know the lower film is a lateral because of the appearance of the bodies of the vertebrae.) Note that the forward inclination of the lower poles of the kidneys and of the upper ureters is well shown.

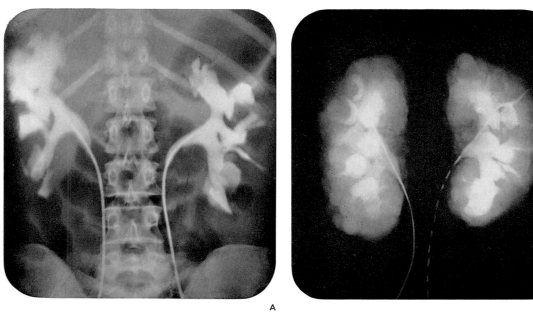

A   B

Figure 12-51. Polycystic kidneys. Bilateral very large kidney shadows on the plain film in polycystic disease of the kidneys should suggest that possibility, confirmed here by retrograde studies (*A*, above). Note the stretched-out appearance of the draining structures and the individual distortion of the calices by the invisible parenchymal cysts. The injected postmortem specimens, *B* (above, right), show the outlines of cysts on the surface of the kidney.

Figure 12-52 (*Unknown 12-2*) (right). You should be able to make a diagnosis from this film. Look back to Figure 2-2*B*, which is the chest film from this patient. Note that it is well to look below the diaphragm in studying a chest film.

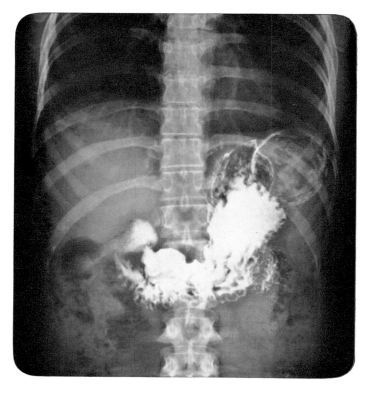

225

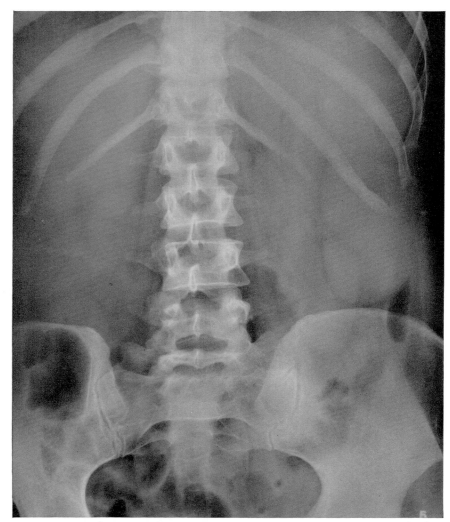

Figure 12-53 (*Unknown 12-3*). Decide as much as you can about this young man's plain film.

Credits: Illustrations this chapter.

Figure 12-5. Courtesy Dr. L. Cole, Blossburg, Pa.

Figure 12-7. Courtesy Dr. A. Melamed, Milwaukee, Wis.

Figures 12-8, 12-9, 12-27. Courtesy Drs. G. Stein and A. Finkelstein, and the publisher, *MR&P* 31:5, 10, 12. (Here and elsewhere in the book are reproduced and preserved the beautiful drawings of the late "Nat" Jacobs of the University of Rochester Department of Medical Illustration.)

Figure 12-10. Courtesy Dr. H. Gray, Memphis, Tenn.

Figures 12-11, 12-12. Courtesy Dr. E. Salzman, Dr. R. Spurck, Mr. G. Mills, and the publisher, *MR&P* 37:2, 3.

Figure 12-13. Courtesy Dr. G. Schwartz and the publisher, *MR&P* 30:55.

Figure 12-14. Courtesy Dr. T. Farrar and the publisher, *MR&P* 30:24.

Figure 12-22. Courtesy Drs. M. Khilnani, B. Wolf and M. Finkel, and the publisher, *Radiology* 79:265.

Figure 12-23. Courtesy Dr. E. Merrill, Rochester, N. Y.

Figure 12-24. Courtesy Dr. O. Weaver, Welch, W. Va.

Figures 12-25, 12-26, 12-39, 12-43, 12-44. Courtesy Drs. J. Hope and C. Koop, and the publisher, *MR&P* 38:32, 35, 36, 47.

Figure 12-28. Courtesy Dr. E. Pirkey, Louisville, Ky.

Figure 12-32. Courtesy Dr. W. Beacham and the publisher, *MR&P* 25:22.

Figure 12-34. Courtesy Dr. J. Dunlap, Waco, Texas.

Figure 12-35. Courtesy Dr. H. Wainerdi, New York, N. Y.

Figures 12-36, 12-38. Courtesy Drs. J. Edeiken, G. Strong and A. Khajavi, and the publisher, *Radiology* 79: 88, 89.

Figure 12-37. Courtesy Drs. T. Tristan, J. Murphy, and H. Schoenberg, and the publisher, *Radiology* 79:733.

Figure 12-41. Courtesy Mr. J. Hill, Lancaster, England.

Figure 12-46. Courtesy Drs. G. Teasley, L. Good, and C. Klein, and the publisher, *MR&P* 33:80.

Figure 12-47. Courtesy Dr. G. Jacobson, Los Angeles, Calif.

Figure 12-48. Courtesy Dr. W. Irwin, Detroit, Mich.

Figure 12-49. Courtesy Dr. J. McCort and the publisher, *Radiology* 78:51.

Figure 12-50. Courtesy Dr. H. Forsyth, Jr., and the publisher, *MR&P* 25:39.

Figure 12-51. Courtesy Dr. N. Alcock and the publisher, *MR&P* 23:27, 28.

Figure 12-52. Courtesy Drs. W. Macklin, Jr., H. Bosland and A. McCarthy, and the publisher, *MR&P* 31:91.

CHAPTER 13 The Abdomen: Distended Bowel; Free Air and Free Fluid

It is midnight. You are interning in a big general hospital in a large midwestern city. Tonight you are on duty alone covering the surgical ward service on two floors, to one of which you are regularly assigned. The head nurse on the other floor calls you; she has a new admission. You find 51-year-old Mrs. A. B. lying on her left side groaning with pain. She tells you she has had cramps in her abdomen off and on for 2 weeks, that they have been much worse for the last 3 days, and that she has vomited everything she ate yesterday and today, usually several hours after eating. She is moderately obese, and her abdomen is somewhat distended with no masses felt. Active bowel sounds are present. History and physical examination yield no other pertinent data. You arrange for an abdominal plain film, Figure 13-1.

Three nights later, on duty again, you inspect a film made that day after a barium enema (Figure 13-2), because Mrs. A. B. is having waves of abdominal pain. To what extent do these films help you to comprehend the developments in Mrs. A. B.? (See text later.)

Figure 13-1

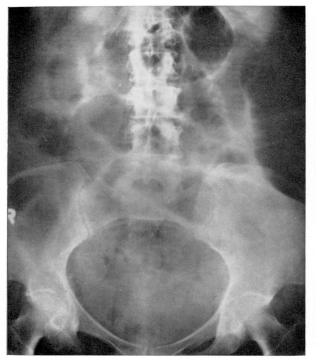

Figure 13-2

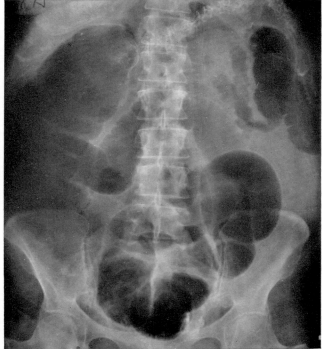

To resume your analysis of the plain film, after you have studied the bones and the soft-tissue zones and profiles, and decided whether there seems to be evidence for organ enlargement or displacement, you should *look at the whole film at once, directing your entire attention to the gas distribution and content.* Normally the air in the stomach will range from the small, round, wrinkled fundal bubble seen on the prone film to a few oblique streaks of antral air which you will see in supine plain films. Actual visualization of the entire organ filled with swallowed air is not the rule. In Figure 13-3 you see the stomach of a child so outlined, but it was filled via a catheter intentionally during pyelography in order to displace the confusing gut shadows downward visualizing the kidneys through the stomach bubble.

In chronic pyloric obstruction, the stomach may be grossly dilated, of course, and often contains a large amount of food and retained secretions. On the plain film such a stomach will appear as an ill-defined density extending across the upper abdomen, and when the radiologist tries to study it at fluoroscopy, the swallowed barium appears to sink into a bog. Attempted examination of such a stomach is futile until the stomach has been emptied.

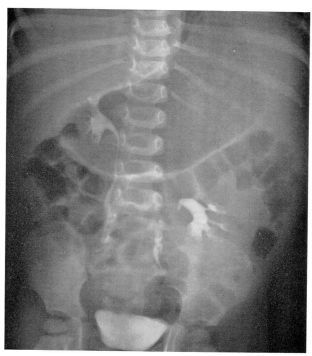

Figure 13-3 (above). Suprarenal mass displaces left kidney, but right kidney is seen through air-distended stomach.

Figure 13-5 (immediately below). The stomach distended with food and barium mixture in a patient with chronic obstruction, the result of scarring after many years of recurrences of his duodenal ulcer. Film was made 4 hours after the administration of the contrast material. Note that there *is* barium in the small bowel, so that some is leaving the stomach intermittently.

Figure 13-4 (below, left). The stomach of an infant with pyloric stenosis, seen obliquely from the right in a projection which should visualize the pyloric canal.

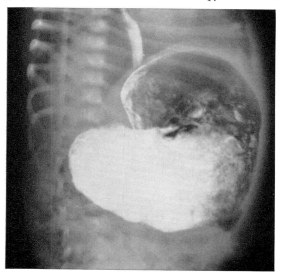

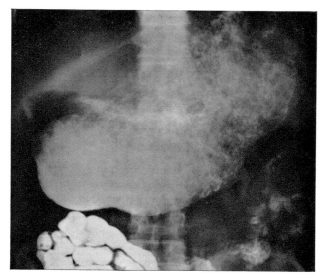

229

As I have said, plain films of hospitalized patients often show a certain amount of air in the small bowel, particularly the ileum, even though there is no clinical evidence to suggest the presence of either ileus or obstruction. You will find that the amount of air in the intestine is increased in plain films made after any kind of painful instrumentation, particularly retrograde catheterization of the ureters. This is unfortunate since such air usually overlies the kidneys, and the intersecting lines produced by the folded walls of air-filled bowel confuse the details of the shadows of the kidney and its draining structures.

Truly distended loops of small bowel will approach and even exceed the caliber of the normal colon. When they are filled with air, their distinctive mucosal markings will usually identify them, but when they are filled with fluid, they will cast vague, sausage-shaped gray shadows across the mid-abdomen, often superimposed in the supine film by a bubble of air.

The colon usually contains some air, particularly its distal half. You may see air outlining solid fecal material within the lumen of the rectum. The cecum and ascending colon more often contain semisolid feces and will be outlined by the characteristic speckled shadow already discussed. Both will show the indented haustrations which generally make identification of the colon easy.

With moderate obstructive distention of the colon, the haustra become shallower but are still visible as serosal indentations, and *more of the colon will be seen continuously outlined with air than is usual.* Thus, when a tumor obstructs at the level of the sigmoid, air may be seen outlining and distending all the colon proximal to that point. With a tumor obstructing at the mid-transverse colon, the proximal half of the transverse colon, hepatic flexure, ascending colon, and cecum will be distended with air. The cecum may eventually balloon up to immense proportions in obstruction of the distal colon, erasing all haustral indentations and appearing as a huge air-filled structure occupying the right side of the abdomen. A neglected patient who comes into hospital after days of large bowel obstruction may have ruptured his cecum, in fact, and free air may be detectable in the peritoneal space.

An important point in the diagnosis of all types of *mechanical obstruction is that the compensatory increase in peristalsis which develops is carried beyond the point of obstruction and results in the clearing of air from bowel distal to that point* (that is, from that portion of the gut which *can* be cleared). Thus, in the obstruction mentioned above at mid-transverse colon, you would expect eventually to find the remainder of the transverse colon, the descending colon and sigmoid, completely empty and, therefore, invisible. In this way it is not impossible to make a strong presumptive diagnosis of large bowel obstruction from a single plain film, with the next step a barium enema and demonstration of the lesion from its distal side.

Figure 13-6. Large or small bowel, or both? (See text next page.)

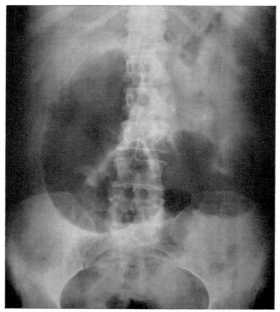

230

When you first look at Figure 13-6, you are struck by the distended loop of bowel which lies across the abdomen. It is apparent from the haustrations that it is colon, and from its distribution it must be transverse colon. If, you reason, it is distended because there is obstruction somewhere near the splenic flexure, then the cecum and ascending colon ought also to be distended. Look more closely at the right flank. There *is* an ill-defined dark shadow present, of smaller caliber than you expect, which represents air within the cecum *above (anterior to) its predominantly fluid content.* Note, too, that there is little or no air in the left lower quadrant. The sigmoid appears to have been cleared of air, further supporting an impression of obstruction in the descending colon.

Is there any appreciable small bowel gas? It is hard to be sure. Now stand the patient up and make an erect roentgenogram (Figure 13-8), and you will have more information. The long fluid levels are in the ascending and transverse colon, and the shorter ones in small bowel. At surgery the patient proved to have an obstructing carcinoma in the descending colon.

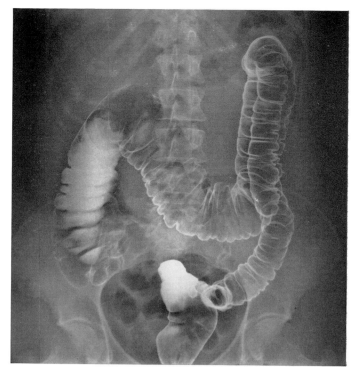

Figure 13-7 (above). Normal colon outlined by a coating of barium on its inner surface and then inflated with air. Use it as a norm in visualizing the accompanying illustrations.

Figure 13-9 *(Unknown 13-1)* (below). Predict the plain film you would expect 4 days after this lesion at the hepatic flexure completely obstructs the colon.

Figure 13-8

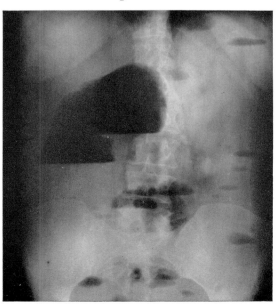

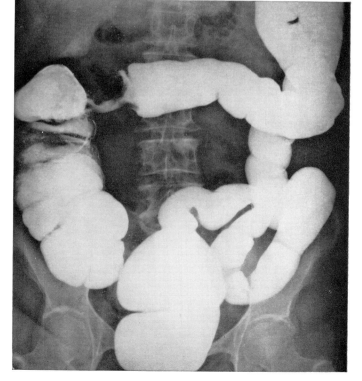

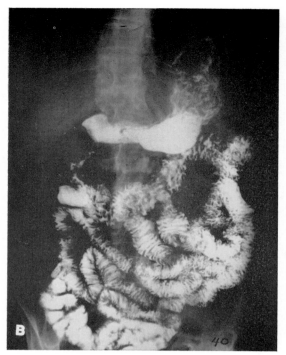

Figure 13-10. Normal small bowel. Barium given by mouth; film B made 45 minutes later.

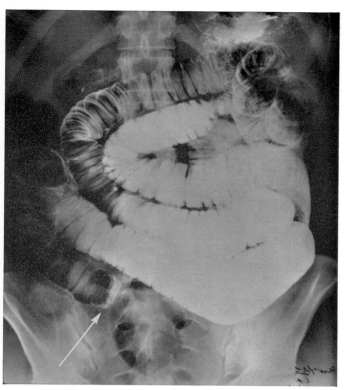

Figure 13-11. Distended small bowel in mechanical obstruction. Note increase in caliber and distinctive markings.

Now look at the two films above. Figure 13-10 shows you the caliber of the small bowel filled with barium in a normal person and can be compared with Figure 13-11, in which obstructed and distended small bowel is seen visualized with barium and air. The arrow indicates the point of obstruction beyond which no barium passed. This is not a standard procedure, and you will not usually be seeing obstructed small bowel outlined with barium, since the addition of insoluble opaque substance to the already retained secretions *above* the obstruction adds to the difficulty of decompression and surgical management. The study of an obstructing colonic lesion by barium enema from its distal side is an entirely different matter, since the barium is readily evacuated.

Nevertheless, the film printed here shows you the caliber of moderately distended loops of jejunum with their characteristic cross striations representing the valvulae conniventes. You will say that they resemble haustra, and

they do, superficially at least. They differ in their periodicity, however, being more numerous than haustra and more narrowly spaced even when the small bowel is distended. They also cross the gut from one side to the other, as opposed to the haustra, which indent but do not cross the colon and are often not precisely opposite the indentation on the other side. In addition, you will be helped in differentiating between obstructed small bowel and large bowel when you observe that small bowel loops tend to line up in rows, three and four parallel loops of bowel appearing close beside each other. The colon, when it distends, very infrequently gives this "stepladder" or "arranged" appearance.

In mechanical small bowel obstruction, precisely the same principle of clearing of gut beyond that point applies which was described for the large bowel. If you make a practice of looking for the colon as soon as you recognize distended small bowel, one of these days you

232

will find yourself looking at an unknown plain film on which you can find no haustrated air shadows, and you will realize that you must be looking at the roentgen findings in mechanical small intestinal obstruction, the colon having been swept clear of gas.

In paralytic ileus, on the other hand, both large and small bowel will be seen distended with air, since peristalsis is generally decreased. This is a far less distinctive roentgen picture than that for mechanical obstruction, and you will find that many plain films with quite obviously distended large or small bowel do not fall neatly into one category or the other. This makes for difficulties, indecision, and a sense of confusion in trying to interpret plain films in patients with abdominal symptoms. However, once you have learned to recognize the picture of mechanical obstruction, when it is clear, you will feel somewhat more comfortable about studying the equivocal findings so often seen in plain films.

Time is the important factor so many of us forget to consider in looking at a single film. It is all too easy, when one is worried about a patient and in quest of diagnostic help, to forget that a single examination is a point on a curve and nothing more, that it represents a state of affairs at only one moment in the course of a patient's illness. *How long* has the obstruction in mid-transverse colon been present? Has it been a complete obstruction *long enough* yet to allow the bowel beyond that point to become cleared of air? If not, then the presence of air in both large and small bowel cannot be distinguished roentgenologically from ileus, which it will closely resemble. By the same token, an *intermittent obstruction* may allow gas to pass into the distal bowel from time to time.

In sum, then, the picture of mechanical obstruction of either large or small bowel, present long enough to allow clearing beyond it, is quite distinctive. When both large and small bowel are seen to be distended, the picture is confusing and may represent either ileus or an incomplete or intermittent obstruction. (Serial films in patients with abdominal problems are often very informative, indicating the developing change more clearly than any other investigative procedure.)

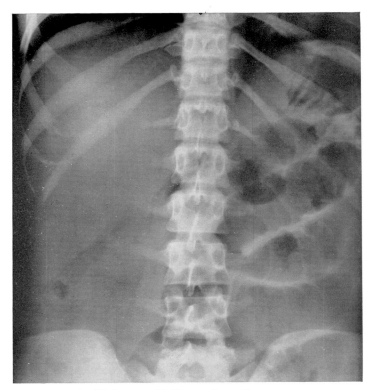

Figure 13-12 *(Unknown 13-2)*. Analyze the gas shadows.

Figure 13-13 *(Unknown 13-3)*. Analyze the shadows of air-filled bowel and explain the appearance of the pelvic soft tissues.

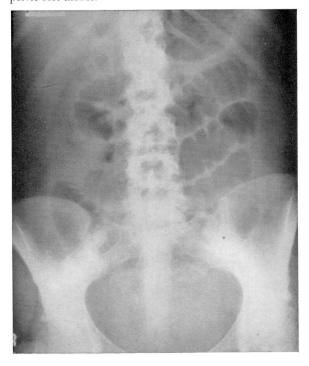

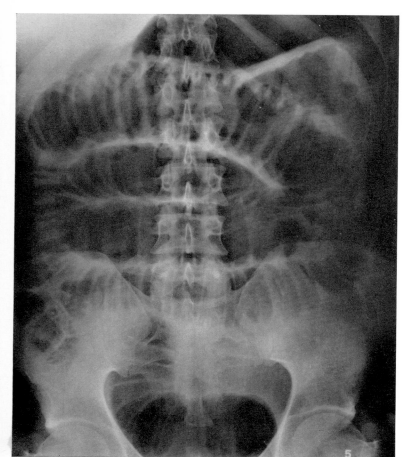

Figure 13-14

LARGE OR SMALL BOWEL?

Analyze the figures to the left before you read this.
Figure 13-14 shows many parallel loops of widely distended jejunum stretched across the abdomen, air in the stomach and cecum, but none in the rest of the colon. Mechanical small intestinal obstruction. Figure 13-15 shows an immense loop of widely distended and still visibly haustrated large bowel, and no air in the rectum. This proved at surgery to be a volvulus of the sigmoid colon, twisted several times and gangrenous. Figure 13-16 shows operative delivery of the volvulus. Arrow indicates the twisted area, the lower part of which can often be shown on the barium enema as a twisted spiral of opaque streaks beyond which no barium will flow.

Figure 13-15

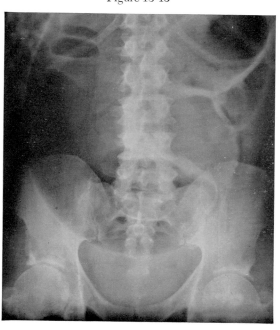

Now go back to the two plain films with which you began on page 228. Figure 13-1 shows a group of distended bowel loops in the upper half of the abdomen, not so clearly arranged as the easier examples on pages 232 and 233, but still clustered in mid-abdomen. The pelvis and lower abdomen look blank, and you must wonder about the presence of fluid-filled small bowel. There are shadows in the right flank which probably indicate a distended cecum, but you cannot be certain of any dilated haustral air shadows in the distal colon, and there is no air in the rectum. The appearance is most consistent with mechanical obstruction near the hepatic flexure.

The second film was made of the same patient 3 days later and shows the right colon and terminal loops of ileum in the pelvis now widely distended with air. The air column ends abruptly at the hepatic flexure. Streaks of barium remaining from a barium enema are seen in the collapsed transverse colon. The barium enema demonstrated a completely obstructing adenocarcinoma at the hepatic flexure which must have been partially or intermittently obstructing for a long time, because the cecum showed considerable hypertrophy of its wall.

When a patient is admitted with abdominal pain and his initial plain film shows both large and small bowel to be distended, the findings are equivocal, as we have said, in that they may represent paralytic ileus or an early or intermittent obstruction. The activity of the bowel sounds repeatedly observed over a period of time may or may not clarify the issue. Serial films may show developments or changes in the roentgen findings which provide helpful clues. If the patient is well enough to stand, the erect film is often informative. One must always bear in mind that a patient with small bowel obstruction and a cleared colon at home the day before yesterday may have developed peritonitis and secondary ileus by the time he is admitted to the hospital. The plain film, like any other roentgen study, can only be interpreted intelligently in the light of a good clinical history.

The standing film itself may provide some additional clues. The small intestine always contains fluid, and when obstructed or paralyzed it accumulates additional fluid and air. On the erect plain film, the air-fluid interfaces inside distended loops of gut will appear as fluid levels, varying in length according to their size and the relative quantities of air and fluid within them. Loops entirely filled with fluid

Figure 13-16

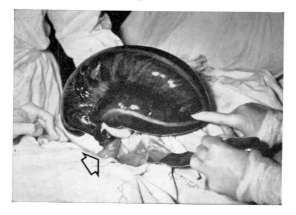

will cast ill-defined gray shadows in both the supine and erect positions. Loops with little fluid and a great deal of air will appear like those in Figure 13-14. Loops three-quarters full of fluid and containing a relatively small amount of air may be very deceptive, since in the erect film they will show short fluid levels and in the supine plain film rather unimpressive bubbles of air superimposed on the indefinite gray of the fluid. You can appreciate the fact that such a patient may not have so startling an initial plain film, and yet be sicker and in a more advanced stage of obstruction than the patient in Figure 13-14. You cannot depend entirely upon the size and appearance of the air-distended gut as an index to the degree of obstruction or to its duration. Moreover, the possibility of the additional presence of free peritoneal air or fluid is always to be entertained in these patients.

One helpful detail about the comparison of standing and supine plain films on the same patient is that, to some extent, the tone of the bowel and its peristaltic activity are appreciable from the plain films. In the patient with paralytic ileus and decreased peristalsis, the loops in either film will *tend* to appear flaccid and of wide caliber with long fluid levels in the erect film. The patient with mechanical obstruction and increased bowel sounds, on the other hand, *tends* to show occasional "hairpin" loops in the erect film. These are so called because ascending and descending limbs are seen filled with air, having short fluid levels on either side, but at different levels, indicating rushes of peristalsis which have dumped fluid from one side of the "hairpin" into the other.

This finding is meaningful when distinct on the plain film of a patient with clinical signs of markedly increased peristaltic activity and on supine and erect plain films which indicate obstruction. Its absence means nothing and does not in any way contradict the mechanical nature of the obstruction. Taken together with the bowel sounds heard clinically, such observations may be useful, and, for example, the development of a suddenly silent abdomen after the roentgen observation of hairpin loops in the standing film might presage bowel perforation and the beginning of peritonitis.

235

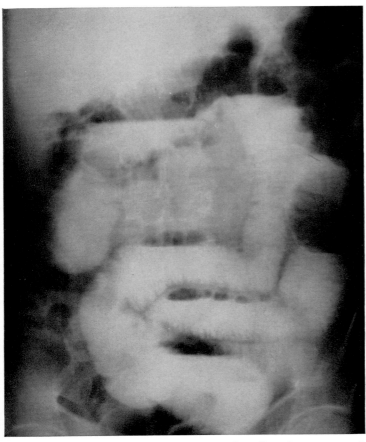

Figure 13-17 (left). Standing film of a patient with low ileal obstruction whose distended small bowel is visualized because she has been given a water-soluble contrast substance. Note the small air bubbles in relationship to the large amount of fluid in the loops. This is how you should think of films like Figure 13-18, being prepared to discount the deceptively small air bubbles and fluid levels.

The over-all grayness of these standing films results partly from the difficulty of obtaining penetration with the usual exposures since the abdomen is pendulous and much thicker erect than it is supine. The gray density of these films is also partly due to the presence of retained fluid within the obstructed loops. You will have noted that in such films the outlines of kidneys and psoas muscles disappear. The same grayness and the same absence of outlines would be seen in a plain film on a patient with free peritoneal fluid in even moderate amounts.

After making any decisions you can with regard to the amount of air-in-gut and its distribution in the course of your systematic survey, direct your attention then to the *general density* of the plain film. To state the oversimplified extremes first, as usual: large amounts of free air in the peritoneal space will increase the radiolucency of the abdomen, just as you would expect, and the film will look darker. Large amounts of free fluid will add to the radiodensity of the abdomen, and the film will appear lighter gray than usual. These statements are true for the conventional exposure techniques used for radiography of the abdomen. Obviously, a film which has been exposed with a relatively more penetrating x-ray beam will have a more uniformly gray appearance, since every structure interposed will have been penetrated effectively. The blackness of any radiograph, however, is a function of total exposure in milliampere-seconds, plus secondary radiation, as well as of the penetration of the beam (kilo-

Figure 13-18 (below). Standing film of a patient with low small bowel obstruction. Arrows indicate a hairpin loop.

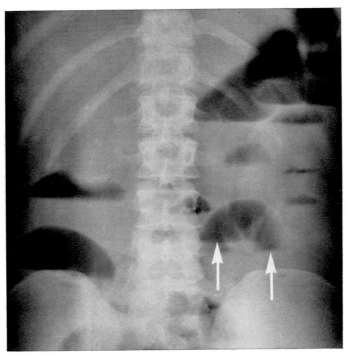

voltage). If the intestinal loops are filled with fluid, the effect is that of adding more thickness to the patient, and for the same exposure factors such a film will be gray and indistinct. This tends to obscure other structures such as the bones. Look at *them,* then, and decide whether they are as well and as clearly shown in their detail as usual; look at the peripheral soft tissues, deciding whether they are overexposed (too black). If these areas are not unusual, then an over-all grayness is meaningful and suggests abdominal fluid.

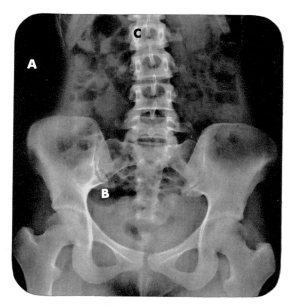

Figure 13-19 (above). Three zones to check. Properly exposed film.

Figure 13-20 (right).
A. Underexposed film.
B. Overexposed film.

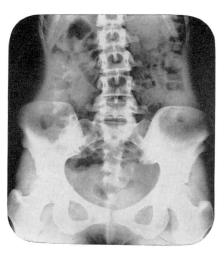

A

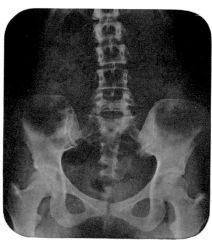

B

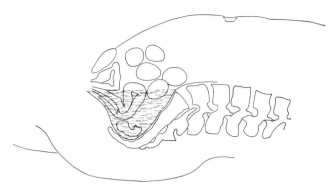

Figure 13-21 (above). Lateral diagram of a supine patient with free peritoneal fluid accumulating in the most dependent part of the abdominal cavity, the pelvic bowl.

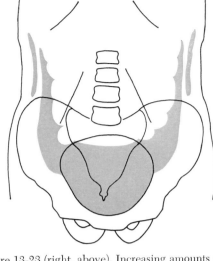

Figure 13-23 (right, above). Increasing amounts of fluid flow into the flanks.

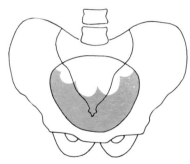

Figure 13-22 (above). Half-moon of gray in the pelvis may mean free fluid (in a patient you *know* had just been catheterized). Scalloped upper margin due to loops of ileum dipping into fluid.

Figure 13-25 (right, below). Plain film made 1 week after pelvic surgery. Retained broken hemostat. Pelvic abscess accounts for density.

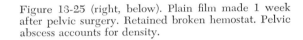

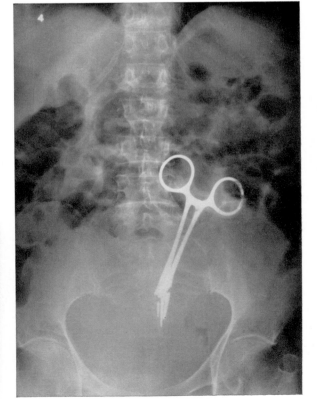

Figure 13-24 (below). Density due to pregnant uterus, 2 months. Fetus not seen until 13 weeks as a rule.

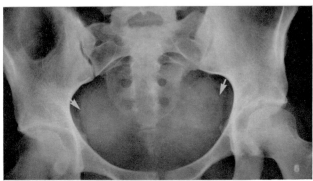

Bme
GT

Loridine ®
CEPHALORIDINE

See last pages of pad for prescribing information.

for many serious
infections encountered
in the hospital

When there is a small amount of fluid free in the peritoneal space, it will gravitate to the most dependent part of the abdominal cavity, which, in the supine patient, is the bowl of the pelvis, as you have seen in the diagram in Figure 13-21. Such relatively small amounts of free fluid probably go unobserved often, because we are more or less accustomed to seeing the pelvis filled with the density of a distended bladder or fluid-containing loops of bowel.

Larger quantities of peritoneal fluid will spill over into the abdominal cavity, flowing up the flanks on either side of the high mid-line ridge of the spine. Fluid collected in the flank displaces the colon medially away from the flank stripe, and with even greater accumulations, air-filled loops of bowel float up under the arched anterior abdominal wall. They are seen on the supine plain film as a cluster of radiolucent shadows in the central abdomen surrounded by the uniform gray of the peritoneal fluid.

Free peritoneal air, on the other hand, fills the highest part of the abdominal cavity (which in the supine position is the anterior part), and massive amounts of peritoneal air strikingly outline the organ masses of liver and spleen including their lateral and superior (diaphragmatic) surfaces. A large amount of free peritoneal air forms a quite distinctive radiolucent, pear-shaped shadow of the whole abdominal cavity which is hard to forget once you have seen it. Small amounts of free air may be quite as important to detect as larger amounts, since they are seen most frequently with perforation of a viscus.

A patient well enough to stand will show crescents of radiolucent air interposed between his diaphragm and liver and spleen, and such a finding is occasionally first detected on an admission chest film.

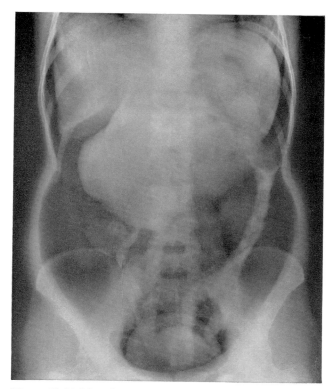

Figure 13-26 (above). Large amount of free peritoneal air fills out the flanks and pelvis, casting a peculiar and distinctive pear-shaped shadow.

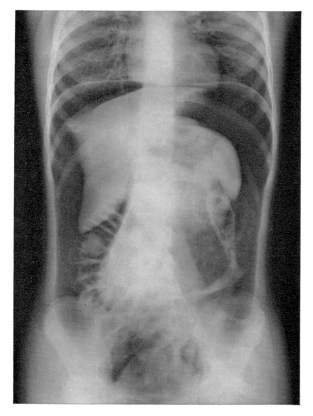

Figure 13-27 (right). Free peritoneal air. Note that you see both sides of the wall of the ascending colon. Why?

Figure 13-28. Lateral abdominal radiography with the patient supine. Question: has the patient free peritoneal air? Dr. Tulp indicates the direction of the beam to two eager residents.

The patient with a perforated viscus is often too ill to stand, and in any event ought not to be disturbed any more than is absolutely vital to a diagnosis. For this reason the search for free air is much more often carried out by decubitus and horizontal beam radiography. The horizontal beam method is demonstrated in Figure 13-28, in which the patient lies supine and is radiographed from side to side, a cassette being placed vertically against his flank. In this way, air free against the under side of the abdominal wall will be appreciable, even in small amounts. A useful variation on this technique places the patient on his left side in his bed or on the examining table, and he is radiographed antero-posteriorly. Free air will rise over the lateral surface of the liver.

You have seen the gut because of air contained within it, in other words because its *inner* surface is rendered visible. With free air in the peritoneal space, *both the inside and the outside of the gut wall may be seen.* This is easy to imagine on a decubitus film with a large amount of free air into which protrude loops of air-filled bowel (Figure 13-29). Both sides

of the wall of a loop of gut may also be seen on a regular supine plain film of the same patient, made, let us say, before there was any suspicion of a perforated viscus (Figure 13-30). This phenomenon is not seen on a normal film.

Finally, you will occasionally see both free fluid and free air in abundant quantities in the abdomen, and their roentgen appearance differs only slightly from what has been described for each. In the supine plain film the air floats on top of the fluid anteriorly under the abdominal wall and is seen on the film as a large, well-defined bubble (Figure 13-33A). In the erect film, the fluid-air interface will be seen as a long, startling fluid level, obviously not within any part of the bowel (Figure 13-33B). The terms "contained" and "uncontained" air are sometimes employed to differentiate the air above fluid levels which are limited by gut wall (in intestinal obstruction) and those which go straight to the abdominal wall and are not confined in any way. "Uncontained air" may also be used to describe air in abscess cavities or fistulous tracts which does not take the shape of any hollow viscus.

240

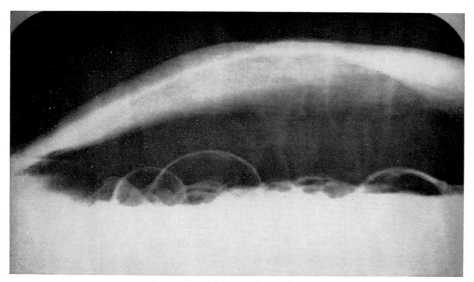

Figure 13-29 (above). Lateral radiograph of the abdomen made with the patient supine. Abundant quantities of free air collected under the abdominal wall outline the serosal side of the loops of bowel.

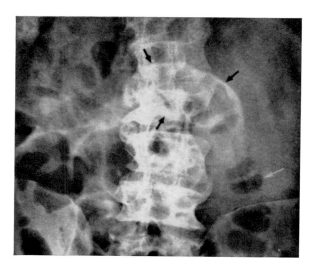

Figure 13-30 (left). Supine plain film on a patient who had free peritoneal air. Note that in this view also both sides of the bowel wall may occasionally be seen. Contrast the loop indicated with black arrows, which is outlined with free air, and others which are not (white arrow).

Figure 13-31 (below, left) and 13-32 (below, right). Two patients with free air over the liver. Radiograph made AP with the patient lying on his left side ("left lateral decubitus").

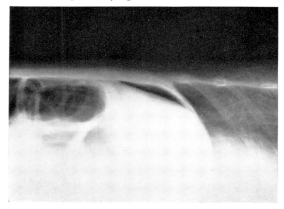

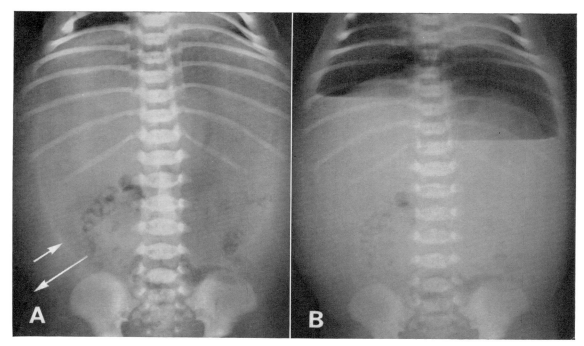

Figure 13-33 (above). Quantities of both free air and free peritoneal fluid. *A.* Supine film shows large bubble with fluid peripherally. Short arrow shows edge of air bubble; long arrow, the margin of abdominal wall. Some of the extra soft-tissue thickness must be free fluid in the flanks. Note how the air bubble margin disappears in *B.* *B.* Erect film, long fluid levels extending to abdominal wall. Air above liver and spleen under diaphragm.

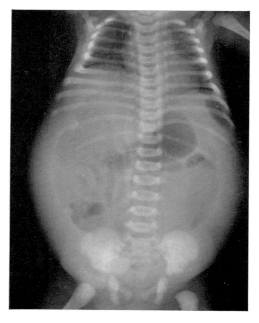

Figure 13-34 (left). Free peritoneal air and fluid seen on a supine film in an infant with meconium ileus and perforation of the small bowel.

242

The next two chapters are devoted to a discussion of abdominal contrast procedures. Chapter 14 explains some of the methods by which the radiologist studies the gastrointestinal tract and will, I hope, make clear to you the basic principles of fluoroscopic observation during barium work. Chapter 15 presents for your interest and information some ideas about contrast studies based on excreted opaque materials. You may want to come back to the chapters on the plain film after you have read Chapters 14 and 15, because air shadows are better comprehended after you have seen their opaque counterparts.

Credits: Illustrations this chapter.

Figures 13-1, 13-2, 13-6, 13-8. Courtesy Dr. L. Love and the publisher, *Radiology* 75:392, 394.

Figure 13-3. Courtesy Drs. J. Hope and C. Koop, and the publisher, *MR&P* 38:9.

Figure 13-4. Courtesy Dr. J. Hope et al., and the publisher, *MR&P* 33:46.

Figure 13-5. Courtesy Dr. D. Haff, Northampton, Pa.

Figure 13-7. Courtesy Dr. E. Ahern and the publisher, *MR&P* 30:8.

Figure 13-9. Courtesy Mr. T. Funke, Lorain, Ohio.

Figure 13-10. Courtesy Dr. C. Nice and the publisher, *Radiology* 80:44.

Figure 13-12. Courtesy Dr. L. Hilt, Eugene, Ore.

Figures 13-13, 13-17. Courtesy Dr. B. Epstein and the publisher, *Radiology* 74:583, 585.

Figures 13-15, 13-16. Courtesy Dr. C. Meckstroth and the publisher, *MR&P* 26:125.

Figure 13-18. Courtesy Drs. F. Fleischner and P. Mandelstam, and the publisher, *Radiology* 70:474.

Figures 13-19, 13-20. Courtesy Mr. C. Brownell and the publisher, *MR&P* 27:115, 119.

Figures 13-29, 13-30. Courtesy Dr. E. Schultz and the publisher, *Radiology* 70:728, 729.

Figures 13-31, 13-32. Courtesy Dr. H. Welsh, Mr. E. Fleming, and the publisher, *MR&P* 34:78.

Figure 13-33. Courtesy Drs. E. Singleton, H. Rosenberg, and L. Samper, and the publisher, *Radiology* 76:206.

Figure 13-34. Courtesy Dr. D. Robinson, Savannah, Ga.

CHAPTER 14 Contrast Studies: Principles, Applications and Scope

Diagnostic roentgenology is entirely based on contrasting the density of adjoining structures. Up to now you have been thinking mostly in terms of naturally occurring density contrasts, and wherever they can be relied upon to produce the desired information, they are preferable to any artificial contrast study. In fact, in the heady and exciting development of modern intracavitary contrast work, the great value of naturally occurring contrast substances like fat and air tends to be overlooked. As dedicated workers in the field of pediatric roentgenology have pointed out, very nearly the same information about, for example, the upper gastrointestinal tract of an infant is available from deductive reasoning about air shadows as from barium studies, and the chances of causing inhalation of vomitus are minimized.

Soon after the discovery of the roentgen ray, the idea of augmenting natural contrast occurred to physicians working in different parts of the world. The ramifications of the many methods of study which were begun even before the turn of the century are still unfolding before us, and the possibilities of new contrast studies seem limitless. The training of a radiologist in these many methods of investigation is lengthy and complex; yet it should always be his concern to examine the patient by the least harmful means available which will produce the information needed. The experienced physician-radiologist knows that complex methods of investigation requiring highly specialized machinery and trained personnel are not *invariably* those best suited to the individual problem, nor will they *invariably* produce more information. While such reservations must influence the choice of the type of examination

planned, one can never lose sight of the fact that a particularly suitable investigative method may be undertaken *in spite of some potential secondary side effect*, as a deliberate risk, in order to make a diagnosis and ultimately secure appropriate treatment for the patient.

Some contrast studies are virtually harmless; others have well-recognized contraindications. Air itself, artificially introduced as in the visualization of the ventricles and outer surface of the brain, is not without discomfort and some hazard to the patient. Other studies incur little risk and minimal discomfort and have become so routinely a part of the diagnostic plan that perhaps too few persons could without effort list half a dozen conditions in which, for example, a gastrointestinal series should *not* be carried out or in which it would be better to postpone the procedure. Barium sulfate in water suspension is itself inert, and none of it is absorbed during its passage through the gastrointestinal tract, but almost any such study involves the taking of numerous films and perhaps repeated fluoroscopic inspections over a period of several hours. The process is fatiguing for the patient, particularly the acutely ill patient. The anxiety of the patient is always an important part of the hazard of the procedure. Such anxiety is allayed to an appreciable extent by intelligent preparation: a referring physician, if he will take the time, can always explain a little about the procedure in advance. The patient suspected of having had a recent coronary occlusion should *not* be sent to the radiology department prematurely for an extended and fatiguing procedure, and the patient with symptoms suggesting large bowel obstruction should not be given barium by mouth.

244

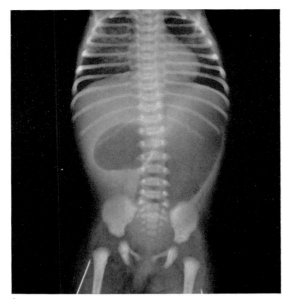
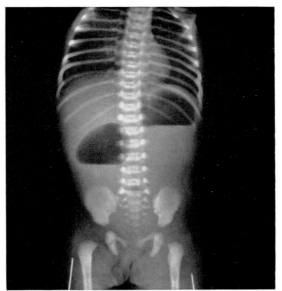

A   B

Figure 14-1. The "double-bubble" phenomenon. In this 4-day-old girl with persistent vomit-ing since birth, the naturally occurring contrast substance, air, provides all the necessary in-formation. There is no need to add barium or other opaque substance. The air shadows alone provide evidence that nothing has passed beyond the duodenum, the remainder of the abdomen showing a blank, uniform gray shadow. The obstruction is not at the pylorus because there are two distinct bubbles of air-distended gut and, in the erect film, two distinct fluid levels. The obstruction must therefore be in the duodenal loop; surgical correction is mandatory. The addi-tion of barium or other opaque substances is pointless, will not alter the indicated treatment, and might be vomited during anesthesia. (A made supine, B erect.)

In sum, then, the complex contrast study should not be requisitioned without consider-ation of the entire clinical problem, nor should it be undertaken when the patient is not in a reasonably safe condition to undergo it. You would do well to observe one example of each of the major investigative procedures for your-self, so that you will understand not only what it will require of your patient in terms of energy and stamina but also the degree to which the patient's cooperation may be re-quired for the success of the procedure. Thus, a patient who is paralyzed may not be able to stand for certain parts of the gastrointestinal examination which are usually carried out in that position. A patient who speaks no English will be particularly difficult to examine be-cause he must hold his breath on command during the exposure of films, and if he does not understand and continues to breathe, the films obtained will often be valueless. Obviously, this kind of difficulty may be prevented by your discussing the procedure with the radiologist before it is carried out. The examination of the paralyzed patient may be modified, and the patient with a language problem may be attended in the fluoroscopy room by someone who can translate and reassure. *If intelligent consideration for the patient is the major con-cern of both radiologist and referring physician, undesirable developments resulting from any sort of procedure will be kept to a minimum.* (Needless to say, this applies no more to radi-ology than to any other branch of medicine.)

Having warned you that clinical judgment must be applied to the selection of contrast procedures, let me give you a somewhat fuller appreciation of what such procedures have to offer as diagnostic tools. Early investigators used a rubber-coated metal wire passed into the stomach with a view to "outlining the curvatures." From such a crude beginning, the polished refinements of modern gastrointestinal studies now comprise a whole branch of radiology. They involve the interpretation of shadows not only of whole casts of hollow structures but also of the far more complex shadows of thin films of opaque substance caught against the mucosal irregularities of the inner surface of the gut. Such *mucosal relief studies*, as they are often called, are carried out with minimal amounts of opaque material, manipulated and spread over the surface of the mucosa during fluoroscopic study, *spot films* being obtained at frequent intervals by mechanically substituting a small cassette for the fluoroscopic screen. The technical expertise required by the procedure and the judgment and experience needed for interpreting correctly the observed shadows constitute one of the most sophisticated accomplishments of the radiologist.

Nevertheless, the conclusions he draws are basically no less logical than everything else you have been learning to appreciate about the field, and in order to comprehend the reliability of the evidence offered by roentgen data obtained from barium studies, you should understand some of the fundamental implications of various kinds of roentgen observations based on such procedures. To that end, examine the hypothetical drawings in Figures 14-2 and 14-3. The gastrointestinal tract is essentially a tube, and the roentgen principles for examining it vary only in degree, even in the stomach, cecum, and rectum, where its tubular structure has been modified by nature. The simple tube in *A*, filled with an opaque substance and radiographed, would produce a shadow like the one you see in *a*, smooth-bordered and uniformly dense. A polyp protruding into its lumen upon a stalk like that in *B*, would produce a barium cast-shadow like that in *b*. A solid tumor growing in its wall like that in *C*, and protruding into the lumen as a sessile growth,

would produce a shadow like *c*. Both of these alterations in the original normal tubular shadow are what are referred to as *filling defects,* or, as they were called earlier, subtraction shadows. This last term has been virtually abandoned in radiologic parlance for filling defect, but it is nevertheless an excellent term, since it describes succinctly the change in the shadow. A part of the expected luminal shadow has been subtracted because barium has been displaced by radiolucent soft tissue.

The growth you see in *D* has entirely encircled the tubular structure being examined, so that a constriction of the lumen is produced. This is often called a *napkin-ring defect,* but times change and the napkin ring has vanished from the dining table, so that possibly we ought to equate this type of filling defect with some more familiar object, like a doughnut. If you prefer, the term *annular lesion* is commonly employed and less gastronomic. In any event, whenever you see a barium shadow like that in *d,* you ought to *reconstruct mentally the rigid annular lesion which has produced it, supplying tumor or other soft tissue wherever the barium has been displaced.* The abrupt and often angular change in the shadow where normal luminal wall meets the margin of a tumor is frequently and aptly referred to as a *shelf,* and its consistent appearance on film after film in the same location is to be interpreted as reliable evidence of rigidity of some sort in the otherwise distensible wall of the gut. (*Aa, Cc* and *Dd* represent the shadows which would be cast if the related segments of gut were *distended* as opposed to being gently filled. Note that the rigid areas remain rigid.)

Figures 14-2 (top), 14-3 (middle), and 14-4 (bottom) (opposite page). Hypothetical examples of gastrointestinal pathology and the changes in the barium cast-shadow produced in each (see text).

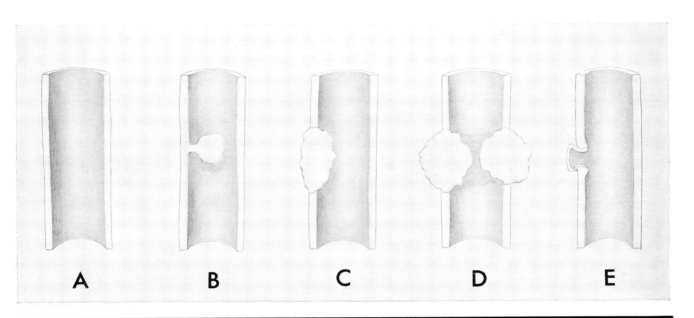

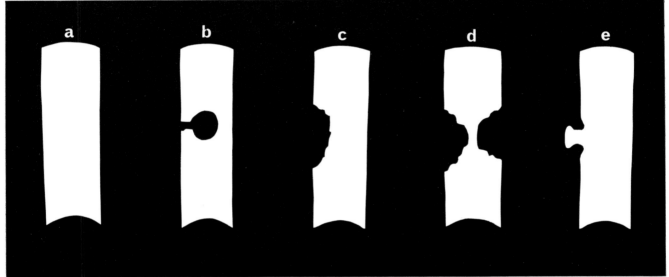

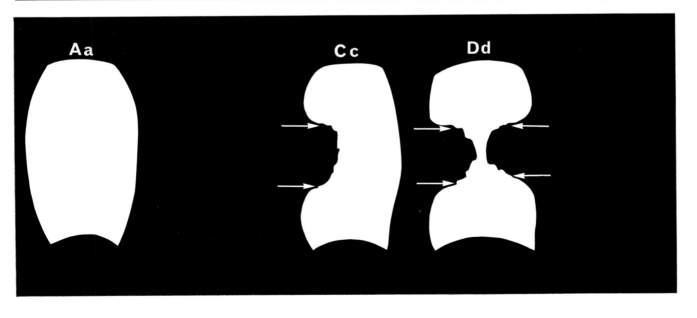

You will find that a filling defect and its shelf-like margin are often so precisely the same from film to film in a series made during the barium study that they may be superimposed over a bright light. Try it. If on two or more such films you can bring into perfect register the margin of a filling defect suspected of representing a malignant tumor, then the probabilities that it is a tumor are greatly enhanced. If, of course, two such films do *not* superimpose, it may mean either that the area in question is not rigid, and therefore changes slightly, or that the two films were made in different projections.

In *Aa, Cc,* and *Dd* (Figure 14-4), the barium casts of our stylized tubular structures are represented as having been distended with fluid from within. The normal (and therefore normally elastic) tube in *Aa* has distended evenly according to the evenly distributed fluid pressures within it. The sessile lesion in one wall in *Cc* is rigid, although the wall above and below it can and does distend. Its barium-outlined profile between the two arrows would be superimposable, bump for bump.

The annular lesion in *Dd* is also rigid and superimposable, although the lumen on both sides of it balloons out with the increase in fluid pressure. Moreover, no change in this demonstrably rigid area would occur in the course of the entire study.

If up to now barium studies have tended to confuse you, if you have wondered how any firm conclusions can ever be derived from them at all, this is the time to tell you that the sobriety and assurance of his interpretations are possible to the radiologist *largely because he has been able to demonstrate a finding repeatedly.* No finding present on a single film only is worth very much, and the resident in training in radiology soon finds that positive diagnostic observations made from barium studies must be consistently demonstrable if they are to be believed. So variable and shifting are the shadows presented by opaque substances within the gastrointestinal tract that it is right that only those consistently present should be taken seriously. This is not less true for other spheres of roentgen investigation, to be sure, nor, for that matter, for other branches of medicine. Any

single positive test, always negative thereafter, is unlikely to weigh much in the balance of evidence, and the principle is no different for more complex investigative procedures.

A

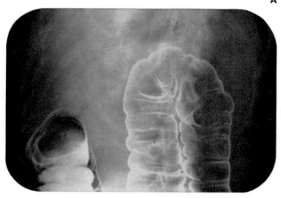

Figure 14-5. *A* (above). The normal splenic flexure unrolled by turning the patient so that there is no overlap. Colon has been filled with barium, evacuated, and inflated with air. *B* (below). The normal mucosal relief pattern of the splenic flexure after evacuation of barium. The collapsed colon shows a wrinkled mucosal lining, and the haustra are closer together. B

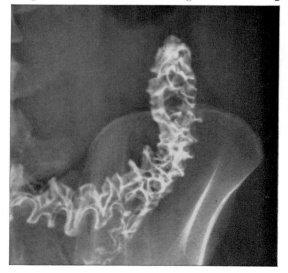

248

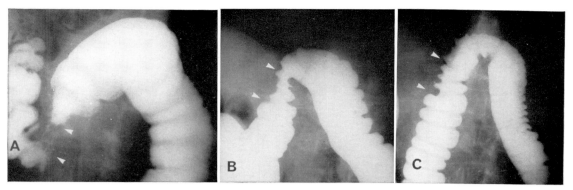

Figure 14-6. *A*. An area of constriction seen just proximal to the splenic flexure at fluoroscopy during a barium enema was present without change for several minutes and then relaxed and changed as you see it in *B* and *C*. The inconstancy of a constriction of the lumen which is due to spasm distinguishes it from a rigid lesion of any kind.

Figure 14-7. A convincing annular constriction near the rectosigmoid junction could not be redemonstrated either fluoroscopically or on films. This is a notorious area for overlap, however, and the patient came to surgery. No lesion was found.

Figure 14-8. An annular area of narrowing just distal to the splenic flexure was constant on all films obtained during a barium enema. Note evidence of low-grade obstruction in the relative dilatation of the transverse colon and splenic flexure, which contain fecal boluses and barium. The descending colon below the lesion shows the pattern expected from collapse of empty colon. Carcinoma was found at surgery.

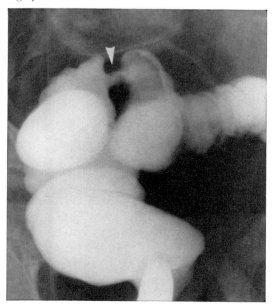

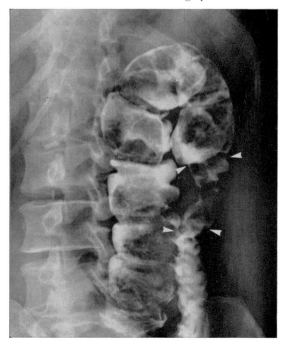

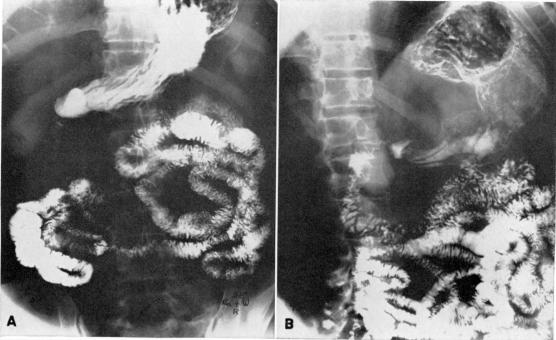

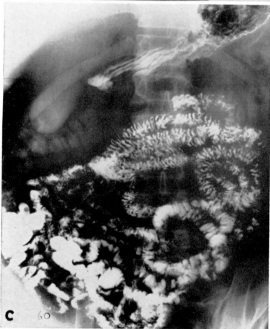

Figure 14-9. Normal upper gastrointestinal series, large films only. The smaller films made in several conventional projections of the stomach and duodenal bulb, and spot films made during fluoroscopy, would complete the series (see text).

The variation of barium shadows within the gastrointestinal tract is well illustrated by the films made during an *upper GI series* which you see in Figure 14-9. *A* was made prone half an hour after 10 ounces of barium suspension had been swallowed and shows the stomach nearly empty and the jejunum and upper ileum filled. *B,* made 15 minutes later in an oblique position, shows most of the small bowel, and *C,* made an hour after the administration of barium, shows the right colon filling. Note the haustrated faint shadows beneath the shadow of the gallbladder. Cholecystography had been done that morning, the opaque medium being given orally the evening before and films made before the commencement of the barium study. There is a single round filling defect within the gallbladder shadow representing the displacement of opaque material by a solitary calculus of lesser density.

You may be inclined to reject the possibility of demonstrating any structure consistently in so changeable a barium pattern, but look carefully at Figure 14-10 *(Unknown 14-1),* four spot films of the stomach and duodenum of a patient who had guaiac-positive stools. She had no hemorrhoids, negative findings on barium enema study, was not anemic, and enjoyed excellent health.

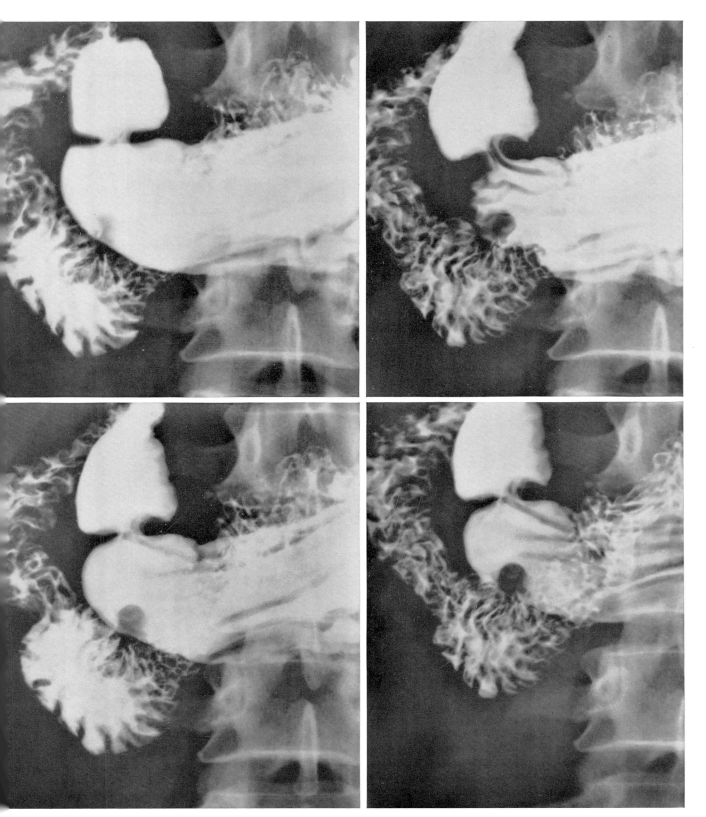

Figure 14-10 *(Unknown 14-1)* Can you spot the consistently present filling defect?

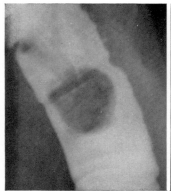
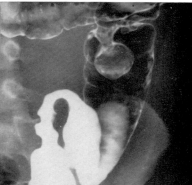

Figure 14-11 (left). Polyps within the colon may be demonstrated as radiolucent filling defects displacing the contrast substance, or, once they have been coated with opaque material, they may be seen protruding into the air-filled lumen after insufflation of the colon. Note that in both the stalk is well seen.

B

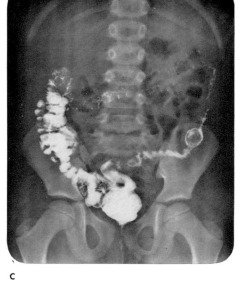

Figure 14-12. Polyp in the descending colon in a boy with bloody stools and crampy left abdominal pain. Note that the polyp is seen demonstrated in three different ways, always in the same location. In A (below) it is seen as a radiolucent filling defect in the opaque barium column. In B (right, above), after evacuation, the polyp is seen because it prevents the collapse of the barium-coated walls of the colon, a regular finding in intraluminal soft-tissue masses. In C (right, below) the polyp, coated with opaque material, is seen outlined by air.

A

C

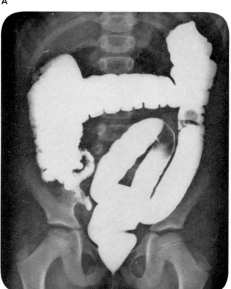

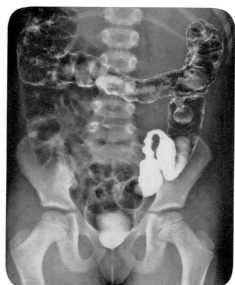

Figure 14-13 (right). *A.* Filling defects along the greater curvature in a patient with pernicious anemia. There is also one inside the duodenal bulb. The patient refused surgery. *B* shows the open stomach and duodenum at postmortem. Polypoid lesions along the greater curvature proved to be adenocarcinoma. There was also a carcinomatous polyp prolapsed into the duodenal bulb from the antrum of the stomach.

A

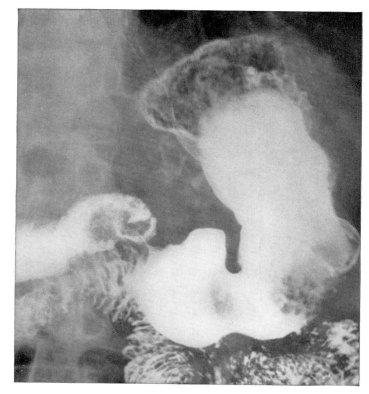

B

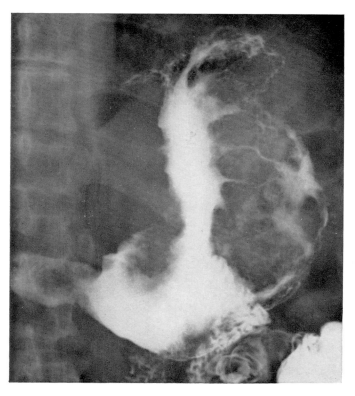

Figure 14-14 (left). Adenocarcinoma of the stomach. The opaque white shadow is all that remains of the lumen. Traces of barium caught at the sides of the large filling defect outline it and the extent of its protrusion into the lumen.

253

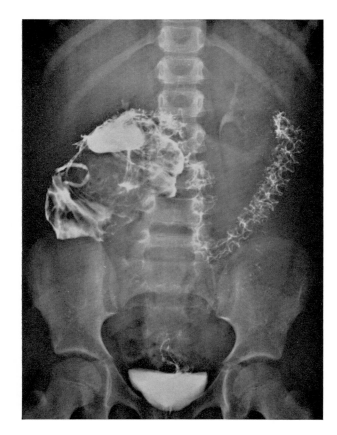

Figure 14-15 (left). Large intraluminal tumor mass filling the ascending colon and preventing its collapse as the barium enema is evacuated. Note that the rest of the colon is normally emptied and collapsed. This proved at surgery to be a lymphosarcoma.

Intraluminal masses, which you see illustrated on these two pages, may take many forms. Polyps range in size from a millimeter to several centimeters. Polypoid tumors may fill up the lumen of the gut. Barium passing between the tumor and the normally distensible wall of the gut will outline the tumor, showing the normal mucosal markings stretched over the tumor. The barium shadows so formed will reflect the irregularities, if any, of the surface of the tumor as well as those of the mucosa lining the bowel. These can often be seen as a double moulage, the one distinguishable from the other, like those in Figure 14-17. Occasionally, matted intraluminal masses are formed of foreign substances like hair or vegetable fibers, becoming too large to be passed and eventually causing symptoms. These are called *bezoars.* They can usually be differentiated from intraluminal soft-tissue masses because barium mixes itself within the matted bezoar giving an appearance quite different from tumor coated with barium.

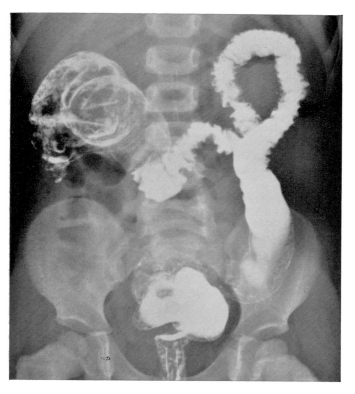

Figure 14-16 (left). Intussusception. Intraluminal mass composed of the patient's own cecum and terminal ileum which have been telescoped inside the lumen of the ascending colon and hepatic flexure, waves of peristalsis forcing it further along the lumen of the large bowel. Early in the illness intussusception may often be safely reduced by barium enema without manipulation. In cases of longer duration, surgery is the treatment of choice.

254

Figure 14-17 (right). Benign tumor projecting into the lumen of the stomach from its sessile base high on the lesser curvature. The normal rugal folds either behind it or in front of it are seen outlined with barium.

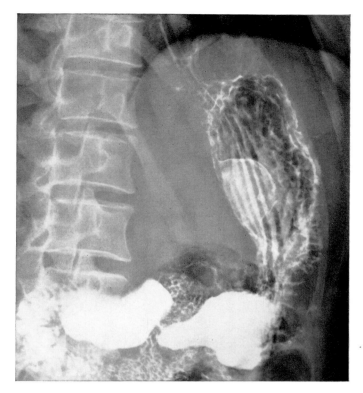

Figure 14-18 (below, right). Numerous ascarid worms outlined with barium are seen filling the small bowel as intraluminal filling defects. A film made the following day will often show a barium study of the gastro-intestinal tract of the worm!

Figure 14-19 (below). Bezoar in the stomach, composed of matted hair, in a little girl known to chew the ends of her pigtails.

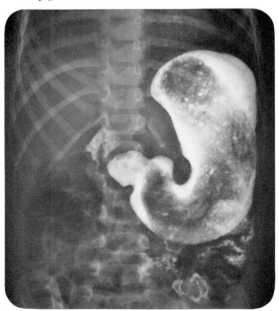

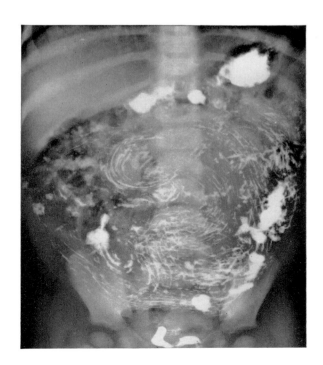

255

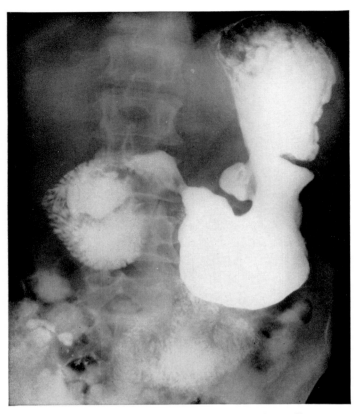

Figure 14-20. Large ulcer crater projecting from the midlesser curvature. Note radiolucent collar of granulation tissue.

The last of the five hypothetical tubular structures in Figure 14-2 shows what might be called an "addition shadow," although that term is not actually used. An ulceration has occurred in the wall of the tube, forming a small additional hollow space into which the opaque substance can flow. The term generally applied to this type of shadow in radiologic parlance is a *niche,* and you will find that term used commonly in reference to the projecting shadow of a barium-filled ulcer crater in the stomach or duodenum. Only when seen in profile, of course, will it be a projection from the normal margin of the gut wall. When a barium-filled ulcer crater is seen *en face* it appears as a *spot of white more dense than the surrounding shadow* because it is frequently encircled by a rolled-up margin of granulation tissue (or tumor, as the case may be). Ulcer craters which are filled with blood clot or food particles at

the time of examination with barium will not be visualized at all. As they heal they fill in from the sides, becoming sharp and thorn-shaped in profile, and finally disappearing altogether.

Because the tubular gastrointestinal tract is flexible, fills and empties in response to waves of peristalsis, and has opposing walls coated with barium, there are myriads of small angular barium shadows in most of the films you examine. To find among them one which can with confidence be labeled a niche requires that it have certain characteristics. A niche is deeper than most of the valleys between the folds of mucosa, in the first place. Therefore its shadow will be *denser* because it represents a slightly greater thickness of barium. Because it is an ulcer it will have no mucosal pattern, and because it is generally surrounded by inflammatory reaction it will be less flexible than the rest of the gut wall. The shadow of the niche will accordingly be *constant in shape and size.* It will be consistently demonstrable in the same place from film to film, and all these characteristics enable the radiologist to find and identify it in the course of his study.

There are numerous other details which also help him in interpreting his findings. For example, when he observes that the nearby mucosal folds in the stomach radiate toward a demonstrable ulcer crater, he may report that the ulcer is almost unquestionably benign and not malignant, because in differentiating these two types of ulcer in the stomach, the *radiation of folds* has proved to be the most reliable indication of benignity. You will hear much about the differentiation of benign and malignant ulcers in the stomach, and you will find that some craters seem to everyone probably benign and turn out to be malignant, while a few benign ulcers of long standing are so imbedded in scar tissue, so rigid, and so reluctant to heal on medical management that they are believed to be malignant by referring physician, radiologist, and surgeon, and only the pathologist with his microscopic evidence can establish the facts.

Do not be discouraged by so negative an assertion, however; many ulcer crater niches on the lesser curvature are reliably and convinc-

256

ingly benign in appearance, and the radiologist will so report them to you. Through repeated barium examinations, watching the behavior of the crater under medical treatment, its rate of healing, and the appearance of its base, together with the comforting convergence of mucosal folds, the radiologist may often safely make the statement that "this crater appears to be benign." If, on the other hand, he finds that the crater changes little with treatment over a period of 2 weeks or so, that it shows a shelf-like margin which protrudes into the barium as a filling defect, and that convergence of the folds is absent, he will report to you that in his opinion the ulcer is probably malignant.

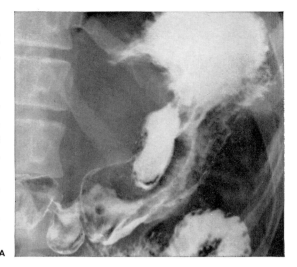

A

Figure 14-21. Natural history of healing in a large benign gastric ulcer. Without the metallic compression device in B, the healing thorn-shaped crater might easily be missed. In C the radiation of folds toward the small remaining crater indicates its benign character. D. Round spot films like this detail study are made during fluoroscopy with a compression cone.

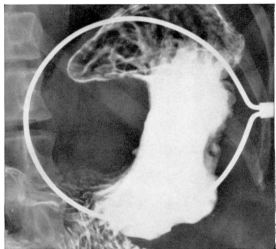

B

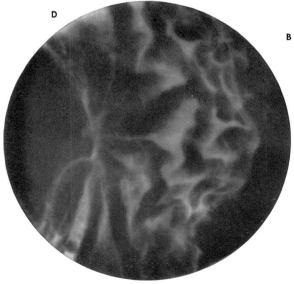

D

C

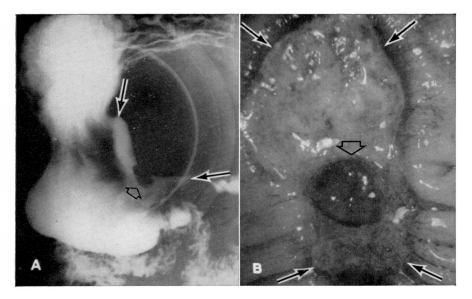

Figure 14-22. Large benign ulcer crater seen in profile on the lesser curvature (the stomach is seen from behind, and the lesser curvature is therefore on your right). Ulcer extended from high on the lesser curvature almost to the pylorus; its dimensions are indicated in both the radiograph, A, and the photograph of the surgical specimen, B, by dark arrows. There is a nodule of granulation tissue in the center of the base of the ulcer (boxed arrows).

Figure 14-23. Four proved malignant lesser curvature ulcers. A. The ulcer is *within a mass,* and there is marked distortion and infiltration of the surrounding mucosa. B. Meniscus sign, a reliable indication of malignancy when present. The meniscus sign consists of a crater outlined by a nodular tumor cuff, both lying *within* the normal profile of the stomach, that is, not truly projecting from its border. The meniscus sign is unfortunately not present in a great many malignant gastric ulcers. A, B, and C would probably be labeled malignant by most radiologists. D is more difficult, but the nodularity of the fold indicated by the arrow is suspicious. No real pronouncements should ever be made from films alone without knowing the dynamic behavior of the stomach at fluoroscopy.

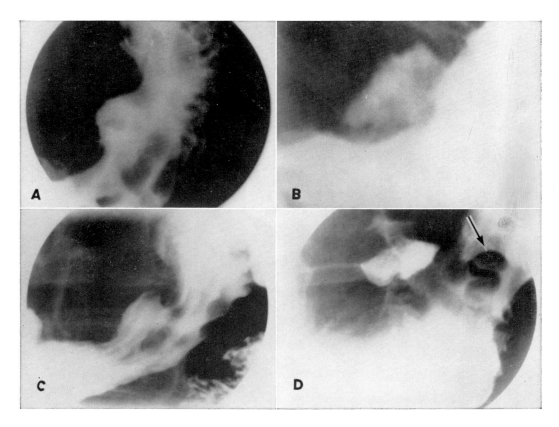

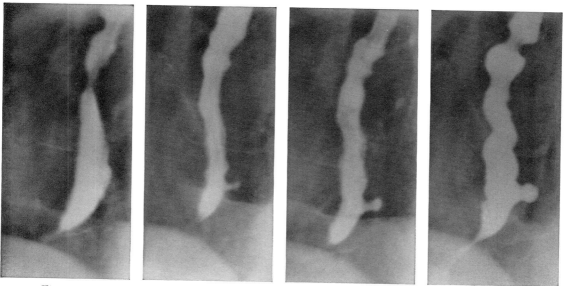

Figure 14-24. An esophageal diverticulum is seen to fill in successive spot films. A diverticulum is also an "addition shadow."

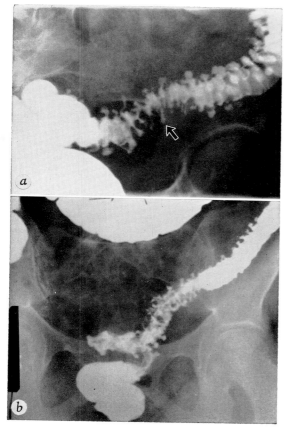

Figure 14-25 (left). Diverticulosis (the presence of diverticula) of the sigmoid colon, shown at barium enema examination.

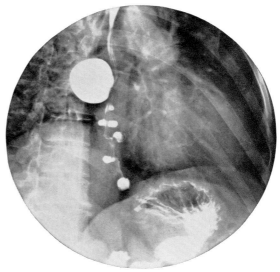

Figure 14-26 (above). Smooth round esophageal diverticula remain filled with barium after passage of the swallowed bolus into the stomach. Such retention of barium is often seen in gastric, duodenal, and other small bowel diverticula as well.

What is true about the identification of stomach ulcers is true about duodenal ulcer craters, in that they are consistently demonstrable denser flecks of barium. However, in the duodenum the problem is somewhat different, since instead of a wide sac the structure to be examined is now a narrow tube with a bulb or ampulla at its commencement distal to the pyloric canal. Although the crater itself is demonstrated in much the same way as it is in the stomach, still more important and informative in the long run are the changes due to scar tissue formation in this characteristically recurrent condition. After several episodes of ulceration and healing, permanent strands of scar tissue develop in the wall of the duodenal bulb, which constrict its lumen and limit its free distensibility in the fashion of a reefed sail. These limiting bands of scar tissue produce distinctive changes in the shape of the shadow of the barium-filled bulb, so that its cavity seems to be divided into several cavities bulging outward from the central point at which the ulcer crater has been present or may still be seen. This appearance has been called the *clover-leaf deformity* of the duodenal cap. However, it is only one of the more advanced scarring patterns in long-standing duodenal ulcers and is present in by no means all of the advanced cases you will see. Another common pattern of scarring is the gradual development of a stenosed apex of the cap eventually producing a high degree of obstruction and usually caused by ulcers which are located at the apex of the cap, where it normally narrows to become the descending limb of the duodenum. Still other patterns of scarring are produced by ulcers which for some reason recur less frequently or heal more easily. In these the bulb is seen to be deformed by a reef of scar tissue on only one side, the remainder of the bulb appearing quite unremarkable.

Several chapters could be written on the subject of duodenal ulcer alone, and you will gradually become familiar with the problems of diagnosing this entity roentgenologically. One very important point to remember is that a duodenal ulcer crater is fairly easy to demonstrate radiologically with barium in its early episodes. However, after scar tissue formation has become fairly well advanced, the crater itself becomes more and more difficult to visualize with each successive attack, and at length the radiologist will find it almost impossible to demonstrate in spite of unquestioned reactivation suggested by the patient's symptoms. For this reason, re-examination with barium is not at all indicated with each new attack in a patient with a well-established diagnosis of duodenal ulcer and typical scarring. Once the diagnosis has been made, the clinician does well to be guided by the patient's symptoms alone. Only with the appearance of a significant change in the patient's long-standing symptoms, or increasing evidence of obstruction, need re-examination be carried out.

The student who looks at radiographs of the barium-filled stomach for the first time often has some difficulty identifying the various parts of the stomach, in particular the pylorus, and this difficulty generally stems from the fact that each of the conventional views of the stomach is made in a different projection with the patient differently positioned. The fluoroscopist usually begins with the patient standing, examines the esophagus and stomach with a small amount of barium to study the mucosal relief pattern. Then he tilts the power-driven fluoroscopy table into the horizontal position, arranges the patient prone and turned up slightly on his right side. The patient drinks more barium and is then turned into the supine position. Spot films are made at intervals whenever the radiologist sees anything on the screen he wishes recorded. Large films are then made by a technician in a series of specified projections. These generally include one made straight prone, one prone but turned to the right slightly (the right anterior oblique), one made in a straight lateral projection with the patient on his right side, and one made supine with the patient rolled to the left slightly so as to fill the antrum of the stomach with air. Study the following series of normal stomachs in various positions, in many of which the pylorus is identified by a long black arrow. Note in each the varying shape of the stomach and of the duodenal bulb, as well as the deep indentations in both curvatures (peristaltic waves which progress when seen at fluoroscopy).

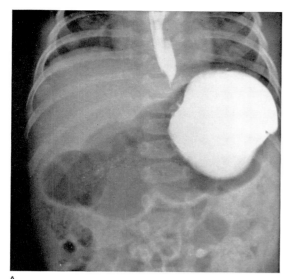
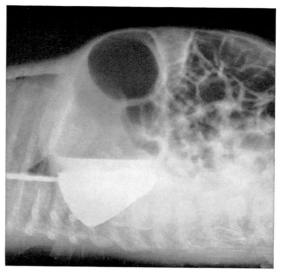

A   B

Figure 14-27. *A.* A baby lying on his back is being fed barium. Note that, just as you saw it in the supine plain films, the antrum of the stomach is filled with air, while the pool of barium collects in the more posteriorly placed fundus of the stomach. *B.* The same baby seen from the side. The ray is now tangential to the air-barium interface, so you see a fluid level. It is easy to understand from these films why babies more readily vomit their feedings when left lying on their backs, and why they are burped upright against the mother's shoulder with the undesirable swallowed air in the fundus.

Figure 14-28. Prone film from a gastrointestinal series in an adult. Arrow indicates the position of the pylorus although you cannot see it because of overlap from barium in the antrum. Note the well-seen duodenal loop, often partly hidden by the antral barium.

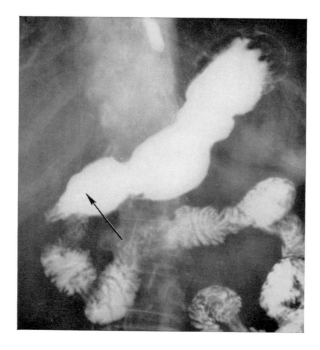

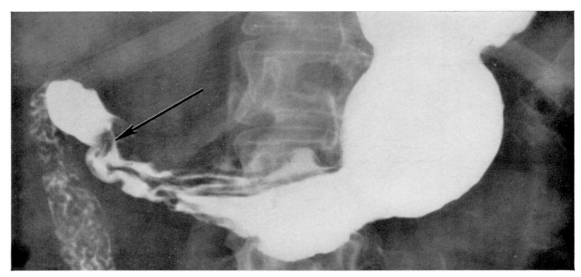

Figure 14-29 (above). Another patient, prone but turned very slightly to the right. Pylorus is seen as barium passes through it.

Figure 14-30 (below). The standard right anterior oblique projection unrolls the antrum, duodenal bulb, and loop. Note obliquity of the vertebrae as a clue to the position.

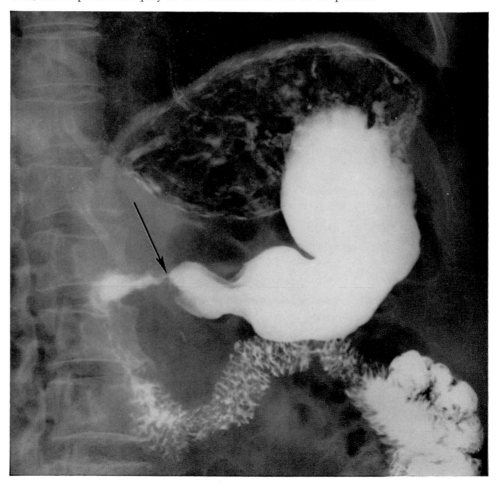

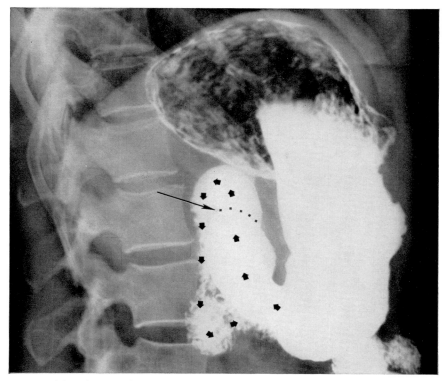

Figure 14-31 (above). Lateral view, the patient now turned straight onto his right side, as you can see from the vertebrae. Arrow indicates position of the pylorus. Base of the cap is indicated in dots. Flow of barium from antrum to duodenal bulb, down the descending limb of the loop, and then forward and to the left is marked with small dark arrows. The descending duodenum in this view usually lies along the anterior borders of the vertebral bodies or overlaps them slightly. Retroperitoneal or pancreatic masses often displace the duodenum forward, a fact best appreciated in this view. Ulcer craters on the *posterior* wall of the stomach are frequently difficult to visualize except in this view.

Figure 14-32 (below). This patient has been turned from the right lateral position onto his back and a supine film made. Air from the fundus has ballooned out the barium-coated antrum. Pylorus indicated by an arrow.

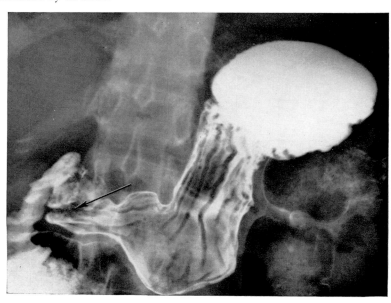

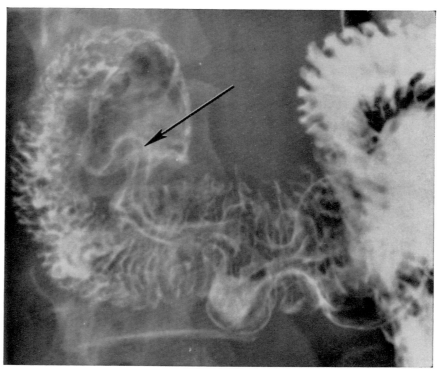

Figure 14-33 (above). Another example of the supine left oblique, a means of studying the stomach antrum and often the duodenal bulb by double contrast, that is, coated with opaque barium and then inflated with air. The antrum is seen here superimposed on the barium coated mucosa of the duodenal loop. Each can be distinguished by its relief markings. Note deep peristaltic waves in the antrum. Arrow indicates the pylorus. Compare this duodenal cap with the one below.

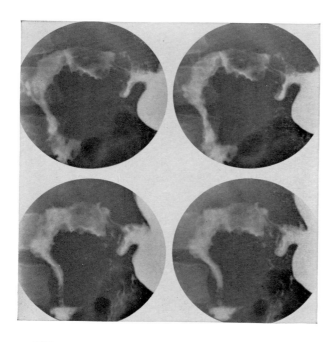

Figure 14-34 (left). Duodenal cap and loop unrolled in the lateral position in four spot films. The pylorus is identified by two fine parallel streaks of barium caught in its folds. The bulb here is radiolucent centrally because it contained a soft-tissue tumor mass, which might have resembled air filling except that it was consistently present in every film no matter in what position the patient was placed.

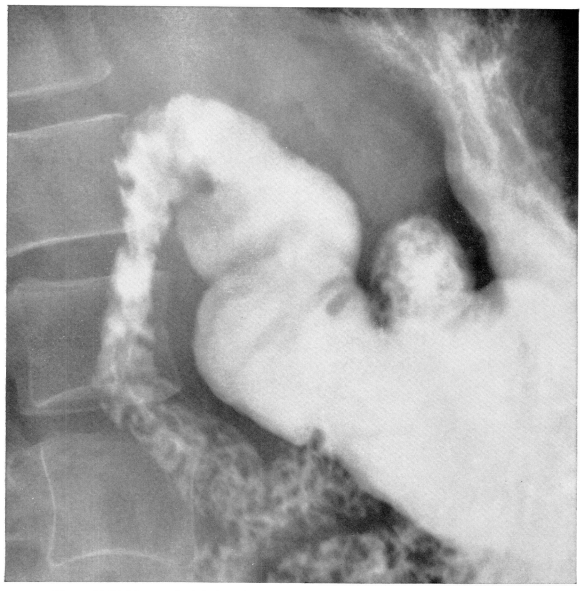

Figure 14-35. The vertebral bodies identify this as a lateral view. Antrum, pylorus, duodenal bulb (indented posteriorly by scar tissue from a duodenal ulcer), and descending duodenum are all easily identified. The apparent projection from the lesser curvature is not an ulcer crater but the duodenum at the ligament of Treitz, recognizable from the pattern of its mucosa.

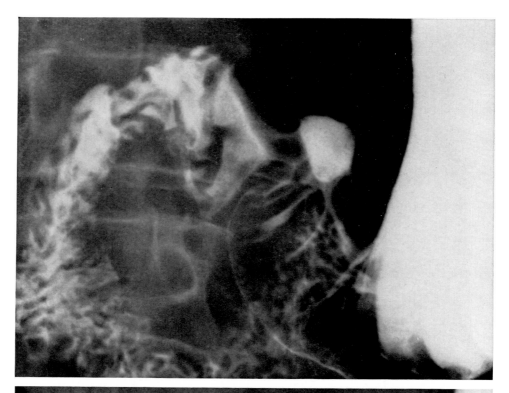

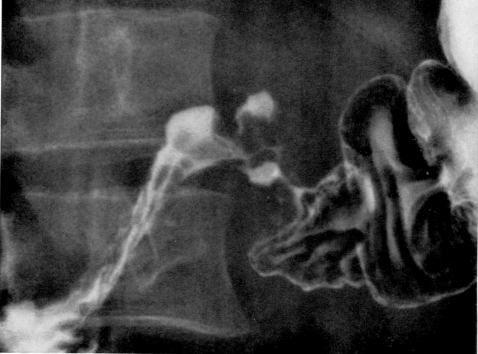

Figure 14-36. Clover-leaf deformity of the duodenal cap. It would be impossible to say from these two films whether there was an active crater present because of the advanced scarring. The behavior of the duodenum under the fluoroscope and the appearance of additional spot films might or might not decide the matter.

Figure 14-37. Large ulcer crater (white arrow) at the apex of the duodenal bulb. The scarring produced by craters in this location is likely to lead to obstruction eventually. Pylorus is indicated by black arrow.

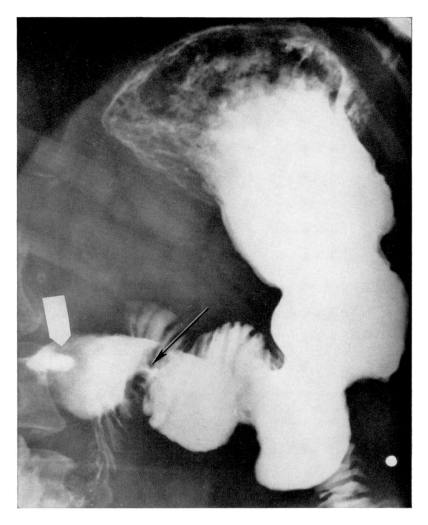

Figure 14-38. Seven ulcer craters on the posterior wall of the duodenal bulb. In both the surgical specimen and the radiograph, the black arrow indicates the largest central crater around which the other six were arranged in a circle. White arrow indicates the pylorus. The duodenal bulb is filling with air so that barium remaining in the craters on the posterior wall is clearly seen.

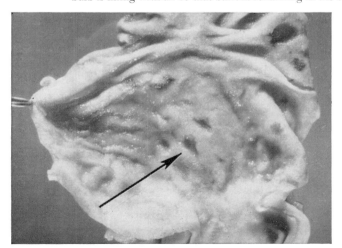 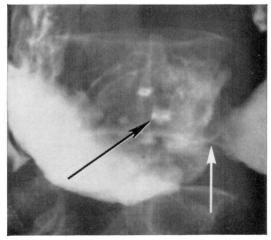

267

In studying the gastrointestinal tract, then, the radiologist looks for a mucosal relief pattern which seems to him to be within the normal limits of variation. He searches specifically for crater niches while manipulating the part through the abdominal wall, his hand protected by a leaded glove. He fills the succeeding parts of the gut with barium, testing their distensibility and looking for areas of rigidity, which may indicate even without any apparent ulceration that the wall is invaded by new growth or scarred by inflammation.

The recognition of an area of rigidity in gut wall is more difficult in many ways than the recognition of a crater, because the wall of the gut varies so much from part to part normally and because early infiltration with sheets of tumor cells does not render the wall entirely rigid but rather limits its elasticity, much in the way a sheet of rubber changes with age. If you can imagine a remarkably distensible organ like the stomach, into the wall of which has been set a piece of rubber which has lost some of its elasticity, you will have a fair idea of the behavior which can be expected from such a segment under the fluoroscope. Barium pushed against it with the gloved hand will fail to produce quite the prompt bulging expected. Barium pushed upward by the examining hand into normal gut shows a marginal pattern of wrinkles or folds as the flexible wall is mechanically displaced; the rigid or infiltrated segment will fold sluggishly and less deeply. Peristalsis, too, will be altered, and as one watches the normal passage of ring-like constrictions along the organ, one sees that they are resisted by the suspicious segment, which indents less readily with the passage of the wave. This is perfectly logical since the contraction of sheets of muscle in the wall is limited by the infiltration of tumor cells, by edema, or by postinflammatory changes, as the case may be.

Decisions with regard to the flexibility of the gut wall, then, are based on the manner in which it is seen to distend with barium, to respond to manipulation, and to contract physiologically. Study the following examples of rigidity, imagining how the gross specimen would look.

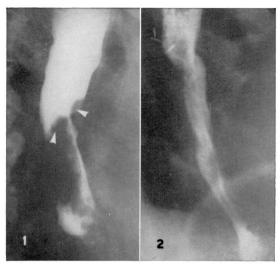

Figure 14-39 (above). Patient with dysphagia. 1. Carcinoma of the esophagus narrowed the lumen to a tunnel a few millimeters wide and 10 centimeters in length, a rigid segment which never changed either at fluoroscopy or on the films. Arrows indicate shelf. 2. Appearance after radiation therapy.

Figure 14-40 (below). Carcinoma of the rectum here forms a rigid filling defect limiting the distension of the ampulla during a barium enema.

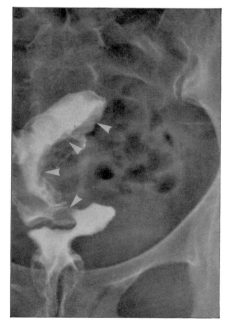

268

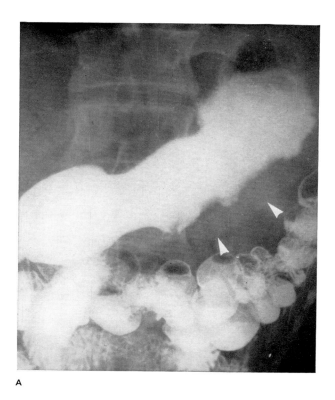

A

Figure 14-41. Radiograph, *A*, shows thickened, rigid stomach wall due to infiltrating carcinoma. Drawing, *B*, indicates the way in which you should try to supply the tumor in imagination when looking at such radiographs. At fluoroscopy no peristaltic waves at all would pass through a rigid segment of this type.

B

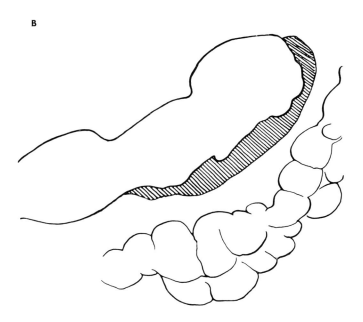

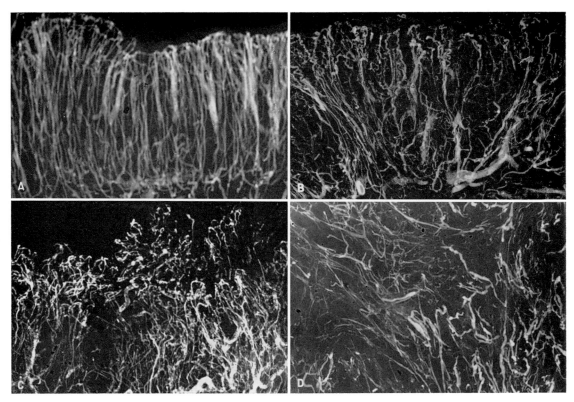

Figure 14-42

Rigidity in the wall of the gut, increasing as invasion by tumor advances, can be even better comprehended by examining the four illustrations above. They are *microangiograms* in which specimens of gut removed at surgery are injected via their arteries with a radio-opaque medium and radiographs made of the frozen sections. Here you see in *A* the normal pattern of the arterioles in the intestinal mucosa, with their narrow straight vessels, terminal arcades, and branching. The other three cuts show this architecture distorted by the invasion of carcinoma in the wall of the gut.

Inflammation in the bowel may result in ulceration or in total loss of mucosa, as seen in regional enteritis with serial barium studies of the small bowel. After long-standing chronic inflammation, scarring and fibrosis may result in localized constriction and intestinal obstruction or in a general loss of elasticity with demonstrable shortening of the involved bowel.

The cecum and rectum, like the stomach expanded sections of the gut, are difficult to examine and present special problems for the radiologist. The cecum should not be considered visualized in its entirety until there is retrograde filling of either the appendix or the terminal ileum. This is a vital point in patients with unexplained anemia in whom carcinoma of the cecum must be ruled out.

Carcinoma of the rectum should be diagnosed by the clinician on physical examination. The radiologist knows that because of the great distensibility of the rectal ampulla it is easy for him to miss entirely a sizable carcinoma in this location, obscured by the barium surrounding and concealing it.

During the barium enema, patients are examined as the barium is being instilled into rectum, sigmoid and descending colon. In the supine position the flexures are studied in various degrees of obliquity. When the colon is filled, a prone film is obtained, and the patient allowed to evacuate the barium, after which a second film is made to show the emptied large bowel and its mucosal relief pattern.

Because of the great redundancy and overlap of the rectosigmoid colon in the pelvis, it is very difficult to "unroll" and thereby visualize every part of this segment of bowel. A number of ingenious maneuvers have been designed by radiologists to help locate malignant lesions in the sigmoid. Patients have been examined at a sharp incline on a table with the head down so that the loops of bowel will be pulled out of the pelvis by their own heavy barium content and the sigmoid straightened. Patients are routinely examined in oblique projections and laterally, and many radiologists use a view in which the central ray is directed obliquely caudad in the sagittal plane in a prone patient (Figure 14-43B). The patient may also be examined sitting up, the ray directed downward through the back as in Figure 14-44. New projections are constantly being evolved for the better visualization of opaque-filled structures. The cooperation of the patient makes a great deal of difference in the success of these procedures. For this reason, it seems to me that it ought to be a rule of thumb with physicians to explain briefly beforehand to the patient approximately what is going to be done.

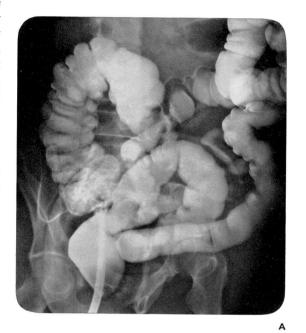

A

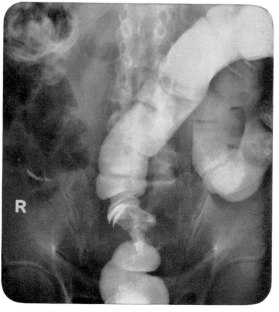

B

Figure 14-43. A. Conventional barium enema examination fails to show the lesion at the recto-sigmoid junction, a carcinoma producing annular constriction which is well seen in the special view, B, made with an oblique sagittal ray.

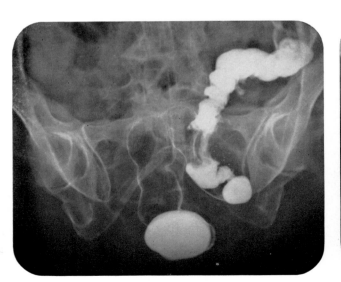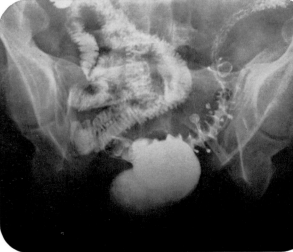

Figure 14-44 (top). A special position in which the patient may be examined in order to unroll the sigmoid colon.

Figure 14-45 (bottom, left). Annular lesion at the sigmoid flexure visualized in this fashion. Note bony structures.

Figure 14-46 (bottom, right). Diverticulosis and diverticulitis of the sigmoid, similarly visualized.

Herniation of the various abdominal structures outside the abdomen is common and has been recorded for every hiatal opening through which structures normally pass. One of the commonest of such herniations is that of a part of the fundus of the stomach through the esophageal hiatus in the diaphragm, the gastric fundus sliding upward through an unusually wide opening. This is the so-called "hiatus hernia," and it may exist throughout life without producing such symptoms as pain or fatal bleeding. It is diagnosed during barium examination of the stomach, often not until the patient assumes the prone recumbent position, and sometimes not without a variety of fluoroscopic maneuvers designed to increase intra-abdominal pressure. The gastric fundus is seldom fixed in its herniated position above the level of the diaphragm, sliding in and out of the hiatus with changes in position or in abdominal pressure. Thus, attempted pronunciation of the letter "K" against a closed glottis increases the abdominal pressure and may show the barium-filled fundus pinched by the diaphragm and visible above it. The hernia is frequently reduced when the patient stands. Here you see two patients in whom the herniated fundus is visualized by such maneuvers in the right oblique recumbent prone position during a gastrointestinal series.

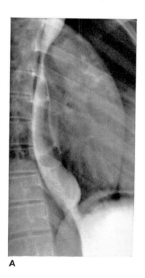  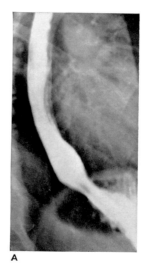 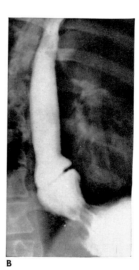

A   B   A   B

Figure 14-47 (above, left). Normal esophagus. *B.* With increased abdominal pressure.

Figure 14-48 (above, right). Hiatus hernia. Note rugal pattern of stomach pinched by the diaphragm with abdominal pressure increased, *B.*

Figure 14-49 (right). Hiatus hernia demonstrated by increasing the abdominal pressure (*B* and *C*).

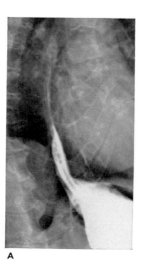 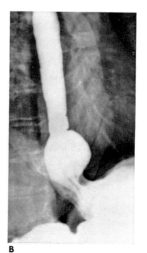 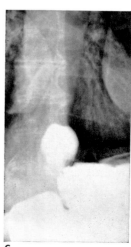

A   B   C

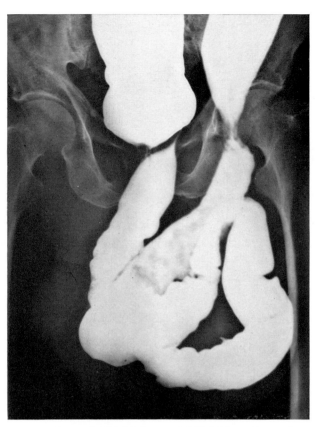

Figure 14-50 (*Unknown 14-2*). Make a diagnosis.

If you go into general practice or into internal medicine as a specialty, the question is sure to arise whether or not you should possess and use a fluoroscope on your own office patients. The late Dr. George Holmes once said that the ownership of a fluoroscope does not make a fluoroscopist, and even the limited information I have just given you about the ways in which the trained radiologist arrives at decisions based on films and fluoroscopic study together may have convinced you of the wisdom of his statement. It is true that there is something dazzling and magical about being able to see through human tissues; it is true that patients are impressed with the procedure; but good judgment in the manipulation of living tissues under the fluoroscope and in the interpretation of the usually vague shadows seen there is obtainable only after years of training and practice.

The use of the fluoroscope also has built-in dangers. Much has been written of late about the hazards of radiation, and there can be no question that any radiation which is unnecessary is ill used, for the sake of physician and patient alike. While the danger involved in diagnostic procedures *not* employing fluoroscopy is minimal, fluoroscopy exposes patient and physician to a much greater amount of radiation, per single procedure, than any examination involving simply the making of films. The radiologist has been specifically trained to limit this exposure in a variety of ways to the smallest amount of radiation which will produce the required information. Studies have been made comparing the measured radiation exposure to both patient and physician when an expert trained in the work is operating the fluoroscope and when a physician unfamiliar with the expected norms and technical maneuvers is fluoroscoping. These studies show that training cuts exposure to a small fraction. *Those who train fluoroscopists feel that since it takes up to 5 years to develop proficiency in these techniques, fluoroscopes should never be used by uninstructed operators.*

There can be no question that the physician is the person in greatest danger. The patient, once the diagnosis is clear, is unlikely to be in need of fluoroscopy more than a few times a year, no matter what his illness. Since injury from radiation is cumulative, however, the physician who uses the fluoroscope only for a few minutes a day can expose himself to a great deal too much radiation in a year's time. Thus, caution and good sense should guide you in making decisions with regard to the avoidability of radiation exposure, both for yourself and for your patients.

So much for the problems you need to be able to recognize with regard to the use of contrast substances in the gastrointestinal tract. Such studies are principally directed toward the recognition of morphologic changes. Other types of contrast studies have important physiologic implications in that the contrast material is excreted by the body. These are cholecystography and intravenous urography, presently, although one may eventually be developed for the pancreas. The next chapter gives you some idea of the deductions one may make based on excretory contrast studies.

274

CHAPTER 15

Special Deductions Possible
from Excretory and Secretory
Contrast Studies

The discovery of cholecystography reads like a detective story, and the details of it are worth giving here because they illustrate so effectively the peculiar combination of intellectual alertness, hard work, and fortunate accident which so often produces a revolutionary new discovery.

When Warren Cole was in training as a surgical resident at the Barnes Hospital in St. Louis between 1921 and 1926, he decided, with Evarts Graham, to investigate the possibilities of producing a radio-opaque drug which would be excreted in the bile. Abel and Rowntree, while searching for a cathartic which could be given hypodermically, had demonstrated that phenoltetrachlorphthalein was excreted almost entirely in the bile.* A few years later Rous and McMaster had shown that the normal gallbladder concentrates bile 8 to 10 times by absorbing water from it. These facts, together with the knowledge that halogenated compounds are very radio-opaque because of their high molecular weights, persuaded Cole and Graham that excretory roentgen visualization of the gallbladder might be feasible.

The first halogenated phthalein compound they were able to obtain from the Mallinckrodt Chemical Works was phenoltetrachlorphthalein. The atomic weight of chlorine is only 35.5, however, compared with 80 for bromine and 127 for iodine, and for this reason they planned early in the experiments to work with the soluble salts of the bromine and iodine compounds. Accordingly, week after week they tried injecting into dogs and rabbits the sodium, calcium, and strontium salts of tetrabromophenolphthalein and tetraiodophenolphthalein.

They injected over 200 animals without obtaining a single shadow of the gallbladder. The animals were injected early in the morning and the radiographs made late in the afternoon to allow time for the excretion and concentration of the opaque-loaded bile. Finally, a very dense shadow of what appeared to be the gallbladder was obtained in one dog, but the finding could not be repeated.

Discouraged, Cole was in the radiology department one afternoon studying that single positive examination (Figure 15-1) to be certain that the shadow did not represent a bone the dog had swallowed. A radiologist, Dr. Walter Mills, happened to see the film and commented at once that it had to be the shadow of the gallbladder and that he believed it could only be a matter of time before the method would be used in humans.

With renewed conviction Cole then interviewed the attendant in the animal house, asking him whether anything different had been done for the dog in question on the day the positive test had been obtained. The caretaker denied that anything unusual had happened, but something about the manner of his reply prompted Cole to press him further, and he finally admitted reluctantly that he had forgotten to feed that dog that day. Expecting a reprimand, the man was startled to have his hand shaken and his back slapped in a vigorous and grateful manner by Cole, who had realized

*Phenolphthalein itself was found to be excreted primarily by the kidneys; phenolsulfonphthalein (PSP) partly by the liver but mostly by the kidneys. Later these data were used by Rosenthal and White to develop the Bromsulphalein test (BSP) for hepatic function.

276

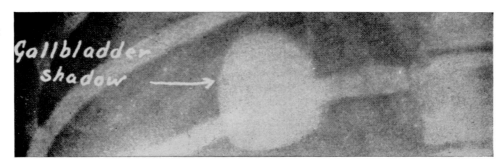

Figure 15-1. The first successful cholecystogram (see text).

Gallbladder Shadow →

at once that all the disappointing negative examinations were probably due to the fact that the gallbladders had emptied prematurely in response to the single daily feeding. The dog who accidentally fasted all day had retained the concentrated opaque bile in his gallbladder until late afternoon when the films were made. After this the studies progressed rapidly, and today, of course, the patient being prepared for cholecystography fasts overnight.

It would be unrealistic not to add to this miraculous story that years of investigative work subsequently went into the perfection of contrast substances which had minimal toxic side effects, could be given safely by vein or by mouth, and would produce roentgen shadows of the gallbladder more and more reliably. Today cholecystography is arranged for in advance, the radiologist supplying the patient with the particular drug to be used if an oral method of administration is planned. The patient, fasting after a light supper, swallows the tablets of opaque drug the evening before the examination and empties his colon with plain water enemas to remove fecal shadows from the right upper quadrant. Cathartics are not used because they interfere with the absorption of opaque material from the small bowel.

Early in the morning the patient, still fasting, reports to the radiologist, and films are made in a prone oblique position (that is, with the gallbladder as close as possible to the film and not superimposed on the ribs).

The absence of a gallbladder shadow on the films obtained does not necessarily imply depressed function. A number of factors influence the successful resolution of this test, just as they did in Cole's original experiments.

The patient may not, after all, have taken the tablets as he was instructed to do. (This is not an absurd premise; it happens too frequently to be amusing.) If he took them, he may not actually have fasted; perhaps his idea of a fast allowed the (surely modest) addition of a cup of tea and two slices of well-buttered toast. If he indeed refrained from food, he may have had some nausea or diarrhea in reaction to the drug, preventing its retention in the small bowel long enough to allow for absorption.

For these reasons the fallibility of the test is checked customarily today in negative cases by re-examination a day later. The patient adheres to a very light, fat-free diet overnight, and a second set of films is obtained the following morning.

A patient suspected of chronic gallbladder disease for some time may have been on a low-fat regimen for months, and will begin the period of the cholecystographic examination with a gallbladder already filled with inspissated bile. It may even be necessary to maintain such a patient on a high-fat diet for a period in order to empty the organ of old bile before cholecystography is attempted.

In the absence of a gallbladder shadow after properly performed cholecystography today, one is justified in assuming (1) that liver function is depressed and the drug is not being excreted; or (2) that there is obstruction somewhere in the biliary tree, cystic duct, or common bile duct, the ducts being distended with nonopaque bile; or (3) that a variety of less well understood technical factors and pathologic changes combine to prohibit opacification of the gallbladder, usually suggesting pathology of that organ.

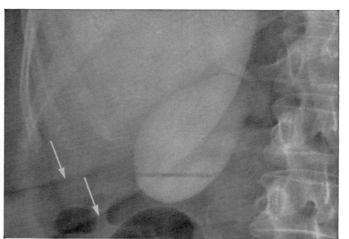

Figure 15-3 (above). A layer of small radiolucent stones seen tangentially in a film made with the patient standing. Arrows indicate crease in abdominal wall and margin of pendulous breast.

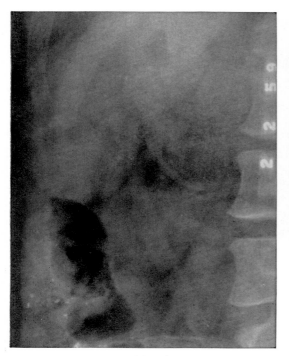

Figure 15-2 (above). Faint shadow of the gallbladder obtained after a single dose of cholecystographic radio-opaque medium. The gallbladder here lies just above the air in the right colon and superimposed on the tip of the eleventh rib.

Figure 15-4 *(Unknown 15-1)* (below). Make a diagnosis.

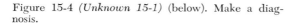
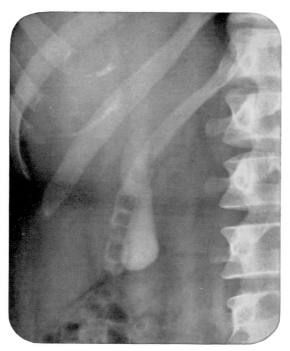

It is important to remember that even when the gallbladder *is* successfully visualized, disease of that structure may be present. The gallbladders of patients with chronic cholecystitis are often successfully visualized for years before a cholecystectomy is done, although the shadows obtained are usually subnormal in density and may show filling defects representing calculi. The prompt contraction of the gallbladder in response to a fatty meal may provide some additional evidence for good "function" and is recorded on a second film. *In sum, then, when you do not see a gallbladder shadow after cholecystography you take it very seriously, but the trouble may be in the liver or ducts. When you do see a shadow, it does not rule out the possibility of inflammation and moderately decreased gallbladder "function."*

Small calculi of low density may present a problem in that often they are not seen on the plain film and are lost to view in a cluster against the anterior wall of the gallbladder even when there is only moderate concentration of the contrast substance. Such small stones may be visualized in the standing position because they drop into the fundus of the gallbladder, displacing a little of the cholecystographic opaque medium. They may also seek a level of their own, above a level of inspissated bile and calcium sand and below a thinner bile containing the contrast material. The stones will be seen in such instances as discs tangential to the beam, and therefore visualized in the stand-ing film as you see them in Figure 15-3. Such erect (or decubitus) films are a routine part of cholecystography in most clinics and often clarify the diagnosis in patients who seem to be having classic bouts of gallstone colic but in whom the cholecystogram is repeatedly nega-tive.

The interpretation of the intravenous uro-gram requires the consideration of a still more complex pattern of physiologic possibilities. The retrograde pyelogram was used long be-fore the development of the excretory urogram in 1929, and its principal value is to study mor-phology. The two types of examination are not at all interchangeable and must be considered quite differently suited to differing conditions. They are often complementary, the retrograde reinforcing or excluding something suggested by the intravenous study. Most clinicians feel that, inasmuch as the excretory study gives certain functional information not provided by the retrograde, it is usually better to begin with intravenous urography, a relatively benign pro-cedure without important contraindications. Retrograde pyelography may be used as a sup-plement where more precise morphologic in-formation is required; it is uncomfortable for the patient and involves at least the trauma of cystoscopy, and ureteral catheterization.

Certainly the discovery of radio-opaque chemicals which were excreted selectively by the kidney revolutionized urologic diagnosis. Renal lesions were visualized which, before that, had only been diagnosed at exploratory surgery, obstruction below the kidney prevent-ing retrograde study. Thus, at once the scope of available morphologic information was ex-panded by the new excretory studies, and at first it was believed, as well, that concentrated opaque material seen in normal-appearing kid-ney draining systems on both sides could be interpreted to mean normal structure and func-tion bilaterally. During the past decade, how-ever, a somewhat more refined pattern of interpretation has been developed for excretory urography. The appearance of the excreted contrast substance has been checked against improved methods of kidney function testing and vascular information.

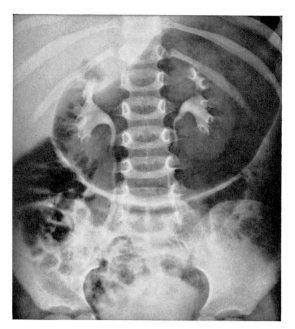

Figure 15-5. Intravenous urogram.

Figure 15-6. Retrograde pyelogram.

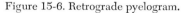

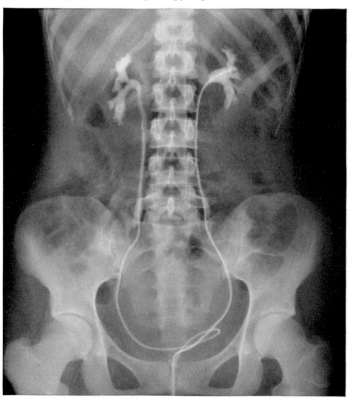

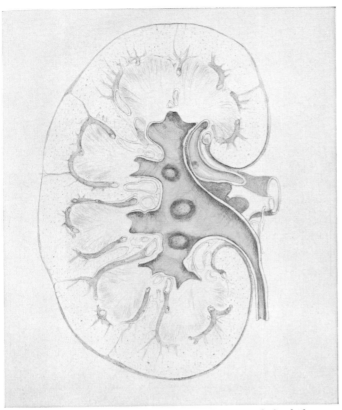

Figure 15-7. Cross section drawing of the kidney to review the anatomy of the draining structures and compare with the excretory urogram seen in Figure 15-8.

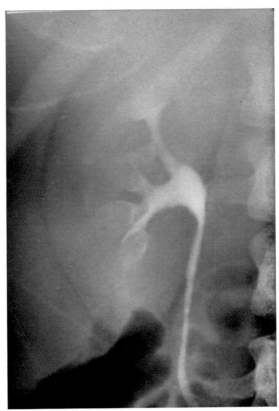

Figure 15-8. Note "nephrogram" density of kidney parenchyma and brush of collecting tubules which compose the papilla emptying into the calix. The cupped shape of the calix is normal. With obstruction this is inverted and caliectasis is said to be present.

One cannot, today, simply equate the density of contrast substance with over-all kidney function. Kidney function is a highly complex matter and consists of many interrelated processes—glomerular filtration, water and electrolyte reabsorption, tubular excretion—all dependent on vascular supply and on normal drainage. *The density of contrast substance in the kidney draining structures must be interpreted in the light of any variation in the fluid flow through the kidney.*

The drugs most widely in use as this is written are excreted by the kidney almost entirely with the glomerular filtrate. This means that within less than a minute after the intravenous injection enough opaque substance is present in the glomerular capsules and kidney tubules within the renal parenchyma to give an appre-

ciable whitening to the kidney shadow on an abdominal film. This is called the "nephrogram phase," and has an important usefulness in certain conditions to be discussed presently.

Between 1 and 2 minutes after the injection, opaque substance may be seen filling the calices, infundibula, and pelves of the kidneys. The radiodensity of the opaque material mixed with urine in the draining structures increases steadily and passes downward into the ureters and bladder. If the patient has voided just before the injection, then most of the urine present will be excreted with the contrast substance cleared from the blood stream. If the patient has not voided, however, there will be some nonopaque urine in the bladder which was excreted earlier and with which the opaque substance gradually mixes. Thus, the bladder shad-

280

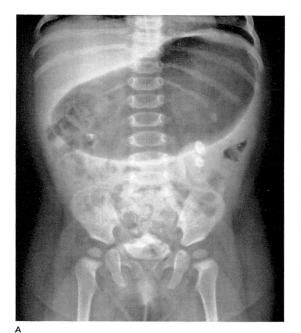
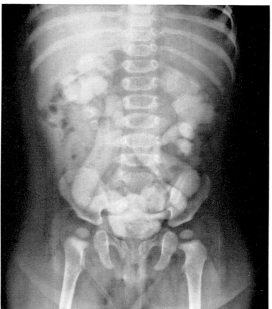

A   B

Figure 15-9. *A.* Fifteen minutes after the injection of opaque medium only a few round areas of density are seen in the kidneys. *B.* Three and one-half hours later the reason for this is evident. This 5½-month-old girl had severe bilateral hydronephrosis and large tortuous ureters.

ow may be seen to be large but faint at first, increasing from film to film in the series in both size and density. The entire length of the ureters is not normally seen filled because they are constantly being swept by peristaltic waves. They may be made to fill more completely by exerting pressure through the abdominal wall against the ureters where they cross the lumbosacral prominence.

The density of the opaque material seen in the draining structures of the kidney, therefore, will be decreased if there is low ureteral obstruction and the ureters are already filled with nonopaque urine. The contrast substance will also be delayed in its time of appearance. In the presence of bilateral ureteral obstruction, then, the faint excretion of opaque medium will be seen only after a lapse of time. The study must be carried on accordingly much longer than the time conventionally devoted to intravenous urography, and much information is available from such late films made after several hours.

Figure 15-10 (*Unknown 15-2*). Six-month-old boy with a mass in the left upper quadrant. This film was made 5 minutes after the injection of contrast medium. Analyze the film.

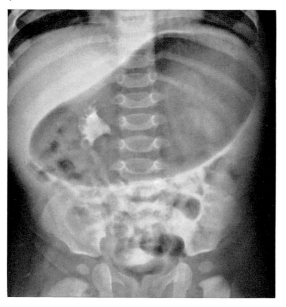

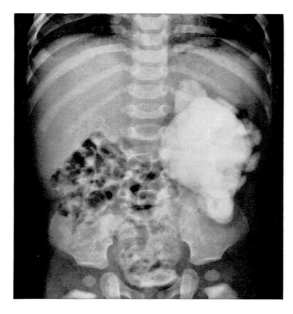

Figure 15-11 (left). This is a film made at 7½ hours after the intravenous injection in the same child you have just studied in Figure 15-10. The mass in the left upper quadrant is now obviously an enormous hydronephrotic kidney. Note that even though much of the opaque medium must have been excreted via the good right kidney, contrast material *was* excreted by the obstructed left kidney, given time.

Figure 15-13 (below). Intravenous urogram. Definite caliectasis, or early hydronephrosis, on the right, possibly caused by pressure on the lower part of the right ureter which is also abnormally full. Note that you must interpret absence of sharp, delicate caliceal cupping in an intravenous study much more seriously than you interpret similar changes in the retrograde study.

Figure 15-12 (below). Retrograde pyelogram. The slight inversion of the caliceal cupping is to be expected in retrograde studies and should not be interpreted as caliectasis or early hydronephrosis. (A cyst is seen deforming the upper pole of the left kidney and distorting the upper and middle calices, which are stretched around it.)

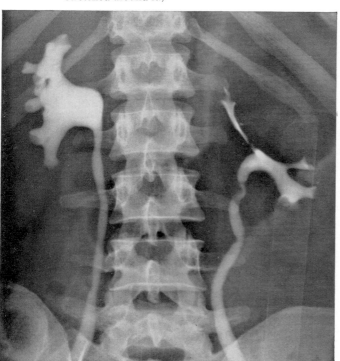

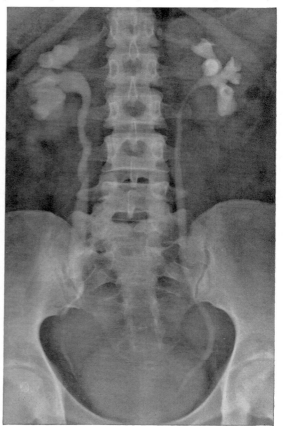

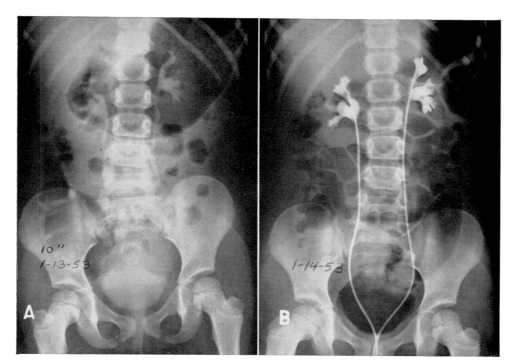

Figure 15-14. *Temporary poor drainage of the left kidney, apparently the result of trauma during a retrograde study. A.* Intravenous urogram, 1/13/53, shows normal sharply cupped calices in both kidneys. *B.* Retrograde study the following day is not abnormal. This degree of inversion of the calices is normal during retrograde pyelography. *C.* Repeat intravenous study the following day shows normal drainage on the right but definitely impeded drainage on the left. This degree of inversion of the calices is distinctly abnormal during an intravenous study. *D.* Poor drainage is not transient and is still present at half an hour after the injection. *E.* Three years later an intravenous study shows sharp caliceal cupping on both sides. (Interim urograms are not available, and, of course, recovery probably occurred after only a few days.)

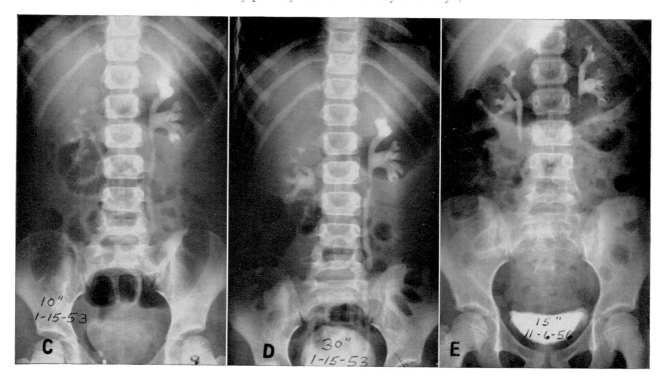

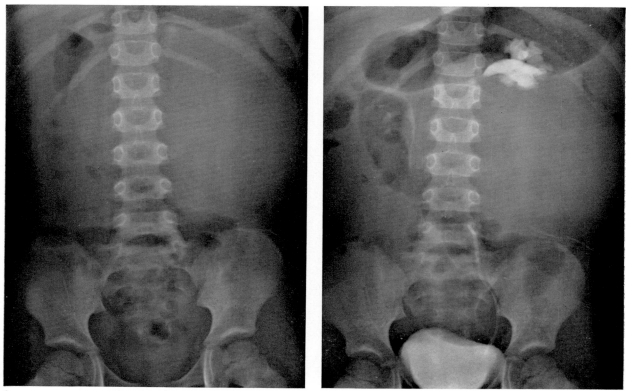

A

B

Figure 15-15 (above). Left upper quadrant mass in a child. Do you think it is a hydronephrotic kidney? *A* (left). Plain film. *B* (right). The 1-hour film from an intravenous urogram (see text).

Figure 15-16 (below and right). <u>Caliectasis</u> without dilatation of the renal pelvis. What conditions might cause it? (See text.)

A

B

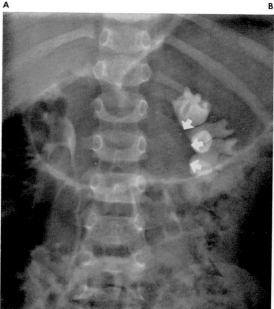

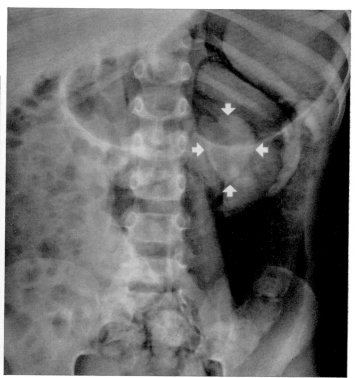

284

The left upper quadrant mass in the child in Figure 15-15 proved to be a <u>Wilms's tumor</u> of very large proportions in the lower part of the left kidney. Note that in the film made at 1 hour the functioning kidney has been displaced upward and that drainage from it is not occurring freely. You know this because of the caliceal blunting which you see and also from the intensification of the opaque shadow which has occurred as a result of water reabsorption in a kidney through which the fluid flow is decreased. Compare the faint shadow of the right kidney which is concentrating urine at a normal rate and must have excreted most of the opaque medium you see in the bladder.

In Figure 15-16 a tumor mass in the left renal hilum obstructs the proper emptying of the calices, which are blunted though still visibly cupped. *B* is a film made after the injection of gas retroperitoneally and outlines the mass in the left kidney hilum clearly.

So far, then, you have seen a variety of examples of unilateral and bilateral obstruction to drainage, producing varying degrees of caliceal fullness and frank hydronephrosis with hydroureter. The appearance of the draining structures in each example is a function of both the level of the obstruction and its degree of completeness. Thus, in Figure 15-9 the obstruction is low because both ureters are seen to be dilated. In Figures 15-10 and 15-11 the obstruction appears to be just below the renal pelvis, while in Figure 15-16 it is higher still and only the calices are seen to be full.

It is surprising that any function occurs in a chronically obstructed kidney which has been converted into a huge sac about which only a rim of much-thinned renal parenchyma remains. Obviously, however, the remaining capacity of such damaged kidneys to excrete urine containing the opaque medium and to concentrate it by reabsorption of water may be clearly demonstrated by making films over a prolonged period of time.

Obstruction to the outflow of urine from the kidney is, of course, only one way in which the fluid flow through the kidney may be decreased. Interference with the blood supply to the kidney also decreases the fluid flow through that kidney, and if this occurs on one side, the op-

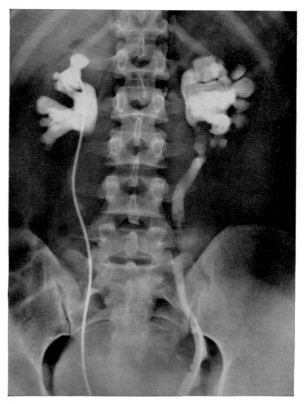

Figure 15-17 *(Unknown 15-3)*. Retrograde pyelogram. Is this hydronephrosis?

posite kidney takes over the work load and excretes a much larger amount of urine than normal. The obvious example would be complete obstruction as in total infarction of one kidney. This does occur, and an excretory urogram will show no opaque medium whatever on the ischemic side. Lesser degrees of interference with the arterial supply produce proportionately less fluid flow than normal through the kidney, and the flow is slower, the urine remaining longer in the tubules before reaching the renal pelvis. This allows more time for water reabsorption so that a smaller amount of more concentrated urine is usually excreted by a kidney whose arterial supply has been compromised in some way.

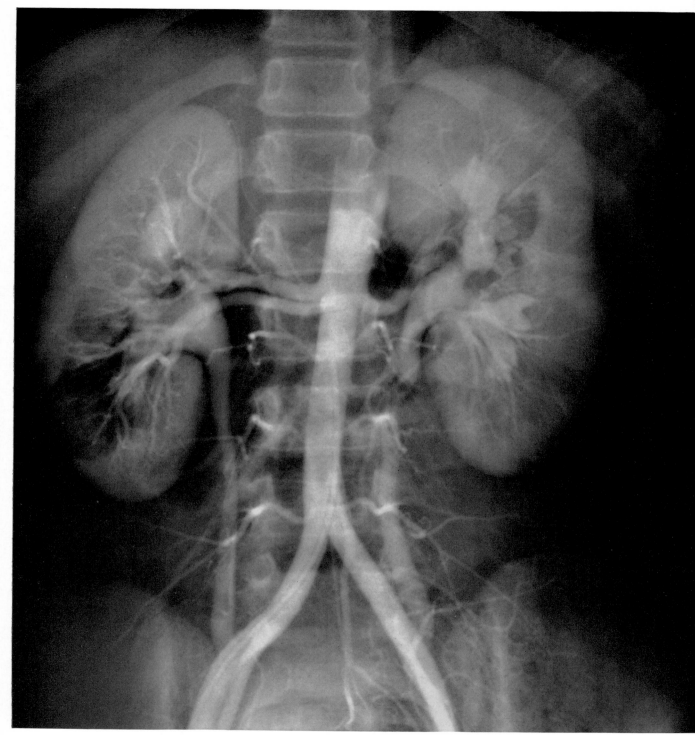

Figure 15-18. Aortagram-urogram. Opaque medium is injected through a catheter passed upward from the femoral artery. The renal draining structures and arterial supply are seen at the same time, as well as an intense nephrogram of the parenchyma, because two spaced injections of the renally-excreted medium have been given. Note the parenchymal defect on the right which could represent a <u>cyst</u>, a <u>cystic tumor</u>, or a <u>large infarction</u>. A tumor having a good blood supply would show a distinctive type of arterial staining quite different from what you see here. (Note the catheter lying in the right iliac artery.)

There are several ways in which the arterial supply to the kidney may be compromised. It may be reduced by extrinsic pressure on the principal renal artery. Intimal proliferation or sclerotic plaques may narrow its lumen, or it may become thrombosed. The restriction of arterial supply may affect the main renal artery or any of its branches. Thus the entire kidney may become ischemic, or only a part of its parenchyma; the entire excretory capacity may be proportionately reduced, or only a small part of it. Ischemia of renal tissue due to some form of decreased arterial supply has been shown in recent years to be related etiologically to the production of hypertension. In persons in whom such a condition can be demonstrated, and who retain good function in the other kidney (as proved by a battery of kidney function tests), hypertension may sometimes be cured or ameliorated by nephrectomy or, where possible, arterial reconstructive surgery.

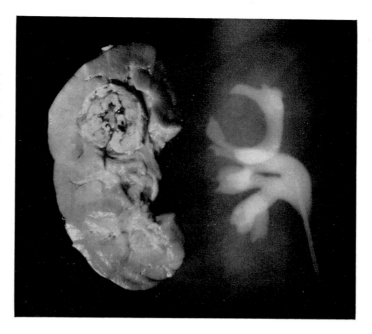

Figure 15-19 (top). Sectioned specimen and radiograph of the same specimen injected with a radio-opaque material before sectioning, to show the caliceal deformity produced by such a tumor mass. Small hypernephroma. Arteriogram would show staining of this mass.

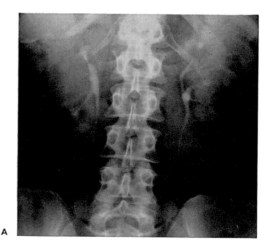

Figure 15-20. A. Intravenous urogram. The right draining structures within the kidney are distorted by a mass of some sort in the middle renal parenchyma along the lateral side. Such a defect could be caused either by a cyst or by a tumor. B. Use of the nephrogram to distinguish the two possibilities. This is a body-section study made very soon after injection of the opaque. It shows the mass to be an avascular cyst which does not share in the parenchymal opacification (nephrotomogram).

A

B

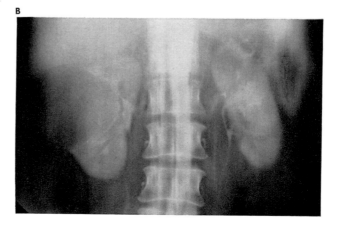

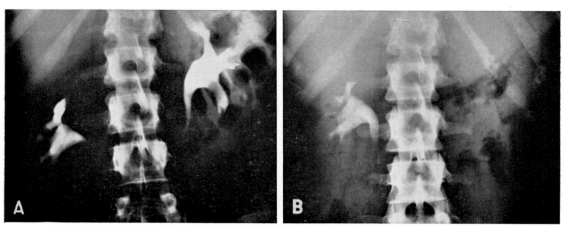

Figure 15-21. Special physiologic study using urographic medium in a hypertensive patient suspected of unilateral vascular disease. *A*, made 5 minutes after the intravenous injection, shows equal concentration of contrast medium on both sides. The right kidney is suspect because its draining structures seem a trifle smaller than those on the left, implying some possible contraction. *B*, made 15 minutes after injection of a mercurial diuretic and 500 ml. of normal saline. There is complete washout of opaque medium on the left, indicating a free flow of fluid through that kidney, while the opaque medium remains in the right kidney. At surgery stenosis of the right renal artery was demonstrated.

Figure 15-22. The same procedure carried out on the same patient following surgical correction by reconstruction of the right renal artery. In *A* the excretion of contrast substance is equal on the two sides, as it was before surgery. However, with the administration of a fluid load, note that the washout is now comparable on the two sides *(B)*, indicating that the fluid flow through the two kidneys is approximately equivalent. Be sure you appreciate the significance of the equal density of the opaque material on the two sides before operation: retarded fluid flow on the ischemic right side allows time for more reabsorption of water and concentration of the opaque material. Equal density of excreted opaque material does not imply equal "function." (In sum, the word "function" is probably too general and too vague to be useful in speaking of so complex a group of physiologic processes as that which occurs in the kidney.)

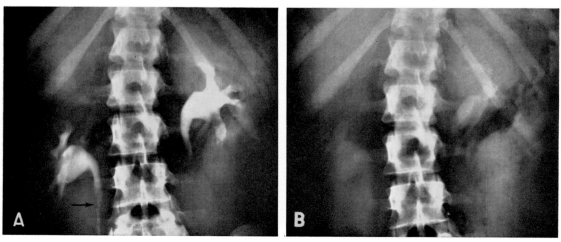

Finally, decrease in the density of opaque medium excreted by the kidney may occur with true depression of renal function, as in chronic glomerulonephritis, in which there is an absolute decrease in the number of glomeruli present. In chronic pyelonephritis, too, there will be delay in the appearance of the contrast substance and it will be diluted, casting a faint shadow. However, most chronically diseased kidneys show morphologic changes, demonstrable on either the excretory study or on the retrograde. These consist of decrease in size of the affected kidney, thinning of the parenchyma, pitting of the surface of the kidney giving an irregular outline in the nephrogram, caliceal erosion, etc. All these changes are predictable if you remember the appearance of such kidneys at the autopsy table, and the morphologic appearance of the kidney shadow on the plain films is quite as important as the kidney's performance in excreting urographic media when you are trying to assay its function.

Integrating chemical and procedural studies of all sorts with the appearance of the kidney on plain films and excretory urograms must eventually lead to a more perfect understanding of renal physiology, and even today no physician should look at an intravenous urogram with nothing but morphologic changes in mind.

Credits: Illustrations this chapter.

Figure 15-1. Courtesy Dr. W. Cole and the publisher, *J. A. M. A.* 82:613, 1924.

Figure 15-2. Courtesy Dr. E. Salzman, Dr. R. Spurck, Mr. G. Mills, and the publisher, *MR&P* 37:2.

Figure 15-3. Courtesy Dr. J. Pepe, Brooklyn, N. Y.

Figure 15-4. Courtesy Dr. P. Barton and the publisher, *MR&P* 31:127.

Figures 15-5, 15-9, 15-10, 15-11. Courtesy Dr. J. Hope et al., and the publisher, *MR&P* 33:49, 50.

Figure 15-6. From *Fundamentals of Radiography*, p. 56, published by Eastman Kodak Co., Rochester, N. Y.

Figure 15-8. Courtesy Drs. F. Fleischner, S. Bellman, and E. Henken, and the publisher, *Radiology* 74:567.

Figure 15-13. Courtesy Miss K. Fengler and the publisher, *J. Mt. Sinai Hosp.*, New York, N. Y.

Figure 15-14. Courtesy Drs. J. Hope and A. Michie, and the publisher, *Radiology* 72:847.

Figures 15-15, 15-16. Courtesy Drs. J. Hope and C. Koop, and the publisher, *MR&P* 38:14, 23.

Figure 15-18. Courtesy Dr. B. Epstein and the publisher, Eastman Kodak Co., Rochester, N. Y.

Figure 15-19. Courtesy Mr. F. Kent and the publisher, *MR&P* 24:3.

Figure 15-20. Courtesy Drs. D. Witten, L. Greene, and J. Emmett, and the publisher, *Am. J. Roentgenol.* 90:117.

Figures 15-21, 15-22. Courtesy Dr. K. Amplatz and the publisher, *Radiology* 79:808, 809.

CHAPTER 16 Skull and Bones

Bones are much more interesting than most people think them during the years in medical school. It is probable that no segment of medical information *could* maintain an aura of fascination against tedium like that felt while memorizing the origins and insertions of muscles. Perhaps the memory of that tiresome and difficult task continues long afterward to cloud the subject of bone at a time of learning when the metabolic disease processes in which bone shares as an organ are being studied. The student cannot afford today to neglect the bones and their function and change, their growth and ultimate microscopic structure. He must be able to imagine what is going on in the bony skeleton in the immobilized patient with a heal-

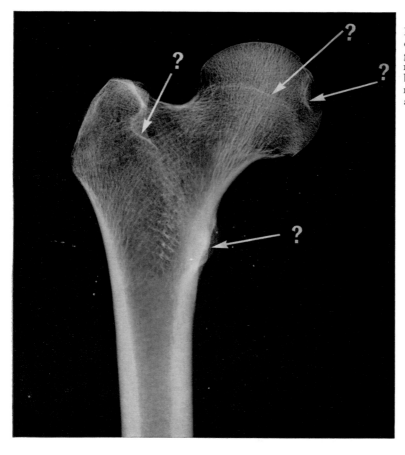

Figure 16-1. Can you explain precisely why the details of the radiographic shadows marked with arrows should have been produced by the anatomical structures they represent? (Rhetorical query; not an unknown.)

ing fracture, and not just at the site of the fracture but throughout the body as a result of enforced inactivity. The physician must be able to predict to what extent invasion of his patient's bones by metastatic tumor, for example, will alter blood chemistry. He must understand the formation of kidney stones in hyperparathyroid patients who develop extensive bone destruction and a significant increase in calcium excretion.

The possibilities for diagnosis available through radiography of the bones were partly anticipated by Roentgen himself in the first months after the discovery of the new ray. The technical improvements made early in the century made possible a much greater sharpness of detail. A finer focal spot which could be kept cool enabled the technician to define the shadows of individual trabeculae in spongy bone. At the same time finer granules of chemical in the gelatin base also improved the photographic properties of radiographic film.

Today bone is studied by x-ray at a gross level, as in routine medical radiography and also at a microscopic level, finely ground sections of compact bone less than 2μ in thickness being radiographed in close contact with high quality, fine-grained film. *Microradiography* in comparative studies of bone in health and disease is rapidly becoming one of the most informative investigative tools in medical research, and collateral autoradiographic studies with radioisotopes such as calcium 45 embellish that information by adding a time record of tagged change, as you shall see later in this chapter.

Begin by understanding at a gross level the radiographic reasons for the appearance of the details questioned in Figures 16-1 and 16-2. If this chapter is to be successful at all it must eradicate completely any lingering feeling of ennui you may have when you think of bones. Radiology can show you better than any other discipline this quite magical part of medical learning.

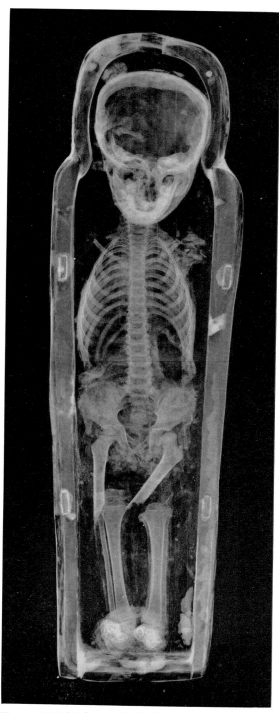

Figure 16-2 (*Unknown 16-1*). Radiograph of a child's mummy undisturbed since about 1000 B.C. What can you determine about the remains? How do you know it is a child? How would experts determine his age in years at the time he died? In precisely what ways is his skeleton abnormal?

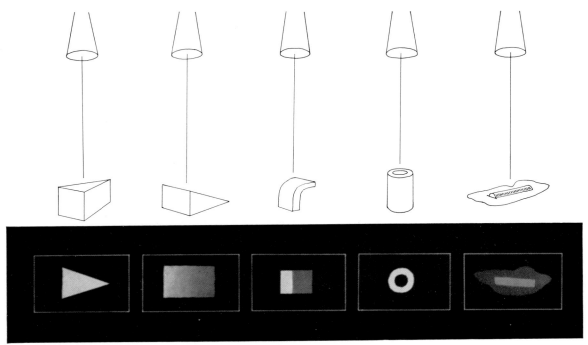

Figure 16-3

Carry forward the general principles about radiographic shadows which you learned in the first chapter from rose petals, now, and apply them to the folds and variations in thickness of the compact cortex which invests the great tubular bones. Examine the several hypothetical examples in Figure 16-3 and the approximate radiographic images below them.

Assuming uniform composition for all five "objects" (which actually you can assume only up to a point for compact bone), the wedge casts a different shadow according to the direction in which the ray traverses it by a simple rule of summation, of thickness. The curved sheet of bone obeys the same principles which applied to the curved rose petal. The cylinder seen end-on becomes a circle in the radiograph and if it were radiographed from the side would produce two parallel lines of tangentially projected "cortex," just as you see it in the lower part of Figure 16-4C. Finally, the sheet of bone with a thicker ridge across it will radiograph as a gray area with a streak of white.

It is just as important to think three dimensionally about the radiograph of a single bone as about the whole chest, for you must add together the shadows cast by all its parts. The shadow of the femoral shaft which you see in the radiograph in Figure 16-4C includes not only the denser shadows of the lateral and medial cortex which has been x-rayed in tangent but also sheets of gray representing the anterior and posterior cortex which has been projected *en face*. You will have identified the fovea capitis in Figure 16-1, but did you account for the white streak which limits it laterally as the cortical bone at the base of the hollow, caught tangentially in this projection? Note that in the lateral projection (Figure 16-4D) the inferior cortex of the lesser trochanter is similarly caught in tangent. You know from 16-4C that the cortex of the bone thickens quite suddenly below that point. For this reason the lesser trochanter appears in *D* as a more radiolucent area above a generally denser one and is separated from it by an even denser white horizontal line which is its own inferior cortex in tangent.

To the folds and thickness of the compact bone, finally, must be "added" the shadow of the trabecular bone inside. As you have seen in Figure 16-1, the trabeculae themselves vary in distribution and thickness within a piece of spongy bone.

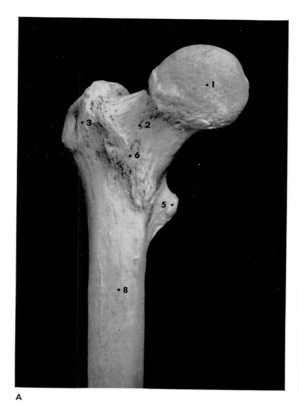

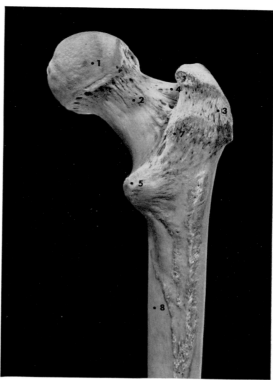

A   B

Figure 16-4. Anterior and posterior photographic views of the upper femur (A and B) help to account for the details of shadows seen in the radiograph (C). A lateral radiograph (D) made at right angles to C provides different shadows because the projection is different, although the same anatomical structures can be identified. (*Unknown 16-2:* Identify numbered points.)

C   D

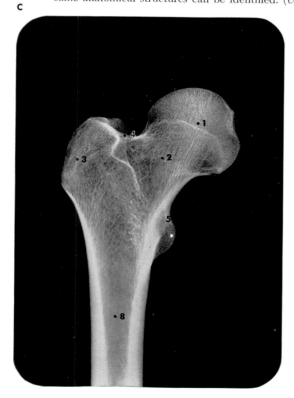

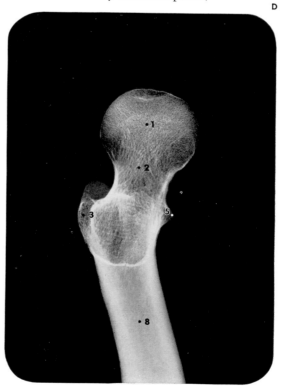

The trabeculae are arranged in the upper femur in a series of arching parallel struts which closely follow the lines of stress developed within this part of the bone in Man, who stands erect and carries the weight of his trunk upon the two femoral heads. The arrangement of these struts to bear weight differs from that of the similar spongy bone within the upper femurs of quadrupeds, and it is interesting to reflect how those trabeculae must have adapted themselves first in *Pithecanthropus erectus*.

Figure 16-5 is a microradiograph of the trabeculae in a coronal 3-millimeter slice of bone from the upper tibia and shows adaptation to weight bearing delivered from above. Note the major struts of bone joined and reinforced by minor horizontal ones which are much more slender. In other areas, of course, spongy bone is more uniform in structure, the trabeculae assuming the form of curved sheets with communicating spaces between them all more or less the same size and radiographing as you would expect, without conspicuous strands of white like those in the upper femur.

When you look at films of bones, therefore, think of the folds and variations in thickness of the investing cortex and then consciously add an inspection of the pattern of the trabeculae inside. For the gross level at which you view routine medical radiographs, remember that optical limitations permit you to resolve shadows of only the larger trabeculae. The myriads of finer ones are not seen as defined white shadows but contribute a diffuse over-all whiteness to the shadow of the bone you are inspecting.

In radiographs made in which there was even the slightest motion during the exposure, you will find that you cannot see any trabeculae at all. You will probably not see them either in films which have been made of an extremity in plaster. Learn to look for the trabecular pattern but to discount its absence in types of examinations in which such a degree of detail was not technically possible.

Learning to think from the gross level of detail in bone films down to the microscopic level and then reversing that process is, in general, the orientation of this chapter.

Figure 16-5. Microradiograph showing trabecular arrangement developed with weight bearing (arrows).

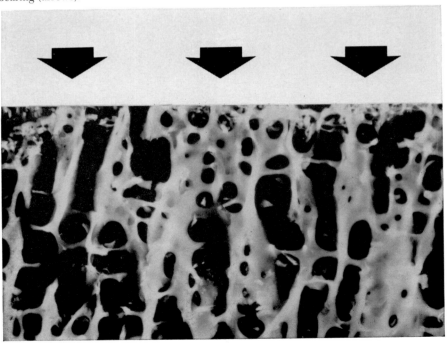

294

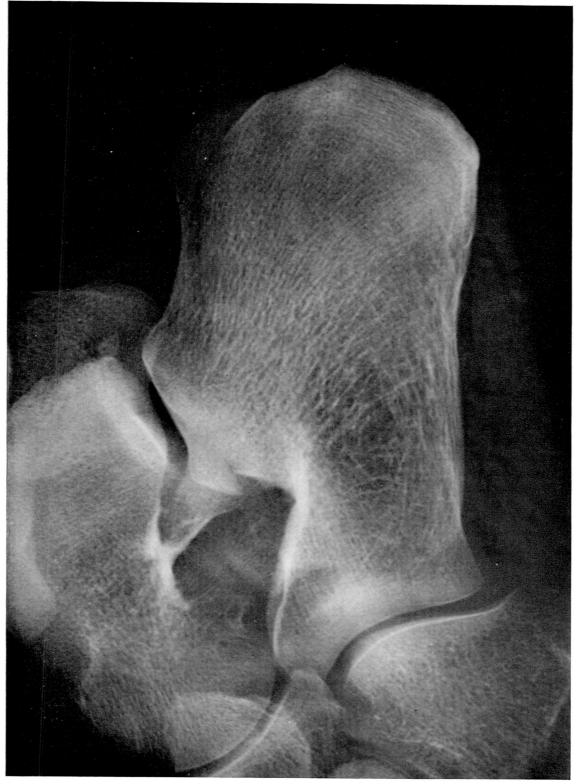

Figure 16-6. Magnification study. Lateral projection of the foot. (Sole of the foot parallel with the side margin of the page.) Note the trabeculae which arch backward and downward from the calcaneotalar joint toward the weight-bearing point under the heel.

Figure 16-7.

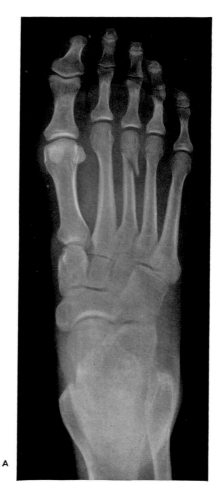

A

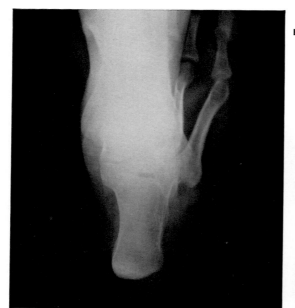

B

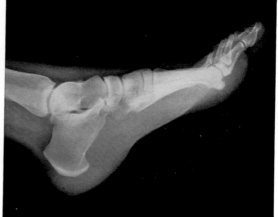

C

Figure 16-8. Three different views of the foot. How would you rearrange Mother Whistler to obtain *B* and *C*? (See text.)

The various projections in which films of the bones are made are largely a matter of convention based upon standard investigations determining which ones combine to produce most information. You will become accustomed to the AP and lateral views which are routine. Additional views often have to be designed in order to show to the best advantage a particular lesion in a particular patient.

Figure 16-8A is the conventional AP view of the foot, made as in Figure 16-7; note that the lower parts of the tibia and fibula are superimposed upon the proximal part of the foot. The added density causes the loss of all detail *at the technical exposure suited to so thin a part as the toes.* Some information about the talus and calcaneus, the ankle joint, and the lower leg is derived from the lateral view *(C),* and if additional AP information is needed about the calcaneus, for example, it can be obtained with view *B,* made by directing the beam downward from above and behind the heel.

With exposure factors calculated for greater penetration and by using the Bucky diaphragm on thicker bony parts, it is usually possible to produce a film with the cortical details of superimposed bones, appearing as though seen through each other. Thus it is often necessary to subtract intellectually the overlapping folds of the cortex of one bone in order to trace the cortex and structure of another which is superimposed upon it in the conventional views.

Familiarity with the anatomical details of the bones is of great help, and by the same token it is possible to learn and review anatomy by "accounting for" the details of the roentgen image. Imagine, for example, the difference in the radiograph of the *hip* which will be produced when the lower extremity is externally rotated compared with the appearance which you would find in a film made with the leg rotated internally as far as possible. The anatomical photographs on page 293 will help you. You will find that in looking at films of bones there are certain key points which, once learned, identify for you the projection you are seeing.

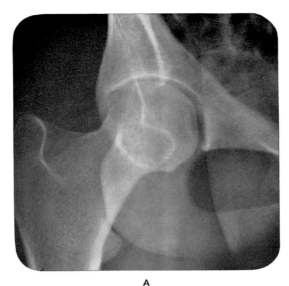

A

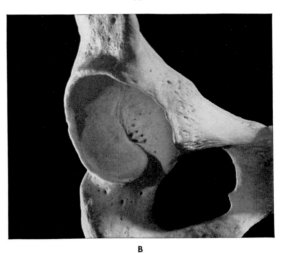

B

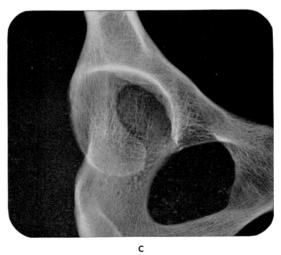

C

Figure 16-9. The shadow of the acetabulum superimposed on that of the upper femur. *A* (top). Radiograph of patient. *B* (middle). Photograph of specimen. *C* (bottom). Radiograph of specimen.

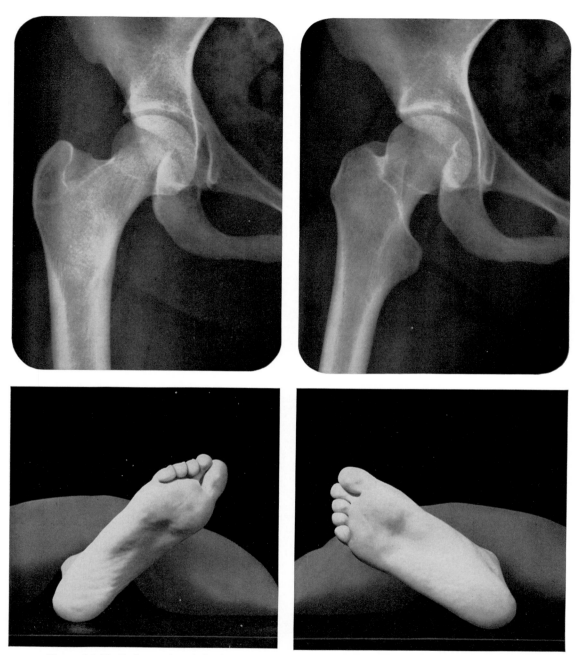

Figure 16-10. Radiographs of the hip made with the lower extremity internally and externally rotated as per text on page 297. Note the changes in the appearance of the trochanters. Compare with the appearance of the hip when radiographed straight AP (Figure 16-4C). The lesser trochanter can thus become an index to the degree of rotation which was present when the radiograph was made.

Fractures appear on radiographs as dark streaks across the white of the bone, of course, because there the continuity of both compact and spongy bone is interrupted, soft tissues and hemorrhage usually separating the fractured fragments slightly. If the fracture is a simple one, a single dark line will be present. If a comminuted fracture occurs with several separate fracture planes communicating, then several lines should be present (Figure 16-11). Sometimes the obvious presence of several fragments indicates that the fracture is comminuted although only one major fracture line can be seen because the additional planes of fracture are so oblique to the direction of the beam used that overlap of bony margins prevents your "seeing through" the planes of the extra fractures. In Figure 16-11 two fracture planes can be seen and one more supposed (that for the fracture of the greater trochanter). Remember that such communicating planes of fracture may curve so that only part of their fractured surface is ever appreciated in a single projection. Remember, too, that while interruption of the continuity of the cortical compact bone is the clearest indication of a fracture, the spongy bone is also fractured and that, depending on the direction and character of the trauma, the surfaces of spongy bone may become impacted. When this happens the fractured trabecular surfaces are jammed into each other, and the trabeculae become enmeshed, so that there are innumerable fragments of bone lying closer together than normal. As you could predict, a radiograph made with the beam parallel to the plane of fracture and impaction will produce an area of increased whiteness because of the greater density existing there.

The radiolucent cartilaginous disc of the epiphyseal plate in immature bones may lie in the plane of the beam of x-rays and so also appear on the film as a linear dark area crossing the bone. It is usually easy to distinguish from a fracture line, however, because it is not an abrupt break in the cortex but smoothly bounded on the epiphyseal side of the radiolucent area by a white line, the denser bony disc of the epiphyseal plate where little or no activity of growth is occurring.

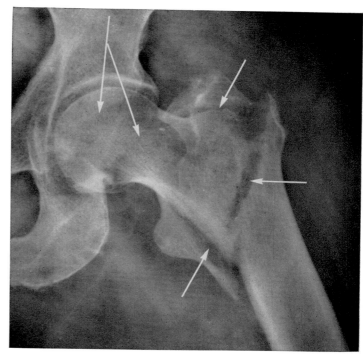

Figure 16-11 (above). Intertrochanteric comminuted fracture of the left femur. Longer arrows indicate the overlapping margins of the anterior and posterior rims of the acetabulum. Shorter arrows indicate three communicating fracture planes, one through the femur at the intertrochanteric line, one through the base of the lesser trochanter, and a third (not clearly seen) through the greater trochanter, its outer cortex showing loss of continuity.

Figure 16-12 (below). Child's hip showing growth plates to be distinguished from fractures. The epiphysis for the femoral head appears before 8 months and fuses at about 18 years, that for the greater trochanter appears at around 2 years and fuses at about 16 years.

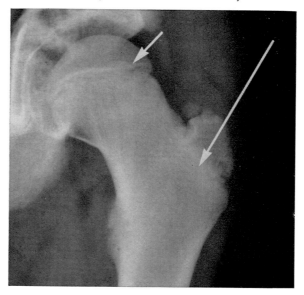

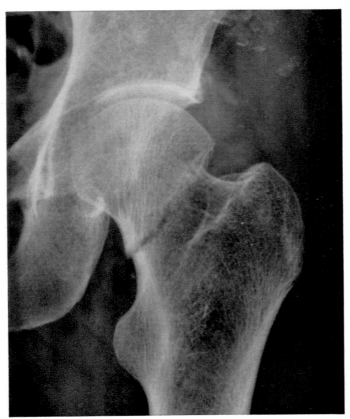

Figure 16-13

You will be able to make a diagnosis of the type of fracture in Figure 16-13 (*Unknown 16-3*). At the same time note the roentgen characteristics of the normal hip joint with its dense white acetabular roof seen in tangent and the radiolucent area just below it which represents the cartilaginous layers lining the acetabulum and investing the femoral head. Compare the thickness of cortex of the head of the femur with that of the acetabulum and of the femoral shaft lower down. Dislocations of joints are often combined with fractures.

When chronic injury to a joint impairs its integrity, the width of the radiolucent zone representing the joint space decreases, while mechanisms of reaction and protection produce increased amounts of dense bone on both sides of the joint. The result is what you see in Figures 16-14 and 16-15, both very common. Figure 16-14 is an example of degenerative arthritis of the first metatarsophalangeal joint with soft tissue swelling (bunion). Here you can use for a normal comparison any of the other metatarsophalangeal joints in the same foot, a procedure you will find convenient in looking at

radiographs of joints and bones. In degenerative joint disease only traces of the interposed cartilage remain, spurs of bone form at the joint margins, and the over-all density of the adjoining bone is increased. Note that there are also fragmentation and hypertrophy of the sesamoid bones found normally about this joint (compare Figure 16-8A, in which, incidentally, there is a fracture of the middle metatarsal).

Figure 16-15 is an example of similar changes about the hip joint, commonly referred to as *malum coxae senile* and understandably frequent in older people after a lifetime of weight bearing. In arthritis which develops in a joint following inflammatory disease, on the other hand, complete obliteration of the joint may occur, and the radiolucent joint space may entirely disappear.

Figure 16-14

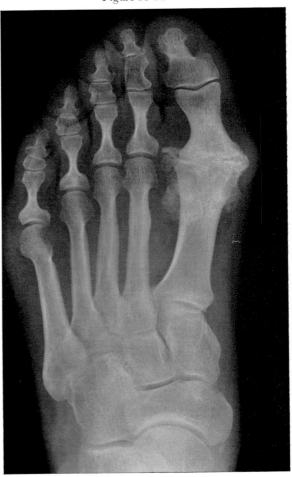

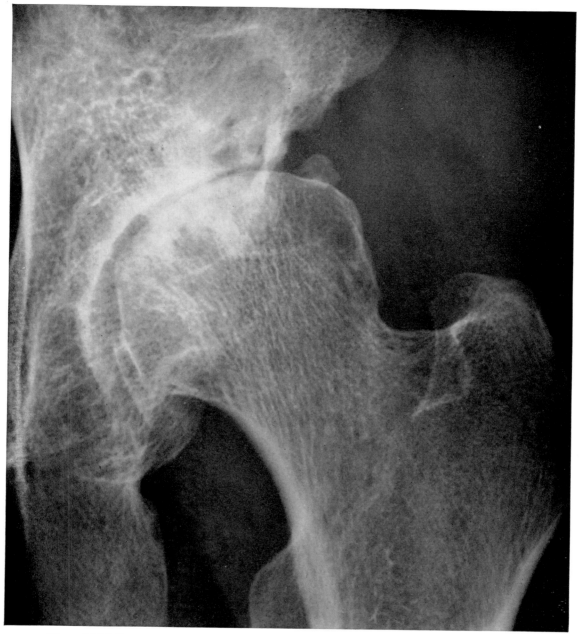

Figure 16-15. Degenerative joint disease of the hip. Note narrowing of the joint space and reactive density of new bone on both sides of the joint.

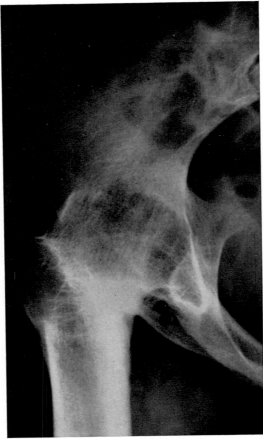

Figure 16-16 (*Unknown 16-4*)

The illustrations on the next four pages comprise an exercise in fracture diagnosis, framed as unknowns because they are more interesting so. *Not every film contains a fracture, however, just as you would find it in the same group of patients if you were seeing them at random in the emergency ward.* The roentgen findings you are looking for are breaks in the continuity of cortex, radiolucent fracture lines, overlap where the added density of cortical bone seen through cortical bone creates a white area, fragments of bone without explanation even in the absence of a visible fracture, and denser areas where impaction has occurred.

Figure 16-17 (*Unknown 16-5*). Lateral view of the knee of a young woman following injury. The skin was not broken.

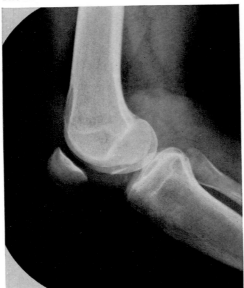

Figure 16-18 (*Unknown 16-6*). Lateral view of a knee made in the reverse projection. Note that two such knees may be used for comparison when you are studying them by looking from one to the other with the mental bias that they are mirror images.

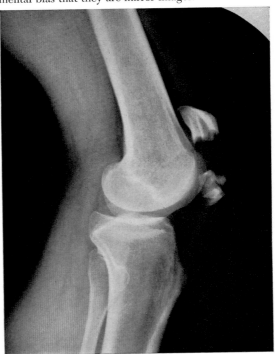

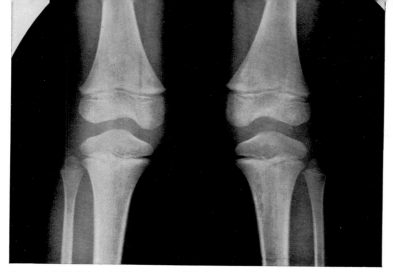

Figure 16-19 (above). The knees of children and adolescents show epiphyseal lines easily distinguished from fractures.

Figure 16-20 *(Unknown 16-7)* (below). Oblique view of the knee following injury. Describe.

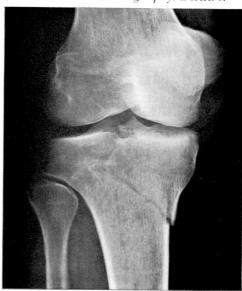

Figure 16-21 *(Unknown 16-8)* (below). Lateral and AP views of the knee following injury. Vertical striations in *B* (right) are from a stationary grid, often used with a portable x-ray unit to improve the quality of films made at the bedside or under difficult circumstances.

B

A

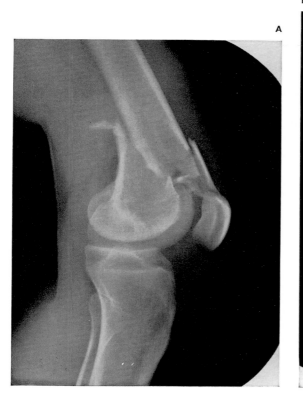

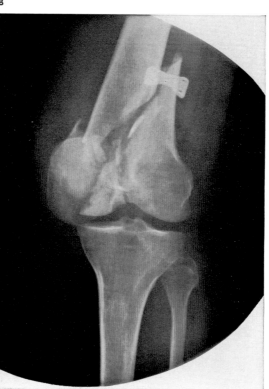

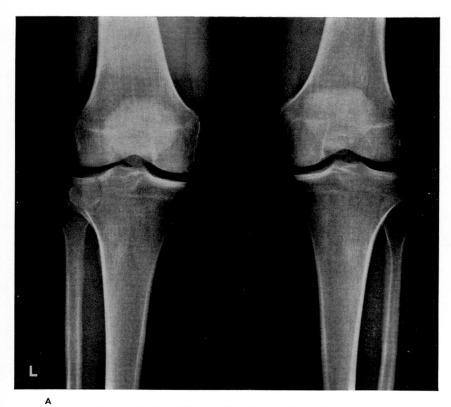

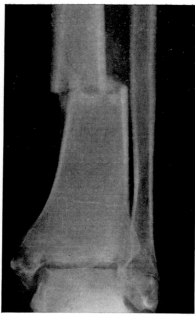

Figure 16-23. Radiograph of a fractured tibia several weeks after the injury. This film was made the day the initial plaster cast was removed. Shadowy, flocculent white material about the fracture site is callus.

A

Figure 16-22 (*Unknown 16-9.*) AP and lateral views of both knees after an injury. One knee is normal.

B

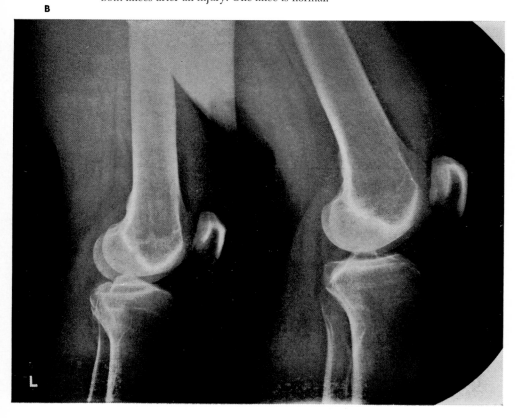

304

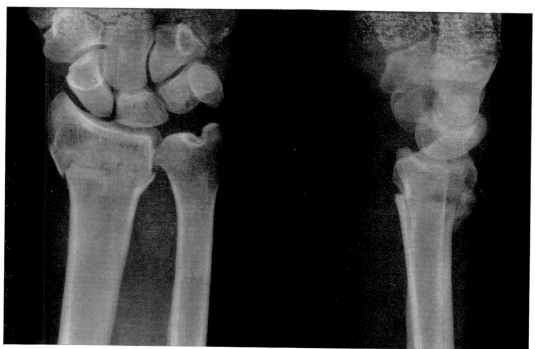

Figure 16-24 *(Unknown 16-10)* (above). Lower forearm and wrist of an adult after a fall on the outstretched hand. What is different about this fracture from the ones you have been looking at? Identify the carpal bones in the two views.

Figure 16-25 *(Unknown 16-11)* (below). Lower forearms and wrists of a boy who had fallen from an apple tree. Note the additional difficulties of fracture diagnosis in the immature individual.

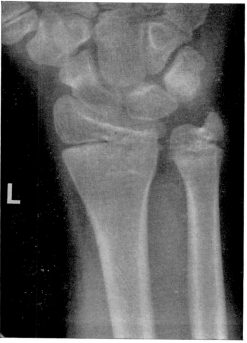
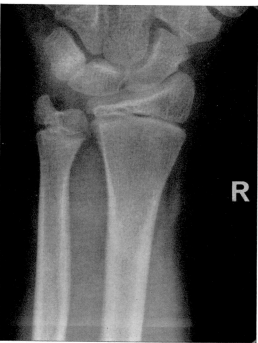

When a fracture appears to have occurred through bone which was already abnormal and may therefore have been abnormally fragile, it is called a *pathologic fracture*. Figures 16-26 and 16-27 are examples.

In Figure 16-26 a cylindrical cuff of bony cortex has been eroded by pressure from within, although you observe the thinning best where you see cortex in tangent medially and laterally. Across the thinned segment of bone at the level of the arrows a jagged fracture has occurred and is seen on the lateral surface as a distinct interruption of the cortex. Note that the bone appears to be expanded by the pressure, a common finding in benign intraosseous tumors and cysts which increase in size so gradually that new bone can be laid down under the periosteum in a protective response to the weakened structure as the erosion occurs from within. This is an example of a unicameral bone cyst, common in children, and occurring, as

you see it here, at the metaphyseal end of the shaft close to the epiphyseal growth plate. Tumor, too, erodes bone and produces a radiolucent area wherever bone has been destroyed.

Figure 16-27 is the upper femur of a patient with Paget's disease, and a transverse fracture has occurred across the shaft several centimeters below the lesser trochanter. Although it characteristically thickens bone, Paget's disease also weakens its structure, and the bone withstands stresses and strains less well than normal sound tubular long bone does. As additional evidence of weakness of the bone, note that this fracture has occurred straight across, whereas it is more usual for sound tubular bone in mid-shaft to fracture irregularly in ragged points and with comminution. Compare the appearance of the cortex in the fractures of previously sound tubular bone you have just seen (or have seen in your own fracture patients) with this very abnormal bone structure.

Figure 16-26

Figure 16-27

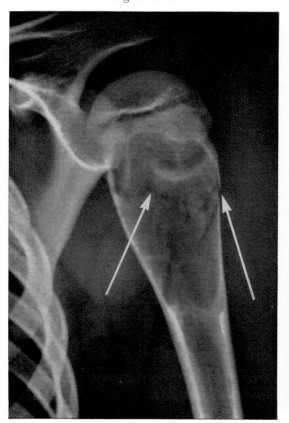

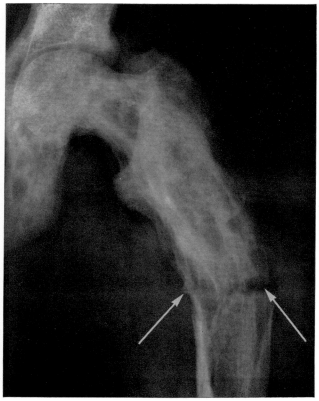

What types of pathologic bony change, then, can be appreciated at the visual level afforded by the conventional roentgen techniques in which the film is placed close to the patient and the bone in question appears approximately life size? There follow examples of various changes matched against specimen photographs of the bones in question.

Figure 16-28. Upper pair: Giant cell tumor of the proximal end of the radius. There is destruction of the cortex for several centimeters down the shaft, but of varying degree. The tumor has not destroyed all the spongy bone within the head of the radius close to the joint surface.

Lower pair: Sarcoma of the tibia. Here the rate of growth has certainly been faster, and the entire medial cortex has been destroyed before a fracture of the bone occurred. The ragged appearance of the destructive border is much more in keeping with the progress of a malignant tumor than the smooth erosion allowing time for expansion of the entire bone in Figure 16-26.

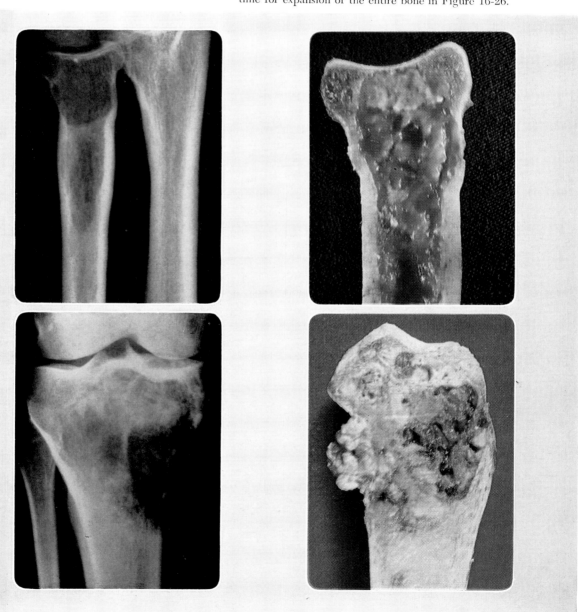

Figure 16-29. The cortex markedly thickened by addition of new bone from beneath the periosteum in a boy with osteoid osteoma. Note that you can follow the old cortex from below upward
in the radiograph to an area about 4 centimeters in length where it has been largely destroyed.
At the center of this segment of destroyed cortex and at a point which is also opposite the thickest
part of the newly superimposed cortical bone, there is an oval area of radiolucency. This represented the nidus of the osteoid osteoma, seen as a reddish pulpy projection from the wedge of
bone removed at surgery.

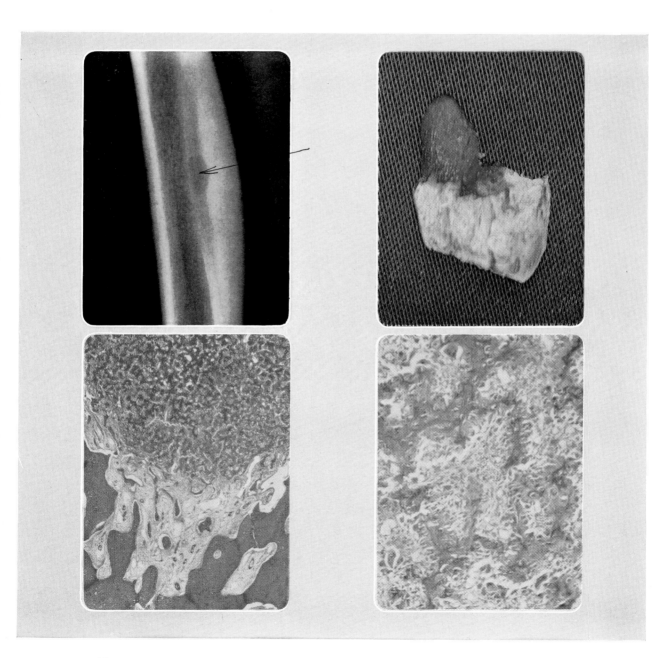

Figure 16-30. Two patients with <u>chondrosarcoma</u>, a relatively slow-growing malignant bone tumor which characteristically shows calcification within the tumor. The two illustrations on the left are from one patient. They show the effect on the upper femur of a chondrosarcoma which <u>is growing principally</u> *outside* <u>the bone</u>. The illustrations on the right are from a patient whose tumor began *inside* the bone and grew slowly enough to expand it. Compare the cortex in the two cases.

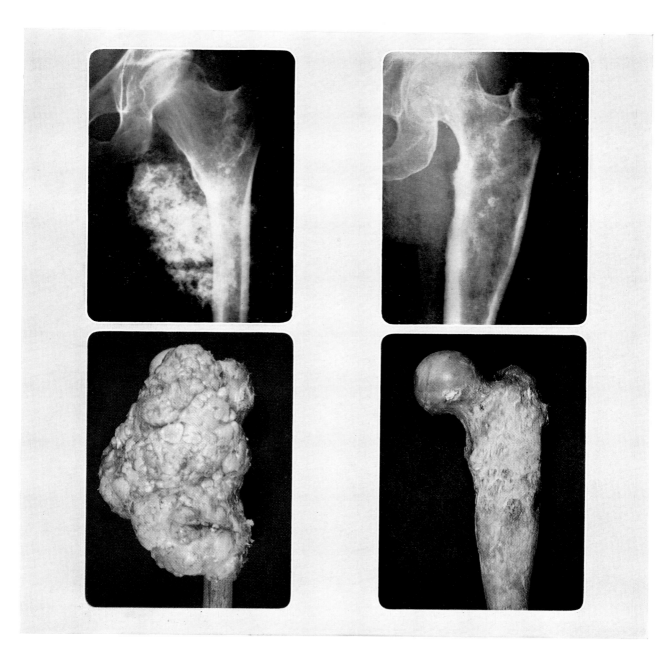

Figure 16-31. This is the lower femur from a child who died at age 4 of lymphatic leukemia. While you see here only the radiograph of the specimen, the same destructive changes would probably have been appreciable in films made shortly before death. Note the numerous radiolucent defects caused by growing lymphomatous tumor in which the thickness of the cortex is generally decreased and also perforated in many areas. Take note, while you are about it, that the cartilaginous part of the growing epiphysis surrounding its bony center is "visible" in the radiograph of the specimen because air surrounds it, whereas in a radiograph of the patient it is not seen because soft tissues and cartilage have about the same radiodensity (compare Figure 16-19). Destruction at the metaphysis close to the growth plate is common in leukemia, and almost all grave illnesses in children are reflected in the appearance of their metaphyses. Hereditary growth faults, vitamin deficiencies, injuries like lead poisoning, and many other pediatric problems may be diagnosed from films of the long bones.

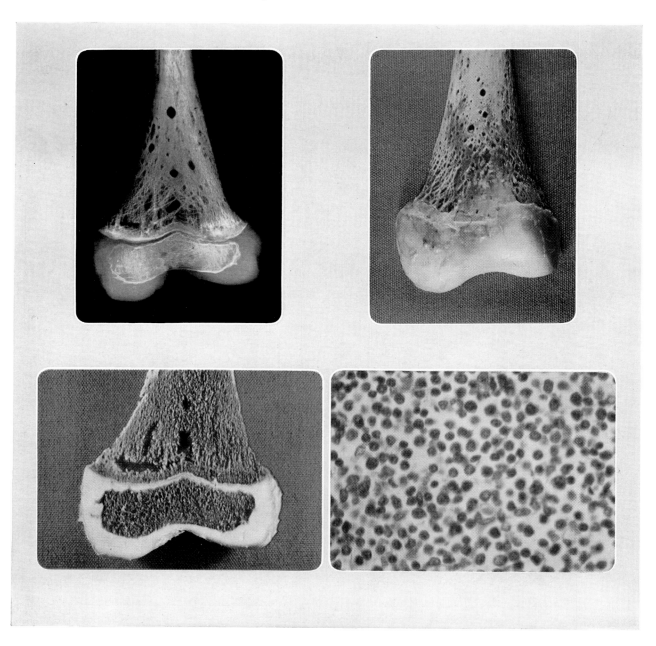

Figure 16-32. <u>Bone destruction in the skull</u>, the result of diffuse involvement of the diploë and perforation of the inner and outer tables in a patient who died of <u>multiple myeloma</u>. Above, photograph and radiograph of the specimen top of the calvarium. Punctate areas of radiolucency like this will be seen antemortem on skull films made in the AP and lateral projections, for example, in patients with <u>myeloma or metastatic malignancy</u>. Below, a specimen of rib from the same patient.

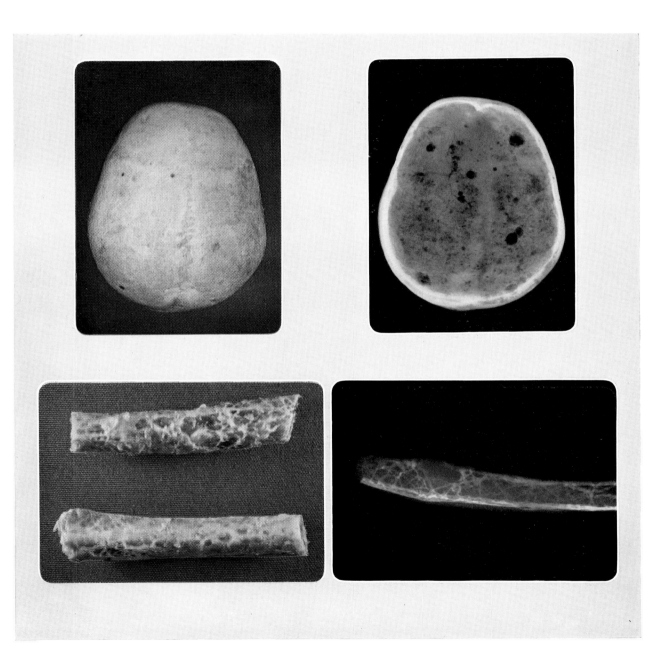

Figure 16-33. Localized destruction of the calvarium in an area involved by a large focus of metastatic neuroblastoma in a young child. Tumor projects upward from the external surface of the skull in the photograph. Note that in the radiographed specimen slice of calvarium the destruction of bone is actually less extensive than one believes on first inspection of the photographs. In radiographs made of the live patient with this type of diploic destruction, spotty loss of density in the diploë and loss of continuity or thickness of the tangentially seen cortical tables may be expected.

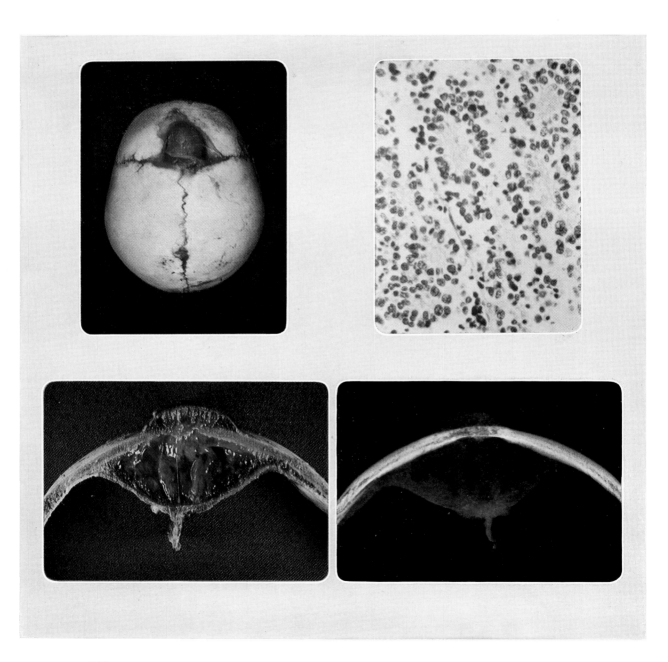

Figure 16-34. <u>Excrescences of new bone arising from the outer surface of the cortex</u> (or extending inward from the meningeal surface of the inner table) will appear as you see demonstrated here in a patient with a <u>calvarial hemangioma.</u> The first illustration is a special tangential view with the technical factors of the exposure decreased for details of the protuberant bone only; note that the skull itself has not been penetrated. Compare this with the radiograph of the specimen and with photographs of the whole fresh specimen and of a slice of that specimen after maceration. The latter can be matched in precise detail against the destruction seen in the radiograph of the specimen.

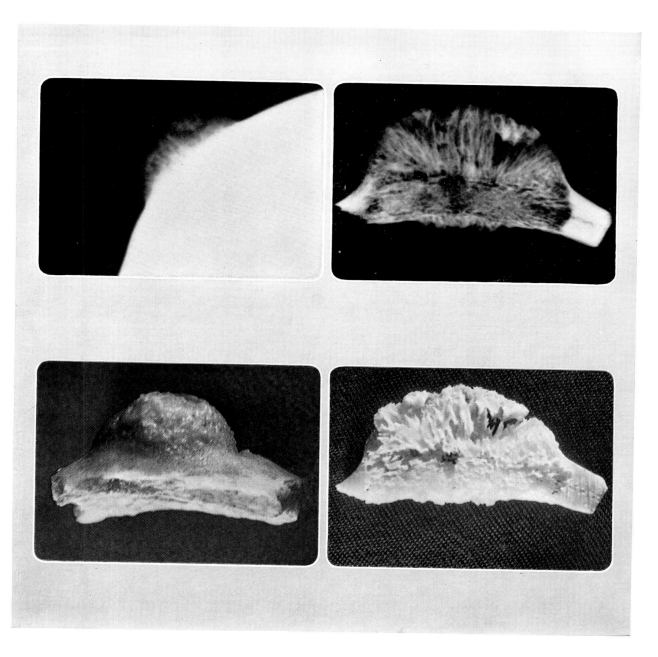

Figure 16-35. <u>Diffuse destruction of spongy bone by tumor</u> usually allows preservation of the shape of the bone for a time, with ultimate collapse when the supporting function of the cortical shell is impaired by erosion and multiple fragmentations. Here, in a patient with diffuse myelomatosis involving the marrow spaces in the spongy bone filling the vertebrae, extensive destruction of the bony trabeculae of cancellous bone and later of the cortical boxy envelope has resulted in varying degrees of vertebral collapse. Note the <u>reciprocal "expansion" of the intervertebral discs</u> whose inclination it is to <u>assume a more spherical shape</u> if destruction of bone above and below allows it.

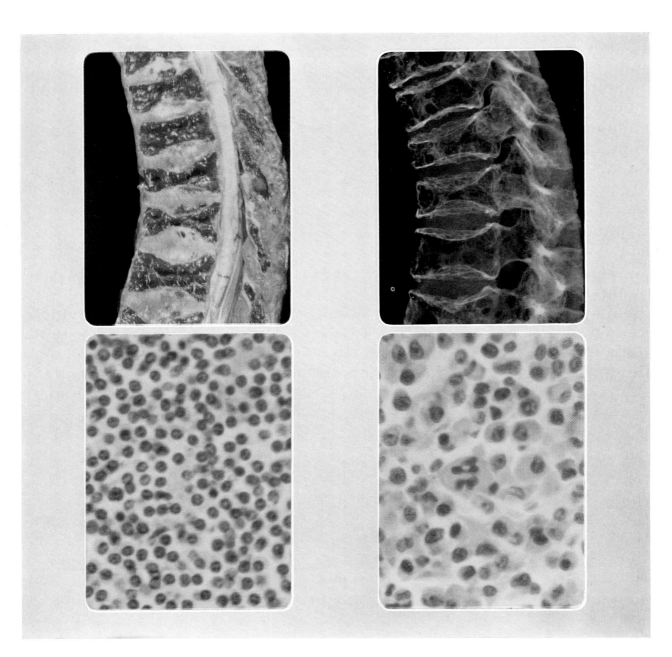

314

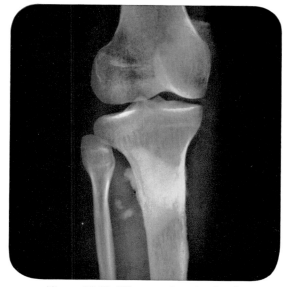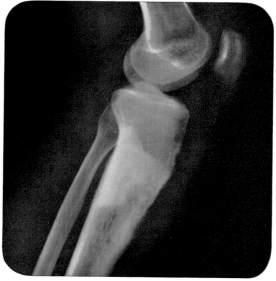

Figure 16-36. When, on the other hand, a tumor invading the marrow spaces between trabeculae of spongy bone characteristically produces dense new bone, as does this osteosarcoma of the tibia, an area of *increased* density will be visualized in the radiograph. In two views at 90 degrees it clearly occupies the central part of the bone. There is also some spotty cortical destruction here, and dense new tumor bone is seen in the soft tissue part of the tumor lateral to the tibia.

In sum, then, conventional roentgen studies of bones will often be able to visualize localized or diffuse *increase* in bone thickness and will also be able to show evidence of localized or diffuse *decrease* in bone mass, either of compact bone or spongy trabeculae, or both. Sometimes the particular location and character of the bone change offer evidence to the experienced viewer which permits him to all but label the disease entity. Sometimes there is nothing characteristic about the changes present, and they can only be described and the possibilities named which fit in with the clinical story.

To give you an example, the diffuse bone loss which occurs in the earlier course of many cases of multiple myeloma cannot be distinguished radiologically by anyone from a similar decrease in bone mass which occurs commonly in patients of the same age group for a variety of metabolic reasons and is termed *osteoporosis*. Once the bone shadows of the myeloma patient begin to show spotty areas of trabecular and cortical destruction (as in Figure 16-35), a much more positive roentgen interpretation is possible in the light of the clinical picture. Early in the course of either myeloma or osteoporosis, the microscopic change in the bone is similar, since it is indeed a diffuse thinning of all bone, though for very different reasons.

Osteoporosis is a term which has been decried by many, but it is not actually a bad description of what occurs, for bone trabeculae do become "porous" when they are perforated by holes. The "sponge" produced is a finer one, then, with relatively more marrow spaces and relatively less bone. In the same fashion, the juxtamedullary part of the compact bone is tunneled into and converted into spongy bone in a patient with developing osteoporosis, so that the much denser compact bony layer under the periosteum is narrowed. Seen in tangent in the radiograph the cortex appears thinned, though it may show a less distinct medullary surface than the cortex you saw in Figure 16-26.

The borderline of the normal in judging the thickness of either compact bone cortex or individually seen trabeculae is not easy to define clearly. It is not easy for either the radiologist or the pathologist when they are considering the problem of a particular patient, because so many factors determine bone thickness. Factors such as genetic heritage, habitual activity, nutrition, and age all influence bone mass, so that a range of differing thicknesses may be normal for each of a group of patients. You can appreciate better this problem in orientation if you now review briefly the microscopic structure of compact bone.

315

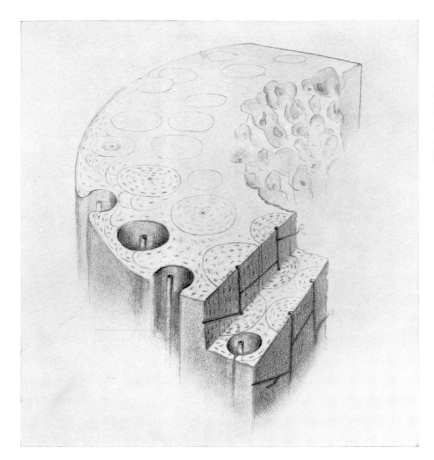

Figure 16-37. The structure of compact bone. Diagram (adapted from Ham) to show both horizontal and vertical cut faces of a full thickness of cortex from the femoral shaft at a level where it begins to be lined with trabecular bone (see text).

Focus down intellectually upon a cross section of the full thickness of the cortex of the femoral shaft you were looking at in Figure 16-1 and you will be seeing the structure which is diagramed above in Figure 16-37. The cross-cut face reveals numerous sectioned *osteones* (or haversian systems) with their central vessels. The vertical cut enables you to recall that the basic functioning adult bone unit is a cylinder between 5 and 7 μ in length. These cylinders, the osteones, are connected with each other via their branching central arteries, and compose, in effect, a breccia of units mortared together to form a mass. They are of a high order phylogenetically and do not exist in the bones of many lower animals. Structurally they produce a type of bone (and there are several types, remember) which is of excellent resilience and beautifully designed for change and adaptation in response to changing needs. Such a composite of arterially connected units begins to be laid down in the bones of the human infant, replacing a far less well-designed type of immature bone, phylogenetically much earlier

in type, and resembling a woven fabric rather than a masonry wall. Even in the infant osteones are found to be concentrated in regions of particular stress such as important tendon insertions. Eventually in the adult most compact bone is composed of osteones mortared together by lamellar bone matrix, as you can see in Figure 16-38, a microradiograph of a thin-ground cross section of the shaft of a long bone which might have been sliced off the face of the diagramed bone wedge in Figure 16-37.

The osteones in such microradiographs are seen as rings of varying density about dark central holes which once contained arteries. Osteones vary in radiodensity because they are of different ages and therefore contain somewhat different amounts of mineral apatite; mineral is precipitated very rapidly into the organic collagen bone matrix when it is first laid down and after that more slowly over a period of several years.

The useful life expectancy of an individual osteone is around 7 years, at the end of which time it is removed by erosion from within until

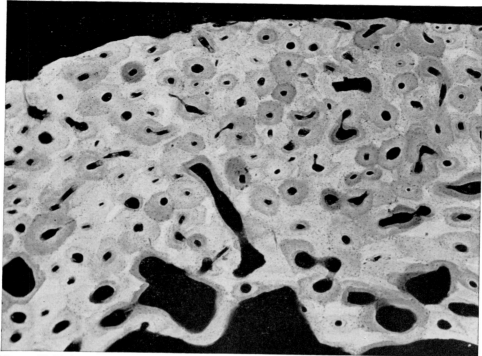

Figure 16-38. Microradiograph of a transverse section of normal femoral cortex. The specimen was not prepared by sectioning decalcified bone but was sawed off and then ground down to a thickness of a few micra in a fresh state retaining its natural calcium content. The radiograph was made with the specimen closely in contact with a photographic film, so that an x-ray shadowgram of the variations in radiodensity of a histologic section of bone is produced.

an empty cylinder exists where it once was, traversed by the central artery and lined by sheets of mesenchymal cells. These differentiate into osteoblasts and lay down new layers of bone matrix concentrically one within another until the central artery is again surrounded by a new osteone. The osteoblasts become engulfed in the bone matrix they elaborate (after which they are called osteocytes), continuing to function via minute canaliculi which radiate from their surfaces in all directions like the spines of a burr. These communicate with the canaliculi of other osteocytes nearby so that bone is able to be transfused with fluid and electrolytes, functioning throughout life as an organ no less important than the liver or kidney. Because the osteoblasts become engulfed in concentric cylindrical layers of matrix, they will appear in cross section as arranged in concentric circles about the artery, just as you see them in the diagram and in the microradiograph. You would *expect* the cells to be radiolucent compared with the mineralized matrix around them and could predict that in the

microradiograph they would appear as minute black dots. Note that some of the osteone circles in the microradiograph are very dark; these are the younger ones less completely mineralized as yet than their white, denser neighbors.

If the patient in Figure 16-38 had recently been given an injection of tagged (artificially rendered radioactive) calcium, the younger osteones which you have identified would now contain much larger amounts of that calcium load, since they are mineralizing at a more rapid rate than their seniors. An *autoradiograph,* made by placing a fine-grained photographic film in close contact with a section of bone like the one which was x-rayed to produce Figure 16-38, would show darker spots in the precise locations of the younger osteones because radioactivity of the calcium isotope produces silver precipitation in the film. When microradiographs, autoradiographs, special stain studies, and photographs made with polarized light *of the same bone section are matched in register,* an invaluable means of studying bone pathophysiology emerges.

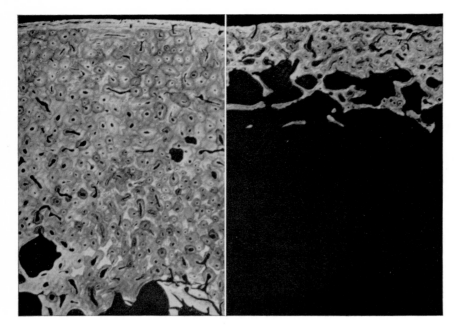

Figure 16-39. Microradiographs of normal cortex (left) and the cortex in postmenopausal osteoporosis (right) taken from precisely the same location on the lateral surface of the femur. The periosteal surface is at the top and the medullary surface below (see text).

By means of such studies the rate at which osteones form and are mineralized, removed, and restored can be recorded for healthy as well as abnormal bone. The gross appearance of a bone is so suggestive of permanence and durability that it is difficult to accept intellectually the degree to which bones are being constantly changed and remodeled throughout life and the extent to which they do reflect and share in virtually every disease condition. In learning to comprehend these changes, it is essential to think clearly of the "flow" prevailing at various periods of life normally in the bones. The infant and young child grow in many ways and at different speeds from year to year, and their growth bone-wise has been charted and documented extensively. However, most of us fail to comprehend fully that bone laid down in one site this year will begin next month to be removed in order to accommodate for developing changes. Take any given tendon insertion site as an example. During growth spurts when the long bones are increasing in length very rapidly, an important muscle tendon inserted at one point soon functions at a disadvantage unless it is moved again closer to the joint it subtends. The adductor muscles, arising from the pubis and inserting into the femur posteriorly along its entire length, powerfully adduct the thigh. However, the adductor longus inserts into the linea aspera on the posterior surface of the bone in about mid-shaft, a location in which little or no change is occurring, while the adductor

magnus inserts further down into a more limited area by a heavy aponeurosis and just above the margin of the epiphyseal growth plate. Here new bone is forming and extending the length of the femur at a very rapid rate indeed. If the tendon insertion of the adductor magnus remained attached at one point it would soon be inserting further up the femur and would adduct the thigh much less efficiently.

The concentration of osteones located along the linea aspera in early childhood and at all tendon sites allows for a mechanism of adaptation. By destruction and reconstruction of osteones at slightly different locations, it is possible to maintain in an area optimal for function the heavy cortex into which tendon fibers insert.

Thus the bones, like every other tissue, adapt and change with growth until maturity. Through the prime years doubtless many individual osteones manage to live out their 7-odd years of usefulness in the same location, but others are removed before that time in order to accommodate to changes pertinent to the habits or activity or health of the individual. If a carpenter gives up his trade and learns another more sedentary one, the heavy concentrations of osteones under the tendon insertions in his dominant arm will gradually be decreased. The young mental patient who recovers after several years of depression and inactivity and takes up the latest dance step must throughout his body increase the rate of bone building.

With the advent of postmaturity and the waning years, however, the normal process of bone replacement flags. The normal stimuli to the maintenance of healthy bone begin to diminish. Activity decreases. The rocking chair takes the place of squash. The appetite declines, and less adequate supplies of proteins, vitamins, and minerals essential to proper bone building are available. Hormonal stimuli to bone maintenance gradually abate with advancing years in both men and women, although these changes, occurring earlier in women, have time to produce the atrophy of bone known as postmenopausal osteoporosis, which might best be thought of as the net decrease in bone mass prevalent in old age.

In Figure 16-39 you can judge for yourself the lengths to which this decrease in bone mass may be carried. The cortex of the woman on the right has gradually been decreased to one-fourth the normally maintained cortex on the left. In serial bone studies taken at different ages this process may be observed to occur in two ways coincident in time. Individual osteones which are removed fail to be replaced adequately, and the cortex takes on the appearance of a Swiss cheese. At the same time the juxtamedullary part of the cortex is gradually converted into spongy bone, the innermost trabeculae being replaced least well and finally disappearing altogether.

Cancellous bone located in the ends of long bones and filling the bodies of the vertebrae, for example, also shares in this attritional process in aging individuals. The high-magnification photographs in Figure 16-40 will give you an unforgettable concept of net decrease and increase in bone mass of cancellous bone, which is not composed of osteones but of sheets of lamellar bone and which is laid down or removed by the surface activity of osteoblasts and osteoclasts.

When you consider that bone mass may be decreased either by failure to replace it when it is removed in the course of normal bone maintenance (osteoporosis) or by some extraordinary process of bone destruction, you will understand that the radiographs of bones in these very different conditions may indeed be indistinguishable. The acceleration of bone

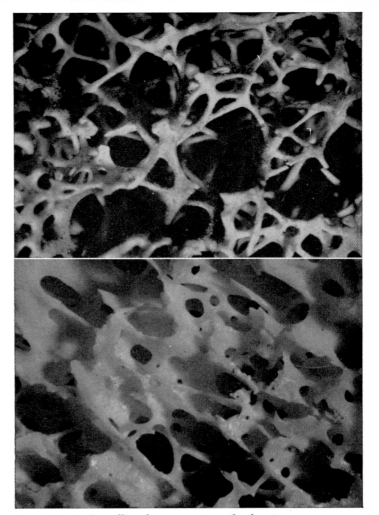

Figure 16-40. Cancellous bone, porotic and sclerotic. The normal is somewhere in between.

destruction occasioned metabolically in hyperparathyroidism is an excellent working example to contrast with the much more gradual loss which occurs in osteoporosis. Both result ultimately in a pronounced decrease in bone mass, but in hyperparathyroidism the decrease occurs relatively rapidly and by a process still incompletely understood in which innumerable osteoclasts appear to destroy bone actively. This occurs in every part of the bone, on the vast total surface of the trabeculae, within the cortex, and also under the periosteum, where no change at all occurs in osteoporosis. The total decrease in bone mass is appreciable in bone radiographs, of course, as decreased radiodensity, but in hyperparathyroidism the distinctive subperiosteal destruction of bone may also be seen on films of the best quality, constituting a dependable diagnostic finding.

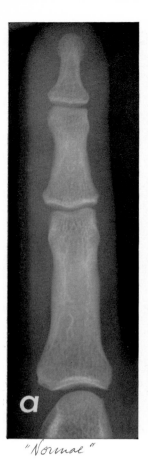

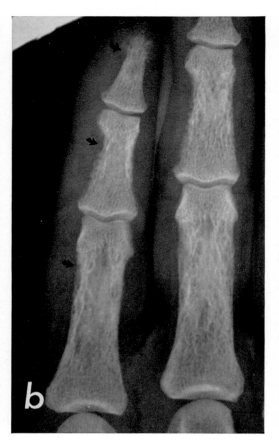

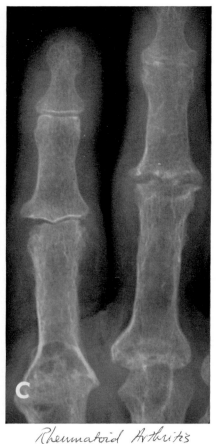

"Normal"

Figure 16-41

Hyperparathyroidism

Rheumatoid Arthritis

Variations in the appearance of cortical and cancellous bone which can be recognized from radiographs may be gauged from the six magnification studies of fingers on this page and the next. The engravings you see here were reduced by a factor of only 1.3 from the original prints and you are therefore seeing the details as though you looked at a routine radiograph of the hand through a low-power magnifying glass.

The finger in _a_ is a normal one from a young man. The relative thickness of compact bone in mid-shaft in the proximal phalanx as well as the size of the individual trabeculae and the marrow space intervals between them are to be compared with the abnormal bones in the other five illustrations.

In _b_ you will recognize the bone destruction occurring subperiosteally in hyperparathyroidism, not to be seen in any other bone disease and therefore distinctive. For this reason films of the hands are often requested in patients suspected of having hyperparathyroidism. Note the erosion of the terminal tuft of the distal

phalanx as well as the appearance of destruction in the areas of compact bone.

In _c_, the fingers of an old man whose activity had been limited for a prolonged period of time by generalized rheumatoid arthritis, the destructive joint changes are the finding which first strikes you. But look also at the cortex and note how thinned it is even in mid-shaft well away from the joints. In _any_ severe generalized illness in which activity is sharply reduced the development of osteoporosis is inevitable. Failure of bone replacement, of course, takes a long time to produce a significant net change in the entire bone mass, so that osteoporosis is to be anticipated in an illness of long duration. However, in very sudden and almost total interruption of activity such as that which occurs in the patient with poliomyelitis or one who is virtually immobilized in plaster following a severe accident, important changes in calcium metabolism largely the result of decreased bone building may have to be watched for, and ultimately osteoporosis develops to a point where it becomes appreciable radiographically. Thus the

320

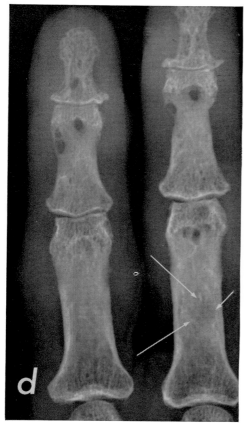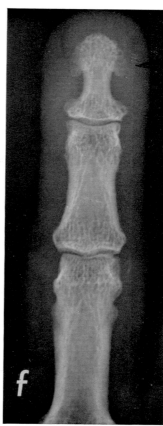

Sarcoidosis

Figure 16-41 (Cont.)
Osteoporosis

Acromegaly

radiographic picture in many bone diseases is complicated by the *additional* development of osteoporosis superimposed on other findings.

In *d* sharply margined areas of bone destruction are seen scattered throughout the bones, the result of pressure from granulomatous foci in a patient with sarcoidosis. Note that when these involve principally the compact bone they are much easier to recognize. When less compact bone and more trabecular bone is being destroyed, as frequently happens in widespread metastatic malignancy, a good deal more bone must be missing before one can see the change radiographically. Something of this sort is going on here in the vaguely lucent area between the arrows. The reason is of course that such areas of loss are masked by superimposed bone above and below. Thus, in a lateral radiograph of the spine, areas of trabecular bone destruction up to 1 centimeter in diameter in the vertebral bodies will not be visible even in retrospect when their presence has been confirmed at autopsy. One must always have such reservations in mind when looking for radiographic evidence of disseminated destructive lesions in the bones.

The patient in *e* had osteopetrosis, or marble bones, an inherited fault in which the maintenance and reconstruction of bone seems to be impaired so that bone accumulates, the cortex is thick and marrow cavities may be obliterated. All bones are affected, and patients who are severely afflicted in early infancy die apparently as a result of failing hematopoiesis. The net bone mass is strikingly increased.

In *f* form is faulty. This finger would be recognized by experts as having the typical alteration of form seen in acromegaly. Compare the widely flanged tuft of the terminal phalanx with the others on these two pages. The bones as a whole are broad, and the bases of the phalanges splayed. Note the distinctive soft tissue changes as well. The classical acromegalic history of increasing sizes for shoes and gloves is as much due to increase in the soft tissues as to increase in the size of the bones. Roentgen findings of this sort may suggest a diagnosis not suspected clinically or confirm one which is.

321

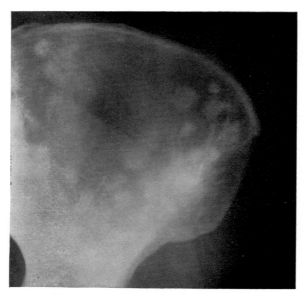

Figure 16-42 (above). Osteoblastic metastases in the wing of the ilium. Such *increased* density is caused by new bone formation locally. Malignant metastases from carcinoma of the *prostate* most frequently produce osteoblastic foci in bone.

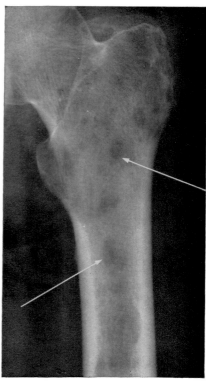

Figure 16-43 (above). Osteolytic metastases in the upper femur. *Decreased* density due to destruction by growing tumor is common in metastases from kidney, lung, thyroid and breast.

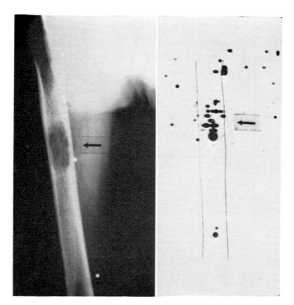

Figure 16-44 (left). Solitary osteolytic metastasis in the shaft of the femur matched against a photoscan of the area after an injection of strontium 85, a radioisotope admirably suited to such studies because of its high rate of uptake in tumors and its rapid decay. Scans are also useful in determining metastatic disease which is not detectable as yet in the radiographs.

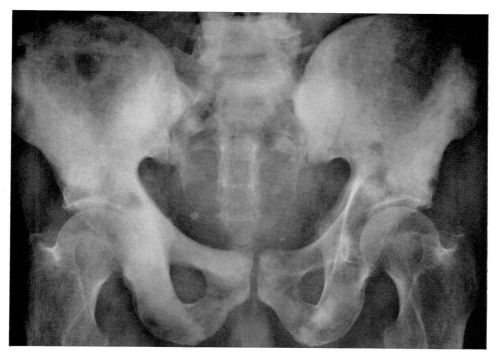

Figure 16-45 (above). The pelvis in a patient with prostatic carcinoma. Dense white areas are involved by diffuse new-bone-forming metastatic disease, rather than the spotty areas in Figure 16-42.

Figure 16-46 (below). The pelvis in a patient with Paget's disease. Note the characteristic linear streaking and enlargement of the bone, not present in Figure 16-45 in which the normal shape and thickness of the pelvic bones are preserved.

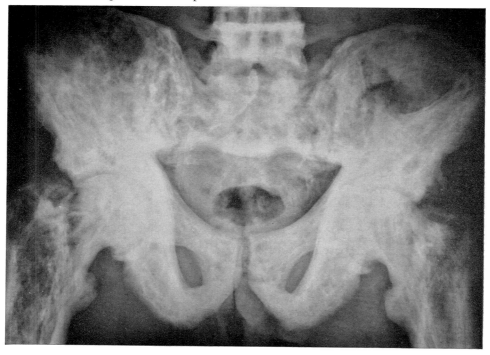

Figure 16-47

Radiography of the skull and brain is already an extensive branch of medical radiology about which many books have been written. The skull film must be viewed, like any other radiograph, while thinking in three dimensions, and the bony parts which are superimposed upon each other subtracted the one from the other. The usual set of skull films comprises a series made AP, PA (in several degrees of sagittal flexion of the neck), lateral (each side in turn close to the plate and one stereoscopic pair), as well as one of the basilar projections in which the ray is directed so that it superimposes the complex basilar structures upon the less complex calvarial cap. The lateral view of the skull shows the two halves of the coronal suture superimposed (Figure 16-49 of a young child). The two parts of the lambdoidal suture are seen as well as the temporoparietal. Sutures remain visible throughout life, distinguishable from fracture lines by their serpiginous character and white margins, while a fracture will be more linear, not at all marginated, and usually more radiolucent.

324

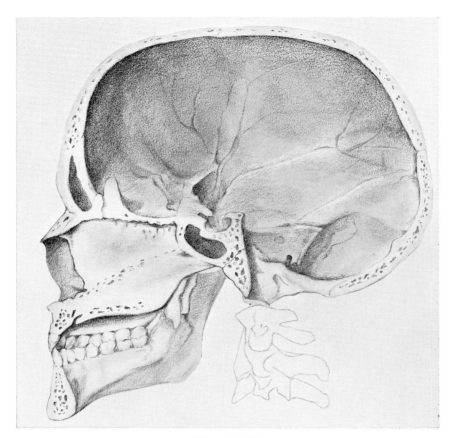

Figure 16-48

Figure 16-49

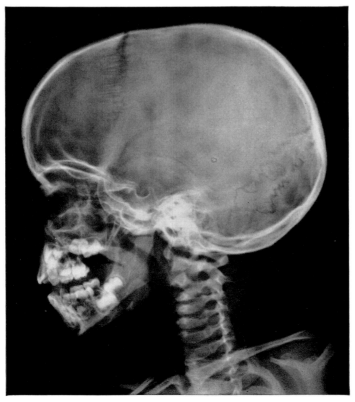

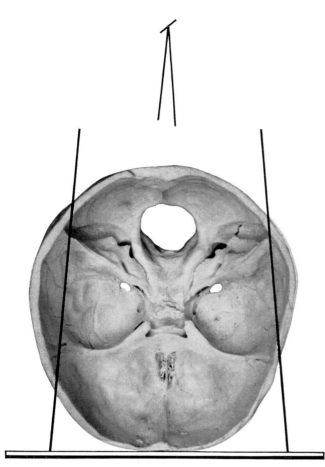

Figure 16-50 (above). PA projection.

Figure 16-51 (below). AP projection.

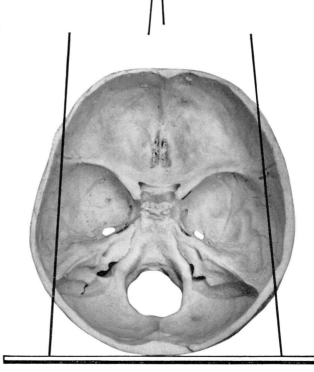

326

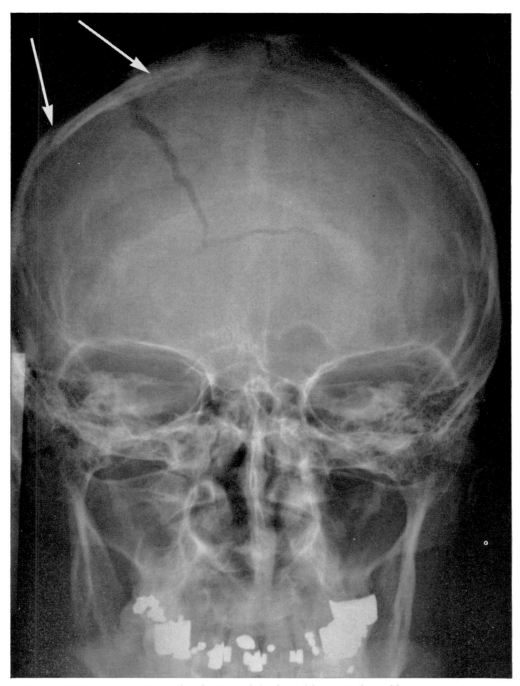

Figure 16-52. PA projection with a fracture of the frontal bone. A plate of bone seen in tangent (between the arrows) is slightly depressed. This is not a simple linear fracture but a comminuted one therefore. Note fillings in the teeth.

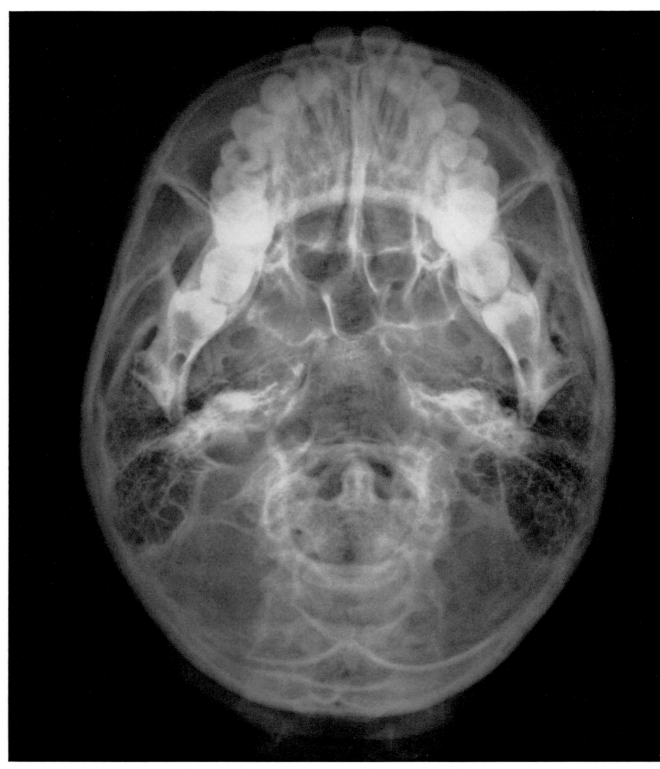

Figure 16-53. Inferior-superior or basilar view of the skull. Normal.

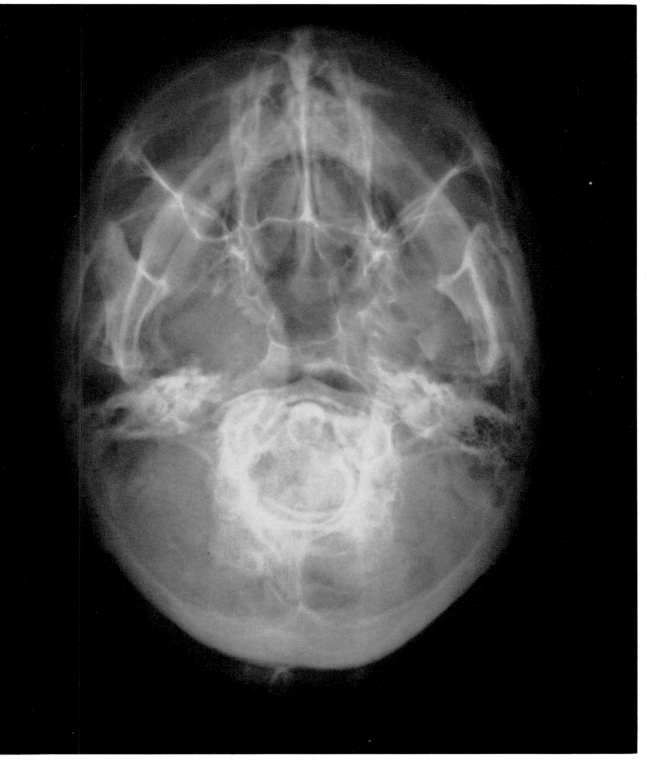

Figure 16-54. Basilar view. Destruction of one petrous tip by metastatic tumor. Look back and forth between the two sides until you see a round area of bone loss the size of a half dollar replacing one foramen lacerum.

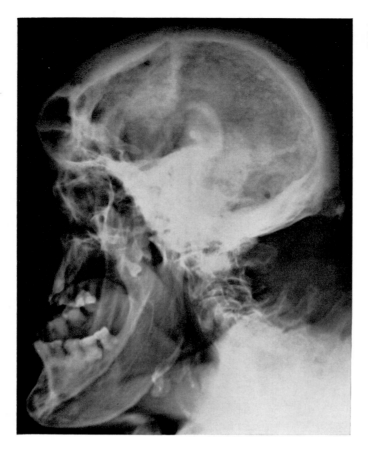

Figure 16-55 (left). Acromegaly with marked overgrowth of the mandible but the sella turcica normal in size.

Figure 16-56. Pituitary tumor with enlarged sella. Note that the posterior clinoids are thinned and tilted backward.

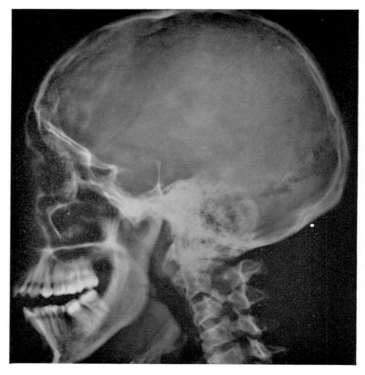

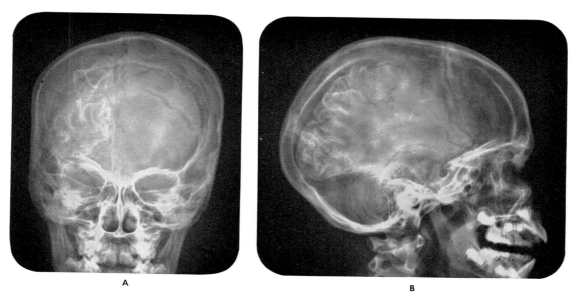

A

B

Figure 16-57 (above). Intracranial calcifications of many kinds have been catalogued, some distinctive for the condition they occur in, others quite unspecific. Here wavy irregular calcifications in the right parieto-occipital part of the brain have an appearance characteristic of that seen in Sturge-Weber syndrome (encephalotrigeminal angiomatosis). The fundamental lesion in this condition is an anomalous development of the blood vessels of the skin, meninges, and underlying brain, with the cutaneous angiomas, or "port-wine marks" occurring in the trigeminal distribution. Calcification has been attributed to disturbance of circulation through the angiomatous channels with focal infarctions. (Locate the intracranial calcification in Figure 16-58 below.)

Figure 16-58 (below).

A

B

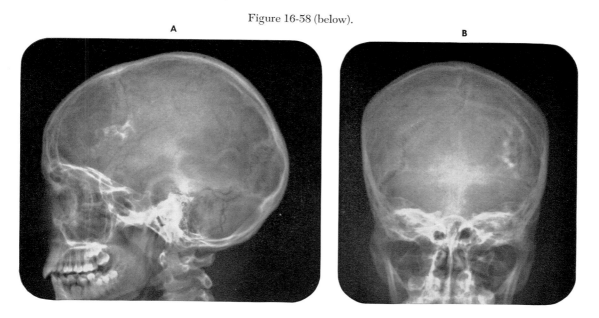

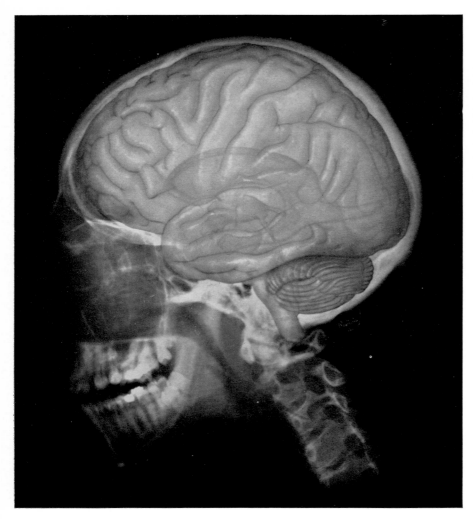

Figure 16-59. A superimposition of the apparently transparent brain and its ventricular system on a lateral radiograph of the skull will help you to visualize the relationships and to think three dimensionally about skull films and air studies. Identify the two lateral ventricles (superimposed in this projection), the third ventricle, the aqueduct, and fourth ventricle.

Radiography of the skull made after air has been introduced into the ventricles of the brain (pneumoencephalography) has proved to be an immensely useful tool in the study and delineation of cerebral lesions of many kinds. If the air is introduced into the subarachnoid space via a spinal tap, the procedure is called an *encephalogram*. If burr holes are made surgically under anesthesia in the bony calvarium and air then introduced into the ventricular system by direct tap, the procedure is called a *ventriculogram*. They are not interchangeable methods of study, however, and each is better adapted to certain disease states.

The air, filling identifiable parts of the ventricular system, casts darker shadows on the films because it is more radiolucent than the fluid which ordinarily fills these chambers and more radiolucent than the surrounding brain tissue. In the presence of space-taking masses some part of the air-filled ventricular system will be seen displaced from its normal position. With obstruction to the downward drainage of the spinal fluid, the ventricles dilate and hydrocephalus will be apparent. During such air contrast studies, films are made with the x-ray beam parallel to the fluid-air interface but with the patient's head variously tilted (Figure 16-60), and also with a perpendicular beam.

Cerebral angiography is a similar spatial tagging system which has gained wide use in the past decade. This procedure is carried out by direct puncture of the carotid or vertebral arteries or by catheterization of the aorta and selective injection of a radio-opaque medium into the aorta itself or one of its branches.

332

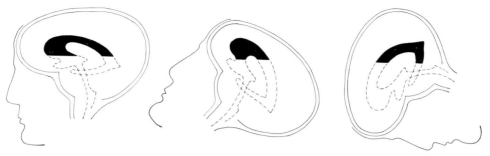

Figure 16-60 (above). Tilting the patient's head with air and fluid in the ventricles produces information about various parts of the ventricular system. Note that here beam is parallel to fluid-air interface, and a fluid level is seen.

Figure 16-61 (below). A (left). Lateral ventriculogram in a patient with an eighth-nerve tumor. The lateral ventricles are slightly dilated and the third ventricle may be seen. B (right). Mid-line body-section study shows with improved detail that there is posterior displacement of the aqueduct and fourth ventricle curving around the tumor. The tumor mass is not seen itself, but its posterior margin becomes "visible" when juxtaposed to air in the ventricular system. Note that here no fluid level is seen. Patient was radiographed as in Figure 16-47 with beam perpendicular to fluid-air interface.

B

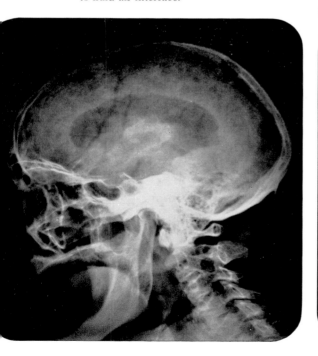

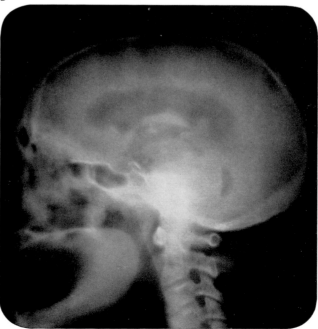

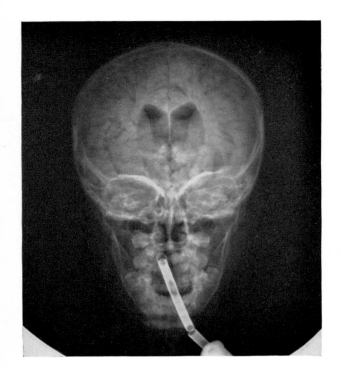

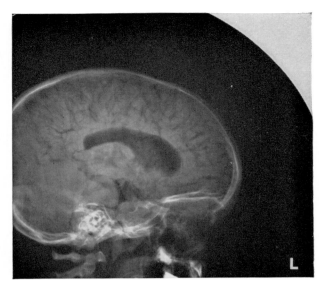

Figure 16-62 (left and above). Pneumoencephalogram demonstrating convolutional atrophy in a 3-year-old child. Note collection of air in the enlarged subarachnoid spaces over the surface of the brain.

Figure 16-63. Hydrocephalus with greatly dilated ventricles and marked thinning of the cerebral cortex.

Figure 16-64. Infant with chronic subdural hematoma. The brain may be seen outlined by air above the fluid level.

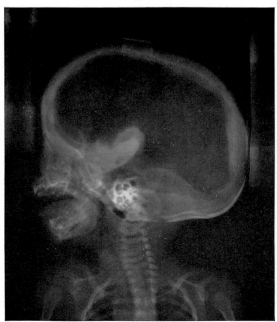

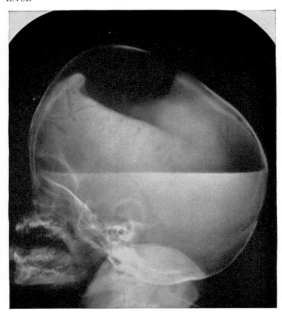

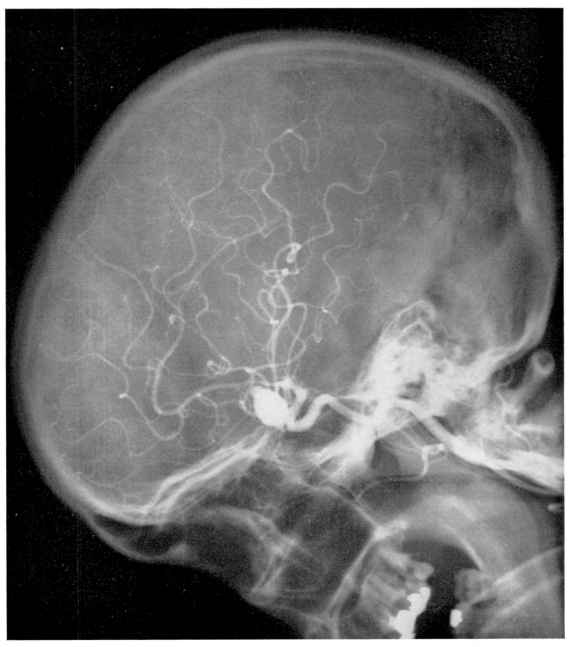

Figure 16-65. Cerebral arteriogram. Follow the course of the carotid upward into the cranial cavity. The large pool of opaque material is in an aneurysm.

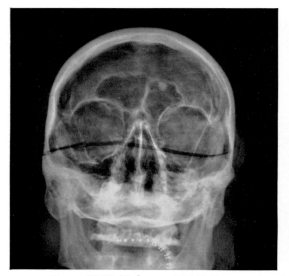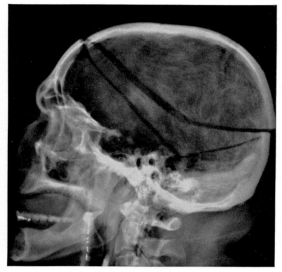

Figure 16-66 (*Unknown 16-12*). Try your hand at radiologic medicolegal detective work. These are radiographs made at the request of the coroner after the prosector had failed to establish the cause of death. The deceased had apparently been beaten to death in a drunken altercation. During the fight he had received multiple cuts from a soft drink bottle, and at autopsy numerous contusions were seen about the face, but there was no evidence of skull fracture or of intracranial hemorrhage. What cause of death, indicated by these films, was established by re-examination of the corpse?

The final unknown serves as a final reminder that roentgen shadows are essentially logical, and that from roentgen density as a clue to composition and from form as a clue to structure even unfamiliar objects may be recognized.

In the same fashion, disease processes whose roentgen appearance you have not yet seen will appeal to you as logical when you do see them, because you think in terms of the pathologic change you know to have occurred. For instance, you will *expect* osteomyelitis to appear as an ill-defined, ragged area of destruction in bone visualized late in the illness since dissolution of a rigid structure takes time to occur. It will not surprise you, therefore, that the patient with osteomyelitis must usually be treated presumptively before the roentgen findings are definite, and that for this reason films are useful and important in following the course and progress of the disease rather than in affording a means of identifying it early.

Bone growth, too, is beautifully documented in serial films, like time-lapse studies of opening flowers. Vagaries of growth can be studied and comprehended through such serial studies. If you want to appreciate the fascinating pathologic implications evident from such studies, hunt out the film envelope of a patient in your hospital who had the familiar classical form of dwarfism, achondroplasia, diagnosed in infancy and followed into adulthood. Compare his films with the pattern of growth in normal bones, measuring in the stunted femurs and square pelvis the failure of cartilage proliferation at the growth plates. Many such adventures in thinking await you in the next few years as you familiarize yourself with the roentgen appearance of normal and abnormal bones.

Credits: Illustrations this chapter.

Figure 16-2. Courtesy Chicago Museum of Natural History, Chicago, Ill.

Figures 16-4, 16-10. Courtesy Mr. C. Bridgman and the publisher, *MR&P* 26:4, 9.

Figures 16-5, 16-38. Courtesy Dr. G. Mitchell and the publisher, *MR&P* 34:6, 7.

Figures 16-6, 16-15. Courtesy Dr. H. Isard, Dr. B. Ostrum, Mr. J. Cullinan, and the publisher, *MR&P* 38:97, 101.

Figures 16-8*B*, and *C*. Courtesy Mr. J. Cahoon and the publisher, *Radiography and Clinical Photography* 22:4, 6.

Figure 16-9. Courtesy Mr. C. Bridgman and the publisher, *MR&P* 27:72.

Figure 16-10. Courtesy Mr. C. Bridgman and the publisher, *MR&P* 26:9.

Figure 16-11. Courtesy Dr. L. Hilt, Eugene, Ore.

Figures 16-17, 16-18, 16-19, 16-20, 16-21, 16-22. Courtesy Mr. T. Funke and the publisher, *MR&P* 36:9, 16, 17, 19, 20, 24, 29.

Figure 16-26. Courtesy Dr. W. Irwin, Detroit, Mich.

Figures 16-27, 16-43, 16-46. Courtesy Dr. D. Wilner, Atlantic City, N. J.

Figures 16-28, 16-29, 16-30, 16-31, 16-32, 16-33, 16-34, 16-35. Courtesy Drs. G. Selin and H. Jaffe, and the publisher, *MR&P* 33:7, 8, 9, 10, 12, 14, 15, 16.

Figure 16-36. Courtesy Drs. G. Wyatt and W. Randall, and the publisher, *MR&P* 24:30.

Figure 16-37. Adapted from Ham, A. W., *Histology*, 3rd ed., 1957, published by J. B. Lippincott, Philadelphia, Pa., p. 295.

Figure 16-39. Courtesy Dr. M. Urist, *Bone As a Tissue*, 37, and the publisher, McGraw-Hill Book Co., Inc., New York, N. Y.

Figure 16-40. Courtesy Dr. J. Luck, *Bone and Joint Diseases*, 1st ed., and the publisher, Charles C Thomas, Publisher, Springfield, Ill.

Figure 16-41. Courtesy Dr. J. Feist, Pittsburgh, Pa.

Figure 16-44. Courtesy Drs. D. Sklaroff and N. Charkes, and the publisher, *Radiology* 80:270.

Figure 16-49. From *Fundamentals of Radiography*, p. 44, published by Eastman Kodak Co., Rochester, N. Y.

Figure 16-53. Courtesy Dr. W. Irwin and the publisher, Eastman Kodak Co., Rochester, N. Y.

Figure 16-54. Courtesy Dr. E. Kalmon, Jr., Oklahoma City, Okla.

Figure 16-56. Courtesy Dr. B. Epstein, New Hyde Park, N. Y.

Figure 16-57. Courtesy Drs. R. Burnip, R. Cohen, and W. Yeider, and the publisher, *MR&P* 27:60.

Figure 16-58. Courtesy Drs. H. Hunt and R. Moore, and the publisher, *MR&P* 27:57.

Figure 16-59. Courtesy Mr. R. Matthias and the publisher, *MR&P* 28:Cover.

Figure 16-61. Courtesy Dr. B. Epstein and the publisher, *MR&P* 32:9.

Figure 16-62. Courtesy Dr. J. Marsh and the publisher, *MR&P* 37:35.

Figures 16-63, 16-64. Courtesy Miss A. Cambern, Dr. D. Shurtleff, and the publisher, *MR&P* 37:9, 10.

Figure 16-65. Courtesy Dr. J. Edwin Habbe and the publisher, Eastman Kodak Co., Rochester, N. Y.

Figure 16-66. Courtesy Dr. C. Dotter and the publisher, *MR&P* 37:19.

Appendices

Answers to Unknowns

Unknown 1-1 (Figure 1-16)

The pair of dice on the right have been loaded by boring holes into the substance of the die, filling with heavy metal, recapping, and re-painting the dots. Bits of lead wire have been used. Of the loaded pair, the die on the left has been x-rayed with the loaded face down as it would tend to fall. The die on the right has been turned on its side and then x-rayed. Note that you are now looking through it from the side, so to speak. The loaded face is down and very dense. The upper part of the die has been evacuated and left empty, increasing its tendency to fall with the "two" facing up — or the "five," depending on whichever is chosen by the tamperer.

Unknown 1-2 (Figure 1-17)

No, not an egg with a nail in it. The oval object could not be an egg because its radiodensity falls away at the edge and is much greater and fairly uniform in the center. Therefore, this must be a solid oval body of considerable density and homogeneous composition, except for the nail, which actually was in the center of it. The dark streaks are air in the interfaces after it has been cracked open. The object was a mineral bolus found in the stomach of a horse. The nail, typical of those used for shoeing horses, had undoubtedly been swallowed and remained in the stomach for many years. The "stone," a concretion like a gallstone, had been built up around it gradually.

Unknown 2-1 (Figure 2-15)

The left shoulder girdle is missing, removed surgically because of a malignant bone tumor. Note that the medial part of the left clavicle is still present.

Unknown 2-2 (Figure 2-16)

Congenital absence of the right femur.

Unknown 2-3 (Figure 2-27)

Radiograph of a mid-line sagittal slice of a female cadaver. It can only be a mid-line slice: the uterus, sternum, and vertebrae are present, while the breasts, rib shadows, and pelvic bones are absent.

Unknown 3-1 (Figure 3-5)

Fractured scapula. The humerus, lying across the rib cage is also fractured obliquely with pronounced over-riding of the fragments. Differences in position from Figure 3-6, used as a normal for comparison, are due to the technical problems implicit in filming a patient who is in great pain.

Unknown 3-2 (Figure 3-18)

The right third rib is congenitally small (hypoplastic), shorter and more slender than those above and below it. Note that when you do not have the rib on the opposite side to use as a normal for comparison, you can use the ribs above and below, a *progression* of structures into which the rib in question does not fit smoothly.

Unknown 3-3 (Figure 3-19)

The ribs are numbered correctly. Structures indicated by white arrows are cervical ribs arising from the last cervical vertebra.

Unknown 3-4 (Figure 3-20)

The eighth rib on the left is fractured close to its vertebral end. There is also a fracture of the lateral margin of the scapula.

Unknown 3-5 (Figure 3-25)

Fractured clavicle. Air from a break in the skin has infiltrated the soft tissues (subcutaneous emphysema).

Unknown 3-6 (Figure 3-29)

The bones are normal. There is no rotation, since the clavicles are symmetrical. The left breast is missing. Note that the left lung field appears darker than the right.

Unknown 3-7 (Figure 3-30)

The tip of the left scapula is fractured, as are the fifth and sixth ribs. There is abundant air in the soft tissues. The injury was a severe blow delivered to the left chest and shoulder. Note that the fifth and sixth ribs are fractured near the posterior axillary line and again in the anterior axillary line. Note streaks of dark air crossing the chest. These are in the pectoral muscles.

Unknown 4-1 (Figure 4-15)

Patient was a male; heavy pectoral shadows may simulate breast shadows. Rounded hilar mass is crossed by normally tapering vessels and is probably not vascular in nature, therefore. Left hilum extends laterally a little farther than one expects it to and may conceal a second mass superimposed partly on the aortic shadow. Close to the left hilum in the mid left lung field (seventh interspace and overlapping the eighth rib) there is a rounded shadow outlined by normal lung around it. The medial posterior portion of the right seventh rib is missing. (All findings were proved due to tumor.)

Unknown 4-2 (no figure in text)

Search the patient's clothing for a straight pin; then order another chest film specifying your reason for doing so. The technician will make sure that there is no straight pin outside the patient. The radiologist will determine whether there is one inside, altogether unlikely in this case, but a chance not to be risked preoperatively. Figure A-1 (pg. 342) shows a chest film in which a hat pin actually was in the left main bronchus. A photograph of the recovered hat pin has been superimposed on the radiograph. This patient, needless to say, was not talking comfortably. Foreign bodies are more commonly seen in the right main bronchus. Why?

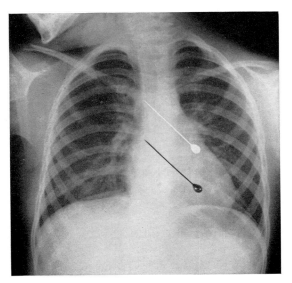

Figure A-1

Unknown 4-3 (Figure 4-22)

You see spotty densities well out in the lung parenchyma which do not taper like vessels. A small circular gray shadow with a darker interior suggests a cavity. Obviously at 23, inflammation of some kind is more likely than tumor or lung insult through employment, neither of which is very plausible from the story. Certainly tuberculosis, a strong possibility, must be ruled out by collateral laboratory procedures. If the chest film made 3 months before (or any other fairly recent film) can be obtained for comparison, it may be easier to judge the age of the process. You can discard consideration of an inflammation 1 day old and probably that of 1 week, since involvement of lung tissue enough to produce infiltrative densities, a cavity, and the story of weight loss indicate a somewhat older process. The best choice would be subacute inflammation 1 month old, although that is not entirely satisfactory either, since earlier changes *might* have been missed on the insurance film.

Unknown 4-4 (Figures 4-23 and 4-24)

Figure 4-23 is the film made after recovery. Note that the hilum in 4-24 made at the height of the illness appears thickened and nodular, probably because its vessels are engorged and because the lymph nodes in and around it are enlarged. The fine reticulum of increased lung markings in the figure is the engorged vascular tree, and the many small round shadows are the innumerable discrete, palpable nodules in the lung which patients with this condition have proven to have at autopsy. You may never see silo-filler's disease again, but you can learn from this patient how to judge change in a hilar shadow which was abnormal and has "improved."

Now, if you saw these two films with no clinical information except that Figure 4-23, the more normal looking film, was made 4 months *before* the other, you would have to assume that whatever process the patient suffered from had progressed rather than healed. The radiologist's report to you would describe an enlarged nodular hilum (developing in the time interval between the two films) and a marked increase in linear markings in the lung with myriads of fine miliary lesions. He might mention that either inflammation or tumor could produce the picture, and he might be willing to suggest verbally to you that miliary tuberculosis and widely disseminated tumor metastases had best be excluded. He would certainly not be justified in entertaining (either verbally or in his written report) the possibility of silo-filler's disease or any other of the rarely seen conditions which may produce a similar roentgen picture until much more probable diagnoses had been unequivocally eliminated by you, the clinician. This is what I mean by the review and reinterpretation of serial films.

Unknown 4-5 (Figure 4-25)

The clavicles are normal. The scapulae, rotated well out, appear normal, their margins seen crossing the upper ribs near the lateral chest wall. The anterior ends of the two first ribs have a curious appearance due to calcification in the costochrondral junction. You will see this often. Clavicles and ribs are symmetrical without distortion due to rotation. The hila and lung markings would pass for normal, with the exception of the lung parenchyma seen in the window formed between the posterior parts of the right fifth and sixth ribs and the anterior tips of the first and second ribs. Here you see some increased density, not present in the comparable interspace window on the left. In a far anterior body-section study (Figure A-2) this density is more clearly seen, placing it near the anterior tips of the first two ribs. It proved to be a malignant tumor arising in the pleura.

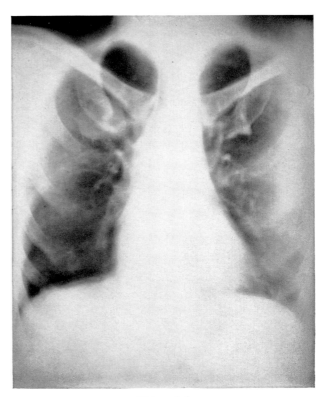

Figure A-2

Unknown 4-6 (Figure 4-26)

One could assume that the density of the shadow in question would be accounted for by calcification. However, it was not in the posterior rib or in any part of the lung superimposed on it, as proved by this far anterior body-section study showing only anterior rib segments (Figure A-3). It proved to be calcification within a benign tumor eroding the under surface of the fourth rib near its anterior end. The vertical shadow is the margin of the body of the scapula. It is projected over the lung field because no attempt was made to rotate it out since the patient was being examined AP referable to the lesion on the rib. Note that, as you would expect, no part of the scapula is seen in the anterior body-section slice.

Unknown 5-1 (Figure 5-15)

Posteriorly. The heart border is clearly seen. Therefore the lung density must be behind the heart in the left lower lobe.

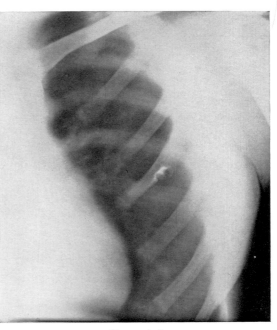

Figure A-3

Unknown 6-1 (Figure 6-10)

These fluid levels could not be inside the thorax, since they extend beyond the rib cage. These are fluid levels inside fluid- and air-containing breast protheses, held in place by the hardware you see, after bilateral mastectomy.

Unknown 6-2 (Figure 6-11)

Child's chest at expiration. The dome of the diaphragm is high at the level of the origin of the seventh rib. The lung fields appear hazy and the heart and mediastinum wide. Figure 6-13 is the same chest at inspiration. Note the diaphragm now at the ninth rib. The heart in this case still appears large and proved to be truly enlarged. Note how the superior mediastinal shadow has narrowed, however, in 6-13.

You see at least three fluid levels in this standing patient. Note one air-gastric fluid level under the left diaphragm and a level between barium and gastric fluid in the antrum of the stomach where the barium (being heavy) has settled. Thus, there are two levels in the stomach which indicate its size and location. There are also air-filled levels in the bowel loops to the right of the barium pool.

Unknown 6-3 (Figure 6-12)

The diaphragm is elevated by large amounts of air below it in the peritoneal space (pneumoperitoneum), one method of putting the lung at rest in pulmonary tuberculosis. The diaphragmatic leaves are seen as thin sheets of muscle, the right at the level of the ninth rib and the left a little lower. Liver and spleen are displaced downward and medially. The patient was unable to pull his diaphragm down well in inspiration because of the air cushion below.

Unknown 6-4 (Figure 6-31)

"The bones are normal, as are the soft tissues in this male patient. The heart and mediastinum appear to be slightly deviated to the left. The diaphragmatic shadows are at the level of the eleventh rib and appear normal. The left costophrenic sinus is normal, but the right is blunted and appears to contain a small amount of fluid since there is a short fluid level there. There is a pneumothorax on the right, the lower and middle lobes being nearly completely collapsed and very dense. The upper lobe is still partly expanded, held to the chest wall by an adhesive band seen overlapping the right second rib. There are mottled densities in the parenchyma of this lobe. The left lung field is not strikingly abnormal except for an area of density in the middle of the sixth interspace measuring about 2 centimeters in its longest dimension." (All this you can say about this film without any clinical information and, you observe, without mentioning any diagnosis.)

If the above report were to reach you, the physician, and you were already pretty sure that your patient had tuberculosis, the points in this report would give you just what you wanted to know, namely, that there is a pneumothorax on the right, as you suspected from your physical examination, and that the disease is probably bilateral, which you may not have suspected. The radiologist would have been thinking the patient had tuberculosis, of course, and might add in summary to his report that the findings are most consistent with that disease, although both you and he know that these roentgen findings could possibly be caused by several other disease conditions. If the radiologist takes a short cut here, and in his summary simply says, "Bilateral tuberculosis with pneumothorax on the right," he is, admittedly, reading from the knowledge based on experience that no other disease is *very* likely to give just this picture. He also assumes that such a patient will not be treated for tuberculosis by you without bacteriologic confirmation.

Unknown 6-5 (Figure 6-32)

Here you can say that the bones and soft tissues are normal. (You know the patient is a child because the head of the humerus is still a growing epiphysis and not yet fused to the shaft.) The right diaphragm is normal at the level of the ninth rib, which could account for the appearance of slightly increased and crowded lung markings at the right base; about these you must reserve judgment. Otherwise the right hilum and lung field appear normal. The probable position of the left diaphragm is visible at the level of the tenth rib, outlined by air in the stomach and bowel underneath it. The left lung field and heart and mediastinal borders are completely masked by density. However, you can hazard a guess that the density most likely represents pleural fluid, in part, at least, since there is a straight fluid level overlapping the third rib, indicating the presence of much fluid and a small amount of air. What may be going on in the lung underneath the fluid you have no way of knowing, but in a child with a massive pleural effusion, of course, you will be planning to consider pneumonia as the primary condition, and much of such a decision will rest on the history you have been given.

Clinically, this child had had pneumonia a week or so before. At thoracentesis, a large amount of purulent fluid was withdrawn from which pneumococcus was cultured. He had a long illness during which he developed a loculated area in his pleural space, sealed off by adhesions, which continued to drain externally. This empyema cavity was outlined by opaque material injected through a catheter (Figure A-4A and B), and it eventually closed. As you look at the opaque-filled empyema cavity, remember that it is flat against the inside of the chest wall, either anteriorly or far posteriorly, and only superimposed on the lung.

Figure A-4C shows the appearance of the child's chest after recovery. Note that you still see thickened pleura along the lateral chest wall and that the costophrenic angle is lost, probably permanently.

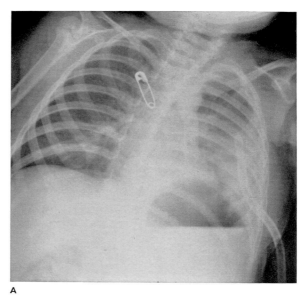

A

Figure A-4

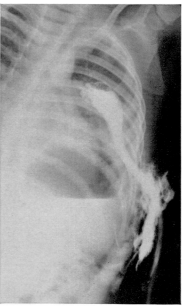

B

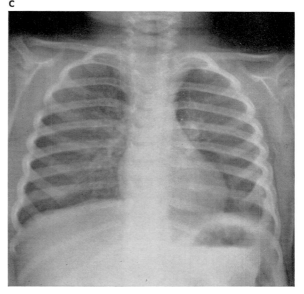

C

345

Unknown 6-6 (Figure 6-33a and b)

Bones, soft tissues, right diaphragm, right lung field, and hilum are all normal. The left diaphragm is not seen because of the density above it. On neither the PA nor the lateral can one be sure of air in the stomach to help locate its position. In the lateral film only one diaphragmatic shadow is seen (compare a normal chest lateral). There does appear to be some increased density posteriorly overlapping the spine on the lateral film, and the posterior location of this density is confirmed by the fact that in the PA view you can see the left border of the heart well outlined with air in the upper lobe, lingular segment. You cannot go further than this without clinical information.

The appearance could be accounted for by pneumonia or tumor of the left lower lobe, and there is no roentgen evidence for fluid in the pleural space, that is, no line curving up along the chest wall laterally and no air-fluid level. Each of the curving lines you do see can be explained as a rib from its spacing and bony trabeculae; when you see the film itself this will always be easier than it is from a small illustration. Finally, in the lateral film that white peak at the middle of the one diaphragmatic shadow you do see is an overlap shadow: the posterior part of the heart plus the high left diaphragm and spleen, plus the anterior part of the dense lower lobe are all added together to absorb the x-rays. Peaked overlap shadows of this sort can be very helpful, and you should look for them and analyze them whenever you see only one diaphragmatic shadow in a lateral chest film.

Unknown 6-7 (Figure 6-34A and B)

A diagnosis of a small pleural effusion on the right was made, and confirmed when thoracentesis produced 130 ml. of fluid. If you have been having difficulty with overlying breast shadows, this unknown should help you. Notice that in A the costophrenic angle seems almost as much obscured on the left as it does on the right, where the fluid was proved to be present. This is due to overlapping breast shadow and would, of course, be somewhat easier to discern on the original full-sized film. Comparing the return of a sharp costophrenic angle on the right in B should help you. Note, too, that the appearance of the left costophrenic angle does not change so much; there may have been blunting from old pleural disease there. Remember that lateral films and fluoroscopy would settle any doubts.

You will find the two lateral films on this patient printed for you on the next page in the text at the end of Chapter 6. Note that one posterior costophrenic angle (the right) is filled in with gray density in the early examination (A); the clearly seen angle represents the normal left sinus. In B, made after recovery, there are two sharp, clear posterior angles and two diaphragmatic shadows which can be traced to the posterior chest wall.

Unknown 7-1 (Figure 7-21)

The absence of the left diaphragm should strike you. Considering the absence of the diaphragm and the apparent depression of the left hilum, there may be some shift of the mediastinum to the left. The lateral view shows only one diaphragmatic shadow, and taking together the two views, this indicates density at the base of the left hemithorax. Some pneumonic infiltrate, some atelectasis, some pleural fluid are all possible. When you are told that the patient had a 3-year history of fever, wheezing, cough, and left chest pain, you are compelled to consider first the presence of chronic infection at the left base, possibly with some decrease in size of the left lower lobe to explain the depressed hilum. You cannot reasonably consider acute left lower lobe atelectasis with this history. The presence or absence of fluid could be established at fluoroscopy.

The film in Figure A-5 was made 2 years later. There is now obvious shift of the mediastinum to the left, both trachea and right heart border being displaced. Neither the left diaphragm nor any part of the heart profile is seen, though there appears to be some aerated lung tissue in the upper part of the left chest. There may be infection and pleural fluid present; you cannot be certain, but at least there is ample evidence now for massive collapse of the left lower lobe and probably part of the upper. At surgery this patient proved to have a tumor in the left lower lobe bronchus, and massive atelectasis was present, both chronic and acute.

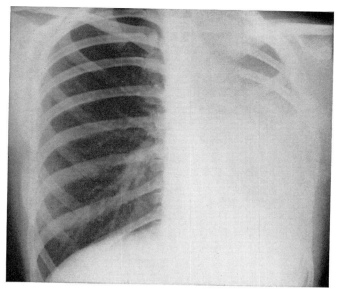

Figure A-5

Unknown 7-2 (Figure 7-22)

The middle lobe is involved. You know this because the density to the right of the heart in the PA view is sharply bounded above by the minor fissure extending straight laterally from the hilum. A normally aerated right upper lobe accounts for the radiolucency above it, and density of the middle lobe for the density below this roughly horizontal plane.

The plane of the minor fissure as seen in the lateral view does not look perfectly horizontal, but enough of it has lined up with the beam to give you that sharp border on the PA view. You know that the base of the lower lobe cannot be dense because you see the profile of the diaphragm so well.

The inferior margin of the slim wedge of density you see in the lateral view is the lower part of the major fissure displaced forward by some degree of collapse in the right middle lobe. The lower lobe behind this part of the fissure has overexpanded, and this is why you still see part of the right heart profile in the PA view: there actually *is* air against much of the right heart. The right heart profile is visible, therefore, although indistinctly. Dense consolidation of a middle lobe retaining its normal size would cause the complete disappearance of this profile.

In summary, your patient may have pneumonia in his middle lobe, but he certainly also has some degree of atelectasis.

Unknown 7-3 (Figure 7-23)

The combination of density in the lower half of the lung beside the heart on the PA view and density anterior to the major fissure in the lateral view tells you that it is the middle lobe which is involved. Here, the major fissure is normal in position, and in this patient you cannot see the location of the minor fissure. Perhaps it may be depressed markedly because the middle lobe is almost totally collapsed, or, on the other hand, perhaps only a part of the middle lobe is involved. Note how smudged and unsharp the right heart profile has become. From the films alone you cannot be certain whether this is inflammation or atelectasis or both, although the radiologist will strongly suspect that atelectasis is present from his experience with the appearance of disease of all kinds in the middle lobe.

347

Unknown 7-4 (Figure 7-24)

The wedge of increased radiodensity in the right costophrenic angle does not have the appearance of pleural fluid. Note its inferior margin curving downward and outward to meet the shadow of the diaphragm. Without any of the story, you would have to consider pneumonia and atelectasis of the lateral segments of the right lower lobe (remember that the middle lobe does not extend so far laterally into the sulcus). With the fragment of tooth clearly wedged in a bronchus on the body-section and the short story of postanesthesia fever, however, you must put first in your differential list "atelectasis beyond a foreign body."

Unknown 7-5 (Figure 7-25)

The wedge of density in the right fifth interspace against the chest wall could be either a patch of atelectasis or a patch of pneumonia from the plain film alone. When you look at the section study, though, you see a cavity with a fluid level, and you must recognize breakdown of lung tissue. Whether the initial insult to lung was infarction, collapse, pneumonia, or tumor, the pathologic process is now a complex one.

Unknown 7-6 (Figure 7-26)

The entire left side of the chest is dense, and you cannot be sure you see the left hemidiaphragm. With the degree of penetration used you cannot be sure you see the trachea, either. There is less right heart visible beyond the vertebral column than normal. You cannot be sure, but you have a right to postulate that there *may* be some displacement of the lower mediastinum to the left and perhaps, therefore, some element of collapse present in the left lung. You can see vague indications that there may be some radiolucent lung tissue in the lower half of the chest, but the upper half is very dense. A

massive effusion seems ruled out, but you cannot say more, nor could anyone else. Any combination of fluid, tumor, atelectasis, and inflammation is possible. (Subsequent studies, including Bucky films and bronchoscopy, showed a carcinoma of the left upper lobe with the upper lobe solidly involved. The trachea was in the mid-line. However, at surgery nodes in the hilum were found compressing the lower lobe bronchus. The lower lobe was partially atelectatic and the heart shifted to the left. There was no pleural fluid present.)

Unknown 7-7 (Figure 7-27)

The findings you can be sure of here are a definite shift of the entire mediastinum to the left, the trachea displaced to the left, and the right heart border not seen at all. The left diaphragm is obscured. There is too much distortion to say anything about the location of the left hilum. However, all signs indicate a collapse of the left lower lobe and possibly a part of the left upper lobe. Postoperative atelectasis is a common surgical complication of importance. What should you do for this patient before you go off duty?

Unknown 8-1 (Figure 8-14)

1. The patient is a child with the epiphyses for the humeral heads as yet unfused.

2. The shadow at *a* is an overlap shadow produced by the soft-tissue overlap of upper arm and upper lateral chest wall.

3. The same principle which applies to masses in the posterior part of the lung applies to masses arising in the posterior part of the mediastinum. The profile of the anteriorly placed heart will often be seen through them. This mass was a tumor of neural origin and located, as neural tumors so frequently are, against the posterior chest wall close to the mid-line. Neural tumors also very often cause pressure erosion of bone (ribs, vertebrae), but none can be seen here.

Unknown 8-2 (Figure 8-15)

You would have to consider all possible causes of superior vena caval obstruction. Tumor could well be present to account for the thickening of the mediastinal shadow. However, this patient actually had a vena caval thrombosis with the formation of extensive collateral pathways for venous return.

Unknown 8-3 (Figure 8-18C)

In Figure 8-18A the left diaphragm was paralyzed and high in position. This together with the aneurysm compressing the left main bronchus must have for some time severely embarrassed the proper inflation and deflation of the left lung. Since the patient was afebrile on admission but complaining of increased dyspnea, and since the entire left side of the chest is now opaque to x-rays, and the profiles of the left heart and diaphragm missing, it is probable that the left lung has collapsed. You do not *know* this from the film alone; it is probable clinically, and the roentgen findings support it. If the radiologist knew nothing of the patient and his story, it would be very improper indeed to make such a diagnosis from this film alone, but, taken together with the film made a year earlier and the history, the most reasonable conclusion for his report at once becomes atelectasis. The possibility of some other process being present as well certainly cannot be excluded on the basis of these films, and, as it turned out, autopsy showed that this patient had tuberculosis and silicosis in addition to his collapsed left lung and aortic aneurysm. (Rupture of the aneurysm with hemorrhage into the left hemithorax might be considered as a dramatic terminal event, but it is actually less probable an explanation for the dense left lung field at the time of admission than atelectasis.)

Unknown 8-4 (Figure 8-31)

Retropharyngeal abscess pushing the trachea forward. With barium in the esophagus you would have been able to see the forward displacement of that structure also. Compare the distance between trachea and cervical spine in the two films. Figure 8-32 shows the normal separation between the posterior wall of the trachea and the anterior surfaces of the vertebral bodies.

Unknown 8-5 (Figure 8-33)

There are overlapping nodular masses in both hila and a mass in the paratracheal region, undoubtedly representing enlarged lymph nodes in this patient with known lymphatic leukemia.

Unknown 8-6 (Figure 8-34)

Many different conditions are accompanied by bilateral hilar nodes and a mass in the paratracheal region. You have already seen two, but in a well person without any abnormal physical findings, the possibility of sarcoidosis should rank high on your differential slate. That is what this patient had, and the films are typical for sarcoidosis limited to the nodes. (Note that to say these films are typical means that sarcoidosis looks exactly like this; it does not mean at all that such a diagnosis could be made exclusively from the films.)

Unknown 8-7 (Figure 8-35)

This patient, too, had sarcoidosis, which obviously improved, since the mediastinal and hilar nodes disappeared and are not seen in the later film. This is the commonest course of events in pulmonary sarcoidosis.

Unknown 8-8 (Figure 8-36)

That patient, too, had sarcoidosis, which, however, progressed to involve the parenchyma of the lung with a miliary infiltration similar to that seen in miliary tuberculosis (see example Figure A-6). The hilar nodes, which were present in an earlier film, have regressed as the lung became involved, a pattern of change also characteristic of this type of sarcoidosis. When even more extensive damage to the lung occurs, with much scar-tissue healing, the patient may eventually present a picture like that in Figure A-7B, with extensive pulmonary invalidism and ultimately a cardiopulmonary death.

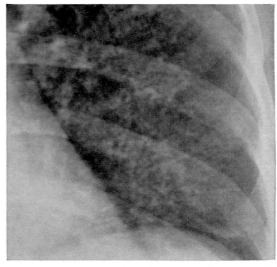

Figure A-6. Miliary tuberculosis, magnification study.

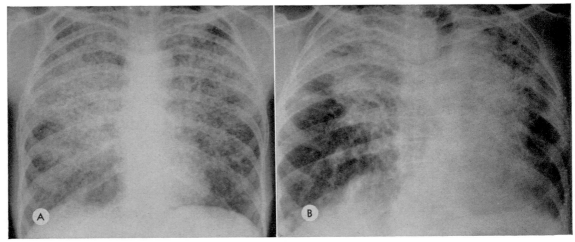

Figure A-7. Another patient with extensive pulmonary sarcoidosis. A. Confluent miliary and nodular pulmonary densities; a much more serious prognosis must be considered for a patient with this degree of involvement than for the patient in whom the demonstrable involvement is limited to the hilar nodes. B. Same patient 6 years later. Note severe pulmonary distortion, the result of extensive fibrosis and particularly marked retraction of the left upper lobe. If the patient is x-rayed for the first time, having reached this stage, the roentgen appearance cannot be said to be distinctive of damage resulting from sarcoidosis, since other grave lung insults can and do result in much the same changes. Thus, sarcoidosis is *one* of the several causes to be considered when you first see a patient with advanced pulmonary damage giving the roentgen appearance of Figure A-7B.

Unknown 8-9 (Figure 8-37)

The right upper lobe is about 50 per cent collapsed, as in Figure 7-17 in the preceding chapter. While a totally collapsed right upper lobe flattened against the right superior mediastinum could certainly resemble a paratracheal mass, this shadow does not. Note its outward curving inferior margin, which is the upward deflected minor fissure. The dense shadow disappeared following bronchoscopic removal of a mucus plug from the bronchus.

Unknown 9-1 (No figure)

Bronchogenic carcinoma may first cause symptoms in a wide variety of ways. You probably have on your list all the following:

1. Silent infiltration of the lung. Likely to be discovered only on routine physical examination or check chest film.
2. Obstruction of a bronchus. May cause cough as the initial symptom, or occasionally hemoptysis. Radiograph may look entirely normal if the mass is small and the obstructed bronchus close within the hilum. Will eventually appear on the radiograph as a mass of increased density within the lung or close to the hilum, and may appear at the time of the first examination as:
3. Atelectasis of the segment of lung distal to the obstructed bronchus.
4. Atelectasis with pneumonia distal to the obstruction.
5. Pneumonia, apparently a simple inflammation clinically, but which does not clear and improve on schedule with appropriate treatment. (You must be very suspicious of repeated episodes of atelectasis in the same lung segment and of recalcitrant pneumonic infiltrations in the lungs of patients in the cancer age group.)
6. Bronchogenic carcinoma not infrequently metastasizes early to the pleura. The patient may therefore appear at your office for the first time complaining of symptoms and presenting signs of pleural effusion, without other complaints or findings.
7. Bronchogenic carcinoma metastasizes to bone very commonly, and if such involvement occurs before other symptoms bring the patient to your office, he may be complaining of bone pain anywhere at all. You may see him because of a fracture which has occurred through bone invaded by tumor.
8. Distant metastases to parenchymatous organs may occur early while bronchogenic carcinoma is still asymptomatic in the chest. Such a patient may therefore present himself for help with symptoms of a brain tumor or with almost total adrenal gland destruction, to mention only two. Radiographic study of his chest may reveal the shadow of the primary tumor, or if the tumor is small and has metastasized very early, the chest films may at first be entirely negative.
9. Bronchogenic carcinoma may metastasize early to lymph glands and bring the patient to you because of pressure from such glands on any of the mediastinal structures. Notable among these patterns of initial difficulty is one in which the trachea is surrounded and compressed by tumor nodes, resulting in dyspnea and wheezing. The vascular structures of the superior mediastinum may also be compressed giving the symptoms of superior vena caval obstruction, for example.
10. Bronchogenic carcinoma may invade the pericardium, presenting initial symptoms of pericardial effusion.

Unknown 10-1 (Figure 10-17)

The visible bones are slender and contrast less sharply than normal with the darker lung fields in this elderly woman. (You will be learning to study bone density in a later discussion.) Because of this, partly, no fractures can be seen to account for the large amount of air under the diaphragm, surrounding the heart and distending the pericardial sac. There are also streaks of air in the soft tissues of the abdominal wall and chest on the left side. The lung fields, elevated diaphragm, and small heart shadow outlined by pericardial air provide no further information.

Unknown 10-2 (Figure 10-37)

This is a right anterior oblique view of the heart, but you are looking through the film in the wrong direction. At first glance this appears to be a left oblique, but you know that it cannot be because of the triangular, flat-backed shape of the heart. When you turn a film like this over, you will be happy about accepting it as a right oblique. Try looking at these two prints reversed in a mirror.

Unknown 10-3 (Figure 10-38)

This is a left oblique seen wrong way through. You know that it cannot be the right oblique as it first seems to be because the posterior surface of the heart is rounded and not flat.

There are other clues, of course: if you turn a patient facing you into the left anterior oblique you would expect the more posterior of his two diaphragmatic shadows to be his left one (seen to your right, of course). Here you have a stomach bubble under the wrong diaphragm. Beware of depending on the aorta to tell you whether you are looking at a right or left oblique, because with the elongation of the aorta which occurs in arteriosclerosis, the unrolled aorta may frequently be seen in the true right oblique projection.

Unknowns 10-4 and 10-5

(Figures 10-46 and 10-47)

Two young women with straightened left heart borders and dyspnea. Only 10-4 shows cardiac enlargement, and her left bronchus is elevated, suggesting that the left atrium is slightly dilated, something which would be easy to confirm by examination of the obliques. This patient actually had mitral stenosis and minimal insufficiency with all the classic physical signs. A mitral commissurotomy was successfully performed. Note the appearance of her hila and vessels (which must be pulmonary veins), suggesting increased intra-atrial pressure.

The patient in 10-5 arrived at the emergency division of a hospital and was examined just at the beginning of one of her biweekly asthmatic attacks. The straightened left border was shown at fluoroscopy and on oblique views to be due to fullness of the pulmonary artery and conus anteriorly, easily distinguishable from the posterior fullness of the other patient. There was no evidence of heart disease.

Unknowns 10-6 and 10-7

(Figures 10-48 and 10-49)

The young man in Figure 10-48 shows borderline cardiac enlargement to measurement, but the concave left border and general shape of his heart suggests left ventricular hypertrophy out of proportion to the given age. The too-prominent aortic knob confirms this impression; it is not the aortic shadow you expect for a young man. This patient had malignant hypertension of some standing.

The young man in Figure 10-49 shows much more cardiac enlargement, also suggesting left ventricular enlargement from its shape, but he has a flat aortic shadow and no knob at all. He was in early failure and dyspneic on the slightest exertion when admitted. His tension was normal (and equal in both arms) and he had femoral pulses. From the heart shape and flat aortic shadow one might suggest coarctation of the aorta in this patient in spite of the absence of rib-notching, but the clinical findings are against it. His history gave one episode of rheumatic fever, and he had a systolic murmur clearly suggesting aortic stenosis. His final diagnosis was pure aortic stenosis of rheumatic origin without mitral disease.

Unknown 10-8 (Figure 10-50)

The heart is grossly enlarged and quite abnormal in shape. The left border is convex with enough additional projection of the apex toward the left to raise the question of left ventricular enlargement. The right border is also abnormally rounded. The hila are partly obscured but suggest engorgement. There are horizontal parallel linear densities in the peripheral lung field, but no frank pleural effusion is seen. The shape of the heart should suggest advanced mitral valvular disease with pronounced insufficiency and enlargement of the left atrium. This is confirmed, even in the single view, by the elevation of the left main bronchus seen through the heart. The oblique views would further confirm the impression by showing posterior displacement of the barium-filled esophagus in the right oblique and filling in of the aortic window by a full left atrium high on the posterior surface of the heart in the left oblique. The lower posterior surface of the heart in the left oblique would show left ventricular enlargement if your impression of the PA arc 9 was correct.

Unknown 10-9 (Figure 10-51)

This heart is patently enlarged to measurement. (Even though you cannot see the lower ribs you can predict their position well enough to estimate the transthoracic diameter.) The left border is straightened, and again you might feel that there is probably expansion of both arcs 8 and 9 (that there is some left ventricular enlargement present). The hila here are distinctly enlarged. The arrow indicates what must be the margin of the left atrium. (This patient had both mitral and aortic valvular disease.)

Unknown 10-10 (Figure 10-52)

In myxedema the heart shadow is frequently enlarged, and, pathologically, this is found to be due to a combination of dilatation of the chambers, some increased bulk of the heart muscle, and, frequently, pericardial effusion. A combination in this patient of a thickened, myxedematous myocardium and arteriosclerotic compromise of its blood supply might well contribute to the advent of failure. Here the angiocardiograms establish the extent to which the increased size of the heart shadow is due to the pericardial effusion rather than to failure with dilatation.

Unknown 10-11 (Figure 10-53)

Fullness in arcs 8 and 9. In the presence of failure as obvious as it is here, the measurably widened heart shadow *may* result simply from dilatation. This was a heart with mitral valvular disease, failure, and right-sided pleural effusion, however. With the advent of failure, characteristics of change in shape become less well-defined.

Unknown 10-12 (Figure 10-54)

Left ventricle, left atrium, and aorta are opacified. Opacification of the atrium implies insufficiency of the mitral valve. The atrium is obviously dilated.

Unknown 10-13 (Figure 10-55)

Left ventricle, left atrium high on the posterior surface of the heart, and aorta are opacified. Again, the visualization of the atrium implies incompetency of the mitral valve.

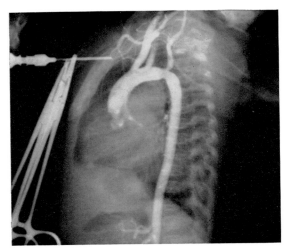

Figure A-8A

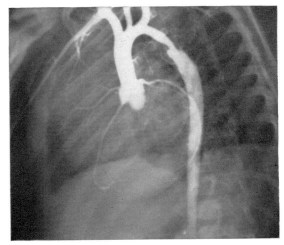

Figure A-8B

Unknown 10-14 (No figure in text)

In coarctation the bolus of opaque-loaded blood will proceed through the right chambers (in the angiocardiogram), through the pulmonary circulation and left chambers in perfect order. The late phase of the levogram will show the outline of the aorta indented at the site of the coarctation, with opacification of the collateral pathways which have been developed. Figure A-8A and B shows *retrograde injections* made directly into the aorta or its branches; no

opaque medium is seen passing through the heart, therefore. Figure A-8A shows a normal aortogram (left lateral projection with unrolled aorta). Figure A-8B is an aortogram in a patient with preductal coarctation (left oblique projection with comparably unrolled aorta and indentation at the site of the defect). The patent ductus itself is not seen opacified.

Unknown 10-15 (No figure)

With an interventricular septal defect (without other defects), if the shunt of blood is predominantly left to right, blanching of the opacified right ventricle may be noted in the dextrogram because opaque-free blood enters the right ventricle from the left. Later, in the levogram, the cleared right ventricle will be *reopacified* when the left ventricle is seen filled with opaque material. In cases in which the shunt is in the opposite direction (right to left, a certain volume of blood passing directly into the left ventricle from the right without passing through the lungs for oxygenation), the left ventricle will be seen to opacify during the dextrogram.

Unknown 10-16 (No figure in text)

In patients with patent ductus arteriosus with a left-to-right shunt (common early in life because of the relatively greater pressure in the aorta), the pulmonary artery will be seen opacified in the frames of the dextrogram, and then *blanching* will be visible in the main pulmonary artery when opaque-free blood enters from the aorta, diluting the opaque material in the pulmonary artery and rendering it, therefore, less radio-opaque. Later, during the levogram, the pulmonary artery will be seen to reopacify when the aorta is filled. If an aortogram is performed with injection through a catheter placed in the brachial artery, the pulmonary artery will be seen to opacify, although no part of the right heart contains opaque medium. Figure A-9A. Opacification of right atrium, right ventricle, and pulmonary arteries in a patient with patent ductus. Figure A-9B. A moment later the main pulmonary arteries are blanched although their branches still contain opaque material. The blanching is due to dilution with non-opaque blood returning from the aorta into the pulmonary artery via the patent ductus.

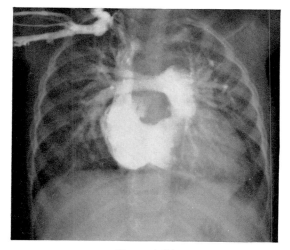

Figure A-9A

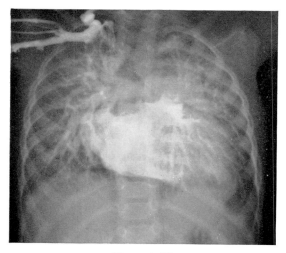

Figure A-9B

Unknown 11-1 (Figure 11-18)

Dark subcutaneous fat can be seen outlining the elbow and flexed forearm and the buttocks. The crescentic gray shadow above the fetus is the placenta in its normal location high in the uterus. Compare the thickness of the uterine wall over the fetal rump.

Unknown 11-2 (Figure 11-19)

The plain film, A, shows a round, sharply demarcated area of radiolucency overlying the sacrum, and the barium study shows the sigmoid colon lifted up over this "mass" and apparently flattened against it posteriorly across the rectosigmoid junction. At surgery, as predicted by the radiologist, a 10-cm. cystic mass was removed which proved to be a dermoid cyst and to contain thick, grumous, fatty material. Note the calcium-dense shadow in both films overlying the sacroiliac joint on the right which was contained in the cyst and consisted of a rudimentary tooth. Teeth are often present in dermoid cysts, and the combination of a circumscribed radiolucent shadow with a density resembling a tooth is dependable roentgen evidence identifying the nature of such masses.

Unknown 11-3 (Figure 11-27)

There is a large round soft-tissue mass in the right upper quadrant which displaces gut. This proved to be a large, benign cyst of the lower pole of the right kidney. Overlying its upper margin there is a long streak of calcium density not seen on most films and representing calcification within a costal cartilage anteriorly. A lateral film would separate it widely from the mass in question. It also extends beyond the mass margin on this view. The right psoas shadow is less well seen than the left. Any equally dense structure lying next to the psoas will render it less well seen. The dark shadows over the iliac wing are probably air-in-gut.

Unknown 11-4 (Figure 11-31)

Cervical vertebra of a giraffe. They, too, have only seven.

Unknown 11-5 (Figure 11-34)

One vertebral body is *not* the expected "empty box," but uniformly dense throughout, although not abnormal in size or shape. The right half of the pelvis shows similar changes. This patient had malignant bone disease with metastases to bone.

Unknown 11-6 (Figure 11-35)

The anterior surfaces of the bodies of the last two thoracic and first lumbar vertebrae show marked erosion in the lateral view. The AP view shows erosion of the left lateral surface of L1, the most extensively involved of the three. The aorta below this level is strikingly calcified, but at the level of L1 it is deviated sharply anteriorly. The patient had a large saccular aneurysm lying against T11 and 12 and L1. Note well the calcified aorta seen through the bones on the AP view.

Unknown 11-7 (Figure 11-39)

The calcium is characteristic of that distributed about the periphery of a spherical structure. Since the patient was a man, you can discard the gynecologic items on your list. This actually represented an aneurysm of the common iliac artery on the right.

Unknown 11-8 (Figure 11-40)

No answer appropriate since structures were to be identified only. The liver was enlarged to palpation.

Unknown 12-1 (Figure 12-6)

Prone, because the round wrinkled fundal bubble is seen filled with air near the diaphragm rather than the lower more mid-abdominal antrum.

Unknown 12-2 (Figure 12-52)

Peripheral calcification in a splenic cyst located close to the diaphragm and indenting the stomach. The patient was a Norwegian housewife and had no symptoms and no important findings. The spleen and cyst were removed surgically, and below you see a radiograph of the entire specimen. Microscopic examination showed no evidence of parasitic infection. The cyst contained clear fluid and may have resulted from trauma many years before.

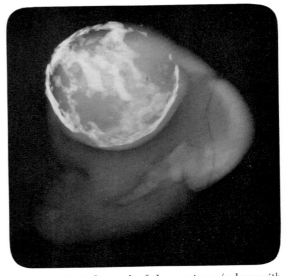

Figure A-10. Radiograph of the specimen (spleen with calcified cyst).

Unknown 12-3 (Figure 12-53)

The upper half of the abdomen is blank and airless. There is no air in the stomach which can be clearly identified. The spleen is obviously enlarged and it lies close against the flank. There is no displacement of the colon away from the left flank stripe. Both kidneys appear to be depressed, as do all air-containing structures. This patient had Hodgkin's lymphoma with massive enlargement of both liver and spleen. That diagnosis could not be made from the film, of course, as there is nothing distinctive about the roentgen findings.

Unknown 13-1 (Figure 13-9)

The narrowing in the barium column at the hepatic flexure was produced by an annular constricting carcinoma of the colon. When the obstruction became complete, you would expect the ascending colon and cecum and some of the terminal ileum to distend with retained gas, and the colon distal to the obstruction to be cleared of air with the increase of peristalsis, so that little or no haustrated shadows would be visible in the expected distribution of the transverse, descending, and sigmoid colon.

Unknown 13-2 (Figure 13-12)

The stomach and several loops of small bowel are seen lying in a row on the left side of the abdomen. The loops lower down are invisible because they are filled with fluid, and the colon is invisible because it has been cleared of air. This was mechanical obstruction close to the ileocecal valve.

Unknown 13-3 (Figure 13-13)

Several parallel loops of jejunum are grouped in the upper mid-abdomen. The lower abdomen and soft tissues of the pelvis appear blank. There are scattered bubbles of air which may be in the colon. This patient had chronic stenosing ileitis, and the lower abdomen and pelvis were filled with fluid-filled loops of bowel. Mechanical ileal obstruction with nearly complete clearing of the colon.

Unknown 14-1 (Figure 14-10)

Four spot films of the antrum of the stomach and duodenum show a small round filling defect arising from the greater curvature about 3 centimeters from the pylorus. The defect is present on all films and represented a gastric polyp.

Unknown 14-2 (Figure 14-50)

Large scrotal hernia containing part of the barium-filled colon.

Unknown 15-1 (Figure 15-4)

Double gallbladder. One part concentrates the opaque material very well and appears normal. The other part contains a number of faceted stones. Both were removed at surgery. Double gallbladder is a rare anomaly.

Unknown 15-2 (Figure 15-10)

Left hydronephrosis delayed visualization of the left kidney. The palpable mass proved to be a huge hydronephrotic kidney. (Later film is shown on page 282, Figure 15-11.)

Unknown 15-3 (Figure 15-17)

Yes, there is more caliceal inversion than is to be accounted for by the procedure alone. But did you "see" the large laminated calculus in the left renal pelvis? A-11, below, shows a plain film on the same patient. *Neither a retrograde nor an intravenous study can ever be properly interpreted without comparing it with a plain film made before the injection of opaque medium.* It is customary in most radiology departments for a radiologist to see the plain film before the injection is made.

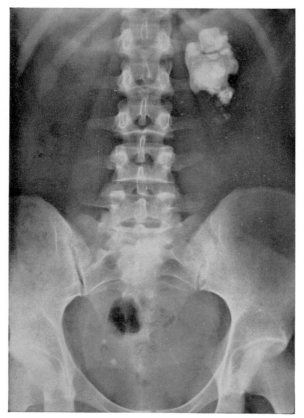

Figure A-11

Unknown 16-1 (Figure 16-2)

The legs have been broken in order to shorten the mummy, doubtless to make it fit into a burial case which the embalmer had on hand. The lower femurs have been removed, and the arms are also missing. The mummy probably dates from a time no later than 1000 B.C. because after that much more packing was used in the preparation of embalmed bodies. Embalmers were often dishonest and left off parts of the bodies entrusted to them, sometimes filling the "trunk" with animal bones and trash and including only the human skull, radiographs have shown.

Unknown 16-2 (Figure 16-4)

(1) Femoral head. (2) Femoral neck. (3) Greater trochanter. (4) Trochanteric fossa. (5) Lesser trochanter. (6) Intertrochanteric line. (7) Intertrochanteric crest. (8) Femoral shaft.

Unknown 16-3 (Figure 16-13)

Fracture of the neck of the femur (subcapital) partly impacted.

Unknown 16-4 (Figure 16-16)

Fused hip, of long standing, following tuberculous arthritis. The joint space and cartilage have disappeared. Note bony trabeculae crossing the region of the joint.

Unknown 16-5 (Figure 16-17)

Sliver of bone, which had been avulsed, lying in the knee joint. The fracture site is not clear.

Unknown 16-6 (Figure 16-18)

Transverse fracture of the patella, and of course you will already have explained why the fragments lie so far apart.

Unknown 16-7 (Figure 16-20)

Fracture of the medial condyle of the tibia, the fracture line extending downward from the joint surface to the medial side of the tibia, with some depression of the fragment. The obliquity of the projection used here may be appreciated from the position of the patella.

Unknown 16-8 (Figure 16-21)

Comminuted fracture of the lower femur extending into the joint.

Unknown 16-9 (Figure 16-22)

Fracture of the lateral condyle of the left tibia and of the left patella. Note white transverse lines in both lower femurs and upper tibias representing recently fused epiphyseal growth plates.

Unknown 16-10 (Figure 16-24)

Impacted fracture of the radius 1½ centimeters from the radiocarpal joint. The typical Colles' fracture adds a fracture of the styloid process of the ulna, not present here. If you subtract the slender shadow of the ulna from that of the radius in the lateral view you will be able to appreciate the degree of impaction, fragmentation, and slight angulation of the distal fragment of the radius.

Unknown 16-11 (Figure 16-25)

Impacted fracture of the distal left radius about 1 centimeter from the epiphyseal line. Compared with the normal right wrist, the streak of increased density of impacted bone is easily seen. In studying fractures close to unfused growth plates it is always important to determine whether there has been displacement of the epiphysis, and for this a lateral view is essential.

Unknown 16-12 (Figure 16-66)

Suffocation. The man is edentulous. A lower denture is in normal place against the mandible, but the upper denture lies vertically behind the tongue. A large fragment of the soft drink bottle was found lodged in the denture.

Credits: Illustrations this chapter.

Figure A-1. Courtesy Dr. E. Emerson and the publisher, *MR&P* 33:112.

Figure A-2. Courtesy Dr. B. Epstein and the publisher, *MR&P* 34:66.

Figure A-3. Courtesy Dr. B. Epstein and the publisher, *MR&P* 34:58.

Figure A-5. Courtesy Drs. V. Condon and E. Phillips, and the publisher, *Am. J. Roentgenol.* 88:551.

Figure A-6. Courtesy Dr. H. Isard, Philadelphia, Pa.

Figure A-7. Courtesy Drs. K. Ellis and G. Renthal, and the publisher, *Am. J. Roentgenol.* 88:1078.

Figures A-8A and *B.* Courtesy Drs. B. Gasul et al., and the publisher, *MR&P* 35, Supplement: 35, 41.

Figures A-9A and *B.* Courtesy Drs. B. Gasul et al., and the publisher, *MR&P* 35, Supplement: 19, 20.

Figure A-10. Courtesy Drs. W. Macklin, H. Bosland, and A. McCarthy, and the publisher, *MR&P* 31:92.

Supplementary Historical Notes

The history of the discovery of x-rays records that crystals of barium platinocyanide *accidentally* lying near a cathode discharge tube fluoresced, giving the first clue to the discovery. But the presence in the laboratory of a cardboard screen coated with barium platinocyanide was not altogether accidental. The fluorescence of this and other chemical substances in response to *cathode rays* was well known. Such fluorescence had been observed by Lenard, among others. It is possible that Lenard himself had not "discovered" the x-rays earlier for the reason that he was employing a fluorescent test chemical which responded only to cathode rays and not to x-rays. Both cathode rays and x-rays were, however, unquestionably being produced simultaneously by such experiments with discharge tubes in physical laboratories in various parts of the world. It was his systematically imaginative quality of mind which enabled Roentgen to eliminate the cathode ray emanations from his apparatus and then to be alerted by the fact that something capable of producing fluorescence still emerged.

Roentgen, in his fiftieth year, with a distinguished experimental career and many papers already behind him, became interested in the work of Hittorf and Crookes and of Hertz and Lenard with cathode rays. He decided to begin by repeating a number of Lenard's experiments, a review procedure which was characteristic of his own experimental work.

Cathode rays are streams of accelerated electrons produced from the cathode of an evacuated glass tube, and the earliest cathode rays were probably produced in 1855 by Heinrich Geissler, a glass blower at the University of Bonn. He had built an efficient mercury vacuum pump with which he had been able to evacuate sealed glass tubes, and he demonstrated beautiful colored effects when these tubes were filled with various gases and high tension discharges passed through them.

In order to study the properties of cathode rays outside the tube in free air, both Hittorf and Lenard had equipped ordinary glass cathode ray tubes with sealed-in, extremely thin aluminum windows, through which the cathode rays could penetrate to the outside. Lenard found that the cathode rays made the air electrically conductive but were absorbed by a few centimeters of free air. He also discovered that they caused certain salts to fluoresce.

As a result of a suggestion of Lenard's, Roentgen determined to experiment further with cathode rays, enclosing the Lenard tube in a tightly fitting cardboard covering encased in tinfoil. This prevented any *visible* light from the tube from pentrating to the outside, but Roentgen observed that the cathode rays still produced fluorescence in a cardboard screen painted with barium platinocyanide. With this experimental setup, however, fluorescence occurred only when the screen was placed fairly *close* to the window in the tube. Roentgen then carried out similar experiments with the thicker-walled, windowless Hittorf-Crookes tube, known to absorb all of the cathode rays. He covered the tube with pieces of black cardboard pasted together to make a lightproof jacket, and to his satisfaction noted that none of the light produced by the tube penetrated the cardboard cover.

Suddenly, about a yard away from the tube, he noticed a weak light shimmering from a little bench located nearby. Not believing this possible, he passed another discharge through the tube and noted the same fluorescence. Roentgen lit a match and found that the coated screen with which he had tested for cathode rays in earlier experiments was the source of the light. The inescapable conclusion from this phenomenon was that *something* emanated from the tube which produced fluorescence at a much greater distance than in his previous experiments, and that that something could not be cathode rays or light.

During the several days that followed these initial experiments, Roentgen found it difficult to believe his own observations and repeated the studies numerous times. He held a piece of paper and then a playing card and then a book between the tube and the screen: the fluorescence with the book interposed was not quite so bright, but it was distinctly present. Convinced, then, that the new type of ray with which he must be experimenting could pass through objects opaque to light, he collected a variety of other materials to test their permeability by the ray. A thin sheet of lead was found to stop the rays completely, but aluminum appeared to be almost transparent. While holding a piece of lead in front of the screen, he observed to his amazement that he could distinguish on the screen the outline of his thumb and finger, within which appeared the shadows of the bones. He was so overwhelmed by the implications of his discovery that he commented to a friend at the time, "I have discovered something interesting, but I do not know whether or not my observations are correct."

In his first communication on the subject (December 28, 1895) he was able to announce that the fluorescence produced by the apparatus was still visible at a distance of 2 meters, that paper was very transparent (even that composing a book of about 1,000 pages), that the printer's ink had no noticeable effect, that thick blocks of wood were transparent as well as sheets of hard rubber and of glass. He noted that the bones could be seen as dark shadows within the finger outlines of the hand and that water and several other liquids could be penetrated by the rays. He announced that lead was practically opaque and that a stick of wood having only one side coated with white lead paint cast a different shadow depending on whether the lead coating was tangential to the rays or placed perpendicular to them! He ob-

served that x-rays produced a direct effect upon a photographic plate encased in a light-tight cassette, and he made photographs of various objects including a series of lead weights still enclosed in their wooden box. He reported that x-rays could not be focused in the usual sense with lenses of various composition. He also had carried out experiments to show that x-rays could not be deflected in a strong magnetic field, although the path of cathode rays was well known to be affected by magnets. He concluded that the x-rays were not identical with cathode rays but were produced in the glass wall of the discharge tube or in the aluminum window.

On New Year's Day in 1896 he addressed copies of the reprint of his communication and some "prints" of the x-ray pictures he had taken, in a letter to F. Exner, a friend and physicist in Vienna, and to certain other physicists in various experimental centers. Exner showed the prints to a group of friends and colleagues, the father of one of whom was the editor of a newspaper in Prague. This man immediately understood the sensational news value of the discovery and printed a summary of the facts in the morning edition of his paper. The report was copied in the first week in January by newspapers throughout the world, and the implications of the new ray which would penetrate objects opaque to light created such a sensation that the press found it necessary to qualify its initial announcement by assuring its readers "that there is no joke or humbug in the matter. It is a serious discovery by a serious German Professor."

Nevertheless, in the course of the next few months, a number of sensational and newsworthy (if now patently absurd) claims were made for the new rays. One reader sent to Edison the hollow eyepieces of a pair of opera glasses, requesting "that he fit them with the x-rays." A New York newspaper reported that "at the College of Physicians and Surgeons the roentgen rays were used to reflect anatomic diagrams directly into the brains of the students, making a much more enduring impression than the ordinary methods of learning anatomic details."[1] A student in Iowa, also possibly with tongue in cheek, claimed to have discovered the philosopher's stone, and said that x-rays would change a cheap piece of metal worth 13 cents into $153 worth of gold in about three hours. Antivivisectionists pointed out that "we are entitled to hope that it (the new rays) will almost put an end to vivisection. There will be no need to put a knife into a live animal when a ray will make its inner workings visible."[2]

Miss Frances Willard, a well-known figure in the temperance movement in the United States, felt that the x-rays might be expected to help the temperance cause because "by this means drunkards and cigarette smokers can be shown the steady deterioration in their systems which follows the practice, and seeing is believing."[3]

"Soul photography" was announced by a French scientist who claimed to have made more than 400 such plates and exhibited them in Munich in 1896. He also stated that he had been able to make "photographic exposures" by thought transmission.

Humorists had a field day. One newspaper predicted that a reasonable advertisement for the future might be: "Competent pedagogue wanted, brain photograph desired." A particularly thin horse was said by a prospective buyer to resemble "one of those roentgen photographs." A student in Munich "had his heart photographed with Roentgen's rays and one discovered in it the following initials: H.B." (a famous Munich beer). The *Literary Digest* for March 1896 averred that "notwithstanding the new photography, it still takes death to discover a man's virtues."

Serious medical experimenters and physicists were at the same time producing a whole spectrum of useful and important roentgen data. Metallic foreign bodies were located and fractures diagnosed, one of such early studies figuring in a litigation in this country. Tuberculosis of the shoulder joint and osteomyelitis of the femur were both observed and studied, and by the fall of 1896 Walter Cannon at Harvard was studying the shadows of radio-opaque buttons and capsules of bismuth salts in the stomachs of experimental animals.

The combination in the various scientific and lay presses of the world of both wild, improbable claims and well-substantiated observations naturally produced a confused press picture on the subject which gradually was sifted and refined so that the true value of the roentgen ray became apparent. Official bodies of professional men felt impelled to caution against too much excitement, and I reprint for your retrospective interest some lines from the editorial page of the *J.A.M.A.,* February 15, 1896:

"The general interest in the recent discovery of Prof. Roentgen, the details of which now fill the daily press and which were at first received with incredulity by the public as probably a scientific hoax, seems to call for some notice....

"In regard to the scientific question as to whether the results obtained by experimenters are due to the previously recognized cathode rays or to a new form of radiation as Prof. Roentgen suggests we can, of course, express no opinion; it is a matter to be decided by physicists. The fact that we have, however, a force, for that is what it may be called, that will act on the sensitive chemicals of the photographic plate through flesh, cartilage, skin, and other tissues of the animal body, is enough to be fertile of practical suggestions to any thinking physician or surgeon. The further fact that these rays go directly through prisms and lenses without modification or change of course adds to their possibilities in a medical point of view; it insures the accuracy of the image from distortion by refractive power of the different solids and fluids of the body. The further fact that in a general way only the density of the medium penetrated seems to affect them is suggestive of practical medical and surgical possibilities; it hints at future valuable physiologic revelations as well as diagnostic aids. It is only a hint, however, and whether it is to be ever realized to any extent is perhaps open to serious question . . . .

"The real utility of the discovery has so far been demonstrated to a limited extent in the field of surgery. A few accounts have appeared in the lay press of needles, bullets, etc., having been detected lodged in the tissues, and some light has been thrown on pathologic diagnosis in one or two cases. In France, M. Lannelongue believes he has been able to show by this method that in a femur affected with osteomyelitis the destruction of bone progresses from the center to the periphery rather than in the opposite direction as had been previously held. When it is considered that the discovery is as yet only a few weeks old, and that students all over the civilized world are laboring to investigate it and to perfect the methods of its application, it may not be unreasonable to hope for much more important results in the near or remote future. At present, however, the limitations of the methods are too great and the medical nature of the discovery is, as yet, a largely unknown quantity. Its surgical utility in certain ways has probably been sufficiently indicated by what has been already done, but enthusiasm as to its future should be tempered by a scientific spirit of moderation that proves all things before building its faith upon them."

Credits:

1. *Science,* New York, 3:436, 1896.
2. *Life,* 27:152, 1896.
3. *Electrical Review,* 38:737, 1896.

4. Most of the material in this appendix is to be found in two biographical works by Dr. Otto Glasser: *Dr. W. C. Röntgen,* published by Charles C Thomas, Springfield, Illinois, 1945; and *William Conrad Röntgen,* published by Charles C Thomas, Springfield, Illinois, 1934.